T0306268

THE WORLD ENCYCLOPEDIA OF
CHEESE

THE WORLD ENCYCLOPEDIA OF
CHEESE

JULIET HARBUTT
WITH RECIPES BY
ROZ DENNY

LORENZ BOOKS

To my mother, who gave me a passion for food and the desire to learn more about it. J.H.

This edition is published by Lorenz Books, an imprint of Anness Publishing Ltd,
Hermes House, 88–89 Blackfriars Road, London SE1 8HA
tel. 020 7401 2077; fax 020 7633 9499

www.lorenzbooks.com; www.annesspublishing.com

If you like the images in this book and would like to investigate using them for publishing, promotions or advertising, please visit our website www.practicalpictures.com for more information.

UK agent: The Manning Partnership Ltd; tel. 01225 478444; fax 01225 478440; sales@manning-partnership.co.uk
UK distributor: Book Trade Services; tel. 0116 2759086; fax 0116 2759090; uksales@booktradeservices.com; exportsales@booktradeservices.com
North American agent/distributor: National Book Network; tel. 301 459 3366; fax 301 429 5746; www.nbnbooks.com
Australian agent/distributor: Pan Macmillan Australia; tel. 1300 135 113; fax 1300 135 103; customer.service@macmillan.com.au
New Zealand agent/distributor: David Bateman Ltd; tel. (09) 415 7664; fax (09) 415 8892

Publisher: Joanna Lorenz
Project editors: Linda Fraser and Dan Hurst
Copy editor: Jenni Fleetwood
Designer: Nigel Partridge
Photography: John Heseltine and William Lingwood
Home economists: Carole Handslip (recipes) and Carol Tennant (cheeses)
Production controller: Claire Rae

ETHICAL TRADING POLICY
Because of our ongoing ecological investment programme, you, as our customer, can have the pleasure and reassurance of knowing that a tree is being cultivated on your behalf to naturally replace the materials used to make the book you are holding. For further information about this scheme, go to www.annesspublishing.com/trees

© Anness Publishing Ltd 1998, updated 2009

All rights reserved. No part of this publication may be reproduced, stored in a retrieval system, or transmitted in any way or by any means, electronic, mechanical, photocopying, recording or otherwise, without the prior written permission of the copyright holder.

PUBLISHER'S NOTE
Although the advice and information in this book are believed to be accurate and true at the time of going to press, neither the authors nor the publisher can accept any legal responsibility or liability for any errors or omissions that may be made nor for any inaccuracies nor for any harm or injury that comes about from following instructions or advice in this book.

NOTES

For all recipes, quantities are given in both metric and imperial measures and, where appropriate, in standard cups and spoons. Follow one set of measures, but not a mixture, because they are not interchangeable.
Standard spoon and cup measures are level. 1 tsp = 5ml, 1 tbsp = 15ml, 1 cup = 250ml/8fl oz
Australian standard tablespoons are 20ml. Australian readers should use 3 tsp in place of 1 tbsp for measuring small quantities.
American pints are 16fl oz/2 cups. American readers should use 20fl oz/2.5 cups in place of 1 pint when measuring liquids.
Electric oven temperatures in this book are for conventional ovens. When using a fan oven, the temperature may need to be reduced by about 10–20°C/20–40°F. Since ovens vary, you should check your manufacturer's instruction book for guidance.
Medium eggs are used unless otherwise stated.

CONTENTS

Introduction

In shops and markets around the world, thousands of cheeses tempt our eyes and challenge our tastebuds. Wrinkled and mouldy, smooth and sunshine yellow, orange and smelly or brilliant white, they are all labelled cheese, and their shapes and sizes, flavours and textures range from the sublime to the truly extraordinary. Yet they are all made from the same basic raw material – milk. What changes this simple product into something so complex and diverse?

Different Kinds of Milk

First, the type of animal yielding milk makes a difference. The cow's milk we drink is slightly sweet, mild and subtle in flavour. Most of it comes from Friesian cows, yet there are more than 50 different breeds whose milk is suitable for cheesemaking. Milk from Guernsey cows, for instance, is rich and pale yellow with larger fat globules than most other types, so this milk tastes smoother and fuller. Water buffalo's milk – used in Italy for making mozzarella – is ivory white, earthy and slightly nutty.

Sheep's milk is also mild but has undertones of roast lamb and lanolin. It is slightly sweeter than cow's milk. As sheep's milk cheese matures, these characteristics are intensified, as exemplified in the hard mature sheep's milk cheeses like the famous Pecorinos of Italy or the Basque and Pyrenees cheeses of France and Spain. Typically they are very nutty – as if fresh milk has been infused with crushed walnuts or brazil nuts – and the sweetness comes through to suggest burnt caramel, sweet fudge or caramelized onions. The aroma of lanolin, like the smell of wet wool, also adds its own distinct personality to the final cheese.

The most misunderstood of all cheeses are those made from goat's milk. There's an explanation for the negative way it is often perceived: if the milk, which is mild with a slightly aromatic background, is handled badly, the microscopic globules of fat suspended in the milk burst and release their contents. These impart a

Above: The milk from cows has a mild, subtle, slightly sweet flavour

bitter, nasty, "billy goat" flavour to the milk. If you have ever been close to a billy or male goat, it is a smell you are unlikely to forget. However, if the milk is handled with care, those same fat globules will gradually break down and will contribute to the delicious, herbaceous taste of the cheese. A good goat's milk cheese tastes as though the milk has absorbed the oils and aromas of tarragon, thyme or marjoram, set against a background of dry, crisp white wine.

There are as many different breeds of goat and sheep as there are cows. In some countries, cheese is made from the milk of llamas, camels or even reindeer, adding yet another dimension to the cheese.

Milk is not produced all year round but only after the animal has given birth. Unlike humans, animals come into season only once a year. Although farmers can control and manipulate their animals' natural urges, sheep and goats are more difficult to persuade to mate out of season than cows. Added to this, they have a shorter lactation period than cows, so there are times when their milk is not available. Some producers freeze goat's or sheep's milk for these times and continue to make excellent cheeses. Others believe in the old ways and simply stop milking their animals. Their cheeses are therefore seasonal. But the type of animal is only one factor that affects the flavour.

The Grazing, the Soil and the Seasons

Of equal significance is what the animals eat. Even the most unobservant amongst us cannot fail to see and smell the difference between fresh grass, wild clover and unspoilt meadows compared with compacted feed, silage, turnips and straw.

You only have to taste the great mountain cheeses of Europe (where, by law, the herds can only graze on natural pastures or sweet hay cut from Alpine meadows), to appreciate the difference. The amount of milk these cows give may be lower than that yielded by animals fed on lush green pastures or carefully prepared balanced diets of dried food supplement and vitamins, but the milk is rich and thick and the flavour is concentrated.

The seasons will also affect the taste and even the texture of cheeses from animals that seek their own grazing and do not rely on their keepers. In spring, the herbage is sweet, moist and green as the young shoots come through; in early summer the grazing is bountiful and varied compared with mid- to late summer when the earth becomes parched and dry and only hardy grasses survive. With the autumn rains comes another burst of new growth before the winter forces many animals inside to become reliant during the winter months on the hay the farmer has cut. The flavour of the milk reflects these differences and changes with the seasons.

The soil and geology of an area will also affect the flavour of the milk and may even govern the type of cheese that can be made. Clay and limestone will support different grasses to volcanic soils and granite. The grasses that grow will absorb different minerals, each making a minute but significant impact on the flavour of the milk. Rainfall, humidity and temperature also affect what will grow and which animals will thrive where.

Making Cheese

Once the milk has been obtained, the skill of the cheesemaker is needed to convert it into a form that will last for days or even years. To achieve this, the cheesemaker must first separate the milk into the solids, protein and fats (known collectively as curds) and the liquid or whey (that consists mainly of water). This process is known as coagulation.

The Starter

If left in a warm place, milk will sour and coagulate or curdle by itself. This souring process is due to the action of millions of tiny bacteria who "eat" lactose (milk sugars), turning them into lactic acid or sour milk. To speed up the process and to stop the milk becoming bitter and unpleasantly sour, a little warm "matured" or slightly sour milk, taken from the previous evening's milk, is added to the new, fresh batch of unpasteurized milk. This speeds up or starts the process of coagulating the milk and is known as a starter or starter culture. It is not unlike adding the culture to yogurt – and in fact some cheesemakers use home-made yogurt as their starter.

If the milk is pasteurized, all these bacteria will have been lost and must be replaced in order for the milk to sour and curdle. The replacements consist of a combination of cultures grown in laboratories. Some the cheesemaker can just tip into the vat of milk; others are a blend specifically requested by the cheesemaker and must be grown in an incubator before they can be added to the milk. These cultures are valuable, but they will never replace the myriad different bacteria naturally present in unpasteurized milk.

Below: The cheesemaker stirring a vat of coagulating milk for Parmesan

Certain types of cheese must use specific cultures if the desired result is to be obtained. Invisible to the naked eye, these cultures work alongside the numerous enzymes on the lactose, protein and fat through all the stages of cheesemaking. Each thrives at a specific range of temperatures and degree of acidity and contributes to the final flavour and texture of the cheese. As the level of acidity changes in the milk (and later in the young curd), some die off or become dormant, while others, preferring the new climate, will spring into action. Their unique characteristics combine to create a kaleidoscope of flavours that no amount of copying can emulate.

The Rennet

Although the starter culture speeds up the process of souring the milk and would eventually cause it to curdle, it produces quite a sharp, acidic cheese, so it is only suitable when making a cheese that will be eaten young. The use of rennet significantly improves cheesemaking techniques, and it was its discovery centuries ago that allowed shepherds to make harder cheeses that lasted through the winter months when their animals and the land were barren.

All milk-fed animals are born with an enzyme in their stomachs that attacks the milk and converts it into solids (which they can digest) and liquid (which is mainly waste). The travelling herdsman probably discovered the effects of the enzyme – rennet – when they stored their milk in sacks made from the stomach of a young kid or lamb and found the warm

Above: Lifting newly formed Parmesan out of the whey using cheesecloth

milk had soured slightly and separated into curds and whey.

If too much rennet is used, there is a risk that the finished cheese will be hard, dry and friable, and have a pronounced bitter taste, especially if acidification is insufficient. When preparing cheese with a rapid coagulation rate, the dosage of the rennet is higher than for cheeses that coagulate slowly.

Rennet also helps to break down the curd into a smooth, even consistency, contributing to the texture and flavour.

The use of this animal product means that many vegetarians are reluctant to eat cheese. Fortunately, manufacturers and chemists recognized that vegetarianism was not a passing fad but represented an increasingly significant proportion of the population and have created non-animal alternatives. Over 85 per cent of cheeses made in Britain and 60 per cent in New Zealand use a rennet substitute suitable for vegetarians. Some traditional cheeses dating back thousands of years use vegetable or fungal alternatives to trigger coagulation. These include the juices or tissues of certain plants, such as thistle and Lady's Bed Straw. Fig juice has also been used to start coagulation.

The Types of Cheese and How They are Made

The type of cheese that is produced by the cheesemaker is determined by the amount of moisture he eliminates from the curd and the size of cheese that he wants to make. The amount of moisture in the curd will also determine what sort of rind or mould will grow on the cheese. The presence of rind is a huge advantage for the consumer. You may not be able to judge a wine by its bottle or a book by its cover, but the essential characteristics of a cheese can certainly be judged by a glance at the rind.

From just a brief glance at the rind and texture of a hitherto unknown cheese you can tell roughly what sort of texture, taste and strength of flavour you can expect. With practice – and the occasional squeeze and sniff – you can even learn to determine the condition and maturity of a cheese. Using the "rind" as a guide gives you an insight into the character, background and probable traits and foibles of virtually any cheese you encounter and enables you to dazzle your friends and family with your expertise.

LOW-FAT CHEESES

Traditional cheeses, such as Parmesan and Single Gloucester, were made with skimmed milk. The cream was skimmed off to use for cooking or to make butter. Today, with the growing obsession with low-fat foods, increasing numbers of cheeses are being made in low-fat versions. The fat, however, is what gives the cheese its texture and depth of the flavour. Consequently low-fat versions of traditional cheeses tend to lack both body and texture. It is far better to use a smaller amount of a traditional cheese than a large quantity of a bland, low-fat substitute.

Try using a soft cheese as they have a higher moisture content and therefore a lower percentage of fat than a harder cheese. Or, simply use less of a more mature, stronger-tasting hard cheese.

Fresh Cheeses

(NO VISIBLE RIND OR GROWTH OF MOULD)
EXAMPLES: *ricotta, feta, Myzlthra, mozzarella, cream cheese, fresh chèvre*

The milk is warmed, the starter culture is added and the acidity starts to increase. For some cheeses, like fromage frais, the starter is sufficient. These are called LACTIC CHEESES. Most cheeses, however, require the addition of rennet. This is stirred into the milk, then left for a few hours until it coagulates and resembles a very floppy milk jelly. The amount of moisture remaining with the whey will determine how soft or hard the final cheese will be.

Fresh cheeses are high in moisture. The young curd is carefully placed in sacks or small perforated containers and drained slowly without pressure for a few hours so that the curd retains much of the whey. Once sufficient whey has been drained off, the curds are either mixed or sprinkled with salt. They are now ready to be eaten. Some fresh cheeses are allowed to mature and grow either a white or bluish-grey mould, which places them in a different category.

Milk was a precious commodity to the herdsmen and their families. It was vital that none should be wasted, so some cheesemakers made cheeses from the whey, which contains small amounts of fat, vitamins and proteins. The most famous of these WHEY CHEESES is ricotta. This is made by boiling the whey, thus causing the small solid particles to float to the top. These are then scooped off, put in basket moulds to drain and sold within a few days. Whey cheeses tend to be used for cooking rather than eating fresh, as are most of these fresh cheeses. Scandinavian cheesemakers boil the whey slowly for hours, reducing it to a sticky toffee-like substance known as Gjetost or Mesost.

The other style of fresh cheeses are STRETCHED CURD CHEESES, with their irresistible stringy, impossible-to-control texture. These came originally from the Middle East, but the best known example today is mozzarella. The young curd is heated in the whey before being stretched or kneaded until the strings do not break when stretched. The pliant curd is then "spun" into balls or plaited and tossed in hot water to seal the cheese.

COMMON CHARACTERISTICS: Fresh cheeses are always mild and high in moisture and therefore low in fat. They have a slightly acidic or lactic taste. Most are used for cooking but some may be wrapped in leaves or dusted with paprika, charcoal or fresh herbs for serving as a table cheese.

WATCH POINTS: A slightly bitter smell, normally accompanied by a greyish brown or thin opaque mould, indicates the cheese is no longer fresh and will taste bitter.

Soft-white Cheeses

(WHITE, FUZZY PENICILLIUM CANDIDUM RIND)
EXAMPLES: *Camembert, Brie, Bonchester, Pencarreg, Chaource*

The floppy curd is ladled gently into moulds and left to drain in perforated moulds in an atmosphere of high humidity so that the curd does not lose too much whey. After a few hours, the cheeses are turned out of their moulds and left to mature for a few weeks. Their high moisture content, coupled with the high humidity, attracts and encourages the growth of the classic white penicillium mould seen on Bries and Camemberts around the world.

The penicillium moulds help to break down the curd and contribute to the flavour and texture of the cheese. The result is a creamy, smooth, voluptuous interior that when perfect looks as though it is almost ready to run.

Originally, the mould would have existed naturally in the atmosphere, along with other wild moulds and yeasts. Today, these need to be introduced into the cheesemakers' ripening rooms. Artisan cheesemakers encourage the growth of these wild moulds. On their cheeses, the white rinds tend to be dusted or impregnated with red, yellow, grey or pink moulds, all of which add to the depth and uniqueness of flavour. The wild moulds, however, do not stand up to the modern hygiene conditions that exist in factories. Here the mould spores have to be continually sprayed into the ripening rooms or even injected into the cheeses, producing a rather one-dimensional flavour.

Common characteristics: Brie is a classic example of a soft-white cheese, with its rich, runny, creamy texture. The taste is reminiscent of soup made from wild mushrooms, with just a dash of sherry. Pasteurized Bries remain white, and smell more like hay and button mushrooms and have a buttery, mushroom taste.

Watch points: A strong smell of ammonia indicates that the cheese has entered second fermentation or has been kept too damp. Soft-white cheeses with long shelf lives have been stabilized to prevent them running. They will consequently taste sweeter and more buttery and will be elastic rather than runny. Soft-white cheeses made with milk that has been enriched with cream before being coagulated will be higher in fat, more solid and have the richness of cream but will seldom develop a great depth of flavour. However, they will feel like melted butter or ice cream in the mouth and will taste delicious.

Exceptions: Blue Bries and other flavoured Brie-type cheeses belong in this category as the classification relates to the *rind* first rather than the cheese's interior. Thus, by looking at a soft flat Brie-type cheese you can tell that its overall character will be that of a soft-white cheese even though only a label or a sharp knife will tell you what is inside.

Natural-rind cheeses

(BLUE-GREY MOULDED RIND, USUALLY GOAT)

EXAMPLES: *Crottin de Chavignol, Saint-Marcellin, Selles-sur-Cher*

The majority of French farmhouse goat's milk cheeses belong in this category, which applies to fresh cheeses that have been left to drain for longer and in a drier atmosphere than the fresh cheeses. These are the cheeses you see piled on wooden trestles in French markets. When young, they have a slightly wrinkled, cream-coloured rind. In time they dry out, the wrinkles become more pronounced and the character and flavour increases, along with the growth of bluish grey mould.

Above: Shelves of unpasteurized Brie de Meaux in a special ripening room where the cheeses will gradually develop their distinctive rind

Common characteristics: Initially, the taste is fresh, almost fruity, with undertones of goat; as the cheeses dry out the flavours intensify, becoming rich and nutty and acquiring a decidedly goaty taste. The mould starts as a discrete hue on the surface, gradually covering the entire cheese in greyish-blue blotches. There are few examples of this variety made in Britain, America or Australasia as the majority of consumers are dubious about moulds.

Watch points: To mature and ripen, these cheeses must be kept dry. Any wetness on the surface should be patted dry immediately or the cheese will become damp and lose its sharp, clean taste.

Washed-rind Cheeses

(ORANGEY-BROWN STICKY RIND)

EXAMPLES: *Epoisses, Herve, Milleens, Stinking Bishop, Munster*

The curd, which may or may not be cut depending on how soft the final cheese should be, is scooped into moulds and left to drain. The high moisture of the curd and the humidity of the maturing rooms attracts a bitter-tasting, grey, hairy mould called "cat fur". To discourage this, the newly formed cheese is rubbed with or dunked in baths of salty water, wine or a similar alcoholic liquid. This produces a rather robust cheese and encourages the development of orange, sticky bacteria that help to break down the curd from the outside, gradually becoming an integral part of the interior, rather than just a skin.

Invented by Trappist monks to enhance their otherwise rather meagre diet on fast days, these cheeses are found right across Europe, but mainly in France, Belgium and (more recently) Ireland.

Common characteristics: Ranging from rather spicy to outrageously piquant in taste and aroma (and once banned on French public transport for that very reason), they can smell yeasty or can be almost meaty. The interior may resemble Brie or be more supple and elastic.

Watch points: A dull brownish rind may indicate that the cheese has been kept too long or has been allowed to dry out. Cracking, if noticed early, can be arrested by wrapping the cheese in clear film to conserve the moisture.

Semi-soft Cheeses

(PINKISH/BROWN TO DARK GREY RIND WITH SUPPLE, ELASTIC "FEEL")

EXAMPLES: *Raclette, Desmond, Gubbeens, Edam, Sonoma Jack, Fontina*

To obtain a firmer cheese, the curd is cut up to release some of the whey before the curd is placed in moulds. It is then often lightly pressed to speed up the draining. After a day or so, the cheese is turned out of its mould and washed in brine. This

ABOVE: Fresh, cloth-wrapped Gruyère curd is placed in the massive, traditional, round wooden hoop

seals the rind before the cheese is placed in cellars or ripening rooms, where other moulds are encouraged to grow. To eliminate the formation of the rind, the cheeses may be sealed in plastic; otherwise the moulds that form are frequently brushed off, gradually building up a leathery rind that may be fine and barely perceptible from the interior, thin orange brown like the rind on raclette or thick grey-brown and leathery like the rind on Tomme de Savoie.

COMMON CHARACTERISTICS: The lower moisture content means the fermentation process is slower, producing cheeses with a round, full-bodied, rather than strong, flavour. Their taste often seems to be embodied with the oils and esters of the wild mountain flowers of Europe. When young, semi-soft cheeses have a firm yet springy, school eraser texture, becoming elastic and supple.

WATCH POINTS: Cheeses that have been dipped in wax to prevent dehydration and splitting may sweat, causing mould to develop under the rind.

EXCEPTIONS: Some semi-soft cheeses are only very lightly pressed and can be eaten within a few days or the cheese may be encouraged to grow a soft-white rind, although this will slowly be corrupted by the more virulent moulds common to this type of cheese.

HARD CHEESES

(THICK RIND, OFTEN WAXED, OILED OR CLOTHBOUND)

EXAMPLES: *Cheddar, Manchego, Cantal, Gruyèye, Cheshire, Parmigiano-Reggiano, Pecorino*

To make a hard cheese the curd must be cut more finely – from small cubes to rice-size pieces – the smaller the pieces, the more whey will be lost from the curd. The curds are then gently heated in a vat to force out more moisture before the whey is drained off. Salt is then added to the curds, which now resemble rubbery, lumpy, cottage cheese. They may be cut again (the process differs for various types of hard cheeses) before being placed in large perforated moulds that are frequently engraved with a unique symbol, logo, pattern or name to identify the finished cheese or its maker.

Most traditional, hard British cheeses are wrapped in cloth, sealed with lard and left to mature for weeks or even years. Hard European cheeses tend to be left in brine overnight (or, in the case of Parmigiano-Reggiano, for up to 21 days) to seal the rind. Then they, like their British counterparts, are placed in "caves" or ripening rooms to mature. Most hard cheeses require at least a

ABOVE: Hundred's of Quicke's Cheddars maturing on ceiling-high shelves in the ripening rooms at their farm in Devon

LEFT: Parmigiano-Reggiano – one of the classic hard cheeses

Above: A newly formed Gruyère cheese is frequently pressed and turned, then it is left in the press overnight

few weeks to mature, if not years, as is the case with good farmhouse Cheddar, Emmental or Cantal.

Hard block cheeses are pressed into shape and then matured in special plastic wrap that allows the cheese to age without the development of either moulds or rind. The moisture that would normally be lost during maturation is also retained. The cheese will mature faster but its texture will be softer than traditionally matured, clothbound cheeses. However, the method for block cheeses is more economical as a hard cheese like Cheddar can lose up to 15 per cent of its original weight if not wrapped.

Watch points: Hard cheeses are user-friendly. They may grow some surface mould, but this can easily be scraped off. The important thing to remember is to keep the cut surfaces of hard cheese tightly covered with foil or clear film (leaving an opening for the rind to breathe) to prevent the cheese from absorbing any taints from the fridge. Fatty substances, particularly cheeses and fat, absorb smells very easily, which is an advantage when the aroma is acquired intentionally, but a drawback if not.

Blue Cheeses

(The rind varies from a fine bloom to a thick gritty rind like that on Stilton, but generally blue cheeses are wrapped in foil)

Examples: *Stilton, Roquefort, Gorgonzola, Cabrales, Maytag Blue, Danish Blue*

Blue cheeses are neither pressed nor cooked. Most frequently the curd is crumbled, eliminating much of the whey, then scooped into stainless steel cylindrical moulds, each with a wooden disk on the top. The curd remains in the moulds for 1–2 weeks and is turned frequently to let the weight of the curds press out more of the whey. Once the cheeses can stand up on their own, they are removed from the moulds, rubbed with salt, then returned to the cellars.

The blue mould is a strain of penicillium that is added to the milk before the rennet is added either in liquid or powder form. The cheese will not turn blue, however, unless it is given air to breathe. This is done by piercing the cheese with rods. The blue then grows along the tunnels and into the nooks and crannies between the loose curd, producing the shattered porcelain look that typifies blue cheese.

Those that are made like Brie have the blue injected into the young curd as the moisture content is so high that any holes made in the cheese would immediately close up, preventing air from penetrating the curd.

Watch points: Most blue cheeses are normally wrapped in foil to prevent them from drying out. This causes the moisture pumped out by the bacteria during fermentation to gather on the rind. Scrape this off before serving.

Speciality Cheese

(Similar to the original cheese used as a base)

Examples: *Gouda with Cumin, Sage Derby, Cheddar with Date & Walnut, Red Leicester with Pecans, Raclette with Peppercorns*

These are made from familiar semi-soft or hard cheeses to which flavourings or other ingredients – nuts, fruit, spices, herbs, even fish – have been added. Traditionally

Above: Bleu d'Auvergne curds draining in their stainless steel moulds – they are left for one or two weeks

the flavourings tended to be cumin, cloves or herbs but in the last five years, particularly in Britain, flavoured cheeses have become a significant growth area of the market. Some combinations are successful, others sublime and a few positively ridiculous.

The Art of Cheese Tasting

The most effective way of putting your new knowledge to the test is to taste a selection of cheeses – preferably one of each of the different types. Buy some cheese, wine and bread, then invite a few friends round to compare the flavours and textures of the cheeses against each other. The categories here are roughly in order of strength so use them as a guide, starting from mild to strong, though as with all rules, there are exceptions and reasons for breaking them. Don't lose sight of the object of the exercise, however, which is to enjoy the gentle art of learning that one "lives to eat, not eats to live".

Below: Once Bleu d'Auvergne cheeses are removed from the moulds, they are rubbed with salt

Wine and Cheese: the Perfect Marriage

As a very general rule, the whiter and fresher the cheese the crisper and fruitier the wine should be. The heavier, richer soft cheeses can be partnered with a big white like a Chardonnay or a light red. The harder and darker the cheese, the heavier and richer the style of wine can be. Most blue cheeses, on the other hand, go superbly with sweet wines.

Perfumed or floral reds are too overpowering. So are heavy tannic wines – the tannin tends to steal the nutty richness of the cheese. If asked to select one grape variety over any other to have with a cheeseboard, the author would go for a Pinot Noir from the New World or a soft Burgundian Pinot Noir. However, white wines are often unexpectedly good partners, allowing the cheese and the wine a chance to show their character in a way that a red wine may often fail to do.

Fresh Cheeses

Try fresh light, crisp white wines like Sauvignon or Chenin Blanc; also try Frascati, Soave or Loire whites. Red wines are too heavy, unless the cheese is part of a spicy dish like a pizza.

Below: Red wine, especially those made with Pinot Noir grapes, makes an ideal accompaniment to cheese

Soft-white Cheeses

With the mild, slightly sharp, salty style try a slightly sweet wine. Those with a richer, sweeter and more creamy taste need a fruitier wine with a good balance of fruit and acidity. A New Zealand or Chilean Sauvignon Blanc would be ideal. The more meaty Bries prefer a full-bodied, fruity red like a Pinot Noir or even a rich white, such as Chardonnay.

Semi-soft Cheeses

Try a full-bodied gutsy white or a light fruity, red. The firmer, more distinctly flavoured semi-soft cheeses need a Chianti, Rioja or Merlot.

Washed-rind Cheeses

The strong, pungent, washed rind cheeses respond well to beer. If you serve wine, make it a spicy Gewurztraminer or a robust red.

Hard Cheeses

They range from the mild to the outrageously tangy, so almost any wine can be a potential match. However a general rule is the stronger the cheese the bigger the wine required.

Mild: something red and fruity – Fitou, Merlot or Chilean reds

Medium: try Côtes du Rhône or a New Zealand Cabernet Sauvignon

Strong: Californian Cabernet Sauvignon or even an Australian Shiraz

Extra Strong: these can handle the rich sweetness of fortified wines, such as Port or Madeira

Blue Cheeses

Milder blues need a light fruity white like a Vouvray, Chenin Blanc or a Rosé, while the more piquant blues prefer robust, spicy reds like the Rhônes or a Shiraz. Better still, serve a sweet wine like Monbazillac or some of the sweeter wines from the New World. The classic marriage is of Roquefort with a Sauterne. The sharp, salty tang of the cheese is softened by the wine, while the sweetness of the sheep's milk is underlined.

Creating the Perfect Cheeseboard

Use the list of cheese types outlined in the introduction as a guide next time you buy your cheeses. Learn to determine which category you prefer and how to offer a balanced cheeseboard. You should have not only a selection from several categories, but also take care to offer a combination of shapes and provide at least one goat's or sheep's milk cheese.

ACCOMPANIMENTS TO YOUR CHEESEBOARD

Bread: There are almost as many breads as there are cheeses. The best are home-made or country-style breads. Walnut and raisin breads are favoured by some, but plain breads are often better with cheese.

Nuts: The Europeans often serve their cheese with fresh walnuts, almonds or hazelnuts in the shell. Pre-shelled nuts rarely have the same sweetness.

Pickles: Serving pickles or chutney with cheese is a very English habit. these accompaniments are suitable for hard, mature cheeses, such as Cheddar, but they can overpower. The best are home-made and sweet, rather than hot and spicy.

Fresh Fruit: Serve seasonal fruit, preferably local. Citrus is too sharp, and tropical fruit generally too sweet – apples, pears and figs are perfect.

Dried Fruit: Dried figs, prunes and raisins are delicious with all style of cheese. The Spanish make a number of delicious fruit pastes or "cheeses" from quinces, figs, almonds and raisins. These are delicious with all their cheeses, particularly the hard cheeses made from sheep's milk.

Savoury Touches: Spring onions, olives, celery, fresh beans and crisp greens like rocket (arugula)or long leaf lettuces can be served with, but not on, the cheeseboard.

Honey: Drizzling blue cheeses lightly with a little wild honey heightens their flavour.

Above: Choose a selection of different cheeses for your cheeseboard and accompany them with bread and fruit

◆ The best cheese board is the one chosen with care and enthusiasm and served on a rough board with chunks of bread, copious quantities of wine and good friends to share it with.

◆ One superb cheese is better than three or four small wedges.

◆ Choosing several cheeses from different categories means you will have a variety of textures. The colours of the rinds will differ, as will the interior of the cheeses.

◆ Colour should come from the rinds of the cheeses and not come from a bunch of grapes or similar fruit. If you want to decorate the board, use chestnut or oak leaves, fresh herbs or wild flowers. Add several different breads.

◆ Biscuits tend to take away from the texture of the cheeses and are often very salty. Try fresh, crusty country-style breads instead.

◆ Serve fresh fruit separately.

◆ There are some wonderful alternatives to the basic round wooden or marble cheeseboard. Experiment with wicker trays, shallow baskets, a piece of driftwood or a tray covered with a linen napkin and grape leaves.

◆ Shapes add interest to your cheeseboard. Where possible avoid having all the shapes of the cheeses the same. Instead, offer pyramids, logs, squares or cylinders. Alternatively, cut the cheese into irregular shapes.

◆ The habit of serving cheese before dessert is practised by the French for the simple reason that this enables the red wine from the main course to be finished with the cheese. The sweet wine can then be served with the blue cheeses (which, because they have the strongest flavour, should be eaten last) and follows through to accompany the dessert.

◆ A cheeseboard can also be served as a main course for lunch. Serve a selection of cheeses with a lightly dressed mixed leaf salad, pickles or chutney, fresh fruit and nuts and country-style bread. If you like, serve a selection of wines.

Cheeses of the World

To taste and record the cheeses of the world would be an impossible, if infinitely pleasureable task. Instead, this reference section includes a cross-section of the world's cheeses. A few are made in huge creameries, but most come from small co-operatives or family-owned farms. Some, such as Roquefort and Cheddar, are found all over the world; others, such as Aorangi from New Zealand, Yerba Santa Shepherd's Cheese from the USA and Cooleeney from Ireland, are recently created, while others use recipes that have remained unchanged for centuries and are rarely found outside the village in which they were first made.

French Cheeses

France has many of the most fascinating cheeses in the world; over 750 of them. Most are traditional cheeses, cherished and fiercely protected.

The earliest recorded French cheese was Roquefort. Pliny, writing in the first century BC, described it as "the cheese that bears away the prize at Rome where they are always ready to compare and appreciate good things from every land". Roquefort continues to be appreciated to this day – all over the world.

During the Middle Ages the cheese-making tradition was kept alive in the monasteries of France. Monks taught the farmers how to keep their animals healthy and their milk clean. It was they who showed the farmers how to mature cheese, usually the peasants' major source of protein. Their numerous fast days gave them the motivation to invent new recipes and in 960AD the first of the monastery cheeses, Maroilles, was created at an abbey in the Thiérache region of northern France. The monks discovered that rubbing the surface of small, soft cheeses with salt created a pungent and quite meaty aroma and taste. The first of the famous Trappist cheeses was born. Munster, Pont l'Evêque, Epoisses and others were to follow.

French cheeses have retained their individual character, allowing the vagaries of nature, combined with the ingenuity of man, to dictate their type, size and final flavour. In the valleys and on the plains small, fresh cheeses were made that could either be eaten by the family or swiftly sold; in the mountains, where cheeses had to be stored until the shepherds could get them to market, large wheels of cheese were made that would not mature for many months or even years. The numerous limestone caves, like those at Cambalou, where Roquefort is made, proved perfect for the making of blue cheeses.

Above: Chevrotin des Aravis (left) and Chèvre Feuille (right)
Below right: Carré de l'Est

Below: Vignotte

Most of the vast number of cheeses made in France today are traditional varieties, but even the French have been unable to resist the temptation to create new cheeses. Most of the new cheeses have emerged from the huge dairy companies that now dominate the French market. Some are dismal, bland variations on traditional cheeses, particularly the standardized, pasteurized Bries and Camemberts; others, such as Chaumes, Saint-Agur and Le Roulé, have been made by adapting traditional methods to the modern factory environment, and offer the consumer a stepping stone to the more complex artisan cheeses they might otherwise shy away from trying.

Surprisingly, it is not Camembert that is the most popular cheese in France. That honour goes to Comté (or Comté Jura), the wonderful, hard, fruity mountain cheese from the north-west corner of France. Second favourite is Roquefort.

Camembert owes its place as the best-known French cheese outside France to two apparently unrelated events. The first was the manufacture of small wooden boxes that proved perfect for packing the soft, fragile cheeses of Normandy, and the second was the invention of the train. Properly packed and rapidly transported to Paris and beyond, Camembert soon became a best seller.

The finest way to discover French cheeses is to travel through France, stopping at markets and fromageries to taste. Failing that, find a good cheesemonger and eat your way to an education.

Abbaye de Belloc (AOC)

Region: *Pays Basque*
Type: *Traditional, farmhouse, unpasteurized, hard cheese*
Source: *Sheep's milk (Manech and others)*
Description: *5kg/11lb fat wheel with natural, crusty, brownish rind with patches of red, orange and yellow. The rind is marked with tiny craters*
Culinary uses: *Table cheese, grating, grilling, sauces*

The Abbaye de Notre-Dame de Belloc was founded by Benedictine monks. For centuries they have made their cheese from milk produced in the locality. In summer, the shepherds follow the ancient tradition of taking their flocks to mountain pastures. Along with other hard sheep's milk cheeses of the area, Abbaye de Belloc comes under the Ossau-Iraty AOC banner. The cheese has a firm, dense, rich and creamy texture. The taste resembles burnt caramel and there is a distinctive lanolin aroma.

Aisy Cendré

Region: *Burgundy*
Type: *Traditional, farmhouse, unpasteurized, semi-soft cheese*
Source: *Cow's milk*
Description: *200–250g/7–9oz round cheese with natural rind covered with a thick coating of ash*
Culinary use: *Table cheese*

To make this speciality, a local cheese (usually a young Epoisses) is immersed in a bed of ashes for at least one month. The best the author tasted was made by a winemaker who washed the cheese in his own marc de bourgogne before burying it in ashes. A few days before serving, the winemaker would brush off the ash, soak the cheese overnight in his precious eau-de-vie, then present it along with the rest of the bottle. Slow to ripen, Aisy Cendré has a white, salty, chalky centre surrounded by a softer, earthy tasting outer layer. Unless you are the sort of person who likes sand with your picnic, you should brush off the layer of ashes before serving the cheese.

Olivet Cendré is a similar cheese.

Ardi-Gasna

Region: *Pays Basque*
Type: *Traditional, farmhouse, unpasteurized, hard cheese*
Source: *Sheep's milk*
Description: *3–5kg/6½–11lb wheel with natural, crusty, yellow rind with greyish moulds*
Culinary uses: *Table cheese, grating, snacks, desserts*

Ardi-Gasna means "sheep's cheese" in Basque, and this cheese has remained virtually unchanged for centuries. There are still a few local shepherds who make the long journey with their flocks up to the high mountain pastures. Here they make their cheese in stone huts in late spring and early summer. Seldom found outside the region, Ardi-Gasna cheeses are highly prized. The cheese has a hard texture, but feels rich in the mouth. The flavour is clean and fresh with the sweetness of mountain flowers and a nuttiness born of age. The finish has a touch of sharpness that increases as the cheese matures.

Similar cheeses include Laruns and Esbareich.

Arômes au Gène de Marc

Region: *Lyonnais*
Type: *Traditional, farmhouse, unpasteurized, natural-rind cheese*
Source: *Cow's and goat's milk*
Description: *80–120g/3¼–4¼oz small, round cheeses. The whitish rind has some mould. The fermenting lees of the marc are pressed into it*
Culinary use: *Table cheese*

Made in various wine-making areas, some two to three months after the grapes have been pressed, these are the result of small immature cheeses such as Rigotte or St Marcellin being macerated or cured in vats of marc (fermenting grape skins and pips). They are then rolled in the marc before being sold. Definitely not for the faint-hearted, the cheeses have a strong, bittersweet, yeasty taste and aroma. When young, the moist, creamy taste of the cheese offers a balance; with age, the cheese becomes hard and flaky, with a formidable pungent taste – not necessarily appreciated by the uninitiated.

Similar cheeses are produced by other villages in the area.

AOC

To preserve and protect the traditions and experience of centuries of French cheesemaking, the AOC (Appellation d'Origine Contrôlée) system was established, as it had been for wine. Each cheese protected by the system must comply with strictly enforced rules that govern the following:

- the area where cattle may graze
- the origin and type of feed provided
- the breed of cattle that furnish the milk
- when the cheese is made (what season)
- how the cheese is made
- the shape and size of the cheese
- how the cheese is stored

The regulations often mean that cattle may only graze on permanent pastures that are organically managed, rather than ploughed and re-sown every year. The use of silage or other fermented or man-made feed is prohibited.

The AOC rules guarantee the quality of France's famous cheeses, protecting them against copies and giving the consumer the confidence to buy raw milk cheeses. Some AOC cheeses are made in huge factories, others on tiny farms, but all proudly respect and uphold the traditions of the area.

Below: Abbaye de Belloc

Above: Banon

Below right: Beaufort

Baguette Laonnaise

Region: *Ile-de-France*

Type: *Traditional, creamery, washed-rind cheese*

Source: *Cow's milk*

Description: *500g/1¼lb oblong loaf with glossy but crusty, orange-brown rind*

Culinary use: *Table cheese*

Created after the Second World War, Baguette Laonnaise has become a favourite with lovers of strong cheese. The sticky, ridged, orange-brown rind hides a supple, yet dense interior.

As the cheese ages it develops a very pungent, spicy nose and taste, and a finish that is reminiscent of the farmyard. In the wrong hands (or a cold fridge) the rind may dry out and the cheese will become quite bitter and unpleasant to eat.

Similar cheeses include Maroilles, Herve and Limburger.

Banon

Region: *Provence*

Type: *Traditional, farmhouse and creamery, unpasteurized, natural-rind cheese*

Source: *Cow's, sheep's or goat's milk, or a combination*

Description: *100g/3¾oz small, round cheese, traditionally sold wrapped in chestnut leaves and tied with raffia*

Culinary uses: *Table cheese*

This cheese takes its name from the market-town of Banon, where cobbled paths wind up past old, stone cottages to the church. Chestnut trees provide welcome shade and also provide the leaves used for wrapping the cheese. The leaves keep the young, slightly acidic cheese moist and impart a fresh vegetable flavour with a hint of wine. As the cheese ages, blue and grey moulds and yeasts are produced on and under the leaves, which contribute to the taste. Banon cheeses range from firm, mild and lactic to soft, creamy and tart, with a nutty flavour. Although traditionally produced from goat's, sheep's or mixed milks, most are today produced in large creameries, from cow's milk. At the weekly market in Banon, you can buy fresh and aged local cheeses.

The local speciality, Fromage Fort du Mont Ventoux, is produced by placing a young Banon cheese (minus chestnut leaves) in an earthenware crock, seasoning it liberally with salt and pepper and pouring over vinegar or local eau-de-vie. The crock is then placed in a cool cellar and the cheese left to ferment, with just the occasional stir. The longer it is left, the more ferocious it becomes.

Beaufort (AOC)

Region: *Savoie*

Type: *Traditional, farmhouse, unpasteurized, hard cheese*

Source: *Cow's milk*

Description: *Large, concave cartwheel, about 60cm/24in in diameter and weighing up to 75kg/165lb. The hard, brownish-yellow, natural, brushed rind is slightly rough*

Culinary uses: *Table cheese, snacks, fondues, grated, in pies*

A member of the Gruyère family, but with a higher fat content, this ancient cheese dates back to the time of the Roman Empire. Made in mountain chalets, it has an irresistible smoothness, despite its hard appearance. It owes its superb flavour to the flowers, sweet grasses and herbs of the high pastures, where, by AOC rules, the cows must graze. Gruyère gets its name from the time when kings sent their tax collectors, known as "agents gruyers", to collect taxes from the cheesemakers. Also known as Gruyère de Beaufort.

Bleu d'Auvergne (AOC)

Region: *Auvergne*
Type: *Traditional, farmhouse and creamery, blue cheese*
Source: *Cow's milk*
Description: *1–3kg/2¼–6½ lb short cylinder. The moist, natural rind has grey and blue moulds*
Culinary uses: *Table cheese, crumbled in salads (with nuts)*

Named after the magnificent mountainous region where it is made, this is a moist, creamy cheese that resembles Roquefort, although it is made with cow's milk, not sheep's milk. It has a piquant smell and sharp, clean taste with a hint of herbs and melted butter. The cheese is composed of pockets and broken threads of bluish-grey mould. With age, the crust becomes sticky and reddish-orange moulds start to develop. These help to break down the interior, which gradually collapses, intensifying the spicy flavour.

Although Bleu d'Auvergne is now made by large creameries, the AOC regulations ensure that tradition and craftsmanship are retained. Some examples of this cheese are still made in farmhouses from raw milk, but they are seldom found outside the region.

Similar cheeses include Bleu des Causses and Bleu de Laqueuille.

Bleu de Haut Jura (AOC)

Region: *Franche-Comté*
Type: *Traditional, farmhouse and co-operative, unpasteurized, blue cheese*
Source: *Cow's milk*
Description: *7.5kg/16½lb wheel with convex edges. The natural rind is dry, rough and thin, with powdery yellow to red moulds*
Culinary uses: *Table cheese, salads*

Unlike most blue cheeses, this is made in the shape of a large, flat wheel, which speeds the ripening process. The result is a cheese that is more supple and less creamy than other blues, with a mild taste that hints of mushrooms, tarragon and fresh milk. The AOC was granted in 1977. Other blues made in the region, such as Bleu de Gex and Bleu de Septomoncel, are now officially named Bleu de Haut Jura.

Bleu de Laqueuille

Region: *Auvergne*
Type: *Traditional, creamery, unpasteurized, blue cheese*
Source: *Cow's milk*
Description: *800g–2.5kg/1¾–5½lb cylinder with natural, pale orange rind, on which the more dominant, white penicillium mould battles it out with the greyish moulds common to blue cheeses*
Culinary use: *Table cheese*

A statue in Laqueuille reminds visitors to the village that Antoine Roussel created this cheese in 1850 after sprinkling young curd with blue moulds he found growing on rye bread. It rapidly became popular, both locally and in Paris. Like a smaller version of Fourme d'Ambert, it tends to develop a soft, white mould on some or all of the rind. The consistency leans towards that of Brie. The blue is chunky rather than in streaks and the flavour is spicy, fresh and creamy, with a slightly salty tang. The smaller version makes an attractive addition to a cheeseboard.

Below: Clockwise from bottom left, Bleu de Laqueuille , Bleu d'Auvergne, Bleu des Causses and Bleu de Gex

Bleu des Causses (AOC)

Region: *Auvergne*
Type: *Traditional, creamery, unpasteurized, blue cheese*
Source: *Cow's milk*
Description: *2.25–3kg/5–6½lb flat cylinder. The sticky, ivory rind has fine reddish-orange and grey moulds*
Culinary uses: *Table cheese, salads*

For centuries, this pungent cheese was made in the Rouergue and surrounding areas, using cow's or sheep's milk. However, since 1947 AOC rules have decreed that it must be made with cow's milk to differentiate it from Roquefort, which is made in the same area. Bleu des Causses, like Roquefort, is matured in limestone caves with natural fissures that allow fresh air currents or "fleurines" to circulate and move the natural moulds through the ripening cheese. The result is a cheese that is firm-textured, but more moist and spicy in flavour than other French blues. Fresh-tasting, with a sharp finish, it is an excellent, less salty alternative to Roquefort.

Bleu des Causses cheeses that attain the required standards of quality are stamped with the AOC symbol before being wrapped in silver foil.

Bougon

REGION: *Poitou-Charentes*
TYPE: *Traditional, creamery, soft-white cheese*
SOURCE: *Goat's milk*
DESCRIPTION: *80g/3¼oz round with fine, white penicillium mould rind*
CULINARY USE: *Table cheese*

Although similar cheeses have been made in various forms in France for generations, Bougon was only recently made commercially. Although *bougon* means "grumpy" in French, this is no reflection on the cheese – it is simply named after the town where it is made. It is a smooth and voluptuous cheese with a taste that has been likened to a blend of tarragon, thyme and white wine. The Camembert shape is the most popular, but it also comes in pyramids, cylindrical logs and mini rounds.

Boulette d'Avesnes

REGION: *Nord-Pas-de-Calais*
TYPE: *Traditional, farmhouse and creamery, fresh cheese*
SOURCE: *Cow's milk*
DESCRIPTION: *150–180g/5–6¼oz cone with natural rind given a dark red colour by the use of annatto or paprika*
CULINARY USE: *Table cheese*

This unusual cheese was originally produced from buttermilk and was made on farms as a by-product of buttermaking. Today, creameries use underripe or less-than-perfect Maroilles or Dauphine cheeses. The soft curd is kneaded and mashed with parsley, tarragon, pepper and paprika. The cheese has a fairly doughy texture and a quite outrageously spicy flavour.

ABOVE: Boulette d'Avesnes

Boursault

REGION: *Ile-de-France*
TYPE: *Modern, creamery, soft-white cheese*
SOURCE: *Cow's milk*
DESCRIPTION: *200g/7oz small half-cylinder with light, white penicillium mould rind with pinkish tones*
CULINARY USES: *Table cheese, canapés*

Invented by Henri Boursault in 1953, about the same time as Boursin, this soft-white-rinded cheese became successful almost overnight. The company is now owned by the cheese giant Van den Berg. The method resembles that used for Brie, but Boursault has a softer and thinner rind. This helps to ripen the cheese, giving off a sweet, mushroomy aroma. The high cream content means that the taste is smooth and almost buttery. The interior is solid rather than supple or runny and the finish is nutty and it has a refreshing citrus tang to balance the richness of the cream. One of the best enriched cheeses, Boursault is also known as Lucullus. Délice de Saint-Cyr is a larger version.

Boursin

REGION: *Ile-de-France and Normandy*
TYPE: *Modern, creamery, fresh cheese*
SOURCE: *Cow's milk*
DESCRIPTION: *80g/3¼oz small half-cylinder without rind, sold in an attractive, corrugated-foil wrapper*
CULINARY USES: *Table cheese, baking, spreading*

Founded in 1957 by a Monsieur Boursin and now produced by one of the major French cheese companies (Van den Bergh), this is a moist, yet creamy cheese with a sweet, rich flavour with a hint of acidity. It melts in the mouth like ice cream. The quality has remained consistently good, both as regards the original cheese and the two well-known variations, one with garlic and herbs and the other rolled in fiery cracked peppercorns.

Boursin was the first cheese advertised on French TV and became a sensational success. The wacky, off-the-wall advertisement showed a famous actor being driven from his bed by his desire for the Boursin that was waiting elegantly in his fridge. Boursin – and the catch phrase "*du pain, du vin, du Boursin*" – became part of French culture.

Made only from rich Normandy milk and cream, the cheese is produced without rennet. Only a starter culture is used and much of the processing is still only semi-automated, to ensure that the texture and quality are maintained. Since Van den Bergh took over, it has invented three more exotic variations, but these are nowhere near as good, or as authentic, as the famous three.

ABOVE: Boursin

LEFT: Boursault

Above: Bresse Bleu

Bresse Bleu

Region: *Rhône-Alpes*
Type: *Modern, creamery, blue cheese*
Source: *Cow's milk*
Description: *125–500g/4½oz–1¼lb cylinder with soft-white rind with penicillium mould*
Culinary use: *Table cheese*

Developed during the Second World War and now owned by the milk processing giant Bongrain, Bresse Bleu became increasingly popular in the 1950s as an alternative to stronger blue cheeses. The interior is rich and buttery. Like Brie, it melts in the mouth, with a sweet, slightly spicy tang. The smooth, white rind has the aroma of button mushrooms. Because of the dense, creamy nature of the cheese, the blue mould must be injected into it, rather than being added to the milk before coagulation. It forms pockets of blue-grey mould rather than fine streaks. Tiny mould spores from the rind may be carried into the cheese when it is injected, forming patches of fluffy, white mould within the cheese.

Individual cheeses are small, so can be sold whole rather than in slices. This fact, together with convenient packaging, means that Bresse Bleu travels well and is therefore widely available outside its country of origin.

Similar cheeses include Blue Brie and Cambazola.

Brie de Meaux (AOC)

Region: *Ile-de-France*
Type: *Traditional, farmhouse, unpasteurized, soft-white cheese*
Source: *Cow's milk*
Description: *2.5–3kg/5½–6½lb wheel. The white penicillium mould rind has reddish-brown ferments. The marks of the straw mat on which the cheese matures are visible*
Culinary use: *Table cheese*

The father of all soft-white or bloomy-rind cheeses. Brie de Meaux was first recorded in AD774 when the gourmet and soldier Charlemagne tasted it in Brie and ordered two batches to be sent to him annually in Aix.

You will know when you have found the perfect Meaux – it is smooth, voluptuous and not quite runny. The aroma is that of mushrooms with the merest hint of ammonia and the taste is of creamy wild mushroom soup with a dash of sherry.

Although the cheese is now protected by AOC regulations, some critics claim these do not go far enough. Regrettably, the Friesian-Holstein cow continues to replace the old indigenous cattle. The richness and character of the milk is therefore not always what it should be. Fortunately, there remain some superb farm-produced Meaux brought to the point of perfection by talented affineurs.

Brie de Melun (AOC)

Region: *Ile-de-France*
Type: *Traditional, farmhouse, unpasteurized, soft-white cheese*
Source: *Cow's milk*
Description: *1.5–8kg/3–18lb wheel with white penicillium mould forming a fine, white crust with a mix of yellow and red ferments*
Culinary use: *Table cheese*

Produced in the same region as Brie de Meaux, Brie de Melun is sharper and more salty. Whereas rennet is used to coagulate Meaux, Melun relies entirely on the action of lactose-loving bacteria. The art of bringing the cheeses to the point of perfection belongs to the affineur. He will watch over row upon row of Bries in various stages of ripeness, each of them sitting on a well-worn wooden shelf lined with a straw mat. The cheese is judged to be ripe when the yellow mould dominates, with just a touch of the red. To attain the perfect balance, the affineur and his team turn as many as 18,000 cheeses twice a week for about two months. They take care not to leave fingermarks and to ensure that no bacteria from their hands are permitted to pass to the cheeses.

A perfect Melun has a supple texture with meadow scents and flavours – quite like an unripe Brie, but with more depth.

Below: Brie de Meaux

Below: Butte

Brillat-Savarin

Region: *Normandy*
Type: *Modern, creamery, fresh or soft-white cheese*
Source: *Cow's milk*
Description: *450–500g/1–1¼lb round cheese. There may be a soft-white rind. The cheese will eventually grow a thick, velvety, white crust*
Culinary uses: *Table cheese, canapés*

Named after the French magistrate, born in 1755, who published a gastronomic tome: *La Physiologie du Goût.* This book bore witness to a lifetime committed to good food. Brillat-Savarin would have approved of this rich triple cream cheese.

Other triple cream cheeses include Le Saulieu, Lucullus and Boursault.

Brocciu/Broccio (AOC)

Region: *Corsica*
Type: *Traditional, farmhouse, unpasteurized, whey cheese*
Source: *Sheep's and goat's milk*
Description: *500g–1kg/1¼–2¼lb cheeses in various shapes, without rind*
Culinary uses: *Served with herbs as a snack or with fruit for breakfast*

This fresh cheese is made with sheep's milk in winter and goat's milk in summer. Traditionally made from whey, although skimmed milk is often used today. The cheese is drained in woven baskets and has a mild flavour. Some cheeses are salted and dried for six months, when the flavour becomes very sharp and pronounced.

Bûchette d'Anjou

Region: *Loire*
Type: *Traditional, farmhouse, unpasteurized, natural-rind cheese*
Source: *Goat's milk*
Description: *80–100g/3¼–3¾oz log with natural rind dusted with salt and charcoal*
Culinary uses: *Table cheese, slicing and grilling, in salads*

These delightful, plain or ash-covered cheeses have been made in the Loire area for centuries. When young they are firm and grainy, with a mild, fresh, citrus taste. Under the watchful gaze of a talented affineur, the interior softens to melting point and the taste becomes redolent of fresh asparagus and wild herbs.

Bûchette de Banon is a similar cheese.

Butte

Region: *Ile-de-France*
Type: *Modern, creamery, soft-white cheese*
Source: *Cow's milk*
Description: *350g/12oz brick with thick, smooth, velvety, white penicillium rind*
Culinary use: *Table cheese*

This takes its name from the shape, which resembles a small hillock. The cheese owes its buttery texture to cream, which is added to the milk before it is coagulated. The fresh cheese melts in the mouth and has a mushroomy aroma and a salty, bitter tang. If allowed to ripen, the rind develops reddish pigmentation, the interior becomes runny around the edges, the aroma becomes acrid and the taste sharper and (to some) more delicious.

Similar cheeses include Grand Vatel and Explorateur.

Right: From the top, Cabécou de Rocamadour, Camembert and Brillat-Savarin

Cabécou de Rocamadour (AOC)

Region: *Midi-Pyrénées*
Type: *Traditional, farmhouse, unpasteurized, natural-rind cheese*
Source: *Sheep's and goat's milk*
Description: *30–40g/1¼–1½oz disc. The natural, soft rind is cream-coloured and wrinkly. It develops pale blue moulds*
Culinary uses: *Table cheese, baking, grilling*

These tiny, round discs, with their creamy white rind, have been made in the area for centuries, ever since the locals domesticated the herds of goats and sheep that once roamed wild on the mountainsides. Today, at the height of the season, the cheeses are sold in flat, wooden, slatted trays, which are piled high on market stalls decked with chestnut boughs. The cheeses are sometimes decorated with tiny sprigs of wild herbs, or sold wrapped in bacon strips, ready for grilling and tossing into a salad of frisée lettuce. When the dense, creamy cheese is grilled (perhaps on a crusty baguette), the nutty taste and distinctly goaty aroma intensify – wonderful when washed down with a bottle or two of local wine. Sometimes the cheese is made with sheep's milk, which gives a nuttier taste with a hint of butterscotch.

The cheese is also known simply as Rocamadour.

Camembert de Normandie (AOC)

REGION: *Normandy*
TYPE: *Traditional, farmhouse and creamery, unpasteurized, soft-white cheese*
SOURCE: *Cow's milk*
DESCRIPTION: *250g/9oz round with thin, white penicillium mould crust that becomes impregnated with red, brown and yellow pigments as it matures*
CULINARY USES: *Table cheese. Anything else would be sacrilege*

Camembert started life towards the end of the eighteenth century as a dry, yellow-brown cheese made for her family by Marie Harel, a farmer's wife. This was around the time of the French Revolution, and the family gave shelter to a priest from the Brie region. Having often talked to his parishioners while they made their cheeses, he was able to repay the Harels' kindness by imparting his knowledge. As a result, the cheese became softer and more earthy, but it would be some years before it acquired the name by which we know it today.

In 1855, one of Marie Harel's daughters presented Napoleon with one of the cheeses and told him that it came from Camembert. The name stuck, but the cheese might still have remained relatively unknown had it not been for three factors. First, the expansion of the railways opened up new markets. Second, small, wooden cheeseboxes proved perfect for protecting the cheeses on their long journeys. Finally, in the 1920s came the discovery of how to isolate and introduce into the ripening rooms the white penicillium moulds. These virulent moulds were capable of fighting off the less aggressive grey and blue moulds that had previously tainted the young cheeses. As a bonus, they prevented the interior from drying out. The voluptuous texture and mushroom aroma of a classic Camembert was finally achieved.

Today, hundreds of producers in Normandy are permitted to make AOC Camembert. The finest have a fragrant aroma and taste of wild mushroom soup, with a slightly yeasty, almost meaty taste.

ABOVE: *Cantal*

BELOW: *Caprice des Dieux*

Cantal (AOC)

REGION: *Auvergne*
TYPE: *Traditional, farmhouse and creamery, unpasteurized, hard cheese*
SOURCE: *Cow's milk*
DESCRIPTION: *35–45kg/80–100lb tall cylinder with natural, straw-yellow to grey crust, dusted with grey and red pigments*
CULINARY USES: *Table cheese, grating, in soups and in sauces*

One of the oldest French cheeses, Cantal was originally produced by putting the curd into *le formage*, the wooden cylinder that is believed to be the origin of the French word for cheese – *fromage*. Cantal Fermier is produced in mountain chalets during the summer months, while Cantal Laitier is a pasteurized cheese made all year round, using milk from nearby farms in accordance with the AOC regulations. Each cheese has a metal badge embedded in the rind, and is stamped with the official AOC logo.

When young, Cantal is moist, open-textured and springy, with a cheese sauce tang not unlike Lancashire. With age, it becomes more like a mature Cheddar. The cheese is sold as *jeune* when it is at least 30 days old. When it is over six months old and has developed a robust personality, it is categorized as *vieux*. Between two and six months old, the cheese is sold as *entre-deux* (between the two).

Caprice des Dieux

REGION: *Champagne-Ardenne*
TYPE: *Modern, creamery, soft-white cheese*
SOURCE: *Cow's milk*
DESCRIPTION: *120g/4¼oz oval, with a smooth, velvety, pure white penicillium rind*
CULINARY USE: *Table cheese*

Milky and rather bland, this cheese looks rather more interesting than it tastes. The texture, too, is somewhat disappointing, being more elastic than supple. However, demand has kept the small, oval boxes on the supermarket shelves and no doubt has provided a stepping stone for many would-be cheese connoisseurs.

Carré de l'Est

REGION: *Champagne and Lorraine*
TYPE: *Traditional, farmhouse, and creamery, washed-rind or soft-white cheese*
SOURCE: *Cow's milk*
DESCRIPTION: *300g/11oz square with either an orange-red, washed-rind or a penicillium mould crust*
CULINARY USE: *Table cheese*

Made in the area for generations, Carré de l'Est is ripened in cellars and encouraged to grow either a soft-white crust or washed in brine and eau-de-vie to produce a pungent, ridged orange rind. Each cheese is turned and washed by hand to spread the colourful bacteria over the cheese. The washed-rind cheeses have a runny interior with a smoky-bacon flavour. The white cheeses have a Camembert-like rind and a flavour reminiscent of melted butter and warm mushrooms.

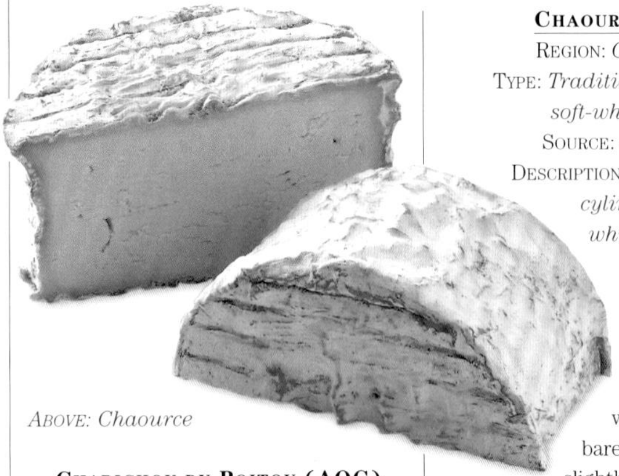

Above: Chaource

Chaource (AOC)

Region: *Champagne*
Type: *Traditional, creamery, soft-white cheese*
Source: *Cow's milk*
Description: *250–450g/9oz–1lb cylinder with downy, white penicillium rind*
Culinary use: *Table cheese*

Some people prefer the cheese young, when the rind has barely formed and is milky, slightly tart and salty. At this stage, the interior is grainy and coarse, rather than smooth. Other cheese-lovers prefer to wait for the rind to thicken and develop red ferments. The rind of the mature cheese has a slightly bitter flavour with a hint of mushrooms, and the interior is buttery and quite piquant, fruity and sharp. Similar cheeses include Ervy-le-Châtel, and Neufchâtel.

Chabichou du Poitou (AOC)

Region: *Poitou-Charentes*
Type: *Traditional, farmhouse and creamery, unpasteurized, natural-rind cheese*
Source: *Goat's milk*
Description: *120g/4¼oz cylinder with a beautiful, bluish-grey mould that overlays the thin, white mould when mature*
Culinary uses: *Table cheese, grilling*

The texture is firm and creamy rather than grainy or gluggy, and the cheese has a fresh ground-nut flavour. Mothais, Saint-Maixent and Sainte-Maure are similar.

Left: Chabichou du Poitou – an unpasteurized natural-rind cheese made with goat's milk

Chaumes

Region: *Dordogne*
Type: *Modern, creamery, washed-rind cheese*
Source: *Cow's milk*
Description: *2kg/4½lb flattened wheel. The soft, thin rind is deep tangerine in colour with a thin, orange-paper cover*
Culinary uses: *Table cheese, grilling*

Based upon traditional Trappist-style cheeses, this has proved to be one of the most popular of the modern French varieties. The soft rind is bright tangerine-orange and the interior is smooth, supple and quite rubbery. Although it looks as though it is about to run, the cheese is actually fairly dense and feels wonderfully rich and creamy on the tongue. The nutty, almost meaty taste and aroma are milder than you might suspect. Port Salut is a similar cheese.

Above: Chaumes

Chèvre Log

Region: *Loire*
Type: *Modern, creamery, soft-white cheese*
Source: *Goat's milk*
Description: *3kg/6½lb log with white, velvety rind, which can become damp, acrid and separate from the cheese*
Culinary uses: *Table cheese, hors d'oeuvres*

First made by a large co-operative in Poitiers and now sold under various brand names, chèvre log, or Bûcheron, is now available throughout Europe. At two days old, it has a lovely, sweet-sour, fruity taste, with just a touch of the almondy character of goat's milk, when the texture is dense with a fine grain. By 10 days, it is firm yet breakable and feels slightly sticky in the mouth. It retains fresh acidity and the aromatic, goaty taste intensifies. It slices easily, so is ideal for grilling.

Below: Chèvre log

Chevrotin des Aravis

Region: *Rhône-Alpes*
Type: *Traditional, farmhouse, unpasteurized, washed-rind cheese*
Source: *Cow's and goat's milk*
Description: *250–350g/9–12oz round with yellowish-orange, floury-washed rind*
Culinary uses: *Table cheese, snacks*

One of the few washed-rind goat's cheeses, Chevrotin is produced in the same way as Reblochon, which it resembles in appearance and texture – smooth, melting, rich and sensuous. It has a mild, goaty aroma and a wonderful complexity of character. The taste is nutty and quite savoury.

Cîteaux/Abbaye de Cîteaux

Region: *Burgundy*
Type: *Traditional, farmhouse, unpasteurized, washed-rind cheese*
Source: *Cow's milk (Montbéliard)*
Description: *700g/1lb 9oz wheel. The fine, leathery crust is pale yellow-orange with a dusting of various moulds*
Culinary use: *Table cheese*

L'Abbaye de Notre Dame at Cîteaux, near Beaune, was founded in 1098 by the Benedictine monks and became the birthplace of the Cistercian movement. The term "Trappist" was not introduced until the 18th century, and it is now used to describe the monastic-type cheeses.

Set in the heart of wine country, the abbey has a herd of around 200 red and white Montbéliard cows and prefers to keep production small, selling most of its cheese locally. The cheese resembles Reblochon, but because the soil and pastures are very different, so is the taste of the cheese. That great 20th-century cheese-lover Patrick Rance describes it as follows: "Cîteaux has a delicious, melt-in-the-mouth, refreshing character all its own, set off by its fine crust, more even in patina than that of Reblochon. Like the crust of the good bread with which it deserves to be paired, it is an important part of the cheese's savour and consistency against the palate, and should never be cut away and wasted."

Coeur de Camembert au Calvados

Region: *Normandy*
Type: *Modern, farmhouse, soft-white cheese*
Source: *Cow's milk*
Description: *250g/9oz round with washed rind covered with fine breadcrumbs soaked in Calvados and decorated with a half walnut*
Culinary use: *Table cheese*

For those not satisfied with the delicious taste of a ripe Camembert, there is this variation. The rind is removed from a semi-cured Camembert, which is then soaked in Calvados. Fresh breadcrumbs are then pressed into the cheese and a walnut garnish is added. The cheese absorbs the heady spirit. The faint apple aroma seems to complement the rich, creamy texture of the cheese.

Comté/Gruyère de Comté (AOC)

Region: *Franche-Comté*
Type: *Traditional, creamery, unpasteurized, hard cheese*
Source: *Cow's milk*
Description: *35–55kg/80–120lb wheel with convex sides. The natural, hard, thick rind is golden-yellow to brown*
Culinary uses: *Table cheese, snacks, canapés, fondues, gratins*

The French make two Gruyères – Beaufort and Comté, both wonderfully large, impressive wheels. Comté is sweeter than Beaufort and has a convex rather than a concave rind. As with their Swiss counterparts, the quality can be judged by the size, shape and condition of the holes. An experienced affineur, with a gentle tap of a special hammer, can detect their condition by the resonance of the cheese. If you find one with a tiny drop or "tear" in one of the holes, it will be as near perfect as you can get.

Comté is a magnificent, unspoilt, mountain chalet cheese. It is very creamy and has a piquant yet sweet, fruity flavour. The bite is firm, dry and slightly granular, while the acidity is fruity and slightly fizzy – like fermenting pears.

These huge cheeses have been made in co-operatives in the Franche-Comté for centuries. Shepherds, with their small herds, have always spent the summer months in remote mountain huts. Due to their distance from the nearest markets, they needed to make a cheese that required months to mature. So they pooled their milk, creating huge cheeses that were often only taken down the mountain at the end of the season.

When the cattle return to the valleys at the end of summer all production of Comté ceases. Instead, they make the equally delicious but very different Vacherin Mont d'Or, now known as Mont d'Or. Both cheeses are governed by the rules of the AOC.

Similar cheeses include Gruyère, Emmental and Beaufort.

Above: Coeur de Camembert au Calvados

Crème Fraîche

Region: *Various*
Type: *Traditional, farmhouse and creamery, matured cream*
Source: *Cow's milk*
Description: *Matured cream, rather than cheese, sold in pots*
Culinary use: *Wonderful to cook with as it curdles less easily than double (heavy) cream when heated*

Crème fraîche isn't a true cheese. It is a matured cream made by adding a culture to fresh cream. The bacteria, similar to those used to make yogurt, thicken and ripen the cream. The result is a truly delicious and exceedingly smooth cream that is rich and nutty with just a hint of lemony sourness.

Above Left: *Crème fraîche*

Above Right: *Crottin de Chavignol*

Coulommiers

Region: *Ile-de-France*
Type: *Traditional, farmhouse, unpasteurized, soft-white cheese*
Source: *Cow's milk*
Description: *400–500g/14oz–1¼lb disc with white penicillium mould*
Culinary uses: *Table cheese, canapés*

Smaller than Brie, Coulommiers ripens more quickly. Some prefer to eat it when the white mould is barely discernible, while others prefer it *affiné* (when the aroma is stronger and more like that of ripe Brie). Commercial versions are pleasant, but lack the depth of an unpasteurized cheese, which can be as good as farmhouse Camembert.

The cheese is also known as Brie de Coulommiers or Petit Brie.

Above: *Coulommiers*

Crottin de Chavignol (AOC)

Region: *Loire*
Type: *Traditional, farmhouse and creamery, unpasteurized, natural-rind cheese*
Source: *Goat's milk*
Description: *60–100g/2¼–3¾oz cylinder with natural rind that ranges from pale ivory to almost black*
Culinary uses: *Table cheese, snacks, grilling, in salads*

The young cheese has an off-white, slightly wrinkled rind with a mere suggestion of white and blue moulds. At eight days, the cheese has a gentle, aromatic, yeasty taste and a fine, moist texture. At 11 days, the interior softens; the taste is nuttier and full-bodied. At 20 days, the cheese is denser and creamier and there is a fruity tinge to the taste. The flavour intensifies when the cheese is grilled, as it often is. Grilled crottin is the basis of a delicious chévre salad that is popular all over France. If the cheese is allowed to mature further, blue and grey moulds will cover the rind, drawing out the moisture. The result is a small, hard, dark grey disc that justifies the name: Crottin de Chavignol means "horse droppings". The interior develops a fruity, bitter taste. Most crottins are, however, sold young.

Dauphin

Region: *Nord-Pas-de-Calais*
Type: *Traditional, farmhouse and creamery, unpasteurized, semi-soft cheese*
Source: *Goat's milk*
Description: *300–350g/11–12oz dolphin- or brick-shaped cheese with brick-red, washed rind*
Culinary use: *Table cheese*

The cheese is said to derive its name from the unusual shape. Usually this resembles a dolphin or fish, although some are small rectangles. A more likely explanation is that when Louis XIV and the Dauphin visited the region and praised the local cheese, the inhabitants settled on both name and shape accordingly.

The brick-red rind gives way to the firm, yet supple interior. Tarragon and pepper are added to the fresh curd, which is then drained and matured. The cheese has a spicy flavour with a yeasty aroma.

Dreux à la Feuille

Region: *Ile-de-France*
Type: *Traditional, farmhouse, unpasteurized, soft-white cheese*
Source: *Cow's milk*
Description: *300–350g/11–12oz round with white penicillium mould rind, enclosed in a chestnut leaf*
Culinary use: *Table cheese*

In size and texture, this cheese, being supple and almost runny when ripe, resembles Coulommiers. The chestnut leaf wrapping imparts a nutty, slightly aromatic taste to the cheese, which is generally a good buy.

Epoisses de Bourgogne (AOC)

Region: *Burgundy*
Type: *Traditional, farmhouse, unpasteurized, washed-rind cheese*
Source: *Cow's milk*
Description: *250g/9oz round cheese with smooth, shiny, brick-red, washed rind*
Culinary use: *Table cheese*

Each cheese is "washed" by hand, using a small brush to spread the bacteria over and into the rind. The final wash is alcohol – usually marc de Bourgogne.

Like many of France's best-loved cheeses, Epoisses are enjoyed at different stages of their maturation by different people. Epoisse Frais (30 days) is a mere shadow of its aged counterpart, being firm, moist and grainy, yet still creamy with a fresh acidity and mild yeasty tang.

At 40 days the rind is orange-brown in colour and very sticky. When the outer edges of the cheese are close to collapse, the interior is not far behind. The pungent, spicy aroma is matched by the strong and strangely meaty taste. Unbelievably good, the cheese deserves to be served with a fine Burgundy or a spicy aromatic white wine. Carré de l'Est, Chambertin, Langres and Soumaintrain are all similar cheeses.

Above: Epoisses de Bourgogne

Below: Dauphin

Above: Etorki

Etorki

Region: *Aquitaine*
Type: *Modern, creamery, hard cheese*
Source: *Sheep's milk*
Description: *4kg/9lb fat wheel with reddish-brown, thin, natural rind*
Culinary uses: *Table cheese, grating, melting*

Until 1984, most of the sheep's milk in this region went to the makers of Roquefort. However, to comply with the strict AOC rules governing the grazing area and the breed of sheep, the region's milk was excluded after that date. Fortunately, the situation was anticipated by Fromagerie des Chaumes (best known for the cheese of the same name). In 1979, they built a factory that now processes most of the sheep's milk in the area into Etorki. The recipe is based on a cheese that has for centuries been made by the local shepherds.

This factory-made cheese has a bright yellow interior, rich texture and a nutty finish and is more close-textured and supple than the hand-made original, but it is nevertheless good, with the burnt-caramel sweetness and creamy texture typical of sheep's milk cheeses. As sheep's milk is abundant only from winter to early summer, the factory makes cow's milk cheese – Lou Palou – for the rest of the year.

Above: Explorateur

Explorateur

Region: *Ile-de-France*
Type: *Modern, creamery, soft-white cheese*
Source: *Cow's milk*
Description: *250g/9oz cylinder with soft-white rind*
Culinary use: *Table cheese*

Invented in the 1950s and named in honour of the first US satellite – Explorer. Explorateur is a firm, creamy cheese with a grainy feel. It has a delicate aroma and a slightly salty, mushroomy tang.

Similar cheeses include Excelsior, Boursault, Brillat-Savarin and Magnum.

Figue

Region: *Aquitaine*
Type: *Traditional, farmhouse, unpasteurized, fresh cheese*
Source: *Goat's milk*
Description: *160–200g/5¼–7oz fresh hemispherical cheese*
Culinary uses: *Table cheese, grilling*

Named for its fig shape, this is similar in taste and texture to the wonderful chèvre cheeses found in the Loire, Aquitaine and Périgord areas of France. Mild and pure with a lemony acidity, it is normally dusted with salt and ash, paprika or herbs.

Fleur du Maquis

Region: *Corsica*
Type: *Traditional, farmhouse, unpasteurized, fresh or natural-rind cheese*
Source: *Sheep's milk*
Description: *575–675g/1¼–1½lb square cheese with rounded corners. The natural rind is covered with chillies, juniper berries, savory and rosemary*
Culinary use: *Table cheese*

If the author were asked to identify her favourite cheese, Fleur du Maquis would be near the top of her list. Not merely because it looks so desirable with its covering of wild herbs, peppers and juniper berries, nor because of its aromatic scent, but largely because it is never the same.

Most Corsican cheeses are superb, thanks to the diverse breeds of sheep and goats and the natural grazing. The island is covered with wild thyme, marjoram and the maquis, a scrubby, aromatic bush on which the sheep graze and which gave its name to this exceptional cheese.

When young, Fleur du Maquis is mild, sweet and lemony. Age brings a richness of character (and a string of superlatives): sweet, nutty, aromatic and creamy. The cheese has a melt-in-the-mouth texture.

Below: Figue

Above: Fleur du Maquis

Fougerus, Le

Region: *Ile-de-France*
Type: *Traditional, farmhouse, unpasteurized, soft-white cheese*
Source: *Cow's milk*
Description: *1kg/2¼lb thick disc with white penicillium mould rind. It is decorated with a piece of bracken or fern*
Culinary use: *Table cheese*

Similar in both size and texture to Coulommiers, this cheese is supple, almost runny when ripe and resembles Dreux à la Feuille. The fern or bracken *fougerus* used to decorate it imparts an earthy charm to the cheese.

Fourme d'Ambert

Region: *Auvergne*
Type: *Traditional, farmhouse and co-operative, blue cheese*
Source: *Cow's milk*
Description: *1.5–2kg/3¼–4½lb cylinder. The natural, white crust develops patches of red and blue moulds*
Culinary use: *Table cheese*

Fourme d'Ambert ("cheese of Ambert") is more supple and dense than most blues. The mould gathers in erratic patches rather than the more usual streaks and the flavour is savoury and nutty. The cheese is easily recognized by its unusually tall, cylindrical shape.

Similar cheeses include Fourme de Montbrison, Bleu de Montbrison, Bleu de Gex and Bleu de Septmoncel.

Frinault

Region: *Orléanais*
Type: *Traditional, creamery, unpasteurized, soft-white cheese*
Source: *Cow's milk*
Description: *120–150g/4¼–5oz round with natural rind covered with ash*
Culinary use: *Table cheese*

Invented by Monsieur Frinault in 1848 at Chécy, this cheese is similar to a Camembert, but matured in wood ash. It has a slightly firmer, less voluptuous texture and a strong, rather spicy taste. The quality varies, however, and the cheese can be bitter if it is allowed to dry out too much. It is quite difficult to obtain. Also known as Chécy, it is similar to Olivet Cendré.

Left: Fourme d'Ambert

Right: Fromage frais

Fromage Corse

Region: *Corsica*
Type: *Traditional, farmhouse, unpasteurized, semi-soft cheese*
Source: *Sheep's and goat's milk*
Description: *500g/1¼lb round. The crusty, washed rind has orange and yellow moulds*
Culinary use: *Table cheese*

Made by the local people for the local people, and thus it has remained for centuries. Even the rennet is still obtained by drying the stomach of a young goat, then slicing it and soaking it in water for two days before it is required. This ancient practice, first discovered by nomadic tribes over 2,000 years ago, gives the cheese added depth.

The rough exterior is pungent, with orange and yellow ferments on a pale beige-yellow background. The interior is supple, sometimes almost runny, with small holes. It has a robust flavour redolent of the wild maquis and herbs that grow on the rugged mountains of the island. The cheese is seldom found outside Corsica, except in Paris. It resembles Niolo.

Right: Fromage Corse

Fromage Frais

Region: *Various*
Type: *Traditional, farmhouse and creamery, fresh cheese*
Source: *Cow's, goat's and sheep's milk*
Description: *Moist, creamy, white, fresh cheese sold in pots*
Culinary uses: *On fresh fruit, for breakfast, as a spread*

One of the first cheeses made by man, fromage frais is simply milk that has been coagulated using a bacteria culture rather than rennet. High in moisture, it varies little except for the fat content, which ranges from *maigre* (very low) to *allégé* (double) and *triple crème*. The culture used is similar to that for yogurt, but, because it is slower-acting, it produces a citrus tingle rather than an acidic taste. The milk is left for around 12 hours to coagulate, the whey is then drained and the fromage frais is strained for two hours before being potted.

Gaperon

Region: *Auvergne*
Type: *Traditional, farmhouse and co-operative, soft-white cheese*
Source: *Cow's milk*
Description: *250–350g/9–12oz cheese shaped like a small, upturned basin and tied with raffia. It has a soft-white rind dusted with white mould.*
Culinary uses: *Table cheese, snacks*

Traditionally, this cheese and others like it were made in homes, rather than by cheesemakers. Buttermilk was originally used, although skimmed milk is more often used today. The curds were kneaded with garlic and peppercorns before being pressed into the bowl-shaped moulds, tied with raffia and hung in the kitchen or cellar to dry.

Mild and milky, the cheese has a gentle acidity and spongy, texture. The aroma of the garlic and peppercorns dominate the flavour.

Left: Gaperon

Grataron d'Arèches

Region: *Savoie*
Type: *Traditional, farmhouse, unpasteurized, washed-rind cheese*
Source: *Goat's milk*
Description: *300–400g/11–14oz thick cylinder with smooth, beige, washed rind*
Culinary use: *Table cheese*

Grataron d'Arèches is one of the few washed-rind goat's cheeses of the Savoie, and it is worth looking out for. The leathery, pale beige rind covers an open-textured, white interior with a wonderful scent of almonds and flowers.

Right: Gris de Lille

Gratte-Paille

Region: *Ile-de-France*
Type: *Modern, farmhouse, soft-white cheese*
Source: *Cow's milk*
Description: *300–350g/11–12oz brick with natural white mould rind*
Culinary uses: *Cheeseboards, baked in pastries with chicken and vegetables*

Invented in the 1970s by a creamery in Seine-et-Marne, this cheese takes its name from *gratte* (to scratch) and *paille* (straw), marking the fact that when bales of straw were carried through the narrow streets in summer, pieces of the straw would become wedged in the walls along the way. Some of the cheeses are sold on small straw mats. The cheese is very good. Rich and exceedingly creamy, it has a pleasant mushroomy flavour. With age comes a slight sharpness.

Right: Gratte-Paille

Gris de Lille

Region: *Nord-Pas-de-Calais*
Type: *Traditional, farmhouse, and creamery, unpasteurized, washed-rind cheese*
Source: *Cow's milk*
Description: *700g–1kg/1lb 9oz–2¼lb square with sticky, pinkish-grey, washed rind*
Culinary uses: *Table cheese, snacks*

Gris de Lille is also known as Puant de Lille or Puant Macéré. The word *puant* means obnoxious or stinking – a term of endearment to those who love the rich flavour of this pungent cheese with its distinctive farmyard aroma. The cheese is similar to Maroilles, although the curing process is different.

La Taupinière

Region: *Poitou-Charentes*
Type: *Traditional, farmhouse, unpasteurized, natural-rind cheese*
Source: *Goat's milk*
Description: *225–250g/8–9oz dome-shaped cheese. The wrinkled, natural rind has a delicate, blue mould*
Culinary uses: *Table cheese, grilling*

La Taupinière means molehill, which aptly describes this unusually shaped cheese. Quite dense, it is ripened for two to three weeks and is deliciously nutty, with a fresh, lemony tang.

La Vache qui Rit

Region: *Various*
Type: *Modern, creamery, processed cheese*
Source: *Cow's milk*
Description: *Small disc with bright red, waxed rind*
Culinary uses: *Snacks, lunch boxes*

The slightly supercilious face of La Vache qui Rit – the laughing cow – is seen on the walls of the Metro, and in supermarkets across France. It may well laugh, for it seems so unlikely that this sweet, bland, buttery, processed cheese should have become a household name in a country famous for its magnificent, pungent cheeses. The tiny discs are a favourite snack with children and adults alike.

Laguiole (AOC)

Region: *Auvergne*
Type: *Traditional, farmhouse, unpasteurized, hard cheese*
Source: *Cow's milk*
Description: *30–50kg/65–110lb cylinder. The hard, mottled brown-grey, natural rind carries the distinctive, red lettering proclaiming its AOC status*
Culinary uses: *Table cheese, snacks, grating, grilling*

With an ancient pedigree (the cheese was certainly made in the fourth century BC and was earlier described by Pliny the Elder), Laguiole has a supple to firm texture. Not as compact as the classic English Cheddar, it has a light, musty aroma that can be quite penetrating when the cheese is fully aged. The straw-yellow interior has

Above: Laguiole

a creamy feel and a taste reminiscent of cheese and onion quiche.

Over the years, economics and the disinclination of sons to follow in the footsteps of their cheesemaking fathers have led to changes in the production of the cheese. The Holstein cow, a prolific milker, was brought in to replace the native Aubrac breed. The number of traditional cheesemakers or *buronniers* has dramatically reduced. At the beginning of this century there were more than a thousand *buronniers*; today there are only four or five producing the cheese.

Laguiole is still a great cheese, especially if you buy one made from *transhumance* milk (produced between late May and mid October, when cows are taken up to the mountain pastures that are covered in gentians, violets, broom and wild herbs). Many people hope that a growing awareness of the need to retain the old ways, coupled with a little assistance from the AOC, will mean that the character of this wonderful, old French cheese will not be lost in the race for progress.

Langres (AOC)

Region: *Champagne-Ardennes*
Type: *Traditional, farmhouse, and co-operative, unpasteurized, washed-rind cheese*
Source: *Cow's milk*
Description: *180g or 800g/6¼oz or 1¾lb concave cone or cylinder with washed rind ranging from orange and sticky to brick-red and dry*
Culinary uses: *Table cheese, also baked and used as a dip for vegetables*

Monks who passed through the region during the Middle Ages probably introduced this cheese. The shape is unusual – a cone or cylinder with a hollow in the top. To form the hollow, the curd is turned only twice during draining. The weight of the whey, and its movement through the curd, causes the centre to subside.

The brightly coloured rind is the result of continual washing; orange bacteria grow on the surface, as well as some white flora or yeasts.

The cheese is notable for its pungent, smoky-bacon aroma. When young, the texture is firm and grainy. With age, the rind starts to break down and becomes smooth-flowing and creamy. The flavour intensifies. Some affineurs pour eau-de-vie into the crater. This gradually seeps into the cheese, adding a new dimension to an already powerful flavour.

Right: Langres

Above: Laruns

Laruns

Region: *Pyrénées*
Type: *Traditional, farmhouse, unpasteurized, hard cheese*
Source: *Sheep's milk*
Description: *5–6kg/11–13lb flattened round loaf with smooth, thin, yellow to ochre, natural rind*
Culinary uses: *Table cheese, snacks, cooking (when aged)*

Named after the local market town, this cheese has been made by shepherds in mountain huts for generations and is now produced by Ossau Valley. When young, it has a supple texture and is mild and nutty; as it ages it becomes hard and brittle, with a sharper flavour. At six months it is best for grating and cooking.

Le Fium'Orbo

Region: *Corsica*
Type: *Traditional, farmhouse, unpasteurized, semi-soft cheese*
Source: *Sheep's and goat's milk*
Description: *400–450g/14oz–1lb round cheese with natural rind*
Culinary use: *Table cheese*

A farmhouse version of Fromage Corse, this has a pungent nose but a more delicate taste, suggesting herbs and flowers. It is an ancient cheese, which has been made by the shepherds for centuries.

Le Brin

Region: *Savoie*
Type: *Modern, creamery, semi-soft, vegetarian cheese*
Source: *Cow's milk*
Description: *150g/5oz small, hexagonal cheese with natural, thin, reddish-orange rind dusted with white penicillium mould*
Culinary use: *Table cheese*

Le Brin was created by Fromagerie Guilloteau in the 1980s as a milder version of the traditional French washed-rind cheeses. It is made by the ultrafiltration method rather than by using rennet to separate the curd from the whey. This gives a higher yield of solids per litre of milk, which means the production costs are lower than when traditional cheese-making methods are employed. *Brin* means a wisp, a breath or a twig – something small or light. The cheese is velvety smooth, like English custard, and has a mild, sweet, almost perfumed aroma and taste. It resembles its soft-white-rinded cousin, Pavé d'Affinois.

Le Terroir is a similar cheese.

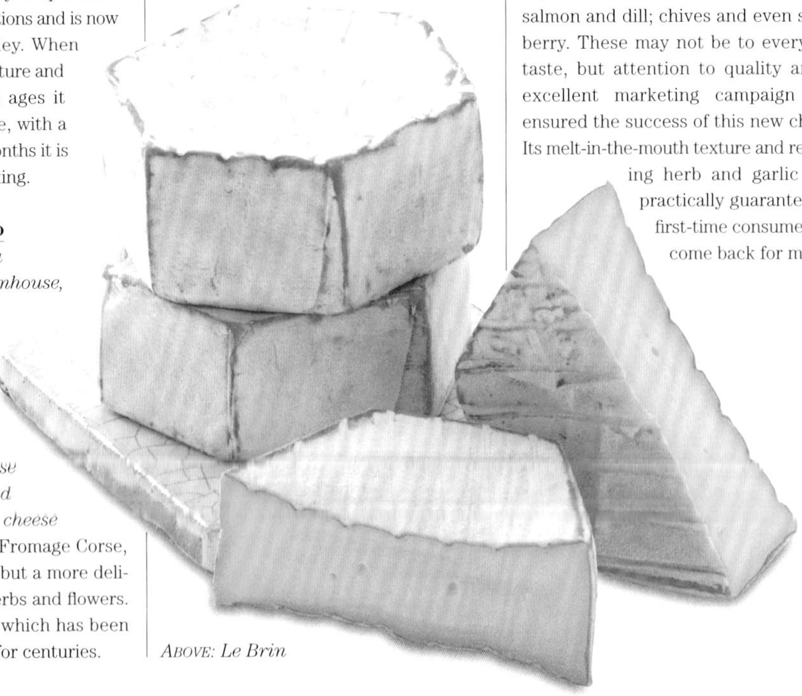

Above: Le Brin

Above: Le Roulé

Le Roulé

Region: *Loire*
Type: *Modern, creamery, fresh cheese*
Source: *Cow's milk*
Description: *Logs of various sizes, rolled in fresh herbs*
Culinary uses: *Table cheese, baking, spreading*

The now familiar logs of Le Roulé with their distinctive green swirl of herbs and garlic, were first introduced in the mid-1980s by Fromagerie Triballat, with the aim of attracting attention to cheese counters in supermarket delicatessens. An overnight success, Le Roulé was rapidly joined by Roulé Light and miniature Roulé logs with numerous exotic combinations: salmon and dill; chives and even strawberry. These may not be to everyone's taste, but attention to quality and an excellent marketing campaign have ensured the success of this new cheese. Its melt-in-the-mouth texture and refreshing herb and garlic layer practically guarantee that first-time consumers will come back for more.

RIGHT: Livarot

LIVAROT (AOC)

REGION: *Normandy*
TYPE: *Traditional, farmhouse and creamery, unpasteurized, semi-soft cheese*
SOURCE: *Cow's milk*
DESCRIPTION: *250g/9oz or 450g/1lb round cheese. The smooth, glossy, brown, washed rind has some white and occasional bluish moulds*
CULINARY USES: *Table cheese, snacks*

This smooth, supple-textured cheese is washed to encourage the orange ferments to grow. These days the wash is a flavourless natural dye, annatto, which may be one of the reasons the cheese is less pungent than it used to be. Heavy in the mouth, it leaves a spicy taste on the finish.

Livarot is jokingly called "the colonel" because of the stripes of sedge grass (today, more often orange plastic) that encircle the cheese. Originally made by the monks in the area, nowadays most Livarot is produced in factories, but the AOC regulations should help to maintain its ancestry.

MÂCONNAIS

REGION: *Burgundy*
TYPE: *Traditional, farmhouse and co-operative, unpasteurized, natural-rind cheese*
SOURCE: *Cow's and goat's milk*
DESCRIPTION: *50–60g/2–2¼oz truncated cone with natural, fine white to pale blue rind*
CULINARY USES: *Table cheese, grilling, in salads*

Small and elegant, this cheese can be made from cow's or goat's milk – or a mixture – depending on the season. When young, it has a dense, flaky interior with a rind of blue and white moulds. The subtle hint of tarragon in the flavour recalls the fruitiness of a young Chardonnay, and the cheese is the perfect partner for a Mâcon white wine. The locals prefer the cheese when it is brittle, almost rancid, savouring it with a generous glass of the local Burgundy or a Beaujolais.

RIGHT: Maroilles

MAMIROLLE

REGION: *Franche-Comté*
TYPE: *Modern, creamery, washed-rind cheese*
SOURCE: *Cow's milk*
DESCRIPTION: *500–675g/1¼–1½lb brick. The finely ridged, orange, washed rind can be slightly damp*
CULINARY USES: *Table cheese, grilling*

The author first tasted Mamirolle at Besançon, where she shared it with the cheesemaker, one of the students at the Ecole Nationale d'Industrie Laitière de Besançon-Mamirolle, where it is made as part of their hands-on experience. She reports as follows: "The supple, smooth interior is encased with a fine, orange rind with a sweet-sour, faintly smoked aroma and taste, although the occasional batch can be as robust and enthusiastic as the students, particularly if it is made towards the end of their academic year!"

The cheese is produced in the department of Doubs and is similar to Limburger.

MAROILLES (AOC)

REGION: *Flanders*
TYPE: *Traditional, farmhouse and creamery, unpasteurized, semi-soft cheese*
SOURCE: *Cow's milk*
DESCRIPTION: *700g/1lb 9oz square cheese with brick-red, smooth, washed rind*
CULINARY USES: *Table cheese, snacks and pies, especially the local goyère*

This is regarded as the forefather of all the Trappist cheeses. It was first made in the tenth century at the Abbaye de Maroilles in northern France, where St Hubert, the patron saint of cheese, is buried.

The cheese has a thickish, damp, brick-red rind with fine ridges. The interior is pale yellow, bouncy and porous, not supple and dense like many similar cheeses. The aroma – powerful and aromatic, with a suggestion of fermenting fruit – is stronger than the flavour, which is sweet-sour in character, with perhaps a hint of smoky bacon. The cheeses can be ripened for up to four months, although many are sold too young, when they are still chalky in the centre and have bitter rinds.

Similar cheeses include Baguette Laonnaise, Dauphin and Gris de Lille.

MIMOLETTE FRANÇAISE

REGION: *Flanders*
TYPE: *Traditional, creamery, hard cheese*
SOURCE: *Cow's milk*
DESCRIPTION: *2–4kg/4½–9lb sphere. The natural rind ranges in colour from yellow-orange to light brown, and is pitted, dry and hard*
CULINARY USES: *Table cheese, snacks, canapés, grating*

This cheese originated in Holland and was probably introduced into France when Flanders was part of that country. Basically, it is a matured Edam that is allowed to ripen for around six to nine months, by which time it becomes so hard and brittle that pieces have to be chiselled off in granite-like chunks. Intensely fruity, with a mouth-puckering tang, it is popular as a cooking cheese, and as a snack to eat with a glass of beer. When young (four to six months), the cheese is firm, compact and slightly oily, with a subtle, fruity aroma and a mellow, nutty taste. Most Mimolette is, however, eaten when aged (*vieux* or *étuvé*).The bright, deep tangerine colour of the cheese is due to the natural dye, annatto.

Mimolette Française is also known as Boule de Lille.

BELOW: Mimolette

MONT D'OR/VACHERIN HAUT-DOUBS (AOC)

REGION: *Franche-Comté*
TYPE: *Traditional, farmhouse and co-operative, unpasteurized, washed-rind cheese*
SOURCE: *Cow's milk (Montbéliard and Pie Rouge de l'Est)*
DESCRIPTION: *500g–1kg/1¼–2¼lb round with a wrinkled, pale-brownish pink, washed rind, dusted with fine, white mould. The cheese is encircled with a band of spruce bark and set in a wooden box*
CULINARY USE: *Table cheese*

In the days when the borders of France and Switzerland were less well defined, the local soft, washed cheese was called Vacherin Mont d'Or, regardless of which side of the mountain it came from. Later, the Swiss (who produce the pasteurized version) laid claim to the name, and the unpasteurized French Vacherin became simply Mont d'Or or Vacherin Haut-Doubs.

A good Mont d'Or has an aroma of chopped wood and mountain flowers, with a faint hint of fermentation and resin. The texture is full and creamy and the flavour suggests wild herbs. Production begins on 15 August, when the cows return from the mountain pastures. The cheese is available only from the end of September through to 31 March. At the moment it may not be exported. Summer milk is taken to one of the local co-operatives to create another great French cheese – Gruyère de Comté.

To check if the cheese is ripe, press gently on the rind. As the soft, runny cheese flows away from the pressure you should see a gentle wave. Carefully remove the "lid" or rind using a sharp knife, then carefully fold back the "lid", scraping off any soft cheese attached. Scoop a dollop of cheese on to a chunk of country bread, and enjoy a superb treat, preferably with a glass of good wine.

Other French Vacherin cheeses include d'Abondance and des Beauges.

BELOW: Morbier

MORBIER

REGION: *Franche-Comté*
TYPE: *Traditional, farmhouse and creamery, unpasteurized, semi-soft cheese*
SOURCE: *Cow's milk*
DESCRIPTION: *5–9kg/11–20lb wheel. The yellow-brown or pale grey rind is thick, moist and leathery*
CULINARY USES: *Table cheese, snacks, grilling, slicing*

Made during the winter months on the lower reaches of the Jura Mountains, Morbier has a horizontal band of wood ash and salt through its centre. The mixture was originally sprinkled over the fresh curds made from the morning milking, left during the day, then covered with the curds from the evening milking. Nowadays the ash layer is more likely to be food colouring, and is purely decorative.

The cheese is elastic and springy, with a pungent, yeasty aroma and a sweet, fruity taste. Traditionally, a half wheel of Morbier would be propped up by the fire. As it started to melt, the cheese would be scraped on to crusty bread or hot potatoes.

Factory-made versions tend to be bland and odourless, but are excellent for melting.

RIGHT: Münster (bottom) and the smaller, Münster Géromé (top)

MUNSTER/MUNSTER GÉROMÉ (AOC)

REGION: *Alsace*
TYPE: *Traditional, farmhouse and creamery, unpasteurized, washed-rind cheese*
SOURCE: *Cow's milk (Vosgiennes)*
DESCRIPTION: *120g/4¼oz; 450g/1lb; 1.5kg/3–3½lb rounds. The sticky, washed rind ranges in colour from yellow-orange to russet*
CULINARY USES: *Table cheese, snacks, grilling*

The Vosges mountains are the backbone of Alsace and home to one of the smelliest and most delicious cheeses on earth. Those made in Alsace are called Munster, while the smaller versions from Lorraine are known as Géromé.

The cheese owes its unique character to the unspoilt pastures of Alsace and the Vosgiennes cows, renowned for giving high-protein milk.

The cheese is constantly rubbed with brine over a period of two to three months. This causes the rind to develop its rich colour and the aroma to intensify.

Don't let the smell put you off. The cheese is wonderful – supple, with a flavour that is both sweet and savoury (almost yeasty), and an intense, spicy, aromatic finish. It is traditional to enjoy the cheese with boiled potatoes, cumin seeds and a glass of local wine.

Munster au Cumin is a popular variation. Langres is a similar cheese, as of course is Géromé.

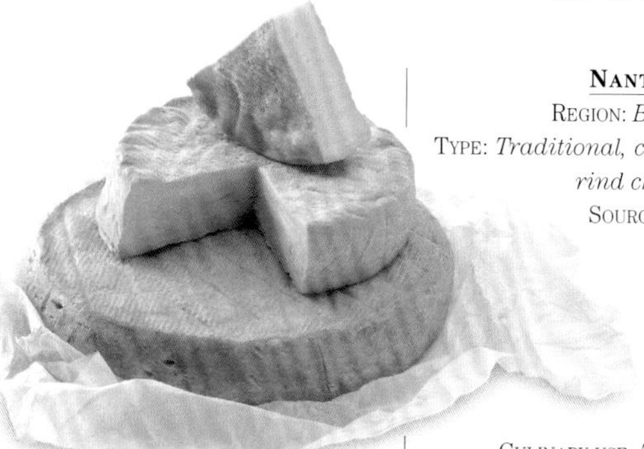

MUROL

REGION: *Auvergne*
TYPE: *Traditional, creamery, semi-soft cheese*
SOURCE: *Cow's milk*
DESCRIPTION: *450–500g/1–1¼lb ring. The thin, smooth, washed rind is mottled pinkish-yellow*
CULINARY USES: *Table cheese, cheese puffs*

This cheese was invented by Monsieur Jules Bérioux, a local affineur. In the 1930s, M Bérioux decided to stamp out a central hole from several young Saint-Nectaire cheeses, ripen the rings and call them Grand Murols, after one of the villages in the area. The cheese is simple and uncomplicated. Supple, creamy and very smooth, it has the sweetness of fresh milk with a delicious, nutty aroma and taste. The unique shape adds a little *je ne sais quoi* to any cheeseboard and the taste appeals to every palate.

The stamped-out holes are not wasted, but are made into Murolait or Le Trou de Murol. These tiny, cork-shaped treats are very soft, but are held in check by a coating of bright red wax. They resemble La Vache qui Rit, but have more flavour.

NANTAIS

REGION: *Brittany*
TYPE: *Traditional, creamery, washed-rind cheese*
SOURCE: *Cow's milk*
DESCRIPTION: *175–200g/6–7oz square cheese with smooth, straw to ochre, washed rind*
CULINARY USE: *Table cheese*

Brittany has no native cheeses and had to wait until the early 1790s for a young priest who was on the run from the French Revolution to introduce cheese-making. This cheese, also known as Curé de Nantais or Fromage de Curé, celebrates that fact. A small, sticky, washed-rind cheese, it has a pungent, yeasty rind. The voluptuous, creamy interior has a rich, smoky-bacon taste and spicy finish. Nantais can be rather good and deserves a weighty Pinot Noir or a strong-tasting Gewurztraminer wine for company.

Carré de l'Est Lavée is a similar cheese.

NEUFCHÂTEL (AOC)

REGION: *Normandy*
TYPE: *Traditional, farmhouse and creamery, soft-white cheese*
SOURCE: *Cow's milk*
DESCRIPTION: *100–200g/3¾–7oz cheeses in various shapes, with natural, downy, white rind, which develops reddish pigmentation*
CULINARY USES: *Table cheese, snacks*

Unlike other soft-white-rinded cheeses, Neufchâtel has a grainy texture. Although it has the aroma and taste of mushrooms, it is also quite sharp and salty. Some lovers of this cheese prefer it when it has been kept until the rind develops reddish pigmentation and a smell of ammonia. At this stage the taste is bitter, salty and acrid.

Neufchâtel is available in various shapes, such as squares, rounds, logs, hearts, loaves and cylinders. Some are available unpasteurized. Gournay is a similar cheese.

LEFT: Neufchâtel – a soft-white cheese with a pleasant, grainy texture

Olivet au Foin

Region: *Orléanais*
Type: *Modern, farmhouse, unpasteurized, soft-white cheese*
Source: *Cow's milk*
Description: *250g/9oz round with soft, dry rind decorated with fine strands of hay*
Culinary use: *Table cheese*

Similar to Camembert, but milder and not as soft when ripe, Olivet au Foin is decorated with fine strands of hay *(foin)*, whose scent is absorbed into the cheese.

Olivet Bleu

Region: *Orléanais*
Type: *Traditional, farmhouse, unpasteurized, blue cheese*
Source: *Cow's milk*
Description: *300g/11oz disc with blue-white, natural rind*
Culinary use: *Table cheese*

Slightly grainy, with a distinct aroma and taste of mushrooms and a salty finish, Olivet Bleu resembles a mild Camembert. "Bleu" refers to the rind, which is so white that it has a blue tinge – like whiter-than-white washing!

Olivet Cendré

Region: *Orléanais*
Type: *Traditional, farmhouse, unpasteurized, soft-white cheese*
Source: *Cow's milk*
Description: *250–300g/9–11oz round with ash-grey, natural rind*
Culinary uses: *Table cheese, snacks*

Olivet Cendré resembles Olivet au Foin, but is cured for three months in wood ash from vines. This gives it a more supple texture and a fairly pungent, spicy aroma. Similar cheeses include Vendôme Cendré and the Cendrés of Champagne and the Ardennes.

Ossau-Iraty-Brebis Pyrénées (AOC)

Region: *Pyrénées*
Type: *Traditional, farmhouse, unpasteurized, semi-soft cheeses*
Source: *Sheep's milk*
Description: *2–7kg/4½–15¼lb wheels with natural rind*
Culinary uses: *Table cheese, grating, soups*

A number of *fermier* (farmhouse), artisan, co-operative and industrial cheeses made in the rugged and majestic Béarn and Basque regions come under this AOC umbrella. The regulations state that the affinage for the mountain sheep's milk cheeses must be at least 60 days for the small and 90 days for the larger ones. Coagulation can only be from rennet, and no milk may be used until 20 days after lambing. These and other conditions must be met before any cheese can carry the AOC label. Those that do not conform must be sold as simple Fromage de Brebis.

Transhumance (the moving of cows in summer to mountain pastures) is still a way of life for the shepherds of this region. The cheeses are still made in small mountain chalets – *kaiolar* – and the hills ring with the sound of the bells worn by the black-faced Manech sheep as they wander across landscapes of spectacular natural beauty.

Other cheeses in this group include Matocq, Ardi-Gasna and Abbaye de Belloc.

Above: Ossau-Iraty-Brebis Pyrénées

Palet de Babligny

Region: *Loire*
Type: *Traditional, farmhouse, unpasteurized, soft-white cheese*
Source: *Cow's milk*
Description: *100g/3¾oz oval with fine, white penicillium mould rind*
Culinary use: *Table cheese*

This tiny cheese packs a lot of punch for its size. Hard and flaky in texture, it has a flavour like that of a fruity, mature Cheddar, yet it melts like chocolate in the mouth and has a hint of chèvre.

Above: Olivet au Foin (left) and Olivet Cendré (right)

ABOVE: Pavé d'Affinois

RIGHT: Pélardon

PAVÉ D'AFFINOIS

REGION: *Lyonnais*
TYPE: *Modern, creamery, soft-white, vegetarian cheese*
SOURCE: *Cow's milk*
DESCRIPTION: *150g/5oz square with ridged penicillium rind*
CULINARY USE: *Table cheese*

This was one of the first cheeses to be made commercially using ultrafiltration – a method of extracting the solids from liquid milk, which gives a much higher yield of solids than when traditional means are used. No rennet is required for the cheesemaking process, only a culture to encourage the lactic fermentation. The technique, together with the packaging and promotion of Pavé d'Affinois and its stablemates Le Brin and Chèvre d'Affinois, has led to excellent sales, but it is to be hoped that this method of preparation is not adopted for the traditional cheeses of Europe.

When young, Pavé d'Affinois is grainy, mildly scented and virtually tasteless apart from a slight hint of mushrooms from the rind. However, if it is allowed to ripen in a warm, humid cellar for two to three weeks, the interior of the cheese literally melts, retaining a firm, slightly chalky centre the size of a quail's egg. The taste is similar to Brie and has hints of Granny Smith apples.

RIGHT: Pavé d'Auge – so-named because it is shaped like "pavé", the squarish French cobble stones

PAVÉ D'AUGE

REGION: *Normandy*
TYPE: *Traditional, farmhouse, unpasteurized, semi-soft cheese*
SOURCE: *Cow's milk*
DESCRIPTION: *675–800g/1½–1¾lb square cheese. The russet-yellow rind can be dry or washed. It is sometimes covered with a white mould*
CULINARY USE: *Table cheese*

Pavé is the name given to the roughly square cobblestones you still see in old marketplaces in France. It is a charming name for this supple, creamy cheese, with its reddish rind. The aroma suggests cool cellars. The flavour is earthy and spicy, but it can be a little bitter.

PÉLARDON

REGION: *Languedoc-Roussillon*
TYPE: *Traditional, farmhouse, unpasteurized, fresh cheese*
SOURCE: *Goat's milk*
DESCRIPTION: *60–100g/2¼–3¾oz disc. The thin, wrinkled, natural rind has white and pale blue moulds*
CULINARY USES: *Table cheese, grilling*

Softer and more mousse-like than most goat's milk cheeses when young, the flavour of Pélardon suggests sour cream infused with walnut oil, balanced by a gentle, salty finish. When aged, the wrinkled, mould-covered rind has a distinct goaty aroma and an intense, Brazil-nut sweetness. The texture is somewhat drier, but the cheese is still very creamy in the mouth.

Pélardon is made in several areas in the Languedoc region and is currently being considered for inclusion among the AOC cheeses of France.

Similar cheeses include Pélardon des Cevennes, Pélardon d'Altières and Pélardon des Corbières.

Below: Pérail

Pérail

Region: *Rouergue*
Type: *Traditional, farmhouse, unpasteurized, natural-rind cheese*
Source: *Sheep's milk*
Description: *80–120g/3¼–4¼oz disc. The soft, wrinkled, natural rind is a pale straw colour with a pinkish tinge*
Culinary use: *Table cheese*

This *fermier* (farmhouse) or artisan cheese has the softest, most delicate of rinds with a nutty aroma. Inside is an even softer, toffee-like centre with the freshness of meadow flowers. The sweet taste of the sheep's milk makes you wish you had bought two – or even three.

Petit-Suisse

Region: *Various*
Type: *Traditional, farmhouse and creamery, fresh cheese*
Source: *Cow's milk*
Description: *30g/1¼oz cylinder without rind*
Culinary uses: *Eaten as a snack with fruit, honey or nuts; also used as the basis of several traditional French desserts*

Normally sold in trays of six, this mousse-like fresh cheese was invented in the late nineteenth century by Charles Gervais, a Swiss cheesemaker. He decided to make a variation on the local cheese, Neufchâtel, by adding cream to the fresh curd and selling the result before the soft white rind could develop. The light, yet creamy texture and charming shape made Petit-Suisse a major success. It is now produced throughout France, although the fat content and quality vary as much as the recipe.

Below: Picodon

Picodon de l'Ardèche/Picodon de la Drôme (AOC)

Region: *Rhône-Alpes*
Type: *Traditional, farmhouse and creamery, unpasteurized, natural-rind cheese*
Source: *Goat's milk*
Description: *50–100g/2–3¾oz round with natural rind that ranges in colour from pale ivory to soft white or pale blue-grey*
Culinary uses: *Table cheese, grilling, baking, fromage fort*

The lower end of the Rhône Valley is too dry for the cultivation of vines, but is ideal for the hardy goats, which attack the tufts of grass and scented scrub with the sort of enthusiasm we might reserve for a gastronomic feast. The milk they yield is the basis of a cheese that varies from area to area, but seldom disappoints. The thin rind has the scent of stone cellars and the hard, compact interior is aromatic. The cheeses are occasionally packed with herbs in jars of the local green olive oil.

Picodon cheeses are very similar to the Pélardon cheeses of the Languedoc-Roussillon region further south.

Above: Pithiviers

Pithiviers au Foin

Region: *Orléanais*
Type: *Traditional, farmhouse, unpasteurized, soft-white cheese*
Source: *Cow's milk*
Description: *300g/11oz round cheese with soft-white rind rolled in strands of hay or grass*
Culinary use: *Table cheese*

Similar to Camembert, Pithiviers au Foin has a mild, milky, caramel flavour. The fine, white rind is delicately rolled in wisps of hay or grass. As such, it resembles Olivet au Foin.

Poivre d'Ane

Region: *Provence-Alpes-Côte d'Azur*
Type: *Traditional, farmhouse, unpasteurized, natural-rind cheese*
Source: *Cow's, sheep's or goat's milk*
Description: *100–120g/3¾–4¼oz round cheese. The natural rind is white with a hint of blue or yellow. It is traditionally covered with a sprig of wild savory*
Culinary uses: *Table cheese, grilling, fromage fort*

This dense, fine-grained cheese has a lovely, aromatic scent and flavour. Any variation comes from the source of the milk: sheep's milk in spring and early summer; goat's milk from the end of spring to the start of autumn; cow's milk virtually all year round.

Banon is a similar cheese.

Pont l'Evêque (AOC)

Region: *Normandy*
Type: *Traditional, farmhouse and creamery, unpasteurized, semi-soft cheese*
Source: *Cow's milk*
Description: *350–400g/12–14oz finely ridged square with greyish-yellow, washed rind*
Culinary use: *Table cheese*

This is probably one of the oldest cheeses of Normandy, an area renowned for the lushness of its pastures. The small Normandy cow has produced some of the greatest French cheeses, including Camembert, Livarot, Pavé d'Auge and Boursin.

Pont l'Evêque is said to have originated in an abbey, though there appears to be no evidence to substantiate this. Despite being granted its AOC status in 1976 to protect its history and good name, only around 2 or 3 per cent of the cheese is *fermier* (farmhouse) made; the majority comes from just two large producers. To comply with AOC regulations and achieve the authentic taste and texture, the cheese must be regularly washed, brushed and turned to encourage the special bacteria to grow on the rind. The milk used for Pont l'Evêque must come from the local area and the curd must be kneaded before it is drained.

The aroma of the cheese has been likened to damp washing, mouldy cellars and farmyards, but the taste is deliciously savoury and piquant, with just a trace of sweetness and a robust tang on the finish. The texture is springy and open and the cheese glistens, thanks to the richness of the milk.

Above: Pont l'Evêque

Right: Pouligny-Saint-Pierre – due to its shape, this elegant, traditional goat's cheese has earned several nicknames. The two most often used are "the pyramid" or "Eiffel Tower"

Pouligny-Saint-Pierre (AOC)

Region: *Berry*
Type: *Traditional, farmhouse and creamery, unpasteurized, natural-rind cheese*
Source: *Goat's milk*
Description: *250g/9oz truncated pyramid with soft, wrinkled, ivory-coloured, natural rind. When this dries out, the wrinkles deepen and grey, white and blue moulds gather. A red label indicates that it is made in a dairy, while a green label means it is farmhouse-made*
Culinary uses: *Table cheese, grilling, in salads*

Named after the eponymous village, this cheese has earned various nicknames because of its shape, the most common of which is "the pyramid". To many people it epitomizes chèvre: wonderfully rustic, yet elegant. The rind is soft and ivory-coloured when the cheese is young. As it ages and dries, the rind becomes reddish-orange and acquires an array of beautiful moulds, providing a magnificent contrast to the firm, pure white, slightly grainy interior.

The first impression is a heady mix of goat, fresh hay and mould. Tasting reveals a complexity of flavours, including herbaceous plants (especially tarragon) and white wine, and a texture that is both creamy and nutty. Like a fine wine, once tasted Pouligny-Saint-Pierre is never forgotten.

RACLETTE

REGION: *Savoie*
TYPE: *Traditional, farmhouse and creamery, unpasteurized, semi-soft cheese*
SOURCE: *Cow's milk*
DESCRIPTION: *7–8kg/15¼–18lb round or square cheese with smooth pink to deep orange, slightly sticky, natural rind*
CULINARY USES: *Sliced and grilled on potatoes or blanched vegetables*

Raclette is an ancient mountain cheese common to the Savoie region in France and the canton of Valais in Switzerland. Although the cheese has a pleasant enough flavour, it is not particularly special until it is heated in front of a fire or under a hot grill. Then the full, nutty, sweet and slightly fruity aroma intensifies and the stringy elasticity of the melting cheese makes it truly magnificent. The rind has a farmyard aroma. When grilled it becomes really crunchy and has a wonderful savoury flavour.

Traditionally, a large cheese was cut in half and leant against a stone with the cut surface facing the open fire. The outer layer of the supple interior was allowed to heat up gradually. As soon as it started to crinkle and change colour, a bowl of steaming potatoes would appear, to be smothered in an avalanche of bubbling cheese. The aroma was irresistible and the rich, nutty, sweet flavour of the cheese was the perfect partner for the potatoes. Nowadays, the dish can be created by heating slices of cheese under the grill.

Bagnes and Conches are similar.

Above: Raclette

Right: Rigotte

Right: Reblochon

REBLOCHON (AOC)

REGION: *Haute-Savoie*
TYPE: *Traditional, farmhouse and creamery, unpasteurized, semi-soft cheese*
SOURCE: *Cow's milk*
DESCRIPTION: *240g/8½oz or 550g/1¼lb round cheese. The yellow to orange, natural rind has fine, white, powdery mould*
CULINARY USES: *Table cheese, melting*

Not unlike Saint-Nectaire or Tamie, Reblochon has a supple, creamy texture that flows over and caresses the palate. The cheese, made in the factories or by co-operatives (*fruitières*), has a warm, yeasty aroma, with the sweet flavour of freshly crushed walnuts, whereas the farm- (*fermier*-) made cheese is both more intense and more complex, and has a distinct savour of fresh spring grass and wild alpine flowers. Do not be deterred by the farmyard aroma of the rind.

RIGOTTE

REGION: *Auvergne and Lyonnais*
TYPE: *Traditional, creamery, unpasteurized, fresh cheese*
SOURCE: *Cow's or goat's milk*
DESCRIPTION: *70–90g/2¾–3½oz cylinder. The rind is very lightly coloured with annatto*
CULINARY USES: *Table cheese, grilling, in salads, fromage fort*

Firm and grainy when a few weeks old, with a mild, lemony freshness and slightly bitter finish, Rigotte becomes quite tart if allowed to dry. Some dry cheeses are marinated in aromatic oils flavoured with peppers and fresh herbs. The cheese absorbs the flavours while becoming creamier, and the result is strangely reminiscent of *saucisson* (sausages) or salami.

Rigottes that are matured in humid conditions develop the classic pale blue moulds. They acquire a more nutty character, but still retain a slight bitterness of taste.

Above: Rollot

Rollot

Region: *Picardy*
Type: *Traditional, farmhouse and creamery, unpasteurized, semi-soft cheese*
Source: *Cow's milk*
Description: *280–300g/10¼–11oz round or heart-shaped cheese with grainy, burnt orange, washed rind*
Culinary use: *Table cheese*

The cheese takes its name from the village of Rollot. Under the tough, sticky rind, the pale yellow interior is firm yet supple, with a rather pungent, yeasty aroma and taste with a fruity bite on the finish. It can be quite salty and bitter if the rind is allowed to dry out.

Below: Roquefort

Roquefort (AOC)

Region: *Rouergue*
Type: *Traditional, farmhouse and creamery, unpasteurized, blue cheese*
Source: *Sheep's milk (Lacaune, Manech, Baso-bernaise; also Corsican breeds)*
Description: *2.5–3kg/5½–6½lb cylinder with sticky, pale ivory, natural rind. Sold wrapped in foil*
Culinary uses: *Table cheese, blue cheese dressings, in salads*

For over 2,000 years, shepherds have been maturing their cheeses in the deep limestone caves of Cambalou, which are famous for the blue moulds that exist naturally in the air.

The traditional way of introducing the mould was to allow it to grow on loaves of rye bread placed beside the cheeses in the caves, and a version of this method is still practised by some cheesemakers today. Loaves of the local rye bread are baked especially for the purpose at the start of the season. The bread is left for 70 days to dry and become mouldy, then it is ground to a powder and tiny amounts are sprinkled on the curds before they are placed in the moulds.

Roquefort has a distinct bouquet and a flavour that combines the sweet, burnt-caramel taste of sheep's milk with the sharp, metallic tang of the blue mould. Crumbly, melt-in-the-mouth, refreshing, clean – all these adjectives and more have been used to describe this great cheese.

Rouy

Region: *Burgundy*
Type: *Modern, creamery, washed-rind cheese*
Source: *Cow's milk*
Description: *250g/9oz square cheese with rounded corners. The smooth, terracotta-coloured rind is slightly sticky and may have some white mould*
Culinary use: *Table cheese*

This is a commercially made copy of the stronger, more pungent, traditional French washed-rind cheeses like Langres or Epoisses. Nevertheless, it is a good buy.

Salers (AOC)

Region: *Auvergne*
Type: *Traditional, farmhouse, unpasteurized, hard cheese*
Source: *Cow's milk*
Description: *30–50g/1¼–2oz cylinder with hard, brown, natural rind that becomes rough and crusty with age*
Culinary uses: *Table cheese, grating, grilling, sauces*

Salers or Fourme de Salers is the *fermier* version of Cantal. Thousands of cheese mites – the sign of a truly great cheese – colonize the thick, brownish-yellow rind, creating a craggy, rock-like surface. The aroma is very meaty, and the rich yellow interior is redolent of wild flowers, including dandelions, and fresh green grass. There is an overlying nutty taste and a strong, savoury, raw-onion bite. Languiole is a similar cheese.

Above: Salers

Sancerre

Region: *Loire*
Type: *Traditional, farmhouse, unpasteurized, natural-rind cheese*
Source: *Goat's milk*
Description: *120–150g/4¼–5oz round. The natural rind is cream in colour, with soft wrinkles*
Culinary uses: *Table cheese, grilling, in salads*

This classic chèvre has a fine, wrinkled rind that hardens over time. It has a light, goaty smell and a slightly grainy texture that becomes dense and smooth. There is a fresh "white wine" fruitiness to the young Sancerre and a strong, nutty, goaty taste when aged. The white wine of the region is a perfect partner for the cheese. Similar cheeses include Crottin de Chavignol and Santranges.

Selles-sur-Cher (AOC)

Region: *Loire*
Type: *Traditional, farmhouse and creamery, unpasteurized, natural-rind cheese*
Source: *Goat's milk*
Description: *150–200g/5–7oz round cheese. The ash-covered rind gradually develops blotches of grey and blue moulds*
Culinary uses: *Table cheese, grilling, in salads*

The Loire is famous for its goat's milk cheeses. They come in a wide array of shapes – pyramids, rounds, truncated cones, hearts, logs and cylinders – but all have the same natural, blue-grey rind and many are lightly dusted with wood ash.

Selles-sur-Cher is a classic example. The ash, mixed with coarsely ground salt, is sprinkled over the cheese, adding to its visual appeal while facilitating the draining of the whey. The concept was probably introduced to the Loire in the eighth century, when the Saracen invaders from Spain reached its southern banks. Most of the invaders were later repelled, but some remained with their goats to provide the foundation for these famous chèvres.

Soumaintrain

Region: *Burgundy*
Type: *Traditional, farmhouse and creamery, unpasteurized, washed-rind cheese*
Source: *Cow's milk*
Description: *350g/12oz round cheese with washed rind. The white of the curd can be seen through the shiny, reddish-brown moulds*
Culinary uses: *Table cheese, fromage fort*

Quite grainy and moist when young, Soumaintrain has a mild, refreshing lemony flavour. After six weeks in a humid cellar, where it is frequently washed in brine, it begins to resemble its more outspoken cousin, Epoisses. The rind becomes more pungent and it develops a strong, spicy tang and a creamier feel. Soumaintrain is sometimes immersed in ash to make Aisy Cendré, a local speciality. Saint-Florentin is a similar cheese.

Below: Sancerre (left) and Selles-sur-Cher (right)

Above: Soumaintrain is often used to make a traditional delicacy called "fromage fort" (strong cheese) – the cheese is steeped in the local wine before if is eaten

Saint-Agur

Region: *Auvergne*
Type: *Modern, creamery, blue cheese*
Source: *Cow's milk*
Description: *2kg/4½lb octagonal cylinder with cream-yellow, natural rind with blue-grey moulds*
Culinary uses: *Table cheese, in salads and dressings*

Created in 1986 by the huge French cheese company Bongrain, Saint-Agur is made from pasteurized milk and has a moist, creamy texture and spicy, blue cheese taste. It is far milder than most other French blue cheeses, with the blue mould evenly spread in patches throughout the cheese. The unique octagonal shape makes this cheese very easy to cut into wedges.

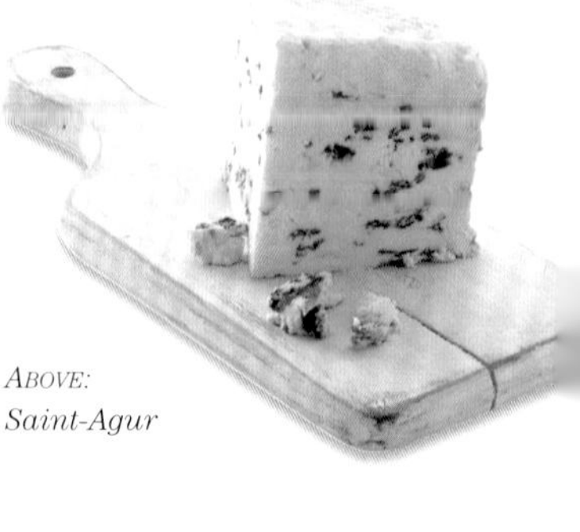

Above: Saint-Agur

ABOVE: Saint-Albray

ABOVE: Saint-Marcellin

SAINT-ALBRAY

REGION: *Aquitaine*
TYPE: *Modern, creamery, soft-white cheese*
SOURCE: *Cow's milk*
DESCRIPTION: *2kg/4½lb round cheese with a hole in the centre. The rind is reddish-brown, overlaid with white penicillium mould*
CULINARY USES: *Table cheese, snacks*

Saint-Albray was invented in 1976 to appeal to those who found the flavour of Camembert too strong, but liked that type of cheese. Twenty years later, it is still found in supermarkets around the world. The stable nature of the cheese means that it can survive the rigours of long journeys and cold cabinets.

Ripened for only two weeks, Saint-Albray develops a moist, rubbery texture and has a mild, creamy, undemanding flavour. The shape makes it very practical for serving: round, with a hole in the middle, it is marked into neat sections by indentations in the rind.

SAINT-MARCELLIN

REGION: *Rhône-Alpes*
TYPE: *Traditional, farmhouse and creamery, unpasteurized, natural-rind cheese*
SOURCE: *Cow's or goat's milk*
DESCRIPTION: *80g/3¼oz round with wrinkly, natural rind dusted with a coating of white yeast. With age, a delicate, blue mould and red and yellow pigments develop*
CULINARY USES: *Table cheese, fromage fort à la Lyonnaise*

Saint-Marcellin is known to have been served to royalty as early as 1461. In those days it would probably have been made from goat's milk, although cow's milk is often used today. The texture of the young cheese varies from firm to very runny, and it has a mild, slightly salty flavour. When ripe, it is irresistible, with a slightly yeasty taste.

SAINT-NECTAIRE (AOC)

REGION: *Auvergne*
TYPE: *Traditional, farmhouse and creamery, unpasteurized, semi-soft cheese*
SOURCE: *Cow's milk (Salers)*
DESCRIPTION: *1.5kg/3–3½lb round cheese. The leathery, natural rind is pinkish, with a covering of pale grey mould*
CULINARY USE: *Table cheese*

This soft, voluptuous cheese is cured on a bed of straw for eight weeks, and seems to absorb some of its earthy, pastoral aroma. Like a large version of Reblochon, a cheese from the Savoie, Saint-Nectaire is creamy and rich, redolent of freshly cut grass, sweet hay, wild flowers and herbs.

When selecting a Saint-Nectaire, look out for an oval, green label that declares it to be a *fermier* (farmhouse) cheese made from raw milk. A square, green label is used on factory-made cheeses, which are usually pasteurized.

BELOW: Saint-Nectaire

Saint-Paulin

Region: *Various*
Type: *Modern, farmhouse and creamery, semi-soft cheese*
Source: *Cow's milk*
Description: *500g–1.5kg/1¼–3½lb or 1.8–2kg/4–4½lb wheel. The thin, washed rind is smooth and leathery. It ranges in colour from pale yellow to bright mandarin orange*
Culinary uses: *Table cheese, melting, snacks*

Based on the Trappist cheese Port-du-Salut, Saint-Paulin has remained a popular cheese since it was first made in 1930. It was the first French cheese produced from pasteurized milk and has remained so, although one producer decided to buck the trend in 1990 and is making a version made with raw milk. Saint-Paulin has a slightly smoky, sweet-sour aroma and taste.

Sainte-Maure de Touraine (AOC)

Region: *Loire*
Type: *Traditional, farmhouse, unpasteurized, fresh or natural-rind cheese*
Source: *Goat's milk*
Description: *250g/9oz log rolled in black wood ash. It develops a blotchy, blue-grey rind with age*
Culinary uses: *Table cheese, grilling, baking*

Saint-Maure is made both on small farms and in large factories throughout Touraine, but the protection afforded by the AOC regulations ensures that the quality is always good. The freshly formed curd is scooped by hand into log-shaped moulds. Farmhouse cheeses have a piece of straw running through the centre. In theory, this makes them easier to pick up; in practice, pulling or lifting the straw often makes the cheese collapse in large chunks.

The ash coating provides a wonderful contrast when the cheese is cut to reveal the stark white interior. Young cheeses are moist and grainy, but as the mould develops the cheese dries, hardens and becomes more dense. Saint-Maure has a lovely musty, citrus flavour that intensifies with age.

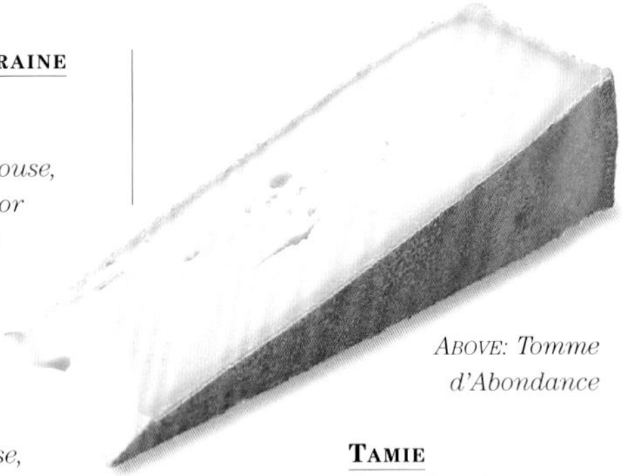

Above: Tomme d'Abondance

Tamie

Region: *Haute-Savoie*
Type: *Traditional, farmhouse, unpasteurized, semi-soft cheese*
Source: *Cow's milk (Montbéliard, La Tarine)*
Description: *500g/1¼lb or 1.3kg/2¾lb round. The fine, leathery, washed rind ranges in colour from pinkish-brown to orange-pink*
Culinary use: *Table cheese*

Tamie, made by the monks of the Abbaye de Tamie, has an attractive rind with a sweet, earthy aroma. Underneath, the cheese is a creamy colour. Initially, the taste is sweet, herbaceous and vaguely nutty, followed by a more powerful tang. The rind should be soft and supple; if it is hard and unyielding, the cheese has probably been kept for too long at too low a temperature and will be past its prime. Such a cheese is liable to be highly acidic without the balancing sweetness.

Similar cheeses include Reblochon and Chambarand.

Tomme d'Abondance (AOC)

Region: *Savoie*
Type: *Traditional, farmhouse, unpasteurized, hard cheese*
Source: *Cow's milk*
Description: *5–15kg/11–33lb wheel with brushed, natural, grey rind*
Culinary uses: *Table cheese, melting*

For centuries, this deep golden cheese has been made in mountain chalets near the border between France and Switzerland. The cheese has a distinct, fruity tang with a hint of yeast. Firm, but supple and slightly grainy, it is made from skimmed milk.

Above: Tamie

Tomme de Romans

Region: *Dauphine*
Type: *Traditional, farmhouse and creamery, unpasteurized, natural-rind cheese*
Source: *Cow's milk*
Description: *200–300g/7–11oz round. The natural rind has fluffy, white and blue-grey mould*
Culinary use: *Table cheese*

These attractive little cheeses are traditionally sold in wooden trays lined with straw. They have a slightly sour, grassy flavour with a delicate, nutty finish.

Tomme de Savoie

Region: *Savoie*
Type: *Traditional, farmhouse and creamery, unpasteurized, semi-soft cheese*
Source: *Cow's milk*
Description: *1.5–3kg/3–6½lb wheel. The thick, furry, grey, natural rind has yellow and orange blotches*
Culinary uses: *Table cheese, grating, grilling*

An ancient mountain cheese from the Savoie, made in winter when the herdsmen have returned from the summer pastures. In summer, the milk goes with the milk from other herds to become Beaufort, but when the weather worsens and yield drops, the herdsman makes his cheese at home. When searching out the best Tomme, look for "*lait cru*" on the label, the numbers 73 or 74 on an oval, red, casein plaque and the logo of four red hearts and the word "Savoie". Don't be put off by the appearance of the rind. Inside, the pale yellow cheese with its few small holes will be firm, yet supple with a gentle flavour hinting at meadow flowers, milk and walnuts.

Above: *Valençay*

Above: *Tourée de l'Aubier*

Tourée de l'Aubier

Region: *Normandy*
Type: *Modern, creamery, washed-rind cheese*
Source: *Cow's milk*
Description: *200g/7oz or 2kg/4½lb round. Sticky, leathery, washed rind with powdery, white mould on its orange red surface*
Culinary use: *Table cheese*

The spruce bark belt gives this washed-rind cheese a unique flavour. Creamy, sweet, yet pungent, it becomes almost runny when mature. Created as a pasteurized copy of the great French Mont d'Or, it is passable as long as it is ripe.

Left: *Tomme de Savoie*

Valençay

Region: *Berry*
Type: *Traditional, farmhouse and creamery, unpasteurized, natural-rind cheese*
Source: *Goat's milk*
Description: *200–250g/7–9oz truncated pyramid with natural, white rind dusted with charcoal ash. With age, the rind develops blue-grey moulds*
Culinary use: *Table cheese*

This elegant pyramid is dusted with fine, black charcoal. When young, the white cheese can be seen through the ash. Gradually, however, the colours merge and blue-grey moulds appear. The taste is at first fresh and citrus-like, but age gives the cheese a nuttier flavour and a distinctly goaty character. The commercially produced version is known as Pyramide.

Vignotte/Les Vignottes

Region: *Champagne or Lorraine*
Type: *Traditional, creamery, soft-white cheese*
Source: *Cow's milk*
Description: *150g/5oz cylinder or 2kg/4½lb thick disc with thick, velvety, smooth penicillium rind*
Culinary uses: *Table cheese, grilling*

This very popular, triple-cream cheese has a light, almost mousse-like texture, thanks to the careful ladling of the young curd into the moulds. The flavour is fresh and creamy, slightly lemony and salty.

Italian Cheeses

For more than six centuries Europe was dominated by the Romans. What began as a few farming settlements in the eighth century BC grew into the city of Rome. In the sixth century BC Rome became a republic, governed by a senate, which was made up of representatives from the influential families of the day. The Romans set about conquering the world as they knew it, and by the second century AD the Roman Empire included all the countries that encircled the Mediterranean, stretching as far as the Persian Gulf in the east, to England, France and Spain in the west, and the countries of North Africa.

Cheese played a major role in the diet of the Romans, as it was convenient, compact and travelled well – even in the knapsacks of the legionnaires – and came in numerous forms. One of the earliest mentions of cheeses was by Pliny the Elder, when he referred to the cheesemaking techniques used by shepherds on the outskirts of Rome to make the sheep's milk cheese that was the forefather of Pecorino Romano. In his writings, Columella also referred to cheese and cheesemaking, demonstrating his understanding of the use of rennet, a significant breakthrough in the art.

Cheesemaking skills were recorded and communicated to shepherds and farmers across Europe who, until the arrival of the Romans, had only a rudimentary understanding of the process, and made mainly soft, fermented cheeses preserved in oil or salt.

It was the legions of Julius Caesar who brought the knowledge of how to make hard cheeses to Switzerland in 400BC, laying the foundation for what were to become some of the world's finest cheeses. Some of the classic English and French hard cheeses also owe their origins to Roman cheesemaking skills.

Roquefort was among the earliest cheeses from the provinces to be mentioned by Pliny in around AD40. The stretched curd *(pasta filata)* cheeses, such as Provolone and mozzarella, are thought to have originated, not in Italy, but with the Bedouin tribes of Persia.

LEFT: Bel Paese, one of Italy's most famous semi-soft cheeses, is now also made under licence in the USA

In a recent survey, nearly 400 Italian cheeses were identified. Some have been given the protection of the DOC (a system of control and protection), while others are yet to be included. They rate in quality and diversity alongside the cheeses of France, but whereas in France cheese tends to be served as a separate course, the great Italian cheeses have found fame for the flavour, style and character they give to Italian food. Enormous volumes of Grana Padano, Parmigiano-Reggiano, Provolone and Pecorino are sent around the world.

It is a shame that most consumers use these wonderful hard cheeses purely for cooking. Once you have eaten a freshly cut chunk of Parmigiano-Reggiano or Pecorino Toscano with fresh figs and Parma ham or simply solo, with a glass of Barolo, you will understand why Italians like to refer to these as table cheeses – the implication being that they should be kept on the table to be eaten whenever wanted.

Many of Italy's greatest cheeses are seldom found outside the areas where they are made, let alone beyond Italy's borders, so the best way to discover them is to take a trip through this wonderful country.

LEFT: Parmigiano-Reggiano

ASIAGO (DOC)

REGION: *Vicenza & Trento*
TYPE: *Traditional, farmhouse and creamery, unpasteurized, hard cheese*
SOURCE: *Cow's milk*
DESCRIPTION: *8–20kg/18–44lb wheel. The natural rind is smooth and glossy. Yellow when young, it deepens to burnt orange*
CULINARY USES: *Table cheese, grating, as a condiment*

Centuries ago, this was a sheep's milk cheese, made by shepherds from the Asiago plateau. However, as sheep gave way to cattle (with their higher milk yields), cow's milk came to be used. There are two distinct types of Asiago. The first is a lightly pressed cheese made from whole milk in small dairies. It is sometimes incorrectly referred to or mistaken for Pressato – a fact that irritates the Asiago producers – and it ripens within 20–30 days. Pale yellow and springy, with a delicate, sweet, undemanding flavour and fragrance, it has achieved significant commercial success with the modern consumer.

Asiago d'Allevo is the mature cheese, and, according to locals, the better form. Although it is made with skimmed milk, the long, slow maturation process creates a fruity, slightly sharp cheese with a compact, granular interior full of small holes. After 12 months it is the colour of liquid honey; after two years it acquires a toffee colour and becomes brittle and intensely flavoured. Like Parmesan cheese, Asiago can, when grated, be used as a condiment.

RIGHT: Asiago

DOC

Like France, Italy operates a system to protect certain indigenous cheeses. It goes under the acronym DOC (Denominazione di Origine Controllata). In 1955 the Ministry of Agriculture and Forestry, in conjunction with a consortium of cheesemakers, set out to identify suitable candidates for DOC regulation. They agreed standards of production and determined areas where the cheeses in question could be made. So far 26 cheeses have been given the DOC classification, and more will undoubtedly follow.

Identifying and promoting indigenous cheeses in this way helps to protect them from being copied, while guaranteeing the consumer a level of quality. It also brings to the attention of the public artisan cheeses that might otherwise have become extinct.

Inspectors regularly visit the cheesemakers. If a cheese sold under the DOC label fails to comply with the regulations, the producer can be heavily fined and legal action may be taken. The DOC symbol is more than a legal requirement, however. It recognizes that indigenous cheeses and their makers have an important role to play in the nation's history. It also acknowledges the places where the cheeses are traditionally made. DOC status is a matter of pride.

What DOC status does not do is guarantee that every cheese that carries the symbol is perfect (or identical with every other cheese of the same type). The character of an individual cheese will depend upon the grazing, the season and the skills of the cheesemaker. DOC status, however, guarantees an overall standard.

BEL PAESE

REGION: *Lombardy*
TYPE: *Modern, creamery, semi-soft cheese*
SOURCE: *Cow's milk*
DESCRIPTION: *2kg/4½lb wheel with shiny, golden, waxed rind*
CULINARY USES: *Table cheese, melting; can be used instead of mozzarella*

Dante referred to Italy as "*bel paese*" – beautiful land. This later became the title of a book, which in turn proved the inspiration for Egidio Galbani when he sought a name for his soft and yielding cheese. Bel Paese is ivory in colour and has a delicately sweet flavour that has won the hearts of thousands around the world. The cheese ripens in one to three months. A version is made in the USA under licence.

BRA (DOC)

REGION: *Piedmont*
TYPE: *Traditional, farmhouse and co-operative, unpasteurized, hard cheese*
SOURCE: *Cow's milk*
DESCRIPTION: *8kg/18lb round. The natural rind ranges in colour from pale straw yellow to deep brownish-yellow and has some surface moulds*
CULINARY USES: *Table cheese, grating, melting*

Like Stilton, Bra is named not for where it is made, but for the place where it was originally sold. The people of Bra (in Cuneo, Piedmont) used to buy young cheeses from the herdsmen of the Alpine valleys. These they matured in their own cellars, either for their own consumption or for selling on. If the cheeses were matured for long enough, they could be substituted for the more expensive and less readily available Pecorino.

Today there are two types of Bra, both similar in appearance but cured in different ways. The traditional, hard version is still the most popular. It is matured for three to six months, when the colour darkens and the flavour intensifies.

The cheese is also sold young, at 45 days, when the paste is still soft. This version is made in small dairies, almost always from pasteurized milk; it is disapproved of by traditional producers.

Caciocavallo

REGION: *Southern Italy*
TYPE: *Traditional, farmhouse and creamery, stretched curd cheese*
SOURCE: *Cow's milk*
DESCRIPTION: *2–3kg/4½–6½lb fat, gourd-shaped cheese, tied at the thin end with a cord for hanging. The rind is oily and smooth*
CULINARY USES: *Table cheese, grating, grilling, melting*

This stretched curd (*pasta filata*) cheese is typical of the south of Italy. The origin of the name has long been debated. *Cavallo* means "horse" in Italian, and some say the cheese was originally made from mare's milk. A more logical, but less romantic, explanation is that the name comes from the method of hanging pairs of cheeses over a pole, as if on horseback.

Usually farm-made, the curd is pulled and stretched until it is stringy but no longer breaks. It is then divided into portions, kneaded into shape and matured. At three months the Caciocavallo is sweet and supple and eaten as a table cheese. Some though are matured for up to two years, when they can be grated. The interior is golden-yellow and close-textured, the aroma is intense and lingering, and the taste is full but mellow. Caciocavallo is sometimes made with a lump of butter in the middle, which oozes out when the cheese is cut. There are also smoked versions.

Canestrato Pugliese (DOC)

REGION: *Foggia*
TYPE: *Traditional, farmhouse, unpasteurized, hard cheese*
SOURCE: *Sheep's milk (Merino or Apulian Gentile)*
DESCRIPTION: *7–14kg/15¼–31lb cylinder. The natural, beige to gold rind is embossed with the intricate pattern of the basket in which it is drained*
CULINARY USES: *Table cheese, grating*

Named after the simple, hand-woven reed basket in which it is pressed and drained, Canestrato Pugliese is a flavoursome Pecorino. After being allowed to mature on a wooden shelf for a month or two, the cheese has an aroma reminiscent of wet wool, lanolin and mould. Although hard and grainy, the texture retains the rich, creamy feel and burnt-caramel taste characteristic of sheep's milk cheeses. The cheese can be left to mature for up to a year, and has a fat content of 45 per cent.

BELOW: Casciotta di Urbino

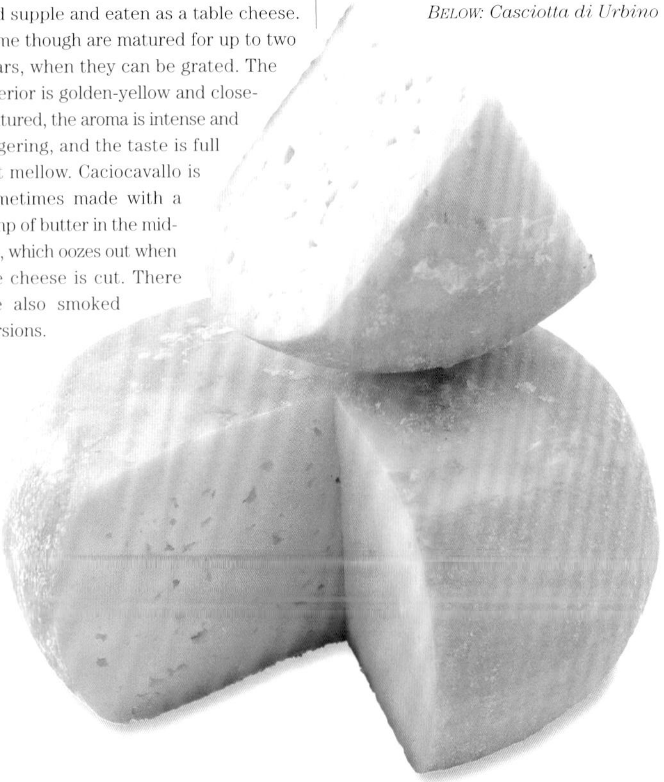

ABOVE: Caciocavallo

Casciotta di Urbino (DOC)

REGION: *Tuscany and Umbria*
TYPE: *Traditional, farmhouse, unpasteurized, semi-soft cheese*
SOURCE: *Sheep's milk (Sardinian and Appennine Brown) plus some cow's milk*
DESCRIPTION: *1.2kg/2½lb round-edged cylinder with thin, polished, yellow to orange, natural rind*
CULINARY USES: *Table cheese, snacks, cooking, in salads*

Casciotta is the name used to describe the many small, artisan cheeses made all over central Italy and in some parts of the south. They can be made with cow's, goat's or sheep's milk (or a mixture) and are popular with both locals and tourists alike. Some have smooth, firm, oiled rinds; others have the basket imprint typical of Pecorinos.

Casciotta di Urbino is said to be one of the best. The yellow rind gives way to a deliciously compact, friable, straw-coloured interior. Sweet-tasting and moist, with the aroma and flavour of warm milk, it is a delicate, subtle cheese with underlying flavours of fresh green grass, nuts and wild flowers.

The makers of Casciotta di Urbino use raw milk and make their cheese only between April and September. It ripens in 15–30 days and has a fat content of 45 per cent. The cheese may be flavoured with garlic, onion or truffles.

Castelmagno (DOC)

Region: *Cuneo*
Type: *Traditional, farmhouse and co-operative, unpasteurized, hard cheese*
Source: *Cow's milk (with goat's or sheep's milk)*
Description: *5–7kg/11–15¼lb cylinder. The reddish-yellow, natural rind is crusty, with some grey moulds and yeasts*
Culinary uses: *After-dinner cheese; also used to make gnocchi*

The first official record of Castelmagno was in 1277, when it was mentioned as a unit of exchange. Production remained steady for centuries and some even found its way to Paris and London, but by the early 1950s demand had dropped significantly. Recognizing the importance of preserving a part of local history, an association to protect Castelmagno was formed and formalized under the DOC system in 1982.

Castelmagno is made from partially skimmed cow's milk, with some goat's or sheep's milk added. The evening milk is left to ripen overnight. Next day, the morning milk is added, which contributes to its strong taste and unusual texture. This has been described as resembling cotton wool, but lovers of Castelmagno prefer to describe it as flaky or compact, but not dense, not unlike young Lancashire.

The cheeses are left to ripen in damp cellars and drying rooms, occasionally being turned and washed to encourage the development of the natural micro-flora that contribute to the pungent, yeasty aroma. Blue moulds, present in the cellars, sometimes penetrate the rind to form fine, blue streaks that impart a more spicy flavour to the cheese. It ripens in two to five months (today's consumers tend to prefer it younger and milder).

Crescenza

Region: *Lombardy*
Type: *Traditional, farmhouse and creamery, fresh cheese*
Source: *Cow's milk*
Description: *1–2kg/2¼–4½lb white square or rectangle*
Culinary uses: *Baking, grilling, in sauces*

The texture of this Stracchino-style cheese varies considerably from one brand to the next and according to the percentage of fat. The best examples are reputed to come from around Milan or Pavia. Sold within a few days of making, they come wrapped in simple, white, greaseproof paper and are quite luscious. Squidgy and so moist as to be almost wet, they have a fresh, clean acidity not unlike that of yogurt. Other Crescenzas are more rubbery, jelly-like or mushy, with a sour, synthetic taste. Low-fat varieties can be grainy.

Crescenza should be ripened for no longer than 10 days and eaten as soon as possible after that. The fat content varies between 48 and 50 per cent.

Dolcelatte

Region: *Lombardy*
Type: *Modern, creamery, blue cheese*
Source: *Cow's milk*
Description: *1–2kg/2¼–4½lb wheel. The moist, natural rind is white, blotched with blue and grey mould*
Culinary uses: *Table cheese, dressings, in salads and on pasta*

The name means "sweet milk" and the cheese has a luscious, sweet taste. Deliciously soft, it melts like ice cream in the mouth. Created by Galbani, a company already famous for Bel Paese, Dolcelatte appeals to those who find the more traditional blue cheeses, such as Gorgonzola and Roquefort, too strongly flavoured, robust and spicy.

The cheesemaking method is similar to that used for Gorgonzola, except that Dolcelatte is made from the curd of only one milking. Produced in factories, the cheese ripens in two to three months and has a fat content of around 50 per cent. It may also be labelled Gorgonzola Dolce. Similar cheeses include Dolceverde and Torta Gaudenzio.

Below: Dolcelatte

Left: *Dolcelatte Torta*

Dolcelatte Torta

Region: *Various*

Type: *Modern, creamery, blue cheese*

Source: *Cow's milk*

Description: *2–3kg/4½–6½lb rectangle with moist, natural rind covered in grey and blue moulds*

Culinary uses: *Table cheese; also used in dips and spreads and over pasta*

Created in the 1960s, this cheese consists of thick layers of mascarpone cream alternating with the mild, Italian blue cheese, Dolcelatte. The cream mellows the blue cheese and the feel in the mouth is soft and gentle, more like ice cream than cheese. Spread it on warm toast, melt it over pasta or keep it for a private feast. Dolcelatte Torta is really too rich – the fat content is a hefty 75 per cent – to serve with ordinary wine, but it is delicious accompanied by a smooth fortified wine, such as Madeira, or even a sweet Italian dessert wine to cut the richness.

In the USA it may also be labelled Gorgonzola Torta.

The success of this cheese has led to the creation of other *tortas*, some good, some almost inedible. One of the best has layers of lightly toasted pine nuts and pesto alternating with the mascarpone – a few chunks of this *torta* melted into hot pasta and sprinkled with fresh chopped basil makes an irresistible appetizer.

Fiore Sardo (DOC)

Region: *Sardinia*

Type: *Traditional, farmhouse and co-operative, unpasteurized, hard cheese*

Source: *Sheep's milk*

Description: *1.5–4kg/3–9lb cylindrical wheel. The hard, ridged, natural rind is golden-yellow to dark brown*

Culinary uses: *Table cheese, grating, cooking, snacks*

Don't be put off by the sour, damp smell of the rind. This is the sweetest of the Pecorinos. Straw-coloured and compact, this hard and grainy cheese has a wonderfully rich flavour, with a caramel sweetness, a mouthwatering, salty tang and a hint of fruit.

Rennet from lamb or kid (goat) is used to coagulate the milk. The method differs from that used for traditional Pecorino in that the curds are not "cooked" or heated in the whey. Once drained, the curds are scalded in hot water to seal the rind. They are then stored on a woven reed shelf, which hangs over the family hearth, absorbing the sweet smoke as they dry. Ripening continues in another room or the attic and the cheeses are periodically rubbed with olive oil and sheep fat to keep them moist and prevent moulds from forming. Fiore Sardo ripens in three to six months and has a fat content of 45 per cent.

Fontina (DOC)

Region: *Valle d'Aosta*

Type: *Traditional, farmhouse and creamery, unpasteurized, semi-soft cheese*

Source: *Cow's milk*

Description: *8–18kg/18–40lb wheel. The thin, uneven, light brown to terracotta rind is lightly oiled*

Culinary uses: *Table cheese, melting, grilling*

In the pastures of the Valle d'Aosta, dominated by the highest mountains in Europe, the very dry summers result in a wide variety of high-quality fodder. There has been a cheese industry here since the eleventh century, when the local cheese was known simply as "caseus" to indicate that it was made from cow's milk.

Today, the name Fontina is used exclusively and proudly to identify cheeses produced in the Valle d'Aosta. The best of these are made in mountain chalets between May and September, when the herds graze the alpine meadows.

Fontina is dense, smooth and slightly elastic. The straw-coloured interior, with its small, round holes, has a delicate nuttiness with a hint of mild honey. When melted, as it frequently is (Fontina being the foundation for that superb fondue-style dish, fonduta), the flavour is earthy, with a suggestion of mushrooms and a fresh acidity.

Each cheesemaker has his own favourite location for ripening his cheeses – caves, tunnels, former military bunkers and even an abandoned copper mine. Fontina ripens in about three months and has a fat content of 45 per cent.

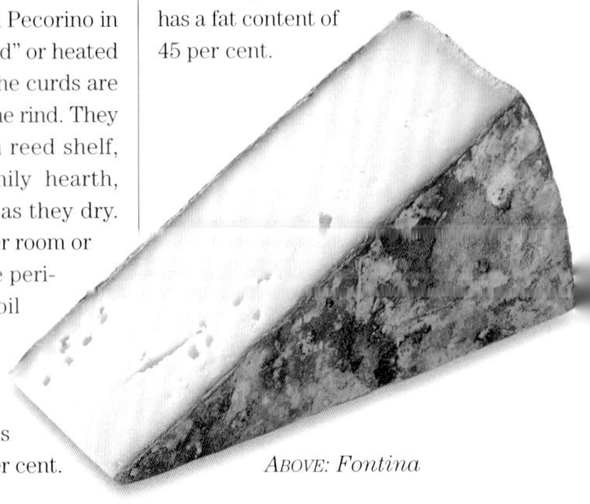

Above: *Fontina*

Gorgonzola (DOC)

Region: *Lombardy*
Type: *Traditional, creamery and co-operative, blue cheese*
Source: *Cow's milk*
Description: *6–12 kg/13–26lb drum with red to orange rind covered with powdery patches of grey and blue moulds*
Culinary uses: *Table cheese, dressings, salads, on pasta or gnocchi*

There are several folk legends to explain how what was originally a winter-made Stracchino cheese became one of the world's first blue cheeses. According to some, it was discovered inadvertently by an innkeeper in Gorgonzola, who found that his young Stracchino cheese had turned "blue" after a few weeks in his cool, damp cellars. Conscious of his profit margin, he decided to dish it up to some passing customers. Far from protesting, they demanded more.

The greenish-blue penicillium mould imparts a sharp, spicy flavour and provides an excellent contrast to the rich, creamy cheese. Gorgonzola is made by over 80 producers – large and small – in the north of Italy. Some use unpasteurized milk and follow the traditional method of allowing the curd to hang overnight so that it can become exposed to the mould naturally, but most Gorgonzola is made with pasteurized milk, to which the mould is added. At about four weeks the cheeses are pierced with thick needles to encourage the spread of the mould. Some are still ripened in the caves at Valsassina and Lodi, which provide ideal conditions for the formation of the mould.

Gorgonzola ripens in three to six months and has a fat content of 48 per cent. The cheese is usually wrapped in foil to keep it moist.

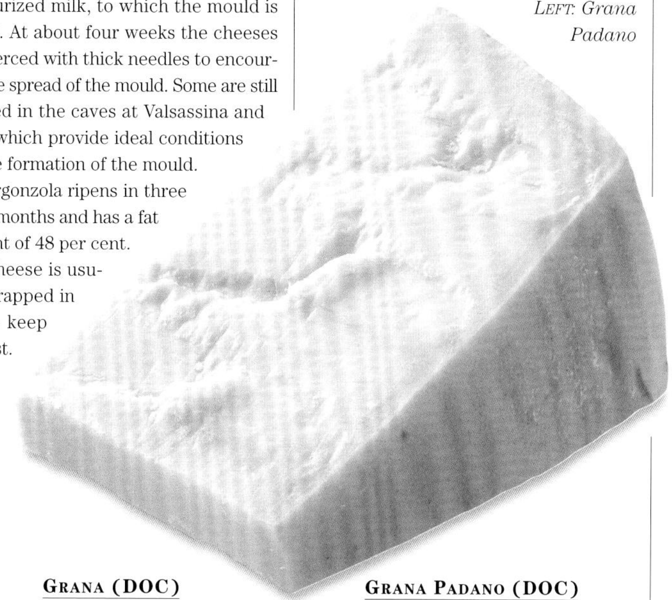

Left: Grana Padano

Grana (DOC)

Region: *Po Valley*
Type: *Traditional, creamery, unpasteurized, hard cheese*
Source: *Cow's milk*
Description: *24–40kg/52–88lb drum with rock-hard, polished, yellow to brown, natural rind*
Culinary uses: *Table cheese, grating, in sauces, as a condiment*

Grana is the generic name for the hard, grainy cheeses that originated in the Po Valley in Roman times. Magnificent, fruity and full of flavour, Grana must be matured for at least 12 months (longer, if covered by DOC controls). The most famous examples of Grana are Grana Padano and Parmigiano-Reggiano, which are listed separately in this book. Grana Lodigiano is characterized by a slightly greenish tinge and the flavour is very strong, even bitter. It is unbelievably expensive to buy.

Left: Gorgonzola

Grana Padano (DOC)

Region: *Specified parts of Piedmont, Lombardy, Emilia Romagna, Veneto and Trentino*
Type: *Traditional, co-operative, unpasteurized, hard cheese*
Source: *Cow's milk*
Description: *24–40kg/52–88lb drum. The smooth, natural rind is extremely hard and thick. Deep yellow and often oily, it carries the official logo*
Culinary uses: *Table cheese, grating, in starters and sauces, on pasta and salads*

Both Grana Padano and Parmigiano-Reggiano are known to many of us as simply "Parmesan". The cheese should taste fresh, fruity and sweet, with a hint of pineapple; never sour or dull. The pale yellow interior should be hard, grainy and crumbly. Although they are expensive, a little goes a long way. These cheeses freeze very well, you can either grate the cheese first and pack in a freezer container, or simply freeze the piece. It can be grated straight from the freezer – a far better convenience food than the unpleasant-tasting pre-packed pots of grated Parmesan that are available.

Grana Padano ripens in 12–48 months and has a fat content of 32 per cent.

Mascarpone

REGION: *Various*
TYPE: *Traditional, farmhouse and creamery, vegetarian, matured cream*
SOURCE: *Cow's milk*
DESCRIPTION: *Pale cream and shiny, sold in pots*
CULINARY USES: *Desserts, baking, with pasta, in savoury dishes*

Technically speaking, mascarpone is not a cheese at all, but rather the result of a culture being added to the cream skimmed off the milk used in the production of Parmesan. It is, however, often described as a curd cheese although it is made in much the same way as yogurt.

After the culture has been added, the cream is gently heated, then allowed to mature and thicken. It develops a magnificent, thick, spoonable texture and is extremely versatile.

Famous as the main ingredient of that most sensuous of all Italian desserts, tiramisù, it also makes an excellent alternative to double (heavy) cream in both sweet and savoury dishes. In southern Italy mascarpone is sometimes made from buffalo's milk. It takes only a few days to ripen and has a fat content of 75 per cent.

BELOW: Mascarpone

Montasio (DOC)

REGION: *Friuli and Veneto*
TYPE: *Traditional, farmhouse and creamery, unpasteurized, hard cheese*
SOURCE: *Cow's milk (with some sheep's milk)*
DESCRIPTION: *5–10kg/11–22lb wheel. The yellow-brown rind is smooth and springy at first, becomes harder and a darker brown with age*
CULINARY USES: *Table cheese, grating, in sauces*

Developed in the thirteenth century at the monastery of Maggio, Montasio was originally made wholly from sheep's milk. Cow's milk is used today. The evening milk is partially skimmed (the cream being used to make mascarpone) and then mixed with the morning milk. The cheese is the same shape as Fontina, but in texture it resembles a young Asiago. Pale yellow or straw-coloured, the body is firm, with small holes. A good Montasio is creamy, rich and fruity, with a hint of pineapple. It should be quite tangy on the finish – not unlike a medium Cheddar. As it matures, the rind becomes very hard and the interior quite granular, even brittle. The fruity taste intensifies.

Montasio ripens in three to 18 months and has a fat content of 30–40 per cent.

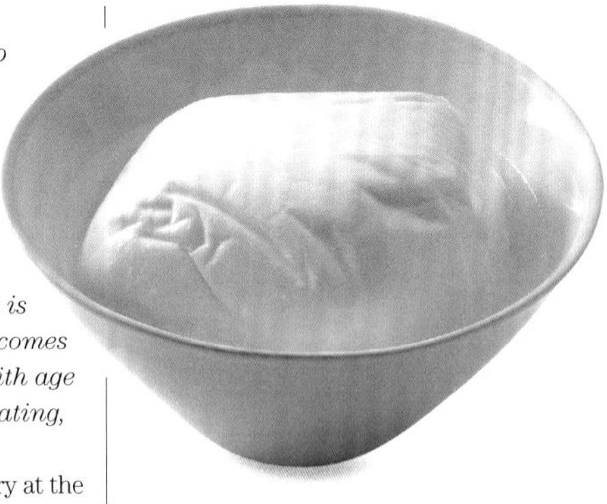

ABOVE: Mozzarella

Mozzarella di Bufala

REGION: *Various*
TYPE: *Traditional, farmhouse and creamery, stretched curd cheese*
SOURCE: *Water buffalo's milk*
DESCRIPTION: *Spherical or oval cheeses in various sizes – wet, shiny and pure white*
CULINARY USES: *Freshly sliced in salads, baked on pizzas, also grilled*

Like most fresh cheeses, mozzarella is used to add texture rather than a specific taste to a dish. The juices, oils and flavours of the other ingredients are absorbed and intensified by the mild, moist, open layers of spun curd. It is this characteristic, together with the fact that mozzarella melts to become wonderfully elastic, that has made the cheese so popular.

The cheese is sold swimming in whey. It should be floppy rather than rubbery and have moisture trapped between the layers of springy curd. Cow's milk mozzarella is not as delicately flavoured as that from water buffalo's milk, nor as soft in texture, but it can be exceptional if well made. A fresh cheese, it should be eaten within a few days of being made.

If the cheese is lightly smoked, it is called mozzarella affumicata. If the cheese is more heavily smoked (a process that dries it out), it is referred to as scamorza. The hard, rubbery "pizza" cheese sold as mozzarella outside Italy may be perfect for pizzas in terms of texture, but will never equal fresh mozzarella in taste. In Italy, the commercial "block" mozzarella is usually called pizzaiola.

Murazzano (DOC)

Region: *Cuneo*

Type: *Traditional, farmhouse and creamery, unpasteurized, fresh cheese*

Source: *Cow's and sheep's milk in 60:40 ratio*

Description: *150–250g/5–9oz round with fine, smooth, yellow rind*

Culinary uses: *Table cheese, grilling*

Named for the village where it is made, this is a typical Piedmontese *robiola* – a soft, round cheese made from a mixture of cow's and sheep's milk. The texture is delicate and supple and the taste fresh and milky, with a hint of the caramel characteristic of sheep's milk cheese. Although it is delicious as it is, it is usually melted on pizzas or crostini or used in sauces or pastries. Murazzano ripens in four to five days and has a fat content of 45 per cent.

Above: *Parmigiano-Reggiano*

Parmigiano-Reggiano (DOC)

Region: *Modena, Parma, Reggio Emilia, parts of Bologna and Mantua*

Type: *Traditional, co-operative, unpasteurized, hard cheese*

Source: *Cow's milk*

Description: *24–40kg/52–88lb drum with thick, hard, yellow to orange rind*

Culinary uses: *Table cheese, grating, in sauces and salads, over pasta and risotto*

In Italy, this wonderful cheese is sold in large, rough, grainy chunks chiselled from the shiny drum that carries its name emblazoned on the rind. The aroma is sweet and fruity, the colour fresh yellow and the taste exquisite – fruity (like fresh pineapple), strong and rich, but never overpowering or vicious. It will keep for months in the fridge, but the rough surface may grow some mould. If you have bought a large chunk and use it infrequently – an unthinkable possibility – freeze it. You can grate it straight from the freezer. In 1955 the rules relating to where Parmigiano-Reggiano could be made were tightened and the method of manufacture strictly specified. The cows whose milk goes into the cheese may have only fresh grass, hay or alfalfa. Enforcing these rules adds to the production cost, but the result is a cheese whose flavour and quality are guaranteed.

The secret of the continuing success of Parmigiano-Reggiano is the determination of the regulating body to maintain the 800 or so local dairy farms producing it. Only on small farms, where the milk does not have far to travel to the cheesemaker, can the close relationship between each batch of milk and its transformation into cheese be maintained.

A surprising feature of this delicious, robust and full-bodied cheese is that it is made from partially skimmed milk. The evening milk is left to rest in vats overnight. Next morning, the slightly soured cream is skimmed off to make mascarpone and the skimmed milk is combined with the fresh morning milk. It is then poured into conical, copper cauldrons so that the cheesemaking process can begin.

To seal the rind, and protect it from drying out over the next 18–48 months, the cheeses are floated in enormous brine baths for around 21 days, then they are moved to the storerooms. Throughout the maturation process, the huge cheeses are carefully brushed, turned, checked and rechecked before being graded by an official representative of the consortium responsible for determining the quality of each one.

The trademark, Parmigiano-Reggiano, is branded all over the rind, so that even a small piece of the cheese can easily be identified. It is one of the finest cheeses in the world.

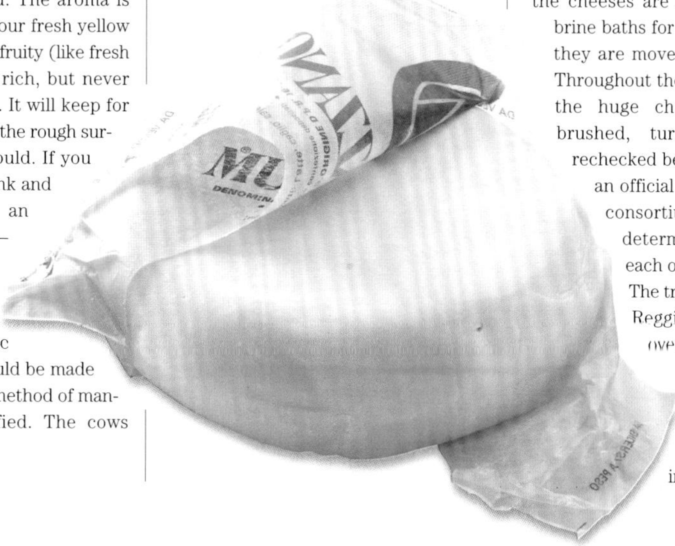

Right: *Murazzano*

Pecorino Romano (DOC)

Region: *Lazio and Sardinia*

Type: *Traditional, farmhouse and creamery, hard cheese*

Source: *Sheep's milk*

Description: *22–33kg/48–72lb drum. The smooth, hard rind is pale straw to dark brown in colour*

Culinary uses: *Table cheese, grating, in sauces, on pasta*

Pecorino is the generic name for cheeses made from pure sheep's milk. Each is characteristic of a specific area and of a particular breed of sheep. For centuries, Pecorino Romano was made in the countryside around Rome, and it remains virtually unchanged to this day.

Since the first century AD the cheese has been widely exported, thanks to its excellent keeping qualities. It was issued to Roman legionaries as part of their rations. Demand continued to grow until the Roman producers could no longer keep up. At that point production spread to Sardinia, where there are now more than 60 factories or dairies compared with only 10 in the area around Rome.

The cheese is made between November and late June, when the sheep graze freely on the natural pastures. Pecorino Romano is larger than most cheeses of this type and must be pressed. It takes eight to 12 months to mature, during which time it develops its characteristic flavour – salty, with a fruity tang that becomes steadily more robust. The rind varies in colour, depending on the age of the cheese, and may have a protective coating of lard or oil. The compact interior is white to pale yellow, with irregular, small eyes. It should feel moist, yet granular and it is a superb grating cheese.

Other Romanos are Caprino Romano made with goat's milk and Vaccino Romano made with cow's milk. Both are hard and have their own individual character.

Pecorino Sardo (DOC)

Region: *Sardinia*

Type: *Traditional, farmhouse, unpasteurized, hard cheese*

Source: *Sheep's milk*

Description: *1–4kg/2¼–9lb cylinder. The natural rind varies in colour from pale straw yellow to deep russet*

Culinary uses: *Table cheese, grating, in snacks, salads and sauces, on pasta*

Only recently brought under the protective umbrella of the DOC system, this cheese has two distinct styles. The delicate and sweet Pecorino Sardo Dolce is matured for 20–60 days and weighs 1–2.3kg/2¼–5lb. The body is white and firm, with a few scattered eyes.

Pecorino Sardo Maturo is matured for up to 12 months and becomes hard, granular and dry. It develops a robust sharpness and a salty tang. A cornucopia of flavours – sweet, nutty and herbaceous – is released when the cheese is grated on to hot foods such as pasta.

Each season can bring a subtle difference in the flavour of the cheese, depending on the flowers, grasses and herbs favoured by the native Sardinian sheep – the *mouflon* – that range over the rocky hillsides of the island.

Below: Pecorino Romano (left), Sardo (top) and Toscano (right)

Pecorino Toscano (DOC)

Region: *Tuscany*

Type: *Traditional, farmhouse and co-operative, unpasteurized, hard cheese*

Source: *Sheep's milk*

Description: *1–3kg/2¼–6½lb wheel. The natural rind ranges in colour from pale straw to brown or black*

Culinary uses: *Pared or grated on pasta or risotto, in sauces and salads*

A young Pecorino Toscano is supple, fruity and aromatic; the complex flavour suggests walnuts and rich, burnt caramel.

Until recently, the name was used to describe any cheese made in Tuscany from sheep's milk or a mixture of milks. New regulations mean that the name is now protected and reserved only for pure sheep's milk cheeses. Mixed milk cheeses are sold as Caciotta.

Generally smaller than other Pecorinos, Toscano ripens more quickly. Those sold young have a yellow rind and are firm, but not hard. The rind darkens to a brownish-red after two to three months. The black-rinded cheese (Pecorino Toscano Crosta Nero) is matured for at least six months and has an intense flavour.

Pressato (DOC)

Region: *Vicenza and Trento*

Type: *Traditional, co-operative, hard cheese*

Source: *Cow's milk*

Description: *Various sizes and shapes with pale straw to golden-yellow rind*

Culinary uses: *Table cheese, melting*

Pressato simply means "pressed" and is a generic name for a family of lightly pressed cheeses made from either skimmed or semi-skimmed milk. These sweet-sour, milky cheeses are sold young, when they are supple and open-textured. Asiago (to the annoyance of the producers) is sometimes wrongly referred to as Pressato.

ABOVE: Provolone

PROVOLONE (DOC)

REGION: *Lombardy*
TYPE: *Traditional creamery stretched curd cheese*
SOURCE: *Cow's milk*
DESCRIPTION: *200g–5kg/7oz–11lb cheeses in various shapes. The thin, hard rind is golden-yellow and shiny. It is sometimes waxed*
CULINARY USES: *Table cheese, grilling, melting*

No one knows precisely where or how this cheese originated, but it was certainly among the earliest cheeses known by the Romans. Local names for Provolone usually reflect the shape or size, which can vary considerably. The cheese can be spherical, pear-shaped, cylindrical or even plaited and the weight depends on the mood of the cheesemaker. The Giganti (monster cheeses), often made for special occasions or trade fairs, can be over 3m/3¼yd long, but the most familiar shape, often found hanging in Italian delicatessens, is the sausage tied with cord.

Dolce (mild Provolone) is aged for two to three months, and it is supple and smooth, with a thin, waxed rind. It is generally used as a table cheese. Picante (piquant) is coagulated with kid's rennet, which gives it a stronger flavour. Aged for six months to two years, it is darker, with small eyes, a hard rind and a strong, spicy flavour. It is often grated as a condiment.

QUARTIROLO LOMBARDO

REGION: *Lombardy*
TYPE: *Traditional, farmhouse and creamery, semi-soft cheese*
SOURCE: *Cow's milk*
DESCRIPTION: *1–3kg/2¼–6½lb square cheese. The tender, pale pink rind hardens with age and acquires reddish-grey moulds*
CULINARY USES: *Table cheese, served with salads and cold meats*

In summer, the abundant grass in the Lombardy valleys was traditionally mown three times. After the final mowing, the cattle would be brought from the mountain pastures to graze on the sweet, new grass (*erba quartirola*) before being turned into the barns for the winter. The cheese made from the rich milk yielded at this time was called Quartirolo Lombardo. Skimmed milk was used (the cream being turned into butter).

Today, the cheese is made all year round, usually from full-cream milk. It looks like a young Taleggio, and has a slightly crumbly, lumpy centre. If eaten within the first few weeks, it has a lemon-fresh acidity and delicate fragrance; after two months it becomes dense, almost runny, and its fruity character is more distinctive. Cheese lovers seek out those made in the mountains – Quartirolo di Monte – which are unpasteurized and slowly ripened. Producers are currently attempting to have the cheese brought under the control of the DOC system to protect its quality and character.

BELOW: Raschera

RAGUSANO (DOC)

REGION: *Sicily*
TYPE: *Traditional, farmhouse and co-operative, unpasteurized, hard cheese*
SOURCE: *Cow's milk (Modicana)*
DESCRIPTION: *10–12kg/22–26lb brick. The thin, smooth, natural, yellow rind is polished*
CULINARY USES: *Table cheese, grilling*

In local dialect, Ragusano (or Caciocavallo Ragusano) is described as a *scaluni* or step. The curd is heated and stretched until it is rubbery. It is then pressed into special rectangular moulds. Once draining is complete, the cheeses are rubbed with salt and left to mature in cellars for up to six months. To stave off insects, they are regularly rubbed with a mixture of oil and vinegar. The pale yellow interior is soft and supple, with a savoury taste that becomes stronger as the cheese hardens and ages beyond six months.

RASCHERA (DOC)

REGION: *Cuneo*
TYPE: *Traditional, farmhouse and co-operative, semi-soft cheese*
SOURCE: *Cow's milk (with sheep's or goat's milk)*
DESCRIPTION: *7–10kg/15¼–22lb round or square. The thin, reddish-yellow crust with white or grey moulds*
CULINARY USES: *Table cheese, grilling*

Named after Lake Raschera, which lies at the foot of Mt Mongioie, this cheese resembles Toma, but is square, the practical shape having been determined in the days when it was transported by mule.

Generally made with the sweet milk of the Piedmontese cow, Raschera has a pale ivory interior scattered with tiny holes which occasionally have a bluish tinge. When young, the cheese is supple and elastic, with a delicate sweet taste that becomes richer, more aromatic and slightly tart. The flavour changes from season to season. Spring and summer cheeses are sweet and fresh, whereas those made in winter tend to be more solid and vibrant. The best is reckoned to be that which comes from the alpine pastures – look for the words "*di alpessio*" on the label.

Ricotta

Region: *Various*
Type: *Traditional, farmhouse and creamery, whey cheese*
Source: *Cow's milk*
Description: *1–2kg/2¼–4½lb basin-shaped cheese, pure white and wet, but not sticky*
Culinary uses: *As a dessert cheese with sugar and fruit; also baked in ravioli or pastries*

When cheese is made, the solids in the milk are separated from the liquid by coagulation. Yet, however careful the cheesemaker, some solids are lost to the whey. To retrieve these, the milk is heated until the solids come to the surface as small, white lumps. These are skimmed off and drained in woven baskets until the curd is solid enough to stick together and can be turned out. The result is a soft, moist, basin-shaped cheese.

Good ricotta should be firm, not solid, and consist of a mass of fine, moist, delicate grains, neither salted nor ripened. One of the finest, Fior di Maggio, has a texture not unlike delicate bread and butter pudding. Only vaguely grainy, it melts in the mouth. Unfortunately, much of the ricotta made today uses semi-skimmed milk instead of whey and the texture can vary tremendously. It can be gritty, lumpy or even wet, causing havoc for those trying to use it in a traditional recipe.

In Italy, ricotta appears in a number of guises. Ricotta Romano is made from sheep's milk and is available only from November to June. Ricotta Salata is a salted and dried version that resembles feta, while Ricotta Infornata is a Sicilian speciality that is baked until it is lightly browned. Northern Italians like their ricotta smoked.

Ricotta ripens in one to five days and has a fat content of around 20 per cent.

Right: Ricotta Salata (left) and fresh Ricotta (right)

Robiola di Roccaverano (DOC)

Region: *Lombardy*
Type: *Traditional, farmhouse and co-operative, fresh cheese*
Source: *Cow's and goat's milk*
Description: *200g/7oz round or square cheese. Pure white when fresh, it becomes pink to orange with reddish ferments if aged*
Culinary uses: *Table cheese, baking, spreading, in sauces*

Roccaverano is a small, typically Italian hillside town. The local cheese was once made exclusively from goat's milk, but a mixture of milks is now permitted and cow's milk can account for as much as 85 per cent. Some Robiola di Roccaverano is still made on farms for family consumption, but the majority is made in small co-operatives, using pasteurized milk.

The cheese can be eaten fresh, at just a few days old, when it is sweet and very moist. Others prefer it once it has matured for up to 20 days. The mature cheese is sharper, but still retains the subtle, taste characteristic of goat's milk. The pasteurized cheese is spreadable, with a smooth texture. It has a sweet-sour aroma and a taste that resembles melted butter, but can be quite salty. The unpasteurized cheese has a much more complex flavour. Rich and meaty, it has a piquant, yeasty aroma.

Above: Scamorza Affumicate

Scamorza

Region: *Various*
Type: *Traditional, farmhouse and creamery, stretched curd cheese*
Source: *Cow's milk*
Description: *Smooth, shiny, white cheese traditionally made in a money-bag shape*
Culinary use: *Cooking*

The producers of Caciocavallo make this cheese when milk is abundant. It matures within a few days and it thus provides a good way to boost their income while waiting for the Caciocavallo to ripen.

A stretched curd cheese, Scamorza resembles Provolone. It is rubbery, with a stringy texture, and is drier than mozzarella. Sold young, within two to three days of making, it has a bland, vaguely milky taste. The smoked version, Scamorza Affumicate, is more popular than the plain and is often used in pasta dishes. It is also served with ham, mushrooms or chargrilled vegetables.

Stracchino

Region: *Lombardy*
Type: *Traditional, farmhouse and creamery, semi-soft cheese*
Source: *Cow's milk*
Description: *Made in various sizes and shapes (usually square). The thin, natural rind ranges from pale cream to reddish-brown, and can be sticky*
Culinary uses: *Table cheese, melting, grilling*

Stracchino is a generic term, used to describe a style of soft cheese that has been made in Lombardy since the twelfth century. The quality varies considerably, so it is wise to taste before you buy. A good Stracchino will have a supple, yielding texture and a deliciously fruity flavour.

Well-known Stracchino-style cheeses include Crescenza, Quartirolo, Taleggio and Robiola.

Taleggio (DOC)

Region: *Lombardy*
Type: *Traditional, farmhouse and creamery, semi-soft cheese*
Source: *Cow's milk*
Description: *2kg/4½lb square with distinctive markings. The rough, rosy crust is imprinted with the official stamp of the consortium*
Culinary uses: *Table cheese, grilling, melting (popular over polenta)*

Taleggio was originally only one of several cheeses referred to as "Stracchino", a term still used to describe the soft, square cheeses of Lombardy. Today, DOC regulations govern both how and where Taleggio is made, and the quality is maintained (as are the basic shape and method of production) despite the fact that the majority of the cheese is now produced in factories from pasteurized milk.

Traditionally, the cheeses were matured in natural caves, which had deep crevices that provided natural air-conditioning and encouraged the spread of the moulds and ferments essential to create Taleggio's unique aroma and taste. Over 30 per cent of the cheeses sold today continue to be matured in these caves, which undoubtedly makes a difference to their flavour.

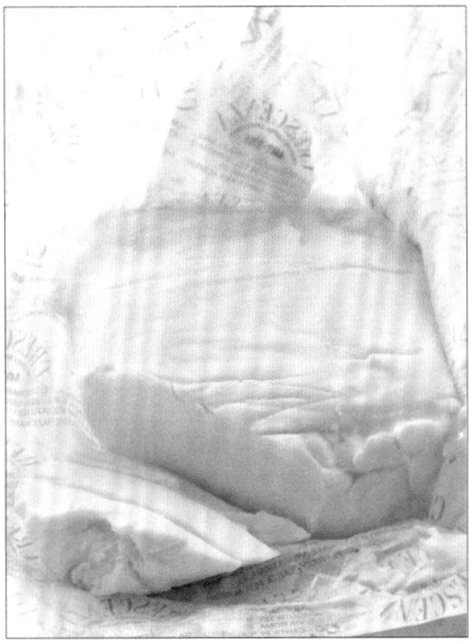

Above: Stracchino

By the time Taleggio reaches your favourite cheese shop it will have developed its rosy crust. The curd will be very nearly at melting point, while the centre will be elastic, with some eyes. The aroma will be gentle, but insistent, redolent of almonds and sweet hay.

In the hands of a talented affineur, the rind will harden and the ivory interior will reveal its magic – to experience it is like smelling and then eating a rich cream of asparagus soup.

Taleggio ripens in 25–50 days and has a fat content of 48 per cent.

Above: Taleggio, which is still matured in caves

Toma (DOC)

Region: *Piedmont*
Type: *Traditional, farmhouse, semi-hard cheese*
Source: *Cow's milk (or mixed milk)*
Description: *Made in various shapes and sizes. The natural rind ranges from thin and pale yellow to thick, grey and crusty*
Culinary uses: *Table cheese, cooking*

Toma has been made in the mountains of Piedmont in various shapes and sizes for generations. Although it now comes under the DOC umbrella, there are as many variations as there are small dairy farms in the Valle d'Aosta, where the finest Toma is said to be made. The young cheese is sweet and milky, but if it is allowed to mature for up to 12 months, the flavour becomes more tangy, often sharp. The Toma Piedmontese available in Britain has a soft, leathery rind and supple texture. It tastes fresh and creamy, with a hint of meadow flavours.

Ubriaco

Region: *Vicenza and Trento*
Type: *Traditional, farmhouse, unpasteurized, hard cheese*
Source: *Cow's milk*
Description: *8–12kg/18–26lb wheel. The deep burgundy, natural rind is rough and hard*
Culinary uses: *Table cheese, grating*

Ubriaco means "drunken" in Italian, and it isn't difficult to see how the cheese got its name. Following local custom, the young cheese is soaked in wine, covered with the crushed grape skins left after pressing and allowed to mature for six to 10 months. The result is a cheese with the heady aroma of fermenting fruit. Ubriaco has a firm, crumbly but open texture that is fairly wet (the moisture tastes distinctly alcoholic and salty) and has a mouth-puckering bite that is reminiscent of ripe pineapple.

English Cheeses

Simple cheesemaking implements dating back to the Iron Age have been found in England, but it was the arrival of the Romans in the first century AD – and the sweeping agricultural changes that ensued – that resulted in the introduction of harder, longer-lasting cheeses.

It is possible that Celtic monks from Wales and Ireland introduced the Trappist cheeses, but no records exist until the arrival of William the Conqueror in 1066. William brought with him Cistercian monks from Cîteaux in Burgundy, who taught the shepherds of the Yorkshire Dales how to make sheep's milk cheeses.

The dissolution of the monasteries during the reign of Henry VIII meant that the monks were forced to find shelter and employment on local farms. Their cheesemaking skills spread further afield. Gradually sheep were replaced by cattle, which yielded far more milk and had longer lactation periods.

England is well suited to dairy farming, and by the sixteenth century nearly every county had its own cheese. Sadly, few of these cheeses exist today. Those that do are known as "territorials", with the best-known example being Cheddar.

The unique texture is obtained by using the traditional "cheddaring" process, whereby the curds are drained, cut into bricks, then pressed numerous times until the texture satisfies the cheesemaker. It is this laborious task that makes farmhouse Cheddar unique.

Left: Today, Cheddar accounts for about 70 per cent of all cheese consumed in Britain

Unlike the other great cheeses of Europe, neither the name of Cheddar nor its method of production is protected, and the cheese has been copied the world over. The "cheddaring" performed in giant factories means that a generation of Cheddar eaters have grown up without the slightest clue as to what this great cheese should really taste like.

Although the origin of its name is still hotly disputed, it was unquestionably the landlord of the Bell Inn in the village of Stilton who put Stilton on the world map in the 1800s by serving the cheese to travellers journeying on the Great North Road from London to Scotland.

Cheshire, mentioned in the Domesday Book, is one of Britain's oldest cheeses. It derives its distinct character from the salt marshes on which the cattle graze. Port records from 1770 show that over 5,000 tons of Cheshire were shipped to London that year. It was considered to be one of Britain's finest cheeses, and by the 1930s there were more than 400 farms producing Cheshire.

Both Double and Single Gloucester have been made in Gloucestershire since the sixteenth century, originally from the milk of the native Old Gloucester cows.

Although still popular in the north of England, Lancashire has all but lost its way since the last century, when it was considered to be one of England's finest cheeses. Leicester – or Red Leicester as it is now known – was, until the late 1700s, produced in volume. However, the production of farmhouse versions of this russet cheese all but ceased before the Second World War. The same can be said of most of England's farmhouse cheeses, which are made only in limited volume and farmhouse varieties rarely exist.

Above: Stilton is one of England's best-loved cheeses

Several factors led to the decline and almost fall of these great cheeses. First was the cattle epidemic of 1860, when thousands of cows were slaughtered and tons of mass-produced American Cheddar was imported, paving the way for the industrialization of the cheese industry.

With the increasing demand for milk, many farmers found it easier to sell their milk rather than make cheese, and the number of cheesemakers declined further.

The ravages of the Second World War devastated the industry. With few men to run the farms and severe food shortages, the Ministry of Food ruled that any excess milk be used to make fast-ripening "National Cheese". When rationing ended in 1954 many farming families were without their menfolk and cheesemaking skills had been lost. Before the war there had been 15,000 cheesemakers; by the time it ended, only 126 remained.

In the past 20 years there has been a revolution. Farmhouse cheesemakers are on the increase, old recipes are being revived and cheeses made with milk from traditional rare breeds of cow are on the increase while sheep and goat's milk cheeses are firmly established in supermarkets.

England can now boast over 400 artisan cheeses. At the 2008 British Cheese Awards, 908 cheeses were entered. Of these, 45 were sheep's milk, 109 were goat's milk and 7 were made from buffalo's milk – as diverse and distinctive as those found in Europe.

ABOVE: Bath Cheese – one of the many recently created British cheeses that is based on an old recipe

ALLERDALE

REGION: *Cumbria*
TYPE: *Modern, farmhouse, unpasteurized, vegetarian, hard cheese*
SOURCE: *Goat's milk*
DESCRIPTION: *2.5kg/6lb small clothbound cylinder. Smooth, dry, grey-brown leathery crust*
CULINARY USES: *Table, grating, grilling*

Carolyn Fairbairn started making cheese at Thornby Moor Dairy in 1979 by adapting a traditional English hard cheese recipe to suit her small herd of goats and the climate. Allerdale, named after one of the dales in the Lake District, was her first cheese. It is matured in cloth for between two to five months when the tightly packed, finely cut curd becomes dense and creamy and the aromatic milk is transformed into flavours reminiscent of fresh walnuts and pear drops with a fruity acidity on the finish.

Carolyn, now helped by daughter Leonie, has since sold the herd to concentrate on cheesemaking and now also makes Smoked Allerdale, Cumberland Farmhouse, from shorthorn cows, Crofton made with cow and goat's milk and a semi-soft sheep's milk cheese Croglin.

BATH CHEESE

REGION: *Somerset*
TYPE: *Modern, farmhouse, unpasteurized, soft-white cheese*
SOURCE: *Cow's milk (Friesian and Ayrshire)*
DESCRIPTION: *225g/8oz square with smooth, white penicillium rind*
CULINARY USE: *Table cheese*

When young, Bath Cheese is mild and slightly tart, with a salty finish. When aged, the soft, furry, white rind yields to a soft interior, which oozes on to the plate as it reaches perfection. The flavour has hints of mushroom and warm milk balanced with a peppery, dandelion bite.

The producers, G. and P. Padfield, who also make Kelston Park, Bath Blue and Wyfe of Bath, developed the cheese after reading Patrick Rance's description of a similar cheese made in Bath a century ago.

Bath Cheese ripens in three to four weeks and has been a consistent medal winner at the British Cheese Awards.

BEENLEIGH BLUE

REGION: *Devon*
TYPE: *Modern, farmhouse, pasteurized, organic, vegetarian, blue cheese*
SOURCE: *Sheep's milk*
DESCRIPTION: *3kg/6½lb cylinder. The rough, crusty, natural rind is slightly sticky and has some patches of blue, grey and white moulds*
CULINARY USE: *Table cheese*

Robin Congdon and Sari Cooper of Ticklemore Cheese are gifted cheesemakers. Their Beenleigh Blue is one of only a handful of blue sheep's milk cheeses made in Britain. A consistent gold medal winner at the British Cheese Awards, it is moist yet crumbly, with the blue appearing as bold blue-green streaks through the white interior. The flavour is steely blue, with the burnt-caramel sweetness characteristic of fine sheep's milk cheese. It melts on the palate, disclosing its strong, spicy character. Don't cook it – eat it. It is wonderful with mead or sweet cider. Beenleigh Blue ripens in six months and has a fat content of 30 per cent. It is available from August to January.

Robin and Sari also produce Harbourne – a blue, goat's milk cheese – and Devon Blue, made from cow's milk. Ticklemore, their hard, goat's milk cheese, has a smooth texture and herbaceous character. These cheeses – and others from all over the country – are available from their cheese shop in Totnes.

BELOW: Beenleigh Blue

Berkswell

Region: *West Midlands*
Type: *Modern, farmhouse, unpasteurized, vegetarian, hard cheese*
Source: *Sheep's milk (Friesland)*
Description: *3.25kg/7lb flattened round. The deep russet-red, natural rind bears the intricate marks of the basket mould in which it is made*
Culinary uses: *Table cheese, grating, in soups*

Stephen Fletcher and his mother make their splendid cheese at Ram Hall, near the Forest of Arden. The milk comes from their flock of East Friesland sheep.

Berkswell is sold at around four months, when the hard, crusty, ridged rind has an aroma of lanolin and damp wool. The cheese is hard and chewy, almost granular, with a fat content of 32 per cent. Each bite reveals more of its complex flavours – roasted nuts, caramelized onions and meadow flowers with a prickly tang.

Winner of numerous accolades it is truly one of the greatest of the modern English cheeses.

Above: Berkswell

Blue Cheshire

Region: *Cheshire*
Type: *Traditional, farmhouse and creamery, vegetarian, blue cheese*
Source: *Cow's milk*
Description: *9kg/20lb truckle cheese. The natural rind is rough and crusty*
Culinary use: *Table cheese*

Traditionally, because of its open, crumbly texture, some Cheshire cheese would develop fine threads of blue during the months spent maturing in cellars. As this occurred naturally it was referred to as "blue fade" and came to be highly prized.

In recent years, the old idea has been revived, particularly by some of the Stilton makers. To guarantee that the blueing occurs, however, the mould is added to the milk before curdling. The young cheese is pierced, which allows in air and encourages the blueing to spread so that it provides an attractive contrast to the orange interior. A dry, dense and crumbly cheese, Blue Cheshire tends to be quite sharp, with a hint of green grass and salt balanced by the creaminess of the milk. The colour, which was originally obtained from carrots or marigolds, is now provided by annatto, a natural dye. Blue Cheshire ripens in two to three months.

Left: Blue Wensleydale (front) and Blue Vinny (back)

Blue Vinny

Region: *Dorset*
Type: *Traditional, farmhouse, unpasteurized, vegetarian, blue cheese*
Source: *Cow's milk*
Description: *2–7kg/4½–15¼lb cylinder. The natural, hard and crusty rind is reddish, with a dusting of white mould*
Culinary use: *Table cheese*

In 1982 Mike Davies set out to revive the old Dorset blue cheese, Blue Vinny, which had all but disappeared, yet about which there were a host of rumours. One claimed the cheese acquired its spidery, blue veining from having had old leather boots placed beside the vats.

Like most rumours, this had little foundation. "Vinny" is the old English word for "veining", and the blue comes from the family of penicillium moulds that occur naturally in the air. These invade the young, moist, open-textured, skimmed milk curd to create what is known as "blue fade". The same mould is attracted to old leather, hence the tall tale.

Today the blueing is not left to chance, and the penicillium mould is added directly to the milk.

Blue Vinny ripens in three to five months. The fat content is 22 per cent.

Blue Wensleydale

Region: *North Yorkshire*
Type: *Traditional, creamery, vegetarian, blue cheese*
Source: *Cow's milk*
Description: *4kg/9lb clothbound cylinder with hard, dry, brown-orange, rough rind*
Culinary use: *Table cheese*

Based on an original recipe that dates back to the eleventh century, this cheese has recently been revived by several creameries in the Yorkshire Dales. Firmer than most blues and slightly crumbly, Blue Wensleydale has a spicy, blue tang with a slightly bitter, dark chocolate and chicory finish.It takes nine to 12 weeks to mature and has a fat content of 34 per cent.

Bosworth

Region: *Staffordshire*
Type: *Modern, farmhouse, unpasteurized, vegetarian, soft-white cheese*
Source: *Goat's milk*
Description: *150g/5oz round cheese with very thin, velvety, penicillium rind dusted with a fine layer of ash*
Culinary use: *Table cheese*

Made by Joe and Stella Bennett of Highfields Farm Dairy, this elegant, soft-white cheese has a firm, breakable texture rather than the usual Brie-like softness. It melts in the mouth, yielding up its sweet, nutty flavours with just a suggestion of goat's milk. It matures in three to four weeks and has a fat content of 21 per cent.

Highfields Dairy also make other unpasteurized goat's milk cheeses, including Bosworth Leaf, which has a fine, grained texture that softens to a velvety smoothness. The taste is reminiscent of vanilla and butterscotch, with a subtle but distinct, almost almondy finish.

Buffalo Blue

Region: *Yorkshire*
Type: *Modern, farmhouse, vegetarian, blue cheese*
Source: *Buffalo milk*
Description: *3.5kg/8lb flat drum with sticky rind covered in grey and blue moulds*
Culinary uses: *Table cheese, salads*

Buffalo Blue, the latest from Shepherds Purse, was created in 2001 by Judy Bell when she was offered some buffalo milk by a local farmer who had discovered it has a high nutritional content and would benefit his son who suffers from cystic fibrosis.

Aged for eight to 10 weeks, it is whiter than cow's milk blues with fine, slightly gritty streaks of blue and a smooth moist texture that is soft enough to spread. The buffalo milk gives it an earthy or mossy character, rather than a sweet or nutty taste like cow's milk, and the flavour is spicy and pleasantly sharp or acidic, leaving the palate feeling fresh.

Button/Innes

Region: *Staffordshire*
Type: *Modern, farmhouse, unpasteurized, vegetarian, fresh cheese*
Source: *Goat's milk*
Description: *50g/2oz round*
Culinary use: *Table cheese*

Twice voted Supreme Champion at the British Cheese Awards, firstly in 1994 and then once again in 2002, Button, or Innes Button, is soft, mousse-like and fragile. It simply dissolves on the palate, trailing a subtle hint of almonds, honey, lemon, white wine and tangerine. One of Britain's finest goat's milk cheeses, it is also available dusted with French salted ash, dusky pink peppercorns, chopped nuts or herbs. Button ripens in five to 10 days and has a fat content of 21 per cent. Innes Button is also available in a larger size, under the name Innes Clifton. Like Bosworth it is made by Joe and Stella Bennett of Highfields Dairy at Tamworth in Staffordshire.

Below: Capricorn Goat

Capricorn Goat

Region: *Somerset*
Type: *Modern, creamery, vegetarian, soft-white cheese*
Source: *Goat's milk*
Description: *125g/4½oz cylinder or 1.2kg/2½lb square cutting cheese with pure white, soft rind*
Culinary use: *Table cheese*

Lubborn Cheese is best known for its Somerset Camembert and Brie cheeses, but Capricorn Goat has made giant strides in convincing the British public that goat's milk cheese can be mild, not vicious, and can have a distinct character without being overwhelming.

The smaller version of this cheese is an attractive cylinder with a delicate, soft-white rind. Slightly chalky, like unripe Camembert when young, it becomes softer around the edges and is sometimes almost runny. The fresh, creamy feel with a background of chicory and nuts is very appealing. The cheese ripens in four to six weeks and has a fat content of 26 per cent. It has won many medals at the British Cheese Awards, most notably winning a gold medal in 2004.

Cerney

Region: *Gloucestershire*
Type: *Modern, farmhouse, unpasteurized, vegetarian, fresh cheese*
Source: *Goat's milk*
Description: *240g/8½oz pyramid dusted with oak ash and salt*
Culinary use: *Table cheese*

Like many of Britain's dedicated artisan cheesemakers, Lady Angus, creator of this distinctive cheese, maximizes the flavour by using unpasteurized milk. Her cheeses are named after the pretty village of Cerney where they are made. Each has a mild, zingy, citrus taste, with a delicate, goaty finish. The light, moist texture resembles that of fromage frais. Each of the small, truncated pyramids is hand-made, and coated with a fine dusting of oak ash and sea salt. Cerney has won many accolades over the years, including the much coveted title of "supreme champion" at the British Cheese Awards in 2001, making it a true superstar of English goat's cheeses.

Cerney ripens in seven to 10 days and has a fat content of 23 per cent.

Below: Cerney's distinctive pyramid shape and dark ash-dusted exterior make it an attractive and delicious addition to any cheese board

Above: Traditional clothbound Cheddars from top right, Green's, Keen's, Quicke's and Montgomery's

Cheddar

Region: *Somerset*
Type: *Traditional, farmhouse, unpasteurized, hard cheese*
Source: *Cow's milk*
Description: *26kg/57lb cylinder with natural rind, bound in cloth*
Culinary uses: *Table cheese; also widely used for cooking in a host of traditional dishes*

Since the sixteenth century, the hard cow's milk cheese made in the Mendip Hills near the Cheddar Gorge has been known as Cheddar. This famous cheese undoubtedly goes back to earlier centuries, perhaps even to the Romans, who first introduced the people of England to hard cheeses.

Over the centuries, the recipe for this West Country cheese has been taken by emigrants to Canada, the USA, Australia,

South Africa and New Zealand. More than any other British cheese, it has been copied and emulated, but it is not really Cheddar unless it comes from the verdant hills that populate Somerset, Devon and Dorset.

To taste a hand-made, unpasteurized, clothbound Cheddar, made from the milk of cows whose daily diet of fresh green grass is diluted only with the occasional buttercup or daisy, is to truly taste a piece of magic. The bite is like chocolate, firm and yielding; the aroma is fresh, nutty and slightly savoury. The flavour differs from farm to farm, but there is always the rich sweetness of the milk, a classic acid tang and a long-lingering kaleidoscope of flavours. Cheddar is generally matured for between nine and 24 months, and has a fat content of 34.4 per cent (50 per cent in the dry matter).

Unlike the great cheeses of Europe, Cheddar's name is not protected, so it has been continuously used and abused. Hundreds of tasteless tonnes of cheese masquerading as Cheddar are churned out in giant factories around the world. Even in Britain, home to this wonderful cheese, both the consumers and the market have conspired against the farmhouse Cheddar makers. Today there are only six cheesemakers left who are still making truly traditional, clothbound English Cheddar:

Denhay (Bridport, Dorset): Hand-made and matured on the farm, Denhay is nutty, and rich with a strong, savoury tang. All the milk comes from the farm's own herd of cows.

Green's (Glastonbury, Somerset): Made by three generations of the Green family on the same Somerset farm, Green's is matured for 12 months or more. Each cheese is hand turned until all reach their peak. Twice winner of a gold medal at the British Cheese Awards, the cheese is savoury (redolent of cheese and onion) and tangy.

Keen's (Wincanton, Somerset): Made on the farm since the turn of the twentieth century, using only milk from its own herd, Keen's has a full-bodied flavour. It is complex, with hints of liquorice and a fresh, green tang. Nutty, smooth and creamy, it melts in the mouth. A past winner of a silver medal in the British Cheese Awards, it is both clothbound and larded.

Montgomery's (Yeovil, Somerset): Twice voted Best Cheddar at the British Cheese Awards, this cheese has a superb richness, a spicy acidity and real depth of flavour to the fruity finish. Montgomery's is the epitome of an artisan cheesemaker and produces only 10–12 cheeses a day.

Quicke's (Exeter, Devon): The only traditional Cheddar makers in Devon, the Quicke family have been farming at Newton St Cyres for over 450 years. Their Cheddar is a regular medal winner at the British Cheese Awards. Firm and chewy, with a buttery texture and tangy, nutty, complex aroma, the cheese, when tasted, suggests green grass and fresh hay. Pasteurized and unpasteurized versions are available.

Westcombe Dairy (Evercreech, Somerset): Firm and biteable, the cheese has a flavour that explodes on the palate. The rind is nutty, the interior is suggestive of cheese and onion with a hint of butter.

Together with Montgomery's and Keen's, Westcombe Dairy has formed the Artisan Somerset Cheddar Presidium, under the auspices of Slow Food, to protect and uphold Cheddar making traditions, and produce cheeses made with animal rennet using only raw milk from their own herds.

CHESHIRE

REGION: *Cheshire*
TYPE: *Traditional, farmhouse, unpasteurized, hard cheese*
SOURCE: *Cow's milk*
DESCRIPTION: *900g/2lb, 8kg/18lb or 20kg/44lb tall cylinders with natural rind with grey moulding, tightly wrapped in cloth*
CULINARY USES: *Table cheese, grilling, snacks, grating*

Fewer than a handful of cheesemakers still make the traditional clothbound Cheshire, using raw milk. Most of the cheeses are factory-made today and lack any real depth of character. The fine, moist texture that is the hallmark of a good Cheshire (but which also renders the cheese susceptible to cracking, crumbling or blueing) is rejected by many supermarkets in favour of cheeses that are creamier and more solid. Changes are afoot, however, and smaller producers are now being encouraged to return to a more traditional style.

Clothbound Cheshire is produced by several traditional cheesemakers, including Applebys, H. S. Bourne, Carron Lodge and Joseph Heler. The classic Cheshire has a crumbly, flaky texture and a sea-breeze freshness with the tang of orange zest and can be white or "red" when it is coloured with annatto.

Cheshire requires up to four months to mature and has a fat content of 33 per cent.

ABOVE: Cheshire

Coquetdale

Region: *Northumberland*
Type: *Traditional, farmhouse, vegetarian, hard cheese*
Source: *Cow's milk*
Description: *650g/1½lb or 2.2kg/5lb round cheese. The fine, leathery, natural rind has yellowish-grey mould*
Culinary use: *Table cheese*

Mark Robinson's cheesemaking urge came in 1985 after he read a book about sheep and their cheeses. At the time he had over 600 ewes on his farm in Northumberland. Over the following five years he built up the herd, changing over to Friesland sheep, then diversifying into cow's milk as well.

On a trip to France, he visited the makers of Saint-Nectaire and decided to develop a similar cheese at home. Once the cheese was placed in the ripening room, however, and came into contact with the natural flora and moulds that live on the walls and roofs, the original recipe began to change. The result is a soft, supple cheese with a wonderful balance of sweet-savoury flavours and a nutty, slightly salty finish.

Coquetdale ripens in 10–12 weeks and has a fat content of 36 per cent. Mark Robinson's Northumberland Cheese Company also produces Northumberland, Redesdale and Brinkburn, a hard goat's milk cheese. These and many other local cheeses are available at their farm shop.

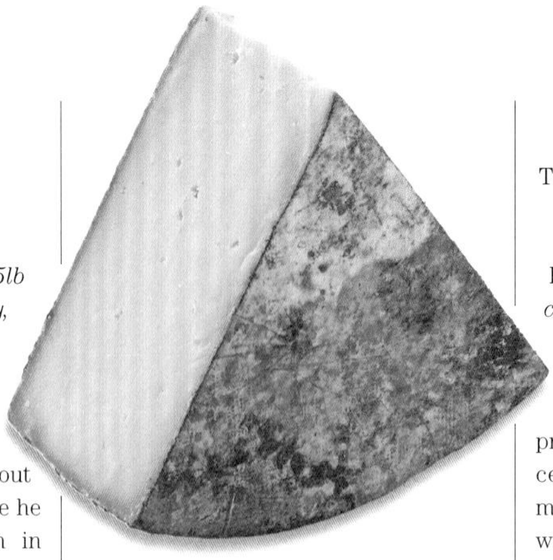

Above: Cornish Yarg

Cornish Blue

Region: *Cornwall*
Type: *Modern, farmhouse, vegetarian, blue cheese*
Source: *Cow's milk*
Description: *6kg/13lb drum with blue-grey slightly sticky rind*
Culinary use: *Table cheese*

Looking for a way to add value to their milk, Philip and Carol Stansfield started making Cornish Blue in 2001. Based on the edge of Bodmin Moor where the warm summers, high rainfall and year-round grazing give their cheese a unique character.

Cornish Blue is softer and higher in moisture than most English blues and almost buttery with streaks of blue. The flavour is mellow with a hint of dark chocolate and melted butter on the finish. Voted Best Blue Cheese and Best English Cheese in 2006 it is one of Britain's best modern blues.

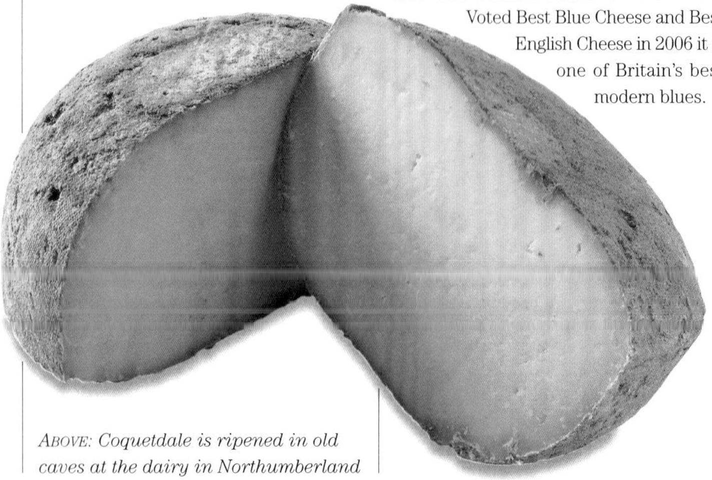

Above: Coquetdale is ripened in old caves at the dairy in Northumberland

Cornish Yarg

Region: *Cornwall*
Type: *Modern, farmhouse, vegetarian, hard cheese*
Source: *Cow's milk (Friesian)*
Description: *900g/2lb and 2.75kg/6lb circular cheeses. The natural rind is covered in fresh nettles*
Culinary use: *Table cheese*

Cornish Yarg is a hand-made cheese produced from a traditional seventeenth-century recipe discovered and initially made by a couple called Gray. When they were trying to find an authentic Cornish name for it, someone pointed out that Gray spelt backwards had a very Cornish ring to it and so Yarg it became.

Catherine Mead of Lynher Dairies now produces this delicious cheese. The nettle wrapping provides an unusual and attractive contrast to the white interior, and gives a unique vegetal flavour to the cheese. Moist but crumbly, Cornish Yarg is not unlike Caerphilly, and has a lovely freshness. As it matures, a greyish hue covers the nettles, the interior softens and the taste is reminiscent of meadow flowers and creamed spinach. Other cheeses made by Lynher Dairies include Cornish Garland and Wild Garlic Yarg wrapped in strips of wild garlic. Cornish Yarg won Best Flavour Added Cheese in 2001. It matures in 10–15 weeks and has a fat content of 31 per cent.

Cotherstone

Region: *Durham*
Type: *Traditional, farmhouse, pasteurized, hard cheese*
Source: *Cow's milk*
Description: *900g/2lb or 3.5kg/8lb round. The cream-coloured, natural rind has some white or grey moulds*
Culinary uses: *Table cheese, grilling*

Made by Joan Cross in Teesdale from an old Dales recipe, Cotherstone is a hard, crumbly, open-textured cheese. Yeasty, with a crisp, white wine acidity and a fresh, citrus tang, it is one of the few traditional Dale cheeses still being made in the wild and beautiful Pennines.

Cotherstone is matured for between two and 10 weeks and has a fat content of 32 per cent.

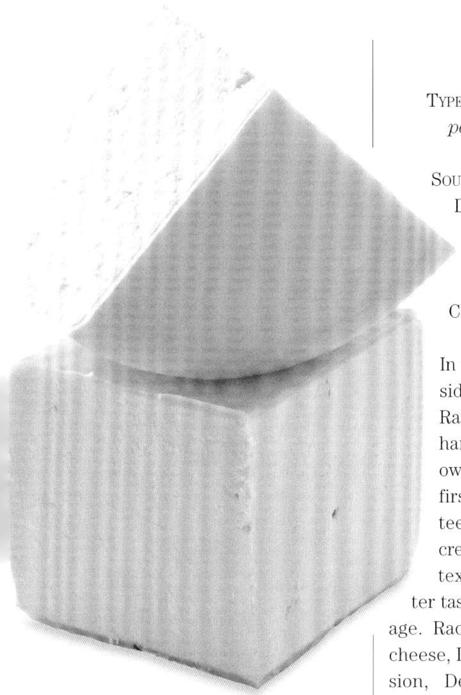

ABOVE: *Coverdale – one of the newly revived old cheeses*

COVERDALE

REGION: *North Yorkshire*
TYPE: *Traditional, creamery, vegetarian, hard cheese*
SOURCE: *Cow's milk*
DESCRIPTION: *1.5kg/3¼lb clothbound truckle cheese with pale yellow rind*
CULINARY USE: *Table cheese*

A mild and buttery cheese, Coverdale has a sharp, clean taste. The texture is firm and open. In recent years many of the old cheese recipes have been revived and new cheeses created in the same style. Coverdale is one such. It reappeared in 1987 after an absence of 50 years. Originally made in Coverdale, it is now produced by Wensleydale Dairy Products. Coverdale matures in four to five weeks.

CURWORTHY

REGION: *Devon*
TYPE: *Traditional, farmhouse, pasteurized, vegetarian, hard cheese*
SOURCE: *Cow's milk (Friesian)*
DESCRIPTION: *450g/1lb and 1.4kg/3lb truckle cheese with natural, firm, grey rind*
CULINARY USES: *Table cheese, grilling, grating*

In the heart of the Devon countryside is Stockbearne Farm. Here Rachel Stevens makes cheeses by hand, using milk from the farm's own Friesian cows. Curworthy, her first cheese, is based on a seventeenth-century recipe. It has a creamy interior with a supple, open texture. The delicate, melted butter taste becomes more rounded with age. Rachel also makes another hard cheese, Devon Oake, and a smoked version, Devon Smoake. Curworthy is matured for three to four months and has a fat content of 32 per cent. Devon Oke is larger than the Curworthy. Aged for up to six months, it has a richer, more full-bodied flavour.

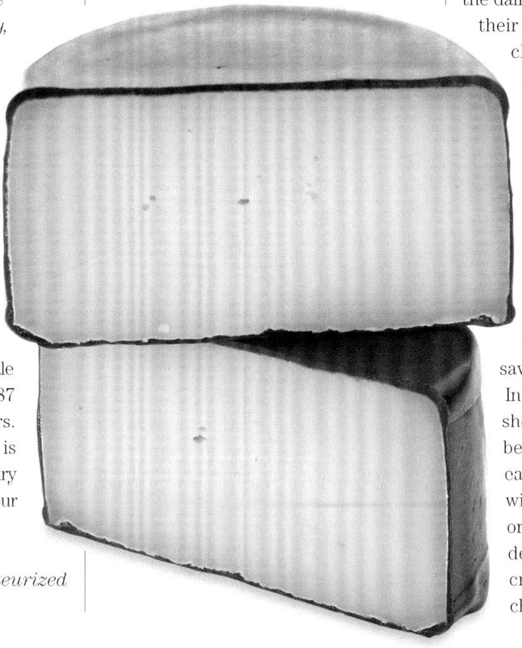

RIGHT: *Curworthy is an unpasteurized vegetarian cheese*

ABOVE: *Daylesford Organic*

DAYLESFORD ORGANIC

REGION: *Gloucestershire*
TYPE: *Modern, farmhouse, animal rennet, organic, unpasteurized, hard cheese*
SOURCE: *Cow's milk*
DESCRIPTION: *2.6kg–10kg/6lb–23lb clothbound truckle*
CULINARY USES: *Table cheese, grating, grilling, sauces*

Made on the Bamford's beautiful estate in the Cotswolds from their organically reared herd of Friesian cows, where the milking parlour sits beside the creamery and the milk can be channelled fresh to the dairy. A Cheddar-style cheese, it was their first cheese created by talented cheesemaker Joe Schneider in 2001 and now made by Clive Curtis, which won Best English cheese at the British Cheese Awards in 2002 and later Best Organic and Best Modern British Cheese. Aged for a minimum of nine months, it is a deep buttercup yellow, with a hard yet chewy texture and a rich cheese and onion tang that mellows out to a delicious, savoury lingering finish.

In 2003 Daylesford opened their first shop in a beautiful converted barn beside the creamery which rapidly earned the respect of food lovers with their own farm produced organic vegetables, as well as wonderful breads and cakes, yogurt, cream, milk and a washed rind cheese called Penyston.

Denhay Dorset Drum

REGION: *Dorset*
TYPE: *Traditional, farmhouse, vegetarian, hard cheese*
SOURCE: *Cow's milk*
DESCRIPTION: *2kg/4½lb clothbound truckle cheese with natural rind*
CULINARY USES: *Table cheese, grilling, grating*

A more diminutive version of the traditional clothbound Denhay Cheddar, Denhay Dorset Drum matures more quickly and has a dense, chewy texture and a delicious, mellow nuttiness. The small size of cylinder, known as a truckle, makes this cheese an excellent gift. It matures in between six and nine months and has a fat content of 34.5 per cent. Denhay traditional Cheddar won Best Traditional Cheese at the British Cheese Awards in 2007.

ABOVE: Denhay Dorset Drum

Derby

REGION: *Derbyshire*
TYPE: *Traditional, creamery, hard cheese*
SOURCE: *Cow's milk*
DESCRIPTION: *4–13.5kg/9lb–30lb cylinder with natural, pale primrose yellow rind*
CULINARY USES: *Table cheese, grilling*

Originally made by small independent cheesemakers on rural farms, in 1870 Derby became the first cheese in Britain to be mass-produced in a factory, which was tantamount to signing its death warrant. However, with the current growing interest in Britain's old cheeses there may well be a resurgence in this once great cheese's popularity.

Similar in texture to Cheddar, but more open, Derby has a softer and flakier curd and a nutty melted-butter taste. Currently very few, if any, farmhouse examples still exist, and those that are sold tend to be too young and lacking in any real flavour.

Derby ripens in between one to six months and has a fat content of 34 per cent. More commonly available is Sage Derby, a green-veined version that is subtly flavoured with herbs.

Devon Blue

REGION: *Devon*
TYPE: *Modern, farmhouse, unpasteurized, vegetarian, blue cheese*
SOURCE: *Cow's milk (Ayrshire)*
DESCRIPTION: *3kg/6½lb cylinder with rough, crusty, natural rind mottled with grey, white and brown moulds*
CULINARY USE: *Table cheese*

Ticklemore Cheeses make three excellent blues, one each from cow's milk, goat's milk and sheep's milk. Available all year round, Devon Blue is milder than the others and has a subtle flavour of new leather overlaid by the spicy blue tang. Smooth, creamy and deliciously herbaceous, it is aged for four to five months, then wrapped in foil to prevent it from drying out.

Other Ticklemore cheeses, made by Robin Congdon, are Beenleigh and Harbourne Blue. They also own and run a superb cheese shop, based in Totnes, selling a wide variety of delicious artisan cheeses.

Double Gloucester

REGION: *Gloucestershire*
TYPE: *Traditional, farmhouse and creamery, unpasteurized, hard cheese*
SOURCE: *Cow's milk*
DESCRIPTION: *3.5–8kg/8–18lb deep round. The hard, natural rind has some grey-blue moulds and bears the marks of the cloth in which it is matured*
CULINARY USES: *Table cheese, grating, grilling, sauces*

Gloucestershire has been home to Double and Single Gloucester cheese since the sixteenth century when they were originally clothbound cheeses made from the milk of the native Gloucester cows. Single Gloucester is smaller, made from skimmed milk and meant to be eaten young. The full-cream milk in Double Gloucester gives it its characteristic, rich, buttery taste and flaky texture. It is firm and biteable, like hard chocolate. The colour is a pale tangerine. It has a wonderful, savoury flavour of cheese and onions. Not as firm as Cheddar, it has a mellow, nutty character with a delicious, orange-zest tang.

Most Gloucester is made in block form by large creameries but some traditional makers are prevailing – try Anstey's, Birdwood, Butlers, Charles Martell, Smart's and Wick Court.

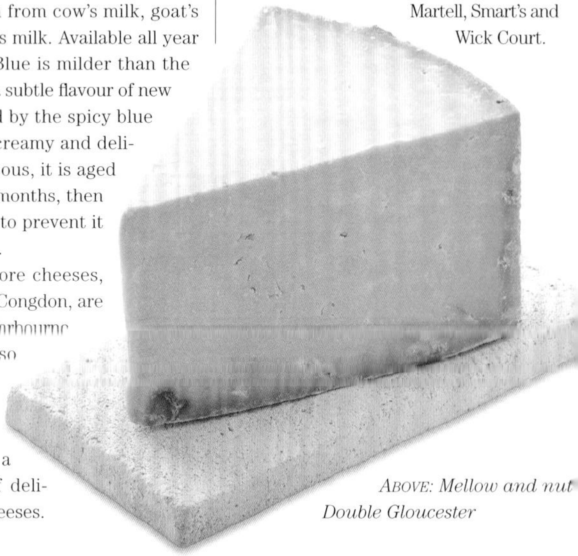

ABOVE: Mellow and nut Double Gloucester

ABOVE: Duddleswell

DOUBLE WORCESTER

REGION: *Worcester*
TYPE: *Modern, farmhouse, unpasteurized, hard cheese*
SOURCE: *Cow's milk (Holstein/Friesian)*
DESCRIPTION: *4kg/9lb cylinder. The hard, natural rind is yellow with some moulding*
CULINARY USES: *Table cheese, grilling, sauces*

A smaller version of Double Gloucester, this is made by Anstey's in the neighbouring county of Worcester. It develops a firm, breakable, flaky texture and deep tangerine-orange interior with a rounded, mellow character and a flavour that is reminiscent of citrus zest.

The Worcestershire farm on which the cheese is made has been in the Anstey family for four generations. Colin and Alyson Anstey decided to diversify into cheesemaking in 1995 and won a silver medal at the British Cheese Awards that same year. Their Double Worcester matures in five to seven months and has a fat content of 35 per cent.

Other cheeses created by the Anstey family include Old Worcester, flavoured with Worcestershire sauce, and a delightful hard goat's cheese called Snodsbury. They have a farm shop and mail order service.

DUDDLESWELL

REGION: *East Sussex*
TYPE: *Modern, farmhouse, unpasteurized, vegetarian, hard cheese*
SOURCE: *Sheep's milk*
DESCRIPTION: *2kg/4½lb truckle cheese with hard, finely ridged, polished, natural rind*
CULINARY USES: *Table cheese, grating (can be substituted for Pecorino)*

The producers of this cheese, High Weald Dairy, are based near Ashdown Forest, the hunting ground of the kings of England since 1372. Mark Hardy and his father Guy have been making a range of sheep's products for over 15 years, including two fresh cheeses called Cowslip and Slipcote that come in a variety of flavours.

Duddleswell is a cheerful-looking truckle whose firm, almost flaky texture seems to melt in the mouth, releasing a sweet, caramel flavour with a hint of Brazil nuts and fresh hay. It is a past winner of various medals at the British Cheese Awards. The cheese ripens in 10–12 weeks and has a fat content of 45 per cent. Sussex High Weald Dairy also produce other sheep's milk cheese, including halloumi and feta.

EXMOOR BLUE

REGION: *Somerset*
TYPE: *Modern, farmhouse, unpasteurized, vegetarian, blue cheese*
SOURCE: *Cow's, goat's or sheep's milk*
DESCRIPTION: *Various sizes and shapes, all with natural rind*
CULINARY USE: *Table cheese*

Ian Arnett makes blue cheeses from cow's, goat's, sheep's and buffalo's milk, each with its own unique character and style. Somerset Blue is made with Jersey cow's milk from two local herds, which gives the cheese a distinctive, Monet yellow colour. The goat's milk comes from the same area, but the sheep's milk is from the Quantocks and Blissful Buffalo from a herd in nearby Devon. Cheesemaking takes place in the original dairy at Willett Farm. All the cheeses are made with raw milk.

FINN

REGION: *Hereford*
TYPE: *Modern, farmhouse, unpasteurized, vegetarian, soft-white cheese*
SOURCE: *Cow's milk*
DESCRIPTION: *225g/8oz round with thick, white penicillium rind*
CULINARY USES: *Table cheese, baking*

This is produced by Charlie Westhead of Neal's Yard Creamery who adds 10 per cent additional cream to the milk just before the cheesemaking starts. It is firm and rich, with a mild, fresh, creamy acidity and just a hint of mushrooms. Finn ripens in two to four weeks and has a fat content of 50 per cent.

ABOVE: Exmoor Blue

Flower Marie

Region: *East Sussex*
Type: *Modern, farmhouse, unpasteurized, vegetarian, soft-white cheese*
Source: *Sheep's milk*
Description: *200g/7oz or 1.5kg/3¼lb square cheese. The thin, soft-white rind has a mushroomy-pink tint*
Culinary use: *Table cheese*

Produced by Kevin and Alison Blunt at Greenacres Farm, near Lewes in East Sussex, Flower Marie has a gentle fragrance like that of fresh mushrooms and a soft rind that envelops the firm yet moist interior. It melts like ice cream in the mouth to reveal a lemony freshness under the characteristic sweetness of the sheep's milk. It ripens in four to five weeks. In 1999 Flower Marie won the British Cheese Awards prize for Best Soft White Cheese.

Golden Cross

Region: *East Sussex*
Type: *Modern, farmhouse, unpasteurized, vegetarian, soft-white cheese*
Source: *Goat's milk*
Description: *225g/8oz log with mould-ripened rind dusted with salted ash*
Culinary use: *Table cheese*

Based on the traditional, French, artisan cheese Sainte-Maure, Golden Cross's exterior is lightly dusted with ash. At first firm and slightly grainy, the cheese softens with age to a velvety texture that is more like gently-melting ice cream. The flavour is a careful blend of sweetness and acidity: vanilla and tones of caramel combine with the bitterness of celery and green grass, and there is a barely detectable goaty finish.

Produced by Kevin and Alison Blunt, Golden Cross ripens in four to six weeks.

Harbourne Blue

Region: *Devon*
Type: *Modern, farmhouse, pasteurized, vegetarian, blue cheese*
Source: *Goat's milk*
Description: *5kg/11lb round. Crusty, natural rind with some moulding*
Culinary use: *Table cheese*

This smooth, yet crumbly blue is one of the great, modern, British cheeses. Like Beenleigh Blue, it is made by Robin Congdon and Sari Cooper of Ticklemore Cheeses and has won numerous medals at the British Cheese Awards.

Harbourne is one of only six English blue goat's cheeses. The aroma suggests tropical fruit, and it finishes with the hot, spicy tang associated with blues. Harbourne Blue needs three to four months to ripen and has a fat content of 33 per cent.

Hereford Hop

Region: *Gloucestershire*
Type: *Traditional, farmhouse, vegetarian, speciality cheese*
Source: *Cow's milk*
Description: *2.2kg/5lb round cheese. The flaky, natural rind of toasted hops is yellow to brown*
Culinary use: *Table cheese*

Charles Martell, a cheesemaker renowned for his love of local history and tradition, revived this old Hereford cheese in 1988.

Above: Hereford Hop

The recipe came from local archives and is made using Hereford hops and milk from his own herd. Supple and Caerphilly-like, with the unusual rind of lightly toasted hops, the cheese makes an attractive addition to any cheeseboard. The hops are crunchy, with the slightly yeasty taste associated with beer, while the cheese is mellow, sweet and buttery. It requires one to three months to mature and has a fat content of 36 per cent.

Hereford Hop is also produced by Malvern Cheesewrights, although each cheese has its own distinct style.

Keldthwaite Gold

Region: *Cumbria*
Type: *Modern, creamery, vegetarian, soft white cheese*
Source: *Cow's milk (Jersey)*
Description: *175gm/7oz round with thick white rind*
Culinary use: *Table cheese*

Winner of the Cheese Lover's Trophy in 2007, this is made with Jersey milk for Cumberland Dairy by Butlers of Lancashire. It is a small cheese that packs plenty of flavour and personality beneath its thick coat and has a delicious button (white) mushroom flavour. The Jersey milk gives it a

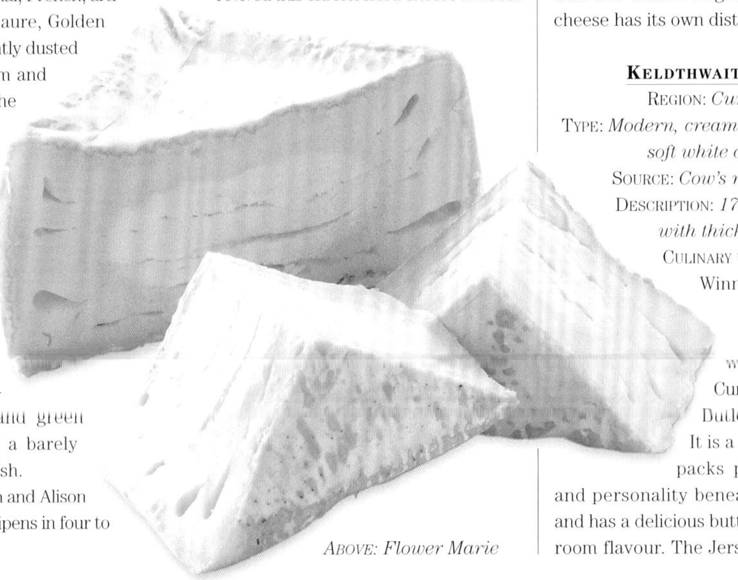

Above: Flower Marie

Above: Keltic Gold

rich, deep yellow colour and a creamier feel in the mouth than similar cow's milk cheeses. When ripe it is runny with a taste like mushrooms in cream, with a slightly meaty taste and a hint of lush green grass.

Keltic Gold

Region: *Cornwall*
Type: *Modern, farmhouse, vegetarian, pasteurized, semi-soft cheese*
Source: *Cow's milk*
Description: *1.4kg/3lb drum, sticky orange brine washed rind*
Culinary use: *Table cheese*

In 1999 Sue Proudfoot embarked on a new career making cheese in a converted corner of a grain store on the Whalesborough Estate. Set on a rugged stretch of the Northern Cornish coastline where the wild grazing contributes to the complexity of this washed curd cheese, winner of the Best Semi-soft Cheese in 2006.

It is curd washed and rind washed in local cider then drained on racks that leave crosshatch indentations in the sticky pink-terracotta rind. Supple and squidgy, every mouthful reveals another stratum of flavour, from hints of bacon and yeast to a more nutty, buttery character. Ripe at around six weeks, it is not as outspoken as other washed rind cheeses and is best eaten with the rind. Other cheeses include Trelawny and Miss Muffet.

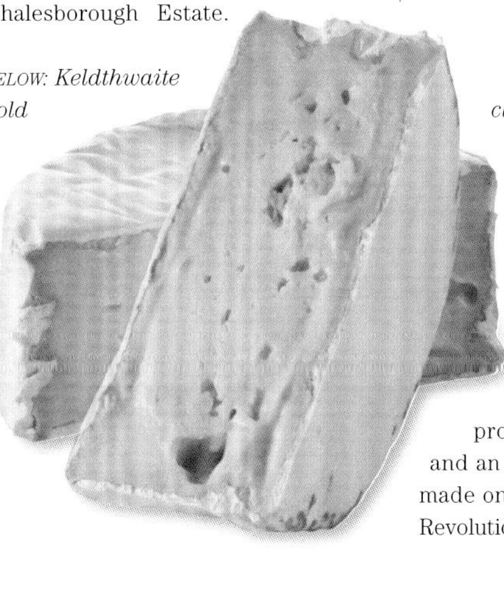

Below: Keldthwaite Gold

Lancashire

Region: *Lancashire*
Type: *Traditional, farmhouse and creamery, hard cheese*
Source: *Cow's milk*
Description: *4–18kg/9–40lb clothbound cylinder. The hard, thin, natural rind is pale gold. It bears the marks of the cloth and has some grey-blue mould*
Culinary uses: *Table cheese, snacks, grilling, grating (a superb melting cheese)*

Only very few of these historic English cheeses are produced in Lancashire today – and an even smaller number are still made on farms. During the Industrial Revolution, Lancashire cheese was the staple food of the mill workers. The first mass produced, factory-made Lancashire cheese appeared in 1913, and today most of this cheese comes from creameries that are scattered throughout the British Isles.

When it is young, this traditional cheese is described as "Creamy Lancashire". At this early stage the texture is moist and crumbly – rather like scrambled egg – with a cheese and chive finish and an excellent balance of fat and acidity. As the cheese starts to mature, the flavour intensifies and the resulting cheese is known as "Tasty Lancashire".

One of the finest of these is Kirkham's Tasty Lancashire, which is made on Beesley Farm near Preston, and was declared Supreme Champion at the British Cheese Awards in 1995. It is a superb example of a genuine farmhouse Lancashire, the award-winning cheese had been matured for nearly six months by Neal's Yard Dairy.

Mrs Kirkham's, Dew-Lay and Leagram Organic are the only three Lancashire makers who use a combination of three days' curd to give a unique, slightly mottled texture to the cheese. As the curds ripen at different times, it acquires a three-dimensional flavour that is both sharp and peppery, with delicious mouth-puckering finish.

Acid or "crumbly" Lancashire, which was introduced in the 1970s, is a faster-ripening cheese that has the bite of a Lancashire, but lacks the depth of flavour that distinguishes a true Lancashire cheese.

Below: Mrs Kirkham's Tasty Lancashire

LEFT: Little Rydings

LINCOLNSHIRE POACHER

REGION: *Lincolnshire*
TYPE: *Modern, farmhouse, unpasteurized, hard cheese*
SOURCE: *Cow's milk (Holstein)*
DESCRIPTION: *20kg/44lb cylinder. The brown rind resembles granite in appearance*
CULINARY USES: *Table cheese, grating, grilling*

Lincolnshire is not an area generally known for its dairy farming. This fact did not deter Simon and Tim Jones, however, when they decided to turn the abundant spring milk from their herd of Holsteins into cheese. One morning the cheese legend, Dougal Campbell, arrived at the farm with a bottle full of rennet. Together they made the first batch of Lincolnshire Poacher. On the following day, Simon found himself in charge of the cheesemaking. That was in 1992. A few years later, the cheese was declared Supreme Champion at the British Cheese Awards from a field of 480 entries. It is also available smoked.

LITTLE RYDINGS

REGION: *Somerset*
TYPE: *Modern, farmhouse, unpasteurized, soft-white cheese*
SOURCE: *Sheep's milk*
DESCRIPTION: *250g/9oz round with fine, uneven, whitish penicillium rind covered with red-brown pigmentation*
CULINARY USE: *Table cheese*

This irresistible cheese is made from March to November by James Bartlett at Wootton Organic Dairy in Somerset. The slightly uneven Camembert-like rind encloses an unpasteurized, soft sheep's cheese that is a deep creamy yellow around the edge. When it is young, the cheese may be slightly chalky and white in the centre.

Like good Camembert, Little Rydings simply melts in the mouth to reveal distinct yet subtle layers of flavour: the sweetness of caramel, a distinct hint of Brazil nut and a slightly "sheepy" taste that is reminiscent of soggy lambswool sweaters or lanolin. Little Rydings matures in three to five weeks and has a fat content of 30 per cent.

LITTLE WALLOP

REGION: *Somerset*
TYPE: *Modern, farmhouse, vegetarian, thermized, aged fresh*
SOURCE: *Goat's milk*
DESCRIPTION: *115g/5oz small round, wrapped in vine leaf with white and orange rind*
CULINARY USES: *Table cheese, grilling*

This is the first cheese created by the Evenlode Partnership, started in 2007 by the author Juliet Harbutt and Blur bass guitarist and now farmer Alex James, and made by White Lake Cheese in Somerset. Washed in Somerset Cider Brandy then wrapped in a vine leaf, it develops a medley of white, grey and orange moulds and a complexity of flavours. At two to three weeks as splodges of white mould start to bloom it is moist, nutty and lemony fresh. Gradually the rind softens, the texture becomes silky, the leaf dries out, the cider works its magic and the underlying character is revealed – yeasty, nutty, almondy with a whiff of brandy to finish and a subtle hint of goat's milk.

Some of the cheeses are tied up with raffia and submerged in olive oil where the cheese develops a firm, smooth, sleek texture and a sweet, marzipan taste with grassy notes from the oil and the vine leaf. These are called Under Wallop. Another in the range is Farleigh Wallop, a soft white goat's cheese with a sprig of thyme pressed into its rind that becomes runny with age and has subtle hints of almonds, hawthorns and thyme.

MALVERN

REGION: *Worcester*
TYPE: *Modern, farmhouse, pasteurized, vegetarian, hard cheese*
SOURCE: *Sheep's milk (Friesland)*
DESCRIPTION: *2.5kg/5½lb wheel with smooth, slightly greasy, yellow rind*
CULINARY USES: *Table cheese, grating, grilling*

Malvern Cheesewrights were the first of the new generation of English cheesemakers to make a sheep's milk cheese in sufficient volume to sell in the supermarket. Firm and dry, yet dense and creamy in the mouth, it has a definite, sweet, butterscotch taste infused with a hint of thyme. The finish is salty and the aroma is of wool or lanolin. Malvern matures in 16 weeks and has a fat content of 32 per cent.

RIGHT: Little Wallop

Mrs Bells Blue

Region: *North Yorkshire*
Type: *Modern, farmhouse, vegetarian, blue cheese*
Source: *Sheep's milk*
Description: *3.5kg/8lb wheel, foil wrapped, sticky grey rind*
Culinary uses: *Table cheese, salads*

Shepherds Purse Cheeses started when Judy Bell, working for an osteopath, became aware of a growing number of clients with intolerance to normal dairy products. After finding the right milk, the first cheeses appeared in July 1989. Now a successful family-run business, they make a range of blue cheeses.

Mrs Bell's Blue is a continental-style ewe's milk blue using milk from local flocks. Pale yellow with blue streaks, it is slightly crumbly becoming dense and creamy with age. Full-bodied yet mellow with a hint of sweetness from the milk, it has a gentle acidity on the finish. It was winner of the Cheese Lover's Trophy in 2000 and 2005.

Yorkshire Blue, made with cow's milk, is less sharp while Buffalo Blue is more earthy, though they are all crafted to a similar recipe and each cheese is nurtured over its 10 week maturation period.

North Wilts Loaf

Region: *Wiltshire*
Type: *Modern, farmhouse, vegetarian, pasteurized, hard cheese*
Source: *Cow's milk*
Description: *2kg/5lb drum with thick grey crust*
Culinary use: *Table cheese*

North Wiltshire cheeses had all but disappeared by the beginning of the twentieth century until they were revived by Ceri Collingbourn in 2006. Ceri produces two hard delicious cheeses, Malmesbury Mold and North Wilts Loaf.

Beneath its thick, grey, crusty and wrinkly rind, dusted with grey and brown moulds, North Wilts Loaf has a texture somewhere between a Double Gloucester and a crumbly Caerphilly. It has a refreshing tang that is lemony and grassy with the bite of horseradish that sneaks up on you on the finish, and is best at around five months.

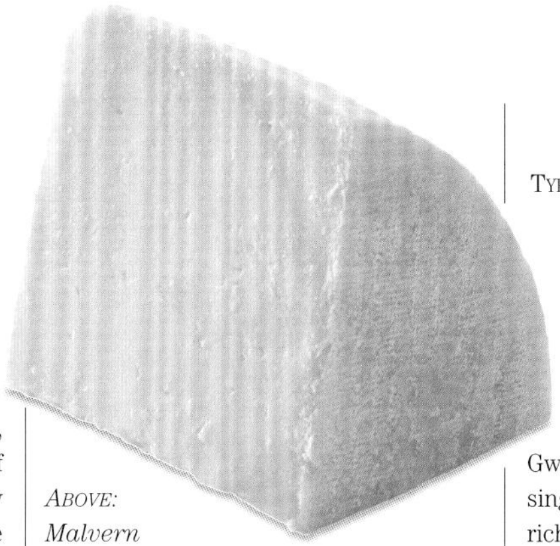

Above: Malvern

Northumberland Original

Region: *Northumberland*
Type: *Modern, farmhouse, vegetarian, hard cheese*
Source: *Cow's milk*
Description: *2.2kg/5lb round. The firm, natural rind is pale yellow, dusted with greyish mould*
Culinary use: *Table cheese*

In 1987 Mark Robertson started making Northumberland, basing it upon a washed curd recipe. It matures slowly in the cellars of a farm where cheesemaking is reputed to have been going on since 1296. A moist, firm cheese with a sweet, fruity nose, Northumberland's flavour is robust, with a tart bite. It matures in 10 weeks and has a fat content of 33 per cent.

Below: Old Sarum

Old Sarum

Region: *Wiltshire*
Type: *Modern, farmhouse, vegetarian, blue cheese*
Source: *Cow's milk (Ayrshire)*
Description: *1.5kg/4lb tall elegant cylinder with thin, dry, grey crust*
Culinary use: *Table cheese*

Loosehanger Cheeses, on the edge of the New Forest, is owned by Ness and Gwyn Williams. All the milk comes from a single herd of cows that graze the herb-rich Hampshire Downs on a nearby farm.

Matured slowly on wooden slats, Old Sarum develops a very smooth texture that melts in the mouth like rich spicy butter. The blue-green veining spreads sparsely through the moist interior creating a gentle aromatic tang on the finish. Subtle but spectacular, it was voted Best British Blue in 2007.

Old Winchester

Region: *Wiltshire*
Type: *Modern, farmhouse, vegetarian, hard cheese*
Source: *Cow's milk*
Description: *4kg/9lb boulder with thin pale sunshine yellow rind*
Culinary uses: *Table cheese, grilling*

The Smales, based at Lyburn Farm in the New Forest, started making cheese in 2000 using milk from their herd of Friesian cows. They decided to make a supple, continental style hard cheese, and Old Winchester is not unlike aged Gouda with its almost brittle texture, crunchy calcium calcite crystals and attractive dandelion-yellow colour.

Winner of the Best Modern British Cheese in 2006, it has a delicious fruity tang that lingers on the palate gradually revealing its inner secrets. They also make Lyburn Gold and a variety of flavour added cheeses.

ABOVE: Oxford Blue

OXFORD BLUE

REGION: *Oxfordshire*
TYPE: *Modern, creamery, vegetarian, blue cheese*
SOURCE: *Cow's milk*
DESCRIPTION: *2.5kg/5½lb round, wrapped in silver foil. The moist rind is cream-coloured and has some grey-blue moulds*
CULINARY USE: *Table cheese*

Baron Robert Pouget is well known to visitors to Oxford's famous covered market, where he has a wonderful, old-fashioned cheese shop. Always searching for something new, he decided to create his own cheese in the style of the French blues, as a distinct alternative to Stilton. After months of experimentation in conjunction with a well-known blue cheesemaker, Oxford Blue was born in 1993. In 2002 it won Best Blue Export Cheese at the British Cheese Awards.

When ripe, the cheese is a luscious, creamy blue with a distinct but not strong, blue flavour. Aromatic and spicy, it has a hints of chocolate, white wine and tarragon. It matures in 14–16 weeks and has a fat content of 30 per cent. Oxford Blue also makes an excellent washed rind cheese, Isis.

PERROCHE

REGION: *Hereford and Worcester*
TYPE: *Modern, farmhouse, unpasteurized, vegetarian, fresh cheese*
SOURCE: *Goat's cheese*
DESCRIPTION: *150g/5oz round or 450–900g/1–2lb log*
CULINARY USES: *Table cheese, toasting, grilling*

Perroche, produced by Charlie Westhead of Neal's Yard Creamery, has a subtle, goaty taste that is clean and slightly almondy. The high moisture gives it a light, almost fluffy feel, but a short shelf life. It ripens in less than two weeks and has a fat content of 22 per cent. It is also made with herbs, such as tarragon, dill, rosemary and thyme.

RACHEL

REGION: *Somerset*
TYPE: *Modern, farmhouse, thermized, vegetarian, semi-soft, washed rind*
SOURCE: *Goat's milk*
DESCRIPTION: *1.3kg/3lb elliptical round with fine orange leathery coat splattered with grey, white and even yellow moulds*
CULINARY USES: *Table cheese, grilling*

Peter Humphries set up White Lake Cheese in 2004 with Roger Longman at Bagborough farm, where Roger farms over 600 goats and a small herd of cows. Peter's love of experimenting means that he, with help from fellow cheesemaker Tim, is continuously creating new cheeses. Some of his best are White Lake, Puddle, Trickle, White Nancy, Sacre Bleu and also Little Wallop, which he makes for the Evenlode partnership.

Rachel, named after an old friend, is an elegant, curvaceous, washed curd and washed rind cheese and was voted Best Goat Cheese in 2007. It has a superb tangy, savoury, cheese sauce taste with the acidity of limes, the sweetness of ground almonds and yeasty fermented fruit finish – like eating Harry Potter's favourite "Bertie Bott's every flavour beans".

ABOVE: Perroche

RED LEICESTER

REGION: *Leicestershire*
TYPE: *Traditional, farmhouse and creamery, hard cheese*
SOURCE: *Cow's milk*
DESCRIPTION: *4–18kg/9–40lb wheel. The bright orange-red rind has fine, powdery moulds*
CULINARY USES: *Table cheese, grilling, grating*

Leicester was produced in volume by the late eighteenth century. The cheese owed its bright orange-red colour to the natural dye, annatto. During the Second World War, however, the practice of adding annatto to Leicester was banned. When the colour was eventually returned to the pale, wartime version of Leicester cheese, it became known as Red Leicester to distinguish it from the tasteless imposter. It was not until 2005 that traditionally made Red Leicester was once again made in the county by David and Jo Clarke of the Leicestershire Handmade Cheese Company. David manages their 150 head of pedigree Holstein-Friesian cows, on Sparkenhoe Farm, located in Upton, a small hamlet in the south-west Leicestershire countryside, where they feed on the farm's lush pastures. Made traditionally with

ABOVE: Red Leicester

raw milk and animal rennet, their Leicester is called "Sparkenhoe" to differentiate it from others made outside the county.

An authentic Red Leicester has a firm body and a close, flaky texture. The flavour is delicately sweet and improves with keeping. There is a mere suggestion of green-grass bitterness behind the more distinct butterscotch and nut flavours. Red Leicester can be eaten young, but it should ideally be left to mature for six to nine months. It has a fat content of 32 per cent.

Ribblesdale Goat

REGION: *North Yorkshire*
TYPE: *Modern, farmhouse, unpasteurized, vegetarian, hard cheese*
SOURCE: *Goat's milk*
DESCRIPTION: *2kg/4½lb wheel with smooth rind covered with white wax*
CULINARY USES: *Table cheese, grating, grilling*

Created in 1982 by Iain and Christine Hill, and now run by their daughter Iona, this goat's cheese is sought after for its fresh and delicate flavour. Its texture is rather like that of a young Gouda, and the taste is mildly suggestive of fragrant chicory and almonds, with a trace of misty hills and wild herbs. The sharp whiteness of the cheese is enhanced by the distinctive, white, wax coating. Ribblesdale matures in between six to eight weeks and has a fat content of 30 per cent. Ribblesdale is also available made with cow, sheep and buffalo milk.

Rosary Goat

REGION: *Wiltshire*
TYPE: *Modern, farmhouse, vegetarian, fresh cheese*
SOURCE: *Goat's milk (Saanen)*
DESCRIPTION: *275g/10oz round or 1kg/2¼lb log – stark white and decorated with a sprig of fresh herbs ash or peppercorns*
CULINARY USES: *Table cheese, melting, spreading*

Chris and Claire Moody have won Best Fresh Cheese numerous times at the British Cheese Awards for their soft, goat's cheeses. Delicate, moist and creamy, their cheeses absorb the flavours of the herbs with which some of them are decorated. Rosary Plain matures in one to two weeks and has a fat content of 25 per cent. Flavoured versions include Rosary Herb, Ash, Pepper and Garlic and Herb.

BELOW: Ribblesdale Goat

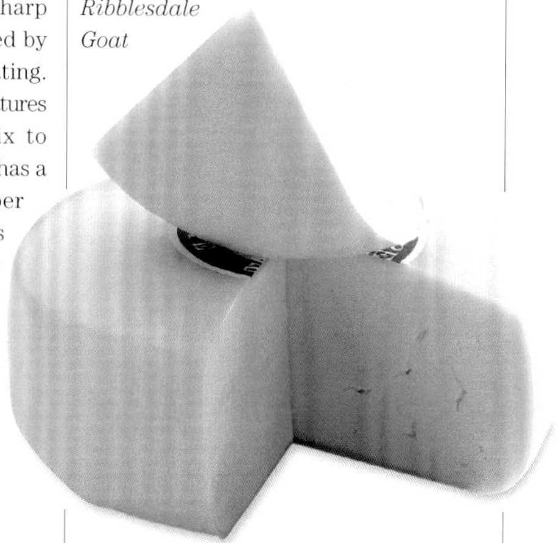

Rustic Chives & Garlic

REGION: *Devon*
TYPE: *Modern, farmhouse, unpasteurized, vegetarian, soft-white cheese*
SOURCE: *Cow's milk (Jersey)*
DESCRIPTION: *2 kg/5lb elliptical round, thin-ridged crust with fine white mould*
CULINARY USES: *Table cheese, grilling*

Sharpham Cheese Company, best known for their cheese of the same name also make this relative newcomer which was voted Best Flavour Added Cheese in 2004 and 2006 and deserves a mention.

Rustic is an unusual flying saucer shape with a thin crust dusted with a beautiful fine white mould that protects the luscious, soft Jersey milk yellow interior. It tastes like cream cheese and fresh chives with a subtle garlic finish. Available in plain or chive and garlic, it is aged for approximately six to eight weeks.

LEFT: Rustic Chives & Garlic

Sage Derby

Region: *North Yorkshire*
Type: *Traditional, creamery, vegetarian, flavour added cheese*
Source: *Cow's milk*
Description: *4–13.5kg/9–30lb cylinder flecked with tiny flakes of sage*
Culinary uses: *Table cheese, grilling*

In the seventeenth century, the custom of adding sage (a herb valued at the time for its health-giving properties) to Derby cheese was begun. As the cheese aged, the savour of the herbs was gradually incorporated. Today, however, most Sage Derby unfortunately consists of reconstituted cheese blended with spinach juice or green vegetable dye and colourless dried sage. The effect is to give the cheese a green-and-white-marbled appearance.

Sage Derby ripens in one to three months and has a fat content of 32 per cent.

Above: Sage Derby

Sharpham

Region: *Devon*
Type: *Modern, farmhouse, unpasteurized, vegetarian, soft-white cheese*
Source: *Cow's milk (Jersey)*
Description: *250g/9oz; 500g/1¼lb or 1kg/2¼lb round or square cheese with smooth, soft, velvety-white rind*
Culinary use: *Table cheese*

The Sharpham estate's permanent pastures undoubtedly give its Jersey milk a unique flavour. This Brie-type cheese is hand-ladled into moulds to retain the soft feel of the smooth Jersey milk, which is so thick that it feels more like clotted cream. It has just a hint of acidity and a whiff of mushrooms. The cheese is made from March to December, ripens in between six to eight weeks and has a fat content of 28 per cent.

Below: Sharpham

Shropshire Blue

Region: *Nottinghamshire*
Type: *Traditional, creamery, vegetarian, blue cheese*
Source: *Cow's milk*
Description: *8kg/18lb cylinder. The deep orange-brown rind has a cocktail of colourful moulds and yeasts*
Culinary use: *Table cheese*

Despite its name, this cheese was invented in Scotland in the twentieth century, and was then introduced to the Stilton makers. It is similar in style to Stilton, but is distinguished by the wonderful, orange colour, created by adding a few drops of annatto, a natural dye, to the vat. The royal blue of the mould provides a distinct colour contrast. The cheese maintains its wonderful blue taste, while the annatto seems to create an underlying hint of rich, buttery, burnt caramel. Shropshire Blue matures for 10 weeks and has a fat content of 34 per cent.

Note: When a blue cheese is wider at the bottom than at the top it has "soggy bottom". This can indicate that it has not been turned often enough, causing the moisture to drop to the bottom and leaving the top of the cheese to dry out. Avoid any cheese like this.

Single Gloucester (PDO)

Region: *Gloucestershire*
Type: *Traditional, farmhouse and creamery, unpasteurized, hard cheese*
Source: *Cow's milk (Gloucester)*
Description: *3.25kg–5.5kg/7–12lb millstone shapes or 1.4kg/3lb truckles. The hard, smooth, natural rind bears the marks of the cloth*
Culinary uses: *Table cheese, grilling*

Traditionally made from skimmed milk from the evening milking, which was then mixed with the morning's whole milk, Single Gloucester is lighter, more crumbly and lower in fat than Double Gloucester. Now protected by the rules of the EU Protected Name Scheme PDO (protected designation of origin) it can only be made in Gloucester by producers who have a registered herd of Gloucester cows. The cheese must be pressed for up to five days and is ready for consumption at around two months. Eventually only those made with milk from the Gloucester cow will carry the name of Single Gloucester.

Cheesemakers who meet the criteria are Charles Martell, Godsell, Smart's Traditional and Wick Farm. Typically Gloucester is firm and biteable with the richness of creamy toffee, vanilla and the occasional suggestion of liquorice on the finish.

Below: Shropshire Blue

ABOVE: Snodsbury

SNODSBURY
REGION: *Worcestershire*
TYPE: *Modern, farmhouse, unpasteurized, vegetarian cheese*
SOURCE: *Goat's milk*
DESCRIPTION: *1.8kg/4lb cylinder clothbound, natural pale grey-fawn crusty rind*
CULINARY USE: *Table cheese*

The latest addition to Anstey's of Worcester range is a wonderful and unusual hard goat's cheese made using a similar recipe to Double Gloucester, giving it a dense, smooth and creamy feel. Unlike the classic French style small goat's cheeses which are nutty and sometimes pungent and "goaty", it develops a more mellow character with hints of marzipan and chicory with a suggestion of wild herbs.

SOMERSET BRIE
REGION: *Somerset*
TYPE: *Modern, creamery, vegetarian, soft-white cheese*
SOURCE: *Cow's milk*
DESCRIPTION: *2.5kg/5½lb cylinder with soft, velvety, smooth, white rind*
CULINARY USE: *Table cheese*

One of the best-selling British soft cheeses, Somerset Brie has a delicious "set custard" texture. The aroma and taste suggest mushrooms with a hint of green grass, with some acidity to give the cheese depth. It does not pretend to be like a French Brie, which is richer and more robust, due to the differences in climate, soil, breed of cattle and production methods. Somerset Brie matures in six weeks, with a fat content of 24 per cent. It is made by Lubborn Cheese Ltd, which also produces Capricorn Goat.

SPENWOOD
REGION: *Berkshire*
TYPE: *Modern, farmhouse, unpasteurized, vegetarian, hard cheese*
SOURCE: *Sheep's milk*
DESCRIPTION: *2kg/4½lb round cheese. The natural rind is firm and crusty. The colour is yellowish-grey*
CULINARY USES: *Table cheese, grating, grilling*

Made by Anne Wigmore of Village Maid Cheese, Spenwood was not only awarded a gold medal at the 1996 British Cheese Awards, but also took the Cheese Lover's Trophy. Hard and seemingly dry, the cheese is creamy in the mouth, melting to release its distinct sweet, caramel flavour, which is superbly balanced with acidity. With age, the flavour of ground nuts becomes more pronounced. Spenwood ripens in six months and has a fat content of 30 per cent.

LEFT: Spenwood

ST OSWALD
REGION: *Worcestershire*
TYPE: *Modern, farmhouse, pasteurized, organic, semi-soft cheese*
SOURCE: *Cow's milk (Montbeliarde and Friesian)*
DESCRIPTION: *300gm/12oz round with firm, deep ridged orange rind*
CULINARY USE: *Table cheese*

Michael and Diane Stacey have been farming at Gorsehill Abbey Farm, between the foothills of the Cotswold hills and the rich fertile ground of the Vale of Evesham, for over 35 years but only started making cheese commercially since 2003. Many of the pastures are at least 150 years old and retain the ridge and furrow pattern developed in the Middle Ages and the addition of Montbeliarde cows in the herd imparts another dimension to the milk.

Protected by the washed leathery rind, the interior is supple and voluptuous and develops a richer, savoury, pungent character like cheese and onion sauce with attitude as it ages. It is matured from around three months, during which time the rind changes from yellow to orange-brown and the flavour intensifies. Voted Best English Cheese in 2007. They also make two other superb cheeses, soft white St Eadburgha, and Cotswold Herb, fresh with herbs.

BELOW: St Oswald and St Eadburgha

Above: Staffordshire Organic

Staffordshire Organic

Region: *Staffordshire*
Type: *Modern, farmhouse, unpasteurized, vegetarian, organic, flavour added cheese*
Source: *Cow's milk*
Description: *3.5–18kg/8–40lb cylinder with firm, Cheddar-like rind*
Culinary uses: *Table cheese, grilling, grating*

Similar to Cheddar it is smooth and creamy, yet firm, with the sweetness and colour of butter. It comes in various guises, the most interesting being made with wild garlic. Whereas most farmers scour their fields to remove any trace of wild garlic, Michael Deaville harvests his, then minces and freezes it so that it retains its zingy freshness when added to the cheese. Staffordshire Organic matures in six to eight weeks and has a fat content of 32 per cent.

Above: Stichelton

Stichelton

Region: *Nottinghamshire*
Type: *Modern, farmhouse, unpasteurized, animal, organic, blue cheese*
Source: *Cow's Milk*
Description: *7kg/16lb cylinder, dry brown and grey crusty rind*
Culinary use: *Table cheese*

Stichelton is a superb new blue cheese made by Joe Schneider, previously of Daylesford Organic, from organic cow's milk at Collingthwaite Farm on the Welbeck Estate in the heart of Stilton country. In fact Stichelton is like Stilton in every respect except it is made from unpasteurized milk, whereas Stilton, according to current PDO specifications, has to be made from pasteurized milk. It is hoped this will not always be the case.

It has a chewily dense yet creamy texture with fruity and appley tones and a spicy aromatic tang that gives way to a long lemony freshness with just a hint of dark chocolate on the finish.

Above: The perfect Stilton will have blue mould spreading out to the rind

Stilton (PDO)

Region: *Nottinghamshire, Derbyshire, Leicestershire*
Type: *Traditional, creamery, vegetarian, blue cheese*
Source: *Cow's milk*
Description: *2.5kg/5½lb or 8kg/18lb drum. The rough, crusty rind formed by a multitude of moulds gives the cheese the appearance of a rock covered in lichen*
Culinary uses: *Table cheese, snacks, soups*

Who first made Stilton has been debated for centuries, but it remains one of Britain's best-loved cheeses, thanks to the foresight of the Stilton makers. In the early 1900s they formed themselves into an association to control how the cheese should be made. As with the AOC system in France, they also specified where Stilton could be made – production is only allowed in the three counties of Nottinghamshire, Derbyshire and Leicestershire.

The rind of good Stilton exudes wonderful aromas of cellars, stone walls and moulds. It is punctuated with tiny holes where it has been pierced by stainless-steel needles to allow air to penetrate the interior. The perfect Stilton should have the blue mould spreading out to the rind so that it looks like shattered porcelain, while the taste should suggest old leather, dark chocolate and an intense spicy "blue" quality, with a hint of white wine and herbs. It should be rich and creamy, not dry and crumbly, with a clean, lasting, tangy finish.

The mistake some producers make is to sell Stilton too young, when it can be bitter and dry. It matures in nine to 15 weeks, with a fat content of 35.5 per cent.

Over the years, some unusual rules of etiquette have developed around Stilton – especially the habit of "digging" pieces out with a spoon. This tradition arose when a whole Stilton used to be served at banquets, where it would be consumed quickly. If you are given a whole or even a half Stilton, don't dig into it unless you are planning to eat all of it within a week, or it will dry out. Instead, work your way down gradually, keeping the surface as flat as possible.

Stilton producers include Colston Bassett Dairy, Cropwell Bishop Creamery, Dairy Crest, Long Clawson, Tuxford and Tebbutt, Websters and the latest addition, Quenby Hall.

ABOVE: Sussex Slipcote

STINKING BISHOP

REGION: *Gloucestershire*
TYPE: *Modern, farmhouse, vegetarian, washed-rind cheese*
SOURCE: *Cow's milk*
DESCRIPTION: *1.8kg/4lb round with glistening, orange-yellow, slightly sticky rind washed in brine*
CULINARY USE: *Table cheese*

A wash-rind cheese dating back to the Cistercian monks who once settled in Dymock, where this wonderfully eccentric cheese was created by Charles Martell. It looks a little like Munster and is washed and rubbed in fermented pear juice made with a local variety of pear called "Stinking Bishop". Wonderfully aromatic, pungent and probably over-the-top for most people.

Consistent winner of the Best Export Cheese at the British Cheese Awards and at a tasting in France, this velvety-smooth, almost spoonable cheese was greeted with amazement. It seems the French still labour under the misconception that the only cheeses made in England are Cheddar and Stilton – a view unfortunately shared by many of the British.

Stinking Bishop requires six to eight weeks to mature and has a fat content of 24 per cent.

ABOVE: Swaledale Cow

SUSSEX SLIPCOTE

REGION: *Sussex*
TYPE: *Traditional, farmhouse, organic, vegetarian, fresh cheese*
SOURCE: *Sheep's milk*
DESCRIPTION: *115g/4oz round or 900g/2lb log. The pure white cheese may form a fine clear "skin"*
CULINARY USES: *Table cheese, baking, spreading*

The recipe is said to date back to the time of Shakespeare, when the young curd would mature too fast and slip out of its cheesecloth coat – hence the name. Today the curd is carefully ladled into moulds so that sufficient whey is retained to give the finished cheese its light, mousse-like texture. Light and creamy, with a suggestion of sweetness from the sheep's milk, Sussex Slipcote is available in three varieties: plain, garlic and herb, and cracked peppercorn. The cheese takes 10 days to mature and has a fat content of 23 per cent.

SWALEDALE (PDO)

REGION: *North Yorkshire*
TYPE: *Traditional, farmhouse, vegetarian, hard cheese*
SOURCE: *Cow's or sheep's milk*
DESCRIPTION: *2.5kg/5½lb round. The hard, natural rind has a blue-grey mould*
CULINARY USE: *Table cheese*

Swaledale is a classic Yorkshire cheese, created by David Reed in the valley of the Swale River. It is soaked in brine before being left to mature in humid cellars, where the rind acquires the attractive mould that prevents the interior from drying out. Softer than Wensleydale and a little more moist, it has the freshness of the misty Yorkshire Dales and wild bracken, along with the typical acidity associated with Dale cheeses.

A frequent medal winner at the British Cheese Awards, Swaledale matures in one month and has a fat content of 48 per cent. Variations of the cow's milk version include cheeses flavoured with fresh chives, garlic and apple mint, and another that is soaked in Old Peculiar ale.

Swaledale Ewe was the first cheese to win the David Reed Memorial Trophy in 2007 for the Best PDO/PGI Cheese at the British Cheese Awards a fitting tribute to his passion for the cheeses of the Dales.

TUNWORTH

REGION: *Hampshire*
TYPE: *Modern, farmhouse, animal, unpasteurized, soft-white cheese*
SOURCE: *Cow's milk (Holstein)*
DESCRIPTION: *250gm/10oz disc, soft-white wrinkled rind*
CULINARY USE: *Table cheese*

Hand-made by two friends, Stacey Hedges and Julie Cheyney, Tunworth has fulfilled a lifelong dream for the two mothers who started their business, Hampshire Cheeses, in their own kitchens in 2002. It is now made in a converted barn in Herriard Village using traditional animal rennet, a cocktail of special cultures and milk from Holstein cows that graze the Hampshire Downs. Winner of Supreme Champion and Best Soft White Cheese in 2006 it has a pale yellow soft creamy interior that feels luscious in the mouth. The aroma is of mushrooms and cellars while the taste is reminiscent of mushroom soup with just a dash of sherry and the finish is nutty with a delicate hint of green grass.

LEFT: Tunworth

ABOVE: Vulscombe, with fresh herbs and garlic (left), with crushed peppercorns and garlic (right), and plain (centre)

TYMSBORO

REGION: *Somerset*
TYPE: *Modern, farmhouse, unpasteurized, vegetarian, soft-white cheese*
SOURCE: *Goat's milk*
DESCRIPTION: *250g/9oz flat-topped pyramid. The natural rind, dusted with black ash, is covered with a fine, white mould*
CULINARY USE: *Table cheese*

When Mary Holbrook's elegant-looking, pyramid-shaped goat's cheese is cut into, a fine layer of black ash is revealed, separating the moist centre of the cheese and the white, mould covered rind. The taste is of lemon sorbet, elderflowers and apples; the finish suggests crisp, fresh fruit with a gentle, spicily aromatic tang. Tymsboro ripens in two to four weeks.

VULSCOMBE

REGION: *Devon*
TYPE: *Modern, farmhouse, vegetarian, fresh cheese*
SOURCE: *Goat's milk*
DESCRIPTION: *170g/6oz round, decorated with a bay leaf or crushed peppercorns*
CULINARY USE: *Table cheese*

Twice winner of a bronze medal at the British Cheese Awards, Vulscombe is produced by Joyce and Graham Townsend. The cheese is unusual in that rennet is not used to separate the milk; coagulation occurs purely through the acidity of the curd. Vulscombe is small, round and elegantly packaged, its stark white appearance offset by a bay leaf or crushed peppercorns. Moist but creamy, it has a fresh, lemon sorbet taste and just the merest hint of goat's milk. It matures in one to three weeks and has a fat content of 25 per cent. Vulscombe is available plain, with fresh herbs and garlic, or sprinkled with crushed peppercorns and garlic.

WATERLOO

REGION: *Berkshire*
TYPE: *Modern, farmhouse, unpasteurized, vegetarian, semi-soft cheese*
SOURCE: *Cow's milk (Guernsey)*
DESCRIPTION: *900g/2lb round. The thick natural, pinkish rind is dusted with white moulds. With age it becomes grey, crusty and wrinkled*
CULINARY USE: *Table cheese*

Made by Anne and Andy Wigmore, Waterloo is a washed curd cheese: sweet, supple and smooth, it is full-bodied in flavour and a rich yellow colour. It starts life mellow and fruity, but time and nature break down the proteins and fat. As the interior reaches the point where it starts to run, the cheese acquires a vegetal taste like young celery leaves and dandelions. These somewhat peppery tastes are balanced by the richness of the milk.

Waterloo matures in four to 10 weeks and has a fat content of 30 per cent. It is a consistent medal winner at the British Cheese Awards.

RIGHT: Tymsboro

WENSLEYDALE

REGION: *Yorkshire*
TYPE: *Traditional, farmhouse, hard cheese*
SOURCE: *Cow's milk*
DESCRIPTION: *4.5kg/10lb or 21kg/46lb clothbound cylinder with natural rind*
CULINARY USES: *Table cheese; also traditionally eaten with apple pie*

The most famous of all the Yorkshire Dales cheeses, Wensleydale is now made by several cheesemakers, including some who have revived the tradition of using sheep's milk. Based on a recipe that can be traced back to the eleventh century, it is wrapped in cheesecloth and matured in cellars.

The best-known example of this cheese is made by the Wensleydale Creamery in Hawes, where it has been produced for almost a century. Production almost ended in the 1990s when the owners decided to close down the creamery. They reckoned without the tenacity of the local community and workers, who fought the closure and have revitalized the company.

Wensleydale has a supple, crumbly and moist texture, similar to a young Caerphilly. The flavour suggests wild honey balanced with a fresh acidity. It matures in two to four months and has a fat content of 32 per cent.

WHITE STILTON

REGION: *Leicestershire, Nottinghamshire and Derbyshire*
TYPE: *Traditional, creamery, vegetarian, hard cheese*
SOURCE: *Cow's milk*
DESCRIPTION: *8kg/18lb drum with pale primrose-yellow, natural rind*
CULINARY USES: *Table cheese, salads*

White Stilton is a younger version of the King of the Blues, Stilton, without the blue. Made by most of the Stilton makers, most are pleasant but undemanding, but when well made it has a wonderful, moist crumbly texture and a sweet buttery taste balanced with a fresh zingy acidity. Matured for three to four weeks and has a fat content of 31 per cent.

ABOVE: White Stilton

WIGMORE

REGION: *Berkshire*
TYPE: *Modern, farmhouse, unpasteurized, vegetarian, semi-soft cheese*
SOURCE: *Sheep's milk*
DESCRIPTION: *500g/1¼lb or 2kg/4½lb round. The thick natural rind ranges from pink to grey-brown and is uneven and wrinkled*
CULINARY USE: *Table cheese*

This is produced by Anne Wigmore of Village Maid Cheese. The curd is washed to remove excess whey, then packed in moulds to drain. This creates a low-acid cheese, which retains the sweetness of the milk and develops a voluptuous consistency. The rind is washed and has a yeasty aroma that penetrates the supple interior of the cheese. The result is a taste sensation, combining floral flavours with burnt caramel, macadamia nuts and roast lamb. Wigmore consistently wins gold medals at the British Cheese Awards.

RIGHT: Waterloo

WOOLSERY GOAT

REGION: *Dorset*
TYPE: *Modern, farmhouse, vegetarian, hard cheese*
SOURCE: *Goat's milk*
DESCRIPTION: *2.2kg/5lb truckle. Thin grey natural rind with some white moulds bearing the imprint of the cloth*
CULINARY USES: *Table cheese, baked, grilled*

To keep up with demand, Annette Lee moved her dairy from Devon to Dorset in 2004, where Woolsery Cheese is now based in the tiny hamlet of Up Sydling near Dorchester. Annette produces a variety of soft and hard cow's and goat's milk cheeses, including a Greek-style feta cheese and a creamy Cheddar.

Her best-known cheese is Woolsery Goat, winner of the British Cheese Award's Cheese Lover's Trophy in 2001. It is best at around four months, when it has a firm slightly crumbly open texture. The squat truckles, which are attractively blemished with streaks of lavender and sulpur-yellow, are available to buy whole or as halves or quarters. Woolsery is ideal for those who are new to goat's cheese, as the distinctive goaty aroma, that can be overpowering in some cheeses, is very subtle with hints of almonds and pine nuts.

ABOVE: Wyfe of Bath

WYFE OF BATH

REGION: *Bath*
TYPE: *Modern, farmhouse, unpasteurized, vegetarian, organic, semi-soft cheese*
SOURCE: *Cow's milk*
DESCRIPTION: *3kg/7lb elliptical cheese with thin, grey, leathery, deeply ridged crust*
CULINARY USE: *Table cheese*

Another excellent cheese by Graham Padfield of the Bath Soft Cheese Company, this is a dense, marvellously gooey, chewy and soft-bodied Gouda-style cheese with small holes and the aroma and taste of melted butter. The finish is sweet and vaguely smoky like warm melted cheese.

In 2005 Wyfe of Bath won the "Tesco Cheese Challenge", a search for Britain's greatest undiscovered cheese. Since this victory production of the cheese has doubled and it is now available to buy in supermarkets across the United Kingdom.

YORKSHIRE BLUE

REGION: *North Yorkshire*
TYPE: *Traditional, farmhouse, vegetarian, blue cheese*
SOURCE: *Cow's milk*
DESCRIPTION: *3.5kg/8lb cylinder with moist, yellow-white, crusty, natural rind*
CULINARY USE: *Table cheese*

Judy Bell of Shepherds Purse produces a range of blue sheep, cow and buffalo milk cheeses on her family farm, near Thirsk in Yorkshire. Yorkshire Blue was added to their range in 1995, and was their first cow's milk cheese, having focused their production on sheep's cheeses in the past. It has been developed using traditional methods dating back to the early Yorkshire cheeses of the eleventh century. It won a British Cheese Awards gold medal in 1997.

A creamy and moist blue, made from fresh cow's milk collected from local farmers, it is mellow but not mild, when at room temperature it develops a slightly sweet tang. When young, it is typical of a young blue Wensleydale – crumbly and flaky with a subtle "blue" flavour – but maturity brings softness and a more pronounced taste. It matures in eight to 10 weeks and has a fat content of 26 per cent.

LEFT: Woolsery Goat

THE BRITISH CHEESE AWARDS

The British Cheese Awards is an annual event that rewards and celebrates excellence within the British cheese industry. Created by the author, Juliet Harbutt, the awards are endorsed by the media, respected specialists and the dairy industry and aim to stimulate awareness of the diversity and quality of cheeses being produced in Britain.

Each year, British cheesemakers are invited to submit their cheeses to a carefully chosen panel of judges including food writers and experts from the cheese, hospitality, retail and food industries. In 2008, over 870 cheeses (including 120 goat's milk, 46 sheep's milk and 200 made with raw milk) were entered for the awards.

Each cheese is judged alongside others produced in the same way and only those cheeses that attain a level of excellence are awarded gold, silver or bronze medals. The award for Best of Category is chosen from the gold medal winners in each category, and an overall Supreme Champion is chosen from the 12 category winners.

The winners of the awards are announced during British Cheese Week, a nationwide campaign held at the end of September to celebrate and raise awareness of all British cheese and its regional diversity.

BELOW: Lady Angus's Aged Cerney won the much coveted title of Supreme Champion at the 2001 British Cheese Awards.

PAST SUPREME CHAMPIONS

YEAR	CHEESE	MAKER
1994	Innes Button	Highfields Dairy
1995	Mrs Kirkham's Lancashire	JJ Kirkham
1996	Lincolnshire Poacher	FW Read and Sons
1997	Milleens	Milleens Cheese
1998	Celtic Promise	Teifi Farmhouse Cheese
1999	Extra Mature Cheddar	Cheddar Gorge Cheese Company
2000	Coolea	Coolea Cheese
2001	Aged Cerney	Cerney Cheese
2002	Innes Button Natural	Highfields Farm Dairy
2003	Organic Stilton	Cropwell Bishop Creamery
2004	Extra Mature Cheddar	JA and E Montgomery
2005	Celtic Promise	Teifi Farmhouse Cheese
2006	Tunworth	Hampshire Cheeses
2007	Seriously Strong Cheddar	Caledonian Cheese Company
2008	Barkham Blue	Two Hoots Cheese

Irish Cheeses

There is a certain magic in the hand-made cheeses of Ireland that is indefinable yet almost tangible. Perhaps it is the touch of the leprechaun or the passion of the Irish for life that comes through the soil. For despite all the past and present problems that are a part of Irish life, the land is still rich and green and fertile.

Since ancient times, the people of this natural dairy land have valued butter and milk, but, curiously, there is no early record of cheesemaking. Even the monks who were responsible for so many of the great European cheeses never inspired in the Irish a love of cheese nor much desire to make it. Most of what is produced today is rather unexciting block Cheddar, mainly made in large factories in Northern Ireland and exported.

The situation is changing, however. A new generation of cheesemakers has arisen, rediscovering traditional old recipes and cheesemaking methods and creating new ones.

There must be something in the West Cork air that has led four of Ireland's best-loved cheese-makers to produce the Trappist-style washed-rind cheese. Perhaps it is the rugged coastline battered by the Atlantic or the gentle mist and rain that have inspired Milleens, Gubbeen, Ardrahan and Durrus. Certainly the presence of Cashel Rock must have influenced the Grubbs to make their robust and spicy Cashel Blue.

The cheese revolution has barely crossed the border into Northern Ireland, where production remains highly industrialized. However, Blue Rathgore, a goat's milk cheese produced by Woodford Dairies in South Belfast, is hopefully the first of many modern specialist cheeses.

Ardrahan

Region: *West Cork*
Type: *Modern, farmhouse, vegetarian, washed-rind cheese*
Source: *Cow's milk*
Description: *400g/14oz and 1.5kg/3¼lb wheel. The ridged, brine-washed rind is encrusted with brown, ochre, grey and yellow moulds*
Culinary use: *Table cheese*

A silver medal winner at the 1995 British Cheese Awards, Ardrahan is made by Eugene and Mary Burns. Beneath the brine-washed rind, the deep yellow interior is firm and slightly chalky. It exudes a wonderful complexity of flavours, the zesty acidity underscoring the buttery, savoury, meaty character. The finish is reminiscent of a young Gruyère. Ardrahan matures in four to eight weeks.

Left: Cashel Blue (left) and Ardrahan (right)

Beenoskee

Region: *Kerry*
Type: *Modern, farmhouse, unpasteurized, vegetarian, hard cheese*
Source: *Cow's milk*
Description: *2kg/5lb wheel with attractive brown-orange rind, brushed daily with whey*
Culinary uses: *Table, grilling*

Maya Binder makes distinct and unusual cheeses in an old stone shed overlooking the sea on the Dingle Peninsula, each contributing to the unique and distinctive character of her cheeses. Beenoskee, winner of the Best Irish Cheese in 2001, is a warm sunshine yellow, firm yet supple with tiny holes and a taste reminiscent of melted butter with a delicious caramelized onion tang on the finish. Maya also makes Dilliskus, with a thin layer of dilisk (or sea-grass) sprinkled through the centre of the cheese, giving it a more salty flavour, and Kilcummin, a smaller semi-soft cheese.

Burren Gold

Region: *Clare*
Type: *Modern, farmhouse, unpasterized, waxed, hard cheese*
Source: *Cow's milk*
Description: *4kg/9lb and 8kg/18lb boulder with a waxed rind*
Culinary use: *Table cheese*

To taste this cheese you will probably have to go all the way to Ballyvaughan, with its rugged limestone hills that are interlaced with rich fertile valleys and the popular Aillwee caves, where visitors find themselves drawn to the well-stocked shop and cheesemaking room run by Ben Johnson. Ben's cheese, Burren Gold, is a beautifully rounded Gouda-style cheese with a smooth, open texture and numerous tiny "eyes". It is buttery, slightly sweet and nutty with a distinct but mellow flavour that lingers on the finish. Also available with fresh ground black pepper, a mixture of chive and garlic or oak smoked. After brine washing, the cheeses are waxed to prevent any moisture being lost.

Above: Coolea

Cashel Blue

Region: *Tipperary*
Type: *Modern, farmhouse, blue cheese*
Source: *Cow's milk*
Description: *1.5kg/3¼lb cylinder. The wet, crusty rind has rampant, grey moulds*
Culinary uses: *Table cheese; also excellent spread thickly on warm walnut bread*

Jane and Louis Grubb are descendants of buttermakers and millers expelled from England in the seventeenth century. Ten years ago they started making the only Irish blue cheese, under the shadow of the Rock of Cashel, a bold outcrop overlooking the Tipperary plains. The milk comes from their own pedigree herd.

When young, Cashel Blue is firm yet moist, with just a hint of fresh tarragon and white wine. With age, its true character emerges, mellowing to a rounder, more spicy style. The interior softens, then – when the cheese is at the peak of perfection – it gives up the battle of the bulge and collapses, providing a challenge for the retailer but a real treat for the cheese connoisseur.

Cashel Blue is available pasteurized, unpasteurized, vegetarian and non-vegetarian. It matures in eight to 14 weeks and has a fat content of 45 per cent.

Coolea

Region: *West Cork*
Type: *Modern, farmhouse, unpasteurized, hard cheese*
Source: *Cow's milk*
Description: *900g/2lb, 5.5kg/12lb and 9kg/20lb cheeses shaped like millstones, with smooth, shiny, orange, natural rind*
Culinary uses: *Table cheese, snacks, sauces*

Coolea is made by the Willems family, immigrants to Ireland from Holland. Their Gouda-style cheese is widely considered to be as good as any made on Dutch farms, while having its own unique character. The rich grazing of this isolated part of Cork produces a rich, nutty cheese with a fruity tang on the finish.

Coolea matures in six to 12 months. Occasionally, the family makes a larger cheese that can be matured for up to two years, when its fruity character intensifies, the colour deepens and the small holes gather drops of moisture. The fat content is 45 per cent.

Cooleeney

Region: *Tipperary*
Type: *Modern, farmhouse, unpasteurized, soft-white cheese*
Source: *Cow's milk*
Description: *200g/7oz or 1.5kg/3¼lb round with soft-white rind*
Culinary use: *Table cheese*

Breda Maher makes this Camembert-style cheese by hand using milk from the farm's Friesian dairy herd. Full-flavoured and grassy, with a distinct aroma earthy of mushrooms when perfectly ripe, Cooleeney's rich, semi-liquid interior benefits from the lush, green pastures for which Tipperary is famous. The cheese is available produced with both pasteurized and unpasteurized milk. The cheese ripens in four to eight weeks and has a fat content of 45 per cent.

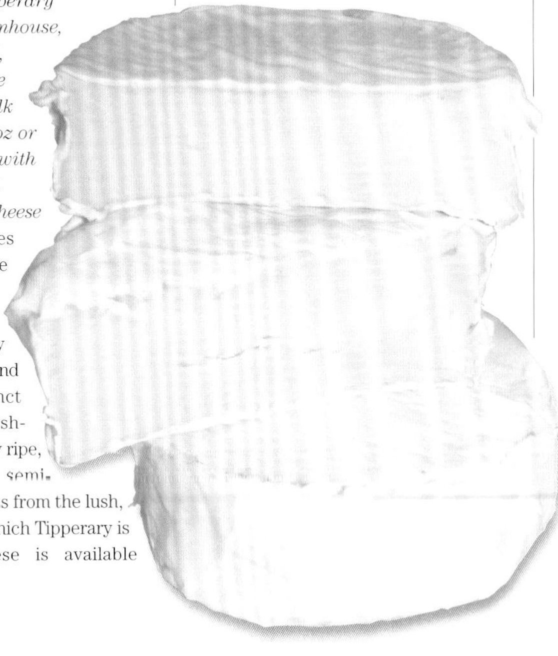

Right: Cooleeney

Cratloe Hills Gold

Region: *Clare*
Type: *Modern, farmhouse, vegetarian, hard cheese*
Source: *Ewes milk (East Friesland)*
Description: *2.5kg/6lb truckle terracotta-coloured smooth crust with some grey, white and blue moulds*
Culinary uses: *Table, grilling, grating*

Sean and Deirdre Fitzgerald have been returning home from the British Cheese Awards with an award on an almost annual basis, including Best Irish Cheese in 2002, 2004 and 2005 for this wonderful rustic yet elegant cheese. Hard, flaky and slightly oily, the interior is almost translucent, becoming darker towards the rind. Each mouthful reveals another layer of flavour from an appley crispness to the sweetness of caramelized onions and undertones of roast lamb in fine port. Irresistible, it reflects the character of the region, the skill of the cheesemaker and wonderful rich sheep's milk produced on their own farm.

Above: Gubbeen

Durrus

Region: *West Cork*

Type: *Modern, farmhouse, unpasteurized, vegetarian, semi-soft cheese*

Source: *Cow's milk*

Description: *1.4kg/3lb round. The zipper-patterned, washed rind is fawn in colour, with blotches of blue, grey and white moulds*

Culinary use: *Table cheese*

Durrus Farmhouse Cheese, made in the beautiful upland valley of Coomkeen, County Cork, is made from milk from a neighbouring farm and is processed in a magnificent copper vat in Jeffa Gill's charming dairy. Over the next few weeks the natural moulds and yeasts in the air gradually form a coat, which both protects the cheese and helps in the ripening process.

When young, Durrus is buttery, mild and slightly acidic, mellowing out to a silky-smooth, compact cheese that resembles a French Tomme. There is the smell of the earth on the rind and the medley of flavours includes caramel toffee, tart apples and a hint of smoke, with a nutty creaminess on the finish. The cheese matures in four to eight weeks and has a fat content of 45 per cent.

Durrus is a consistent medal winner at the British Cheese Awards.

Gabriel

Region: *West Cork*

Type: *Modern, farmhouse, unpasteurized, hard cheese*

Source: *Cow's milk*

Description: *6.75–27kg/15–60lb wheel with sharp edges. The natural rind is smooth, dark brown or khaki and very hard*

Culinary use: *Table cheese*

This wonderful, Gruyère-type cow's milk cheese is full of flavour and has a strong, fruity zing. Gabriel is lightly salted in brine and is cured for many months with neither wax nor plastic to hinder its slow path to maturity. It seems the damp climate of this part of West Cork lends itself particularly well to these slow-ripening, hard cheeses, of which this is one of the best.

Gabriel's makers, Bill Hogan and Sean Ferry of West Cork Natural Cheese Limited, produce two other hard cow's milk cheeses: Desmond, which is similar to Gabriel but slightly smoother, with a sharp, resonant finish, and Mizen, a huge cheese, often over 45kg/100lb in weight, which is very hard, in fact almost brittle, and not unlike the Swiss cheese Sbrinz or Italian Parmesan.

Right: Durrus (top) and Gabriel

Gubbeen

Region: *Cork*

Type: *Modern, farmhouse, vegetarian, semi-soft cheese*

Source: *Cow's milk*

Description: *1.5kg/3¼lb round. The terracotta, brine-washed rind has fine, white and pale blue moulds*

Culinary use: *Table cheese*

Tom and Gina Fergusson's washed rind cheese has twice won silver medals at the British Cheese Awards. There is a wonderful, earthy sweetness to Gubbeen, as the yeasts and moulds work to produce the rugged rind. The taste of this dense, full-bodied cheese is rich and savoury. The finish is of burnt onions and grilled cheese.

Knockdrinna Meadow

Region: *Kilkenny*

Type: *Modern, farmhouse, vegetarian, semi-soft, washed-rind cheese*

Source: *Sheep's milk*

Description: *2.5kg/6lb wheel with thin pink, sticky rind*

Culinary use: *Table cheese*

With the extraordinary growth in goat and ewe's milk cheese in Ireland, the Finnegan family saw an opportunity for small-scale producers and decided to expand their farming activities into cheesemaking. Their first cheese was made with cow's milk, but they continued experimenting with ewe's milk, and in 2007 introduced Knockdrinna Meadow, a ewe's milk cheese washed in white wine. Elastic but slightly crumbly, it is deliciously moreish with hints of cashew nut and caramel undertones.

Lavistown

Region: *Kilkenny*
Type: *Modern, farmhouse, unpasteurized, vegetarian, hard cheese*
Source: *Cow's milk*
Description: *1.4kg/3lb and 3.5kg/8lb cheeses in the shape of millstones. The natural rind is smooth and firm*
Culinary use: *Table cheese*

Made to a Swaledale recipe, Lavistown resembles a Cheddar but is less compact. It is crumbling and fine with a sharp acidity and a green, leafy taste.

Olivia Goodwillie of Lavistown House, a beautiful Georgian house and farm that offers a range courses in culinary and craft pursuits, made Lavistown cheese for 25 years until recently handing it over to the capable hands of Helen Finnegan of Knockdrinna Cheese. The Finnegans, who also make Knockdrinna Meadow, are continuing with Olivia's good work and ensuring that this delicious Irish cheese is not lost forever.

Milleens

Region: *West Cork*
Type: *Modern, farmhouse, unpasteurized, semi-soft cheese*
Source: *Cow's milk*
Description: *225g/8oz or 1.4kg/3lb rounds, with wrinkled, rather uneven, pinkish-orange, brine-washed rind*
Culinary use: *Table cheese*

Veronica and Norman Steele have been making Milleens on the Beara Peninsula for more than 25 years, and it is seldom the same twice, though never disappointing. The aroma is of farmyard, wet rocks and heather, the heather recurring in the flavour of the firm, supple, sweet cheese, which also has subtle hints of cream and butterscotch. At its peak, the runny paste becomes almost fluid, and the taste is yeasty and deliciously savoury, with a strong, herbaceous tang and a suggestion of wild sea breezes. Milleens has the sweet-sour taste associated with genuine Trappist cheeses. It matures in four to 10 weeks and has a fat content of 45 per cent. It was awarded the title of Supreme Champion at the 1997 British Cheese Awards.

Moon Shine Una

Region: *Westmeath*
Type: *Modern, farmhouse, vegetarian, organic fresh cheese*
Source: *Cow's milk*
Description: *150g/5oz jars*
Culinary uses: *Grilling, spreading*

Gerry and Mary Kelly farm on the shores of Lough Ennell in Co Westmeath and started making cheese from their organic milk in 2005. All their products are created on favourable days in the moon's cycle, hence the name Moon Shine Dairy Farm.

Their cheese, sold in glass jars, is as much about texture as taste as it is so light and creamy you can almost lick it like an ice cream. The lemony fresh curd seems almost to have been whipped, while the sunflower oil makes it nutty and so rich it is almost sinful. Made in several flavours, my favourite is Una with large chunks of sun-dried tomatoes and olives on the top that give it a wonderful Mediterranean feel.

Their products can be found in good shops all over Southern Ireland and at the local Mullingar Farmer's Market that is held every Sunday.

St Killian

Region: *Wexford*
Type: *Modern, farmhouse, vegetarian, soft-white cheese*
Source: *Cow's milk*
Description: *250g/9oz hexagonal cheese with velvety, smooth, soft, white rind*
Culinary use: *Table cheese*

Attractively boxed, this Camembert-style cheese has taken the market by storm. Although the rind can be a little whiffy, the prevailing smell is of mushrooms and cellars, while the soft, nearly melting interior has the rich flavour of warm butter, with a bite that suggests green grass. St Killian is produced by Patrick Berridge.

St Tola Log

Region: *Clare*
Type: *Modern, farmhouse, vegetarian, organic, unpastuerized, aged, fresh cheese*
Source: *Goat's milk*
Description: *150g/5oz or 1kg/2lb logs with a thin, wrinkled pink-tinged rind dusted with white mould*
Culinary uses: *Table cheese, grilling, spreading*

St Tola has been made since the early 1980s, originally by Meg and Derrick Gordon. The business was taken over by their neighbour Siobhan Ni Ghairbhith in 1999, whose herd now comprises around 220 Saanen, Toggenburg and British Alpine goats. An attractive log, St Tola owes much of its unique and distinctive flavour to the herb-rich grass and hay, supplemented with organic grains for the winter.

Voted Best Organic Cheese in 2002 and winning a silver medal at the 2008 British Cheese Awards, it is at first pale, fresh, mousse-like and lemony. Then it becomes denser, creamy and appealingly golden-rinded, yielding up its distinct, aromatic goaty nature and sweeter, nutty overtones.

St Tola also produce fresh goat's cheese buttons, a hard, Cheddar-style goat's cheese, and also a crumbly feta-style cheese. Despite all this delicious variety their original cheese, St Tola Log, is still my favourite!

Right: St Tola Log

Scottish Cheeses

Scotland has only a small number of indigenous cheeses. A harsh climate and rugged terrain are not conducive to the development of a cheese industry, although some soft cheeses were made by the crofters (tenant farmers). Caboc, the oldest of these, can be traced back to the fifteenth century. Crowdie, another soft cheese, is thought to have been introduced by the Vikings.

Dunlop, the only indigenous hard cheese, was first made in the time of James II by Barbara Gilmour, the most influential figure in Scottish cheese history. She learnt how to make cheese in Ireland, where she was driven at the time of the religious troubles. On her return to Scotland around 1688, she started making a sweet, milk cheese, which was named after the village in which she lived. The making of Dunlop went on to become a flourishing industry in the eighteenth and nineteenth centuries, then all but died out until Anne Dorward revived the tradition in the mid-1980s.

In the last 15 years there has, however, been a revolution in the Scottish cheese industry. Today there are over 30 different artisan cheeses. Ironically, the very qualities that mitigated against the industry in the past have become its strength. It is the toughness of the climate and terrain and the hardy nature of the milking animal that makes the new Scottish cheeses worthy of mention.

Caboc

Region: *Ross and Cromarty*
Type: *Traditional, farmhouse, vegetarian, fresh cheese*
Source: *Cow's milk*
Description: *900g/2lb chubby log rolled in oatmeal*
Culinary uses: *Table cheese; also spread on oatcakes*

Made with cream-enriched milk, Caboc is buttery and wickedly rich. The toasted oats give it a nutty, yeasty flavour. This is one of Scotland's indigenous cheeses, made to an ancient recipe. According to legend it was created by Mariota de Ile, daughter of a fifteenth-century MacDonald, Lord of the Isles. Caboc was popular for many years, but then went into decline. It was revived by Susannah Stone, a descendant of Mariota de Ile, in 1962.

Caboc ripens in five days and has a fat content of 69 per cent.

Cairnsmore

Region: *Dumfries and Galloway*
Type: *Modern, farmhouse, unpasteurized, hard cheese*
Source: *Sheep's milk (East Friesland)*
Description: *1.4kg/3lb truckle. The hard, crusty rind has rusty red ferments. Available with natural rind or clothbound*
Culinary use: *Table cheese*

This delicious sheep's milk cheese from Galloway Farmhouse Cheese looks irresistible with its sometimes slightly lopsided shape and wonderful, furry moulds that develop as it reaches maturity. The aroma hints of old leather and moss while the texture is firm, rather like Cheddar but slightly higher in moisture. Beautifully aromatic and decidedly nutty, with the sweetness of caramel and burnt toffee, Cairnsmore ripens in seven to nine months and is only made from April to October.

Criffel

Region: *Dumfries and Galloway*
Type: *Modern, farmhouse, unpasteurized, vegetarian, washed rind cheese*
Source: *Cow's milk*
Description: *1.6kg/3.5lb deeply ridge square with terracotta orange sticky rind and some grey moulds*
Culinary use: *Table cheese*

Loch Arthur Creamery make a superb hard cheese of the same name, a semi-soft cheese that looks like a dinosaur's tooth and this outstanding cheese with its pungent sticky orange rind and distinctly meaty aroma and taste. The firm, supple texture breaks down to a dense creaminess around the edges and the flavour becomes fuller and more pungent.

Above: Cairnsmore (left) and Caboc

Crowdie

Region: *Ross and Cromarty*
Type: *Traditional, farmhouse, vegetarian, fresh cheese*
Source: *Cow's milk*
Description: *125g/4½oz log; also packed in tubs*
Culinary uses: *Table cheese, baking, snacks and breakfast*

The author's wonderful Scottish granny, one of many pioneers to brave the long sea voyage to New Zealand in the late nineteenth century, used to make her own hand-churned butter by skimming the cream off the milk. The buttermilk went into her exquisite scones and from the skimmed milk she would make Crowdie.

Crowdie is thought to have been introduced into Scotland by the Vikings in the eighth century. It is called Gruth in Gaelic. Slightly sour-tasting, it has a creamy yet crumbly texture and collapses gently on the palate.

Cheesemaker Susannah Stone recently introduced a blend of Crowdie and double cream called Gruth Dhu (Black Crowdie). This is formed into oval shapes and covered in toasted pinhead oats and crushed peppercorns.

LEFT: *Dunlop*

DUNLOP

REGION: *Ayrshire*
TYPE: *Traditional, farmhouse, unpasteurized, vegetarian, hard cheese*
SOURCE: *Cow's milk (Ayrshire)*
DESCRIPTION: *250g/9oz round with pale yellow, natural, rind finely dusted with moulds*
CULINARY USE: *Table cheese*

Scotland's own hard cheese, originally made by Barbara Gilmour in the early eighteenth century, had all but disappeared until Anne Dorward started making traditional Dunlop again in the late 1980s. She was inspired when she discovered that she was living at the farm where it was first established. Firm yet springy, it is very mild and buttery, with the sweetness of fresh milk and a gentle acidity on the finish. It ripens in six months. Since then other Scottish cheesemakers have started making Dunlop, including Connage, Wester and Lawrenceton.

DUNSYRE BLUE

REGION: *Lanarkshire*
TYPE: *Modern, farmhouse, unpasteurized, vegetarian, blue cheese*
SOURCE: *Cow's milk (Ayrshire)*
DESCRIPTION: *1.4–1.8kg/3–4lb cylinder wrapped in foil. The moist, white rind attracts a variety of moulds*
CULINARY USE: *Table cheese*

Dunsyre Blue is wrapped in foil to keep its rind moist. When aged, the smooth, creamy-coloured interior is penetrated by chunky streaks of blue green mould that impart a delicious spicy tang to the cheese. The flavour is suggestive of the clover and grasses of the pastures where the cows graze. Dunsyre Blue ripens in six to 12 weeks and has a fat content of 45 per cent.

GALLOWAY GOAT'S MILK GEMS

REGION: *Dumfries and Galloway*
TYPE: *Modern, farmhouse, unpasteurized, fresh cheese*
SOURCE: *Goat's milk*
DESCRIPTION: *20g/3-4oz spheres*
CULINARY USES: *Table cheese, grilling, spreading, salads*

These tiny, pure white balls of fresh goat's cheese are marinated with fresh herbs and garlic in jars of olive oil. Although garlic is the overriding flavour, you can still identify the freshness of the herbs and the herbaceous, lemony character of the milk. The same cheese is available as a 450g/1lb round, coated in yellow wax. Very moist and crumbly, it melts in the mouth and has a subtle, goaty aroma and taste, with a slightly smoky finish.

ISLE OF MULL

REGION: *Isle of Mull*
TYPE: *Traditional, farmhouse, unpasteurized, hard cheese*
SOURCE: *Cow's milk*
DESCRIPTION: *25kg/55lb cylinder. The pale yellow rind bears the marks of the cloth in which it is bound*
CULINARY USES: *Table cheese, grating, grilling*

The milk from this part of Scotland produces a pale cheese, but its taste does not suffer from a lack of colour. Jeff Reade, who also makes Iona Cromag, a delicious ewe's milk cheese that is washed in Iona whisky, uses traditional methods but with a local twist: his herd, mainly Friesians with the odd Ayrshire and Jersey, are fed with hops in the winter months. The cheeses, having been bound in cloth, are matured for up to 12 months. Isle of Mull is very dense and packs a powerful punch – the classic Cheddar tang being laced with savoury overtones of garlic and onions, and a barely perceptible flavour of parsley and coriander (cilantro). It is also available in a gift size, flavoured with herbs, caraway seeds or peppers.

LANARK BLUE

REGION: *Lanarkshire*
TYPE: *Modern, farmhouse, unpasteurized, vegetarian, blue cheese*
SOURCE: *Sheep's milk*
DESCRIPTION: *1.4–1.8kg/3–4lb cylinder wrapped in foil. The moist, white rind has some grey and blue mould*
CULINARY USE: *Table cheese*

Cheesemaker Humphrey Errington, who also makes Dunsyre Blue, was the first person this century to milk sheep commercially in Scotland. His flock of 400 graze the wild heather pastures some 300 metres above the Clyde Valley. The unique grazing, coupled with Humphrey's skill and enthusiasm, produces an aromatic, slightly sweet yet pungent, Roquefort-style cheese. The superb, green-blue veins spreading through the cheese are the result of a Roquefort mould having been sprinkled into the milk vat before the cheese is curdled. It is then moulded by hand and allowed to mature for three months.

Lanark Blue is a past winner of a silver medal at the British Cheese Awards. It has a fat content of 45 per cent.

ABOVE: *Isle of Mull*

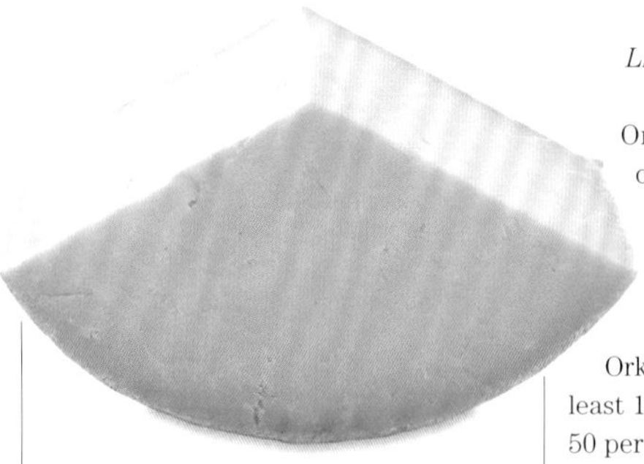

LEFT: Loch Arthur Farmhouse

LOCH ARTHUR FARMHOUSE

REGION: *Dumfries and Galloway*
TYPE: *Modern, farmhouse, unpasteurized, organic, vegetarian, hard cheese*
SOURCE: *Cow's milk*
DESCRIPTION: *9kg/20lb clothbound cylinder with pale brown-grey, natural rind*
CULINARY USE: *Table cheese*

Made by Loch Arthur Creamery, this is a traditionally made, clothbound Cheddar. Firm and quite dry, it melts in the mouth like hard chocolate, revealing a wonderful, nutty character overlaid by fresh, green shoots and a strong, fried-onion tang on the finish. Loch Arthur Farmhouse is less aggressive than mature Cheddars, so the fragrance and subtleties of the organic milk are able to come through.

Loch Arthur Farmhouse ripens in six to nine months and has a fat content of 48 per cent.

ORKNEY EXTRA MATURE CHEDDAR

REGION: *Orkney*
TYPE: *Traditional, creamery, hard cheese*
SOURCE: *Cow's milk*
DESCRIPTION: *20kg/44lb block cheese, without rind; also made in smaller rounds*
CULINARY USES: *Table cheese, grating, salads, snacks, sauces*

Produced on the island of Orkney, which is renowned for the richness and flavour of its milk, this was declared Best Scottish Cheese at the British Cheese Awards in 1996. An excellent example of a creamery-made cheese, it is strong-bodied and biteable, with the tiny crystals of calcium lactate sometimes found in well-aged, hard cheeses like Parmesan. Orkney Extra Mature is nutty and creamy, with a savoury, burnt-onion taste. It is no surprise that it has achieved around 9 per cent of the UK market, despite the distance it must travel.

Orkney Extra Mature is matured for at least 12 months and has a fat content of 50 per cent.

SERIOUSLY STRONG CHEDDAR

REGION: *Dumfries and Galloway*
TYPE: *Traditional, creamery, hard cheese*
SOURCE: *Cow's milk*
DESCRIPTION: *20kg/44lb block cheese, without rind*
CULINARY USES: *Table cheese, grilling, grating, sauces*

This blockbuster of a Cheddar is aged from 18 to 24 months and the flavour is strong and savoury, with a mouthwatering tang to balance the creamy richness. The texture is sometimes slightly crunchy, due to the calcium lactate crystals that form in old, hard cheeses. For the Scottish market it is coloured with annatto, while a "white" version is available for those on the English side of the border.

SKYE BLUE

REGION: *Ross-shire*
TYPE: *Farmhouse, blue cheese*
SOURCE: *Cow's milk*
DESCRIPTION: *900g/2lb drum with a thin, hard crust covered in a mix of blotchy grey and white patches*
CULINARY USE: *Table cheese*

Since the late 80s Kathy and David Biss have been making a wide variety of cheese, from cow's, goat's and ewe's milk in the isolated but beautiful Scottish Highlands.

Unable to resist experimenting, Kathy makes numerous cheeses and Skye Blue is her most recent. Chunks of widespread grey blue streaks through the smooth interior of this small drum give the cheese a salty, spicy tang that has hints of tarragon as it melts in the mouth.

STRATHDON BLUE

REGION: *Ross and Cromarty*
TYPE: *Modern, farmhouse, vegetarian, pasteurized, blue cheese*
SOURCE: *Cow's milk*
DESCRIPTION: *2.9kg/7lb round, creamy, golden and crusty*
CULINARY USE: *Table cheese*

When Ruaraidh Stone took over the management of the dairy from his parents in 1994, he was keen to introduce a blue cheese and in 1998 launched Strathdon Blue. Softer and milder than traditional English blues, it has a sticky rind that plays host to a multitude of moulds. The blue veins are well spread though not dense through the buttery interior, and the overall effect is a delicious, mellow aromatic blue.

SWEET MILK

REGION: *Morayshire*
TYPE: *Modern, farmhouse, unpasteurized, vegetarian cheese*
SOURCE: *Cow's milk*
DESCRIPTION: *3–4kg/7–9lb cylinder, deep yellow in colour*
CULINARY USES: *Table cheese, grilling, grating, sauces*

Pam Rodway at Wester Lawrenceton is passionate about food and especially traditional Scottish food so it was almost inevitable she would start cheesemaking with a classic Dunlop although Pam decided to call hers "sweet milk". An attractive tall cylinder, it is very sweet, buttery and mild with a lemony freshness on the finish that in late summer seems to take on the scent of the wild heather that gives the Scottish landscape its unique colour. Deep yellow in colour, it is smooth and dense with a texture slightly softer than Cheddar.

ABOVE: Orkney Extra Mature Cheddar

Welsh Cheeses

The most famous Welsh cheese – and the only traditional one still made – is Caerphilly, named after the Welsh mining village where it was first produced in 1831. With its high moisture content and raised salt content, it was the ideal cheese for the miners, replacing the salt lost as they sweated far below the pastures.

The economic advantages of this quick-ripening cheese were quickly recognized by the major Cheddar makers of Somerset. Cheddar, which was made in huge cylinders, took months to mature, occupying valuable space and creating cash-flow problems in the interim. Caerphilly, on the other hand, weighed less and, thanks to its high moisture content, ripened in a week but would keep for two to three months. The Somerset cheesemakers could make the small, Welsh cheeses in the summer months when milk was abundant, and still produce their Cheddars.

By the end of the Second World War production had all but ceased in Wales, having been taken up by the large factories in England. Uniformity of feed and pasteurization eroded the subtleties of Caerphilly, and in its block form it became almost indistinguishable from the other "crumblies" – Wensleydale, Lancashire and Cheshire.

Fortunately, with the revival of the old ways by a new generation of cheesemakers, including recent immigrants from Italy and Holland, authentic Welsh farmhouse Caerphilly is back on the shelves. New cheeses, such as Llangloffan and Pant ys Gawn are there too, together with Teifi, a buxom Gouda. Sheep's and goat's milk cheeses are on the increase and the fire is back in the Welsh dragon's tail.

Acorn

Region: *Cardiganshire*
Type: *Modern, farmhouse, unpasteurized, vegetarian, hard cheese*
Source: *Sheep's milk (East Friesland)*
Description: *1.8kg/4lb truckle with golden, crusty, natural rind*
Culinary uses: *Table cheese, grating*

Acorn is loosely based on an old-style Wensleydale. Firm yet crumbly, it melts in the mouth, releasing the flavours of cream caramel and crushed nuts, with a citrus finish. The cheese ripens in three to six months. It has a fat content of 52 per cent.

In addition to Acorn, cheesemakers Karen and Don Ross produce Skirrid, which is soaked in mead.

Above: *Caerphilly*

Caerphilly

Region: *South and West Wales*
Type: *Traditional, farmhouse, unpasteurized, vegetarian, hard cheese*
Source: *Cow's milk*
Description: *900g/2lb and 3.25kg/7lb wheels, with ivory-white rind dusted with fine flour. As the cheeses are aged in a moist cellar, the white and grey moulds become thicker and more leathery*
Culinary uses: *Table cheese, grilling, grating*

One of the four British cheeses fondly known as "the crumblies", Caerphilly is only lightly pressed and has a higher moisture content than other traditional British cheeses. It was first made in Caerphilly (Castle Town) in about 1831. The brine baths in which the cheese was soaked overnight sealed in the moisture, and the cheese proved popular with Welsh miners who had lost salt during their labours.

One of the best-known producers today is the Duckett family of Walnut Farm in Somerset, who have been making traditional Caerphilly for generations. When young, their Caerphilly has a fresh, citrus taste with a background of crushed bracken and riverside reeds. The texture is moist, friable yet supple, like a school eraser. With maturity, the edges become wonderfully creamy, and the flavour becomes more rounded. Duckett's Caerphilly won a silver medal at the 1996 British Cheese Awards.

Other traditional makers include Caws Cenarth, Glynhynod Farmhouse Cheese, Nantybwla and Abergavenny Fine Foods. Caws Cenarth has converted an old barn into a cheese room with a special viewing gallery for visitors.

While a good factory-made Cheddar can still retain some of the character of a traditionally made cheese, the same cannot be said of Caerphilly. It is worth seeking out the traditionally made cheese, which is not only delectable in its own right, but also makes a marvellous ploughman's lunch or Welsh rarebit.

LEFT: Gorau glas

Celtic Promise

REGION: *Carmarthenshire*
TYPE: *Modern, farmhouse, unpasteurized, vegetarian, semi-soft cheese*
SOURCE: *Cow's milk*
DESCRIPTION: *500g/1¼lb round. The smooth, brine-washed rind ranges from orange to terracotta and has a dusting of moulds*
CULINARY USE: *Table cheese*

John and Patrice Savage-Ontswedder only recently started making this small, dumpling-shaped, washed-rind cheese under the guidance of the "inventor", James Aldridge. James is one of Britain's most talented cheesemakers, who willingly passes on his legendary knowledge to those who are willing to work hard and listen attentively.

Once drained, the young, freshly shaped curds are washed, rubbed or smeared with brine to encourage and spread the growth of the orange-pink moulds that contribute to the taste and texture of the final cheese. Supple, smooth, spicy, aromatic and pungent, Celtic Promise is absolutely delicious and is a past winner of a bronze medal at the British Cheese Awards. Available only from some specialist cheese shops, it ripens in about eight weeks.

Cilowen Organic

REGION: *Carmarthen*
TYPE: *Modern, farmhouse, vegetarian, organic, hard cheese*
SOURCE: *Cow's milk (Jersey/Friesian)*
DESCRIPTION: *3.5kg/8lb truckle. Natural, thin grey crust with a dusting of white and brown moulds*
CULINARY USES: *Table cheese, grilling, baking*

Sue and Huw Jones of Llanboidy Cheesemakers began cheesemaking in 1985 using unpasteurized milk from their herd of Red Poll cattle. However, in 2007 they sold their herd to concentrate on making Cilowen, a truly tasty organic cheese from their Jersey and Friesian herd. Winner of the British Cheese Award for Best Organic Cheese in 2001 and also for Best Welsh Cheese in 2002, it has a hard, compact, Cheddar-like texture but with its own distinct savoury character that hints of wild onions and fresh green pastures. Their cows graze on organic land and the use of red clover as a natural fertilizer gives the cheese a special flavour.

LEFT: Celtic Promise

Gorau Glas

REGION: *Anglesey*
TYPE: *Modern, farmhouse, vegetarian, blue cheese*
SOURCE: *Cow's milk*
DESCRIPTION: *400g/16oz drum. Thin sticky rind covered in a coat of blue-green mould*
CULINARY USES: *Table cheese, salads*

With a herd of over 100 Friesian cows producing an abundance of beautiful milk it was almost inevitable that Margaret and Richard Davies turned to cheesemaking in 2002 when the price of milk dropped to an all-time low. Like many new cheesemakers, Margaret started with a Camembert style but quickly decided she wanted to make a blue and so Gorau Glas was born. Beneath its rustic crust the thick streaks of blue-green mould work their magic turning the firm, dense interior into a soft, almost squishy cheese with a sharp and tangy finish that hints of wild herbs, the apricot scent of gorse flowers and rugged pastures.

Lancych

REGION: *Dyfed*
TYPE: *Modern, farmhouse, vegetarian, organic, hard cheese*
SOURCE: *Cow's milk*
DESCRIPTION: *1.8–2.2kg/4–5lb drum. Smooth, natural grey-beige rind with imprint of the cloth*
CULINARY USES: *Table cheese, grating, grilling*

Gwynfor and Thelma Adams have been farming in the heart of west Wales for over 40 years. Their cheesemaking business, established in 1987, is acknowledged to have led to the revival of Welsh Farmhouse Caerphilly, and Caws Cenarth is now the oldest established producer of this cheese.

Lancych is a Cheddar-style cheese but with a more open texture that feels smooth and buttery in the mouth. It is mellow and creamy with a pleasant, tangy acidity and a suggestion of fresh green grass.

Llanboidy

REGION: *Pembrokeshire*
TYPE: *Modern, farmhouse, unpasteurized, vegetarian, hard cheese*
SOURCE: *Cow's milk (Red Poll)*
DESCRIPTION: *4.5kg/10lb wheel. The crusty yellow rind has some mould*
CULINARY USES: *Table cheese, grilling*

Sue Jones, the cheesemaker, is a past winner of a silver medal at the British Cheese Awards for this Cheddar-like cheese. It is firm yet crumbly and has a dense and creamy consistency. The aroma is of fresh cut hay and meadows and the cheese has a mouthwatering, sharp, green and grassy tang. Llanboidy ripens in two to four months.

RIGHT: Pant ys Gawn

Pant ys Gawn

REGION: *Monmouthshire*
TYPE: *Modern, farmhouse, vegetarian, fresh cheese*
SOURCE: *Goat's milk*
DESCRIPTION: *100g/3¾oz disc or log*
CULINARY USES: *Table cheese, snacks, grilling, spreading, salads*

This small, delightful, goat's milk cheese has a very clean, fresh, citrus flavour with a tantalizing suggestion of tarragon. The texture resembles that of fromage frais.

The soft, moist curds are carefully drained in tiny moulds and are ready for sale in only a few days, yet with clever packaging the cheeses have a remarkably long shelf life. Pant ys Gawn is now sold quite extensively in supermarkets throughout Britain – its mild, goaty flavour has a wide appeal. Varieties of the cheese include mixed herbs, cracked black peppercorns, and garlic and chives. The producer, Abergavenny Fine Foods Limited, also makes Castle Meadow Caerphilly, Welsh Goat's Log (a log-shaped version of Pant ys Gawn), St David's (a spicy semi-soft cheese), and a number of blended or speciality cheeses.

Perl Las

REGION: *Dyfed*
TYPE: *Modern, farmhouse, vegetarian, organic, blue cheese*
SOURCE: *Cow's milk*
DESCRIPTION: *600g–2.5kg/1.5–7lb rounds. Thin dry rind covered in grey and blue moulds*
CULINARY USES: *Table cheese, salads*

Another great cheese from Caws Cenarth and winner of the Best Export Cheese in 2005, this is almost as dense and firm as Stilton, becoming softer with age. Thick purple-blue blotches and streaks run through the buttery yellow interior giving it a stronger, snappy, peppery bite with a finish like burnt onions and a hot lingering peppery acidity.

Sancler Organic

REGION: *Carmarthen*
TYPE: *Traditional, farmhouse, vegetarian, organic, fresh cheese*
SOURCE: *Cow's milk (Dutch red and white cows)*
DESCRIPTION: *150g/5oz pots*
CULINARY USES: *Grilling, baking, spreading, snacks, soups, dips*

The milk comes from a single herd of Dutch red and white cows that graze the valleys along the rugged, windswept coast of South West Wales, warmed by the sea currents of the Atlantic. A lactic cheese, it is coagulated not by rennet but by a probiotic yogurt culture giving the cheese a delicate, fine, almost weightless texture that seems to float over the palate. It is milky with a refreshing citrus zing and although salt is added you can almost taste the sea breezes. Sancler is also available with chives, or basil and garlic. It has a fat content of 24 per cent.

Teifi

REGION: *Carmarthenshire*
TYPE: *Modern, farmhouse, unpasteurized, organic, vegetarian, hard cheese*
SOURCE: *Cow's milk*
DESCRIPTION: *450g/1lb, 900g/2lb and 3.5–4.5kg/8–10lb millstones with smooth, polished, natural rind*
CULINARY USES: *Table cheese, snacks, grating*

Similar to Gouda in both shape and texture, Teifi has a deep sunshine-yellow interior. Firm, dense and fairly fruity when young, the cheese becomes hard and almost flaky when mature. The flavour intensifies and tingles the tastebuds with a suggestion of bitter chocolate and young celery. Made by John and Patrice Savage-Ontswedder, Teifi ripens in two to nine months. A smoked version of the cheese is also produced, as are versions flavoured with nettles and cumin.

Spanish Cheeses

Wherever you go in Spain, from the vast, barren plains of Extremadura to the majestic beauty of the Sierra Nevada, you will find wonderful cheeses. At the last count, there were more than 600, many owing their idiosyncratic nature to the numerous varieties of indigenous sheep, cows and goats that have developed over the centuries.

In 1988, aware that this marvellous heritage could easily be lost as a new generation of Spaniards turned its back on tradition and moved to the cities, the government initiated an ambitious survey. Its aim was to catalogue every cheese made in Spain. Much of the survey had to be carried out on horseback or on foot, in order to reach artisan cheesemakers in isolated, mountain regions whose cheeses had been made for centuries, but were unknown in the wider world.

Recipes were compared, and eventually 81 distinct varieties of cheese were identified. A national quality-control system, Denominación de Origen (DO) was introduced. This regulates where a specific cheese must be made, which breed of animal must supply the milk, exactly how the cheese must be made and what size it must conform to. It also details any distinguishing characteristics. Similar to the systems that exist in France and Italy, it protects producers and consumers from inferior or foreign copies, as only those cheeses that meet the criteria may carry the official stamp on their rind.

Discovering this astonishing bounty can be a wonderful pilgrimage for the cheese lover. Northern Spain, from Galicia on the Atlantic coast to Catalonia on the Mediterranean, offers the most extensive choice, but the Basque Country, with over 40 different cheeses, should not be neglected. Follow St James' Way, a network of byways that stretches for about 800km/500 miles over Roman causeways, medieval cattle tracks, through ruins and walled cities, and discover delectable cheeses that have been made in virtually the same way for over a thousand years.

The Spanish are warm and welcoming. The food is fascinating and enjoying it amounts to a way of life. Stop in one of the many tapas bars and sample slivers of the local cheese with slices of air-dried Serrano ham, a dish of marinated red peppers and some fresh anchovies. Add a glass of fino sherry – heaven!

Below: Mahon

Afuega'l Pitu

Region: *Asturias*
Type: *Traditional, farmhouse, unpasteurized, fresh cheese*
Source: *Cow's milk*
Description: *500g/1¼lb cone or pumpkin-shape. The rind is buff to deep orange in colour and has a dusting of white mould*
Culinary use: *Table cheese*

When the author was first offered a taste of this innocent-looking cheese in a tapas bar, she was unaware of its reputation. Local Asturians hooted with laughter as she took a bite – then reached for a glass of fruity León wine to quench the fire. It was only then that they translated the name: Afuega'l Pitu means "a fire in the gut". Fresh red chilli pepper is added to the cheese and more is rubbed into the rind as the cheese is allowed to mature. The pumpkin or bishop's mitre shape is obtained by straining the cheese in a cloth that is knotted at the top, rather than folded. A plain version of the cheese is also made. Both are well worth trying.

Burgos

Region: *Castile-León*
Type: *Traditional, farmhouse and creamery, unpasteurized, fresh cheese*
Source: *Cow's and sheep's milk*
Description: *1–2kg/2¼–4½lb wheel with corrugated grooves down the sides and ridged wedges marked on the top and bottom*
Culinary uses: *Baking; also often eaten for dessert, with sugar and honey*

This fresh cheese takes its name from the Castilian city that used to hold a weekly market. Throughout the winter and spring, farmers from the surrounding areas would gather at the market to sell their sheep's milk cheese. Ready within hours of being made, Burgos, also known as Requeson, is pure white, smooth and slightly rubbery. It tastes of fresh milk, with a hint of acidity and salt. If you can, find a hand-made example. The markings on the cheese come from the moulds into which the fresh curd is pressed.

Cabrales (DO)

Region: *Asturias*
Type: *Traditional, farmhouse, unpasteurized, blue cheese*
Source: *Cow's, sheep's or goat's milk*
Description: 3kg/6½lb cylinder with natural rind, wrapped in either maple leaves or foil
Culinary uses: *Table cheese; also served for dessert, with honey*

This, Spain's best-known blue cheese, is made by hand in the north-east corner of the Picos de Europa (Peaks of Europe) where rugged mountain peaks tower above beech, oak and birch forests. The best cheeses are produced in spring and summer, when the shepherds take their animals to the high pastures and the cheese is made from a mixture of cow's, goat's and sheep's milk. In winter, when only cow's milk is available, the cheese lacks the wonderful complexity of the mixed-milk version.

The cheese was traditionally wrapped in maple or plane tree leaves, which covered the coarse, sticky, orange-yellow rind, with its pervasive aroma. Today, foil is used as it holds the cheese together better. The inside can be off-white or yellow, with brown around the edges. It is streaked like a banana cake, with irregular lines and patches of crunchy, grey-green to purple-blue mould. The texture is unusually complex: soft and creamy, yet grainy and almost crumbly. The pungent smell suggests fermenting fruit, moulds and yeast, and the cheese has a spicy, lip-smacking finish.

Cabrales is ripened in natural limestone caverns for two to three months. The rind is penetrated with rods to encourage the blue mould naturally present in the caves (*Penicillium glaucum*) to penetrate the rind. The locals are said to prefer the cheese at six months old, when it is almost totally blue and *con gustano* (with maggots). This the author has not experienced, nor does she intend to!

Similar cheeses include Picos de Europa and Valdeon.

Castellano

Region: *Castile-León*
Type: *Traditional, farmhouse and creamery, unpasteurized, hard cheese*
Source: *Sheep's milk (Churro and Castilian)*
Description: *1–3kg/2¼–6½lb round (half cylinder). The pale fawn, natural rind is marked with the zigzag pattern of the draining hoop*
Culinary uses: *Table cheese: serve with the classic Spanish quince cheese – membrilla – whose fruity tang makes it the perfect companion*

Castile-León is now the largest cheesemaking region in Spain, accounting for 85 per cent of pure sheep's milk cheeses. Like Manchego, Castellano is a hooped cheese, which means that the fresh curds are drained in special plastic hoops, which leave distinctive zigzag marks on the rind. The top and base of the artisan cheeses also carry a motif or design from the carved wooden or plastic bases, which are placed below the cheese as it drains in the hoops. The motif (a flower, geometric pattern or pair of initials) identifies the cheesemaker – or did. Today, as more of the cheeses are made in factories or cooperatives, the size and shape of Castellano is becoming more uniform, confusing shoppers accustomed to recognizing their favourite cheese by the markings on the rind.

Extremes of climate, the distinctive milk of the Churro and Castilian sheep and the origin of the individual cheesemaker's recipe all contribute to the character of the artisan cheese. The pale yellow interior of a good Castellano is firm and dense. Compared to Manchego, it is quite moist, and has a few rice-sized holes. The wonderfully delicate, cream-caramel taste is perfectly offset by the fresh acidity and hint of salt.

Cuajada

Region: *Various*
Type: *Traditional, farmhouse and creamery, fresh cheese*
Source: *Sheep's and goat's milk*
Description: *Sold in pots of various sizes*
Culinary uses: *Use instead of yogurt; often served with honey or fruit for breakfast*

Cuajada originally came from northern Navarre, where the shepherds used the local thistle rather than animal rennet to coagulate the milk. This gave the traditional cheese a unique and more floppy consistency than the modern equivalent, which is made, like junket, by adding rennet to fresh milk and then heating it gently. The mixture is poured into small, earthenware or plastic pots, where it sets lightly.

Left: Cuajada – this fresh cheese is widely available in Spanish supermarkets

Above: Garrotxa

Garrotxa

Region: *Catalonia*
Type: *Modern, farmhouse, unpasteurized, hard cheese*
Source: *Goat's milk*
Description: *1kg/2¼lb round with natural rind covered in thick, furry, grey mould*
Culinary use: *Table cheese*

Disillusioned with the stress of city life, a steady stream of professionals in many industrialized countries have moved to the country, bringing their entrepreneurial skills to a range of enterprises, including cheesemaking.

Although this cheese is based on an old recipe, it has been developed and marketed using modern methods by several groups of what the Spanish people refer to as "neo-rurals" working together as a co-operative in a village north of Barcelona.

Garrotxa is one of the author's favourites. The pure white milk seems to have absorbed the flavour of fresh walnuts and the scent of mimosa, while retaining the fresh crispness of young grass. The texture is firm yet springy, becoming smooth and velvety as you reach for more.

Idiazabal (DO)

Region: *Basque and Navarre*
Type: *Traditional, farmhouse and co-operative, unpasteurized, hard cheese*
Source: *Sheep's milk (Lacha and Carranzana)*
Description: *1–3kg/2¼–6½lb cylinder. Pale yellow to amber in colour, the natural rind is smooth and hard*
Culinary uses: *Table cheese, grilling, grating, tapas*

For centuries Idiazabal has been made by shepherds in the high mountain pastures of the Urbia and Aralar mountains. It was traditionally sold at the end of September, when the shepherds and their herds of sheep were forced down from the mountains by the first snows of winter.

The cheese has a compact texture, with a few pinprick holes. It is dry, but not crumbly, and feels pleasantly oily in the mouth. The rind carries the marks of the wooden moulds in which it is drained.

The characteristic, smoky flavour was originally the result of the cheeses having been stored near the shepherds' night fires. There were no chimneys in the simple mountain huts, so the cheeses absorbed the sweet, aromatic smoke.

Artisan cheesemakers continue to make the cheese in the way their fathers and grandfathers did, but Idiazabal is also produced industrially. Producers wishing to carry the DOs stamp of approval must, however, adhere to traditional methods.

Mahon (DO)

Region: *Minorca*
Type: *Traditional, farmhouse and creamery, unpasteurized, hard cheese*
Source: *Cow's milk (Friesian)*
Description: *1–4kg/2¼–9lb square with rounded edges. The hard, orange rind carries the imprint of the cheesecloth and tends to be greasy*
Culinary uses: *Table cheese, grating (especially over pasta), snacks*

This cheese comes from Minorca, one of the Balearic Islands off the north-east coast of Spain. It was originally made from the local sheep's milk, but during the brief British occupation in the eighteenth century, cattle were shipped in and the local cheesemakers were persuaded to change to cow's milk.

Although the unpasteurized cheese is sold fresh, a few days after being made, it is at its most bold and delicious when age has given it a hard and slightly granular texture, like that of Parmesan. The ivory interior, with its small, irregular holes, contrasts with the bright orange rind whose colour comes not from bacteria, but from being rubbed with butter, paprika and oil. The taste is sharp, with a salty tang due to the proximity of the grazing to the sea. Some of the traditional cheesemakers add a small proportion of sheep's milk to their cheese.

The curd is piled in the centre of a cloth square, alternate corners are knotted and twisted together and the cheese is pressed for a few days. This gives the cheese its characteristic "cushion" shape and the indentation in the centre.

Mahon is sold at various stages of maturity. If fresh, it must be consumed within 10 days. The semi-cured cheese has been matured for at least two months, while the cured cheese has been matured for five months and the aged cheese for 10 months. Pasteurized Mahon is also available. It is usually sold young, when the texture is smooth and supple and the aroma is sweet and fruity.

Right: Idiazabal

Manchego (DO)

Region: *La Mancha*
Type: *Traditional, farmhouse and creamery, hard cheese*
Source: *Sheep's milk (La Mancha)*
Description: *2–3.5kg/4½–8lb cylinder with flat surfaces. The natural rind is distinctively patterned*
Culinary uses: *Table cheese, grating, grilling*

The plains where the legendary Don Quixote tilted at windmills and protected the shepherds from attack by marauding bandits are now irrigated. There are vineyards where once only the hardy La Mancha sheep survived. Much has changed, but the sheep are still there, grazing on the shrubs and grasses of the Dahesa and producing the thick, aromatic milk that gives Manchego its character.

This remarkable cheese has been made in La Mancha since the time of the Romans. However, it is now produced in large, modern co-operatives and the milk is frequently pasteurized, but this has not markedly altered the flavour.

To qualify for the famous Manchego label, the cheese must be firm and dry, yet rich and creamy. Only sheep's milk from La Mancha may be used. The distinctive pattern on the waxed rind – originally the result of encircling the curd with a plaited (braided) band of esparto grass – must be visible. (The colour of the wax denotes the age of the cheese.) The interior should be ivory in colour, with small, irregular eyes. The complexity of the flavour will depend on the age of the cheese, but there should be a richness, reminiscent of Brazil nuts and burnt caramel, with a slightly salty finish. The aroma should suggest lanolin and roast lamb.

Manchego is sold at various stages of maturity: at the age of 13 weeks, it is described as *curado* (cured) and when over three months old, it is referred to as *viego* (aged). There is a peppery bite to cheeses that have reached a great age.

Below: Manchego, from left, aged for 4 months, 6 months and 10 months

Mato

Region: *Catalonia*
Type: *Traditional, farmhouse, fresh cheese*
Source: *Goat's and cow's milk*
Description: *1–2kg/2¼–4½lb bowl-shaped cheese; also sold in pots*
Culinary uses: *Cooking, as a breakfast cheese, snacks*

This fresh cheese resembles fromage frais. It has a delicate citrus and herb tang. No salt is added before it is potted or drained in basketweave moulds shaped like pudding basins, so it does not keep long. Often made at home, it is used for both savoury and sweet dishes, and is freqently served with honey, aniseed and fruits.

Penamellera

Region: *Asturias*
Type: *Traditional, farmhouse and co-operative, natural-rind cheese*
Source: *Cow's, goat's or sheep's milk*
Description: 500g/1¼lb disc. The thin, wrinkled, yellowish-orange crust has a dusting of fine, white mould
Culinary uses: *Table cheese, snacks*

Named after the high peak that rises behind the village where the cheese has been made for centuries, Penamellera has a slightly greasy appearance and oddly meaty smell. The interior is more elegant. Supple and dense, with a few small, irregular holes, it has a mellow, vaguely nutty taste. The finish is fresh and lemony.

Similar cheeses include Quesuco, Porua and the locally produced Rozagas. In 1984 concern that the number of local producers was gradually dwindling led some Asturian farmers to form a co-operative to market their unique cheese. Production has increased and Penemellera is now well known throughout northern Spain.

Picos de Europa (DO)

Region: *Cantabria*
Type: *Traditional, farmhouse and creamery, blue cheese*
Source: *Cow's milk*
Description: *3kg/6½lb cylinder with natural rind wrapped in plane tree leaves*
Culinary uses: *Table cheese, often eaten with wild honey*

The recipe for this creamy, moist cheese is thought to have been brought to Spain by early French pilgrims as they followed St James' Way to the Atlantic coast.

Picos de Europa is usually made from cow's milk, but farmhouse cheesemakers will add a little goat's or sheep's milk, as available. The cheese has blue-green veins, a pungent aroma, a pleasantly salty bite and a clean, piquant finish. Wrapped in plane leaves, it gives a cheeseboard a rustic yet elegant look. If the rind darkens and becomes sticky, pat it dry and leave it in a cool place to breathe for a few hours.

Also known as Valdeon, Picos de Europa ripens in two to three months and has a fat content of 45 per cent.

Queso Iberico (DO)

Region: *Central Spain*
Type: *Modern, creamery, hard cheese*
Source: *Cow's, goat's and sheep's milk*
Description: *3kg/6½lb wheel. The hard, dry rind bears the marks of the esparto (plaited/braided grass) bands used in the draining process*
Culinary uses: *Table cheese, grating, grilling, snacks*

The mixture of cow's, goat's and sheep's milk gives this modern, uniquely Spanish cheese a truly three-dimensional character. Regulations require that it contain not less than 25 per cent and not more than 40 per cent of any one type of milk, and the flavour has elements of all three.

The creamy texture melts in the mouth gradually, releasing a rich, full-bodied nuttiness before delivering a fruity tang on the finish. It is made by large consortiums, in much the same way as Manchego. It is sometimes mistaken for Manchego, partly because the cheese looks very similar and also because the words "Manchego Blend" appear on some labels. Queso Iberico ripens in one to six months.

Queso Ibores

Region: *Extremadura*
Type: *Traditional, farmhouse and co-operative, unpasteurized, hard cheese*
Source: *Goat's milk (Retinta and Verata)*
Description: *3kg/6½lb round. The smooth, reddish-brown, natural rind is rubbed with oil and paprika*
Culinary uses: *Table cheese, tapas*

Queso Ibores takes its name from the area in Extremadura – Los Ibores – where it has been made since Roman times. The unusual, deep red of the rind provides a wonderful contrast to the pure white interior. The aroma of the paprika is distinctive and penetrates the cheese as a subtle spicy tang. This is offset by the aromatic and creamy nature of the goat's milk.

Queso Majorero

Region: *Fuerteventura*
Type: *Traditional, farmhouse and co-operative, unpasteurized, hard cheese*
Source: *Goat's milk*
Description: *5–7kg/11–15¼lb cylinder. The pale amber, natural rind has a geometric pattern printed at top and bottom*
Culinary uses: *Table cheese, grilling*

Also known as Queso Fuerteventura, from the barren yet beautiful island on which it is made, this cheese is one of the author's favourites. Firmly pressed to create the hard texture, its tough rind bears the traditional marks typical of many Spanish cheeses. Although the interior seems dense, it melts in the mouth to leave a trail that suggests wild honey, the scent of wild thyme and almonds. The finish is peppery and rounded, like a fine, red wine. It is excellent with a fino sherry or robust red wine.

Fuerteventura, like all the Canary Islands, is short of water, yet the prickly pear, thistles, cacti and straggly bushes provide the native goat with a veritable feast. The arid conditions mean a reduced milk yield, but the flavour of the milk is intensely aromatic, almost perfumed.

Below: Queso Iberico

Above: Queso Majorero

Queso de Murcia

Region: *Murcia*
Type: *Traditional, farmhouse and co-operative, fresh cheese*
Source: *Goat's milk*
Description: *1–2kg/2¼–4½lb pure white, round cheese with indented ridges from the wooden bases on which it drains*
Culinary uses: *Table cheese, cooking*

Driving through hot, barren Murcia, one could be forgiven for wondering what the straggly flocks of sheep and goats find to eat in the gravelly soil. Closer inspection reveals tough scrub and intensely scented wild thyme, oregano, rosemary and other hardy plants, each contributing to the flavour of the milk. The low moisture content of the grazing also means that the yield of milk is low, but rich and thick and ideal for cheesemaking.

Queso de Murcia is pure white, with innumerable small holes. The texture is spongy and the cheese is subtly flavoured with rosemary and tarragon, balanced by a refreshing acidity. The fresh cheese has been made in the same way for centuries, but because it has a short shelf life and does not travel well, the local government decided to create a cured or aged local cheese that would keep well and have a wider appeal outside the region and abroad. The result was Queso de Murcia al Vino, a delicious and highly successful cheese, made by washing the cheese in the local red wine. The naturally porous rind takes on a deep burgundy colour and the cheese absorbs the fruity, slightly spicy flavour and aroma of the wine.

QUESO DEL MONTSEC

REGION: *Catalonia*
TYPE: *Modern, farmhouse, unpasteurized, vegetarian, soft-white cheese*
SOURCE: *Goat's milk*
DESCRIPTION: *2kg/4½lb round with rustic-looking, patchy rind coated with wood ash*
CULINARY USE: *Table cheese*

Like Garrotxa, this was developed by a group of young professionals who were looking for a more meaningful lifestyle for themselves and their families. The press dubbed them "neo-rurals" and did not always take them seriously, but had to reconsider when they successfully made and marketed Montsec.

The cheese has a dense, fairly grainy texture that feels very creamy in the mouth, yet has a definite bite. The distinctive taste of goat's milk is instantly apparent, and the cheese has a strong, herbaceous, spicy finish.

Queso del Montsec requires two to three months to ripen. It is also known as Cendrat.

QUESO DEL TIETAR

REGION: *Avila*
TYPE: *Traditional, farmhouse, unpasteurized, fresh or hard cheese*
SOURCE: *Goat's milk*
DESCRIPTION: *Fresh – in pots; aged – in 2.5kg/5½lb cylinders. The natural rind on the aged cheese is blue-grey*
CULINARY USES: *Table cheese, cooking (fried with the local pequilla peppers, garlic and plum tomatoes, it makes a perfect partner for pasta)*

Seldom found outside Avila, Queso del Tietar comes in two distinct styles. The fresh cheese is called Cabra del Tietar. Sold when it is only a few days old, the cheese is pure white and rindless, with a lemon-fresh flavour that hints at the aromatic goat's milk. It is often mixed with wild thyme, oregano and rosemary or paprika.

If the cheese is aged for two to three months, the texture hardens. It resembles Sierra de Zuheros and is firm but spongy, with a pronounced, nutty flavour.

RONCAL (DO)

REGION: *Navarra*
TYPE: *Traditional, farmhouse and co-operative, unpasteurized, hard cheese*
SOURCE: *Sheep's milk (Lacha and Aragon)*
DESCRIPTION: *2kg/4½lb wheel with hard, natural rind covered with a velvety-smooth layer of blue-grey mould*
CULINARY USES: *Table cheese, tapas, grating, grilling*

Roncal was the first Spanish cheese to be awarded the protection of the Denominacion de Origen, but regulation of its production goes back to the thirteenth century, when the local council controlled the movement of the indigenous Lacha and Aragon sheep. In July, the animals were taken to the summer alpine pastures, returning at the end of September. On 13 October they were on the move again, this time to the winter pastures in the south of Navarre, where they remained until 15 May.

This migratory pattern (transhumance) is still practised by a few shepherds, but change of ownership or usage of the land makes it difficult. In 1974 a cheese factory was set up near Pamplona to ensure that this delicious cheese would continue to be produced.

Roncal is aged for at least four months and has a fat content of 45 per cent. The firm, elastic interior is slightly grainy, with small, irregular holes. The flavour owes much to the richness of the milk. Distinctly "sheepy" and quite pungent, it retains a sweet, herbaceous flavour, thanks to the natural pastures of wild grasses, herbs and flowers on which the sheep graze.

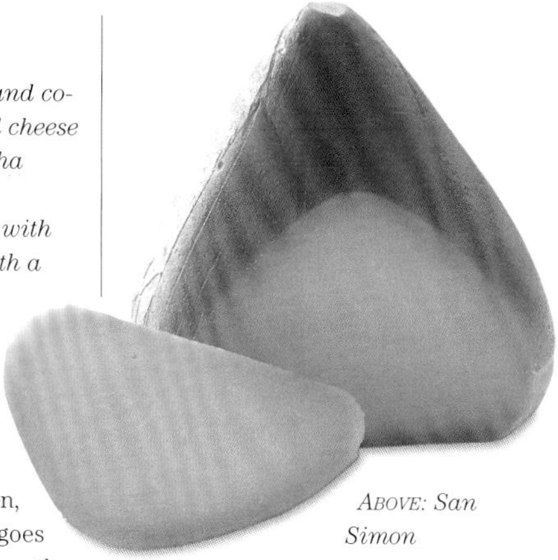

ABOVE: San Simon

SAN SIMON

REGION: *Galicia*
TYPE: *Traditional, farmhouse and creamery, semi-soft cheese*
SOURCE: *Cow's milk (Galicia)*
DESCRIPTION: *1–2kg/2¼–4½lb pear shape with glossy, honey-coloured, natural rind*
CULINARY USE: *Table cheese*

Another quirky Spanish cheese, this has the shape of a bullet or a pear. Enquiries as to the origin of its shape provoke wide grins or unprintable stories, but it has been made for generations on the western tip of Spain, where the lush, green pastures nourish the Galacia cows.

San Simon is lightly pressed, then smoked. It has a supple, open consistency and an attractive, polished rind, which ranges in colour from honey to reddish-brown. The smoke gives the cheese a woody taste to add to the buttery quality and slight acidity from the milk.

ABOVE: Queso del Montsec – also known as Cendrat

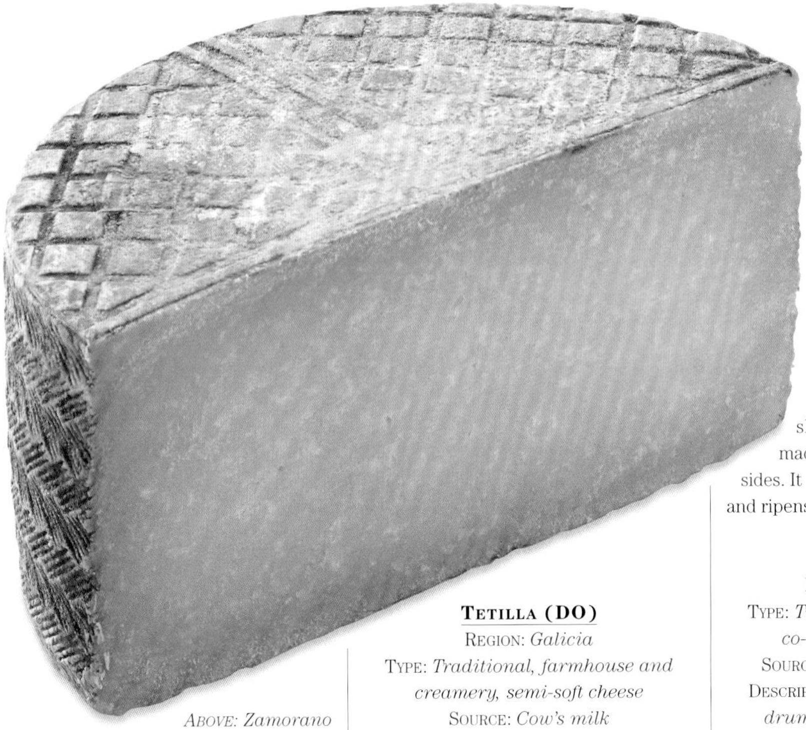

ABOVE: Zamorano

SIERRA DE ZUHEROS

REGION: *Andalusia*
TYPE: *Traditional, farmhouse and creamery, hard cheese*
SOURCE: *Goat's milk (Murcia)*
DESCRIPTION: *1kg/2¼lb cylinder with smooth, pale yellow, hard rind*
CULINARY USES: *Table cheese, tapas*

Sierra de Zuheros is made from the milk of the Murcia goat on small farms and co-operatives near the old town of Trujillo. Like many Spanish cheeses, it was traditionally moulded in hoops made of plaited (braided) esparto grass. Today, these are slowly being replaced by plastic moulds, which have the distinctive pattern imprinted on the inside. They look rather incongruous hanging up against ancient stone walls.

The cheese is dry, fine and almost crumbly. It has a discernible but not pervasive goaty character, with hints of sweet smoke, wild thyme and lemon zest. The rind of Sierra de Zuheros is sometimes rubbed with paprika and oil, which gives the cheese a spicy finish.

TETILLA (DO)

REGION: *Galicia*
TYPE: *Traditional, farmhouse and creamery, semi-soft cheese*
SOURCE: *Cow's milk*
DESCRIPTION: *750g–1.5kg/1¾–3¼lb pear-shaped cheese with pale yellow, ridged rind*
CULINARY USE: *Table cheese*

Tetilla looks like a large, finely ridged fig or breast – hence the name. Made from cow's milk, it has a mellow, fresh, lemony taste with a hint of green grass. The consistency is supple, with a creamy feel on the palate. It ripens in two to three weeks.

TRONCHON

REGION: *Aragon*
TYPE: *Traditional, farmhouse and creamery, semi-soft cheese*
SOURCE: *Sheep's, cow's or goat's milk*
DESCRIPTION: *600g–1.5kg/1⅓–3¼lb flattened globe with deep crater. The natural rind is smooth, glossy and the colour of butter*
CULINARY USES: *Table cheese, grilling, snacks*

In terms of texture, Tronchon resembles a young Caerphilly. The taste is aromatic, with a background of white wine acidity. The origin of the shape is obscure, but it is replicated today with special moulds.

ULLOA

REGION: *Galicia*
TYPE: *Traditional, farmhouse, semi-soft cheese*
SOURCE: *Cow's milk (Galicia and Friesian)*
DESCRIPTION: *1kg/2¼lb round with smooth, waxy, pale yellow, natural rind*
CULINARY USE: *Table cheese*

Ulloa is almost identical to Tetilla, differing only in the shape and the area where it is made. Ulloa is round, with convex sides. It has a fat content of 45 per cent and ripens in about one month.

ZAMORANO (DO)

REGION: *Castile-León*
TYPE: *Traditional, farmhouse and co-operative, hard cheese*
SOURCE: *Sheep's milk (Churro)*
DESCRIPTION: *2 or 3kg/4½ or 6½lb drum. The hard, dry, natural rind is covered in a thin, grey mould*
CULINARY USE: *Table cheese*

A hard sheep's milk cheese, Zamorano has something in common with both Castellano and Manchego, but is less grainy. It is matured in conditions of high humidity in order to encourage the growth of the natural, grey mould rind. The flavour has the appealing intensity of burnt caramel and green grass, balanced by the buttery nature of the milk.

Until late this century, Zamoran shepherds and their families were itinerant cheesemakers, trekking from farm to farm with their rennet, hoops, hand-carved wooden boards and curdling vats. The cheeses they made were often matured in the deep, humid, underground "caves" of neighbouring vineyards, which imparted a musty yet fruity character to the cheese and encouraged the growth of a thick, grey mould rind. This practice is frowned upon by modern winemakers.

Zamorano ripens in three to nine months and has a fat content of about 50 per cent.

Portuguese Cheeses

Unlike Spain, Portugal avoided invasion by the Goths, Vandals and Moors, thanks largely to the Atlantic ocean on one side and the high mountains of the east. This led to the development of a proud, independent race, who to this day value and preserve the old ways.

With a long expanse of coastline, it was inevitable that the Portuguese would become great sailors. In the fifteenth and sixteenth centuries they led the search for new trade routes. The Azores, off the coast of Portugal, were the last port of call for the great explorers on their long journey to the New World. In the fifteenth century, a small settlement was established on the islands. The climate was more temperate than that of the mainland, and a herd of cows was soon established to provide hard, long-lasting cheese, similar to Cheddar, for the seafarers and the islanders. The cheese is known as Queijo da Ilha (island cheese).

The climate on mainland Portugal does not lend itself to cheesemaking and dairy products play a very minor role in the national cuisine. Those cheeses that are made, however, are outstanding: ancient cheeses produced on small farms or dairies in the isolated valleys and mountainsides, where agile, tenacious goats thrive on a diet of wild herbs, scrub, gorse blossoms and brambles. Their milk is thick, luscious and aromatic, and makes superb cheese. The milk from the woolly sheep of the magnificent Serra da Estrela in the centre of Portugal is equally rich and fragrant and shepherds have for centuries used it to make Queijos de Serra. Several similar cheeses, including Queijo Serpa, are made in other areas.

As in other parts of Europe, milk was a precious commodity, and the whey was made into a ricotta-type cheese called Requeijao. Wrapped in fig or cabbage leaves and sold fresh in local markets and small village shops, it is equally useful in desserts or savoury dishes.

During the 1960s and 70s, Portugal underwent rapid social and economic change. The tourist industry boomed and there was a vast migration of people from rural areas to the new coastal developments. This stimulated a need for a more sophisticated dairy industry and large factories were built to bottle fresh milk and produce yogurt and copies of foreign cheeses, such as Camembert, chèvre and Edam.

In the last decade, however, the Portuguese have seen the Spanish revive and revitalize their cheese industry, and have started a drive to do something similar in their own country. 10 Portuguese cheeses recently qualified for Protected Designation of Origin (PDO) and Protected Geographical Indication (PGI) status in Europe (a scheme to recognize and preserve indigenous cheeses, introduced by the European Community and based on the French AOC system). Some, like Queijo Evora, are small discs made with goat's milk; others are made from cow's milk, like Queijo de São Jorge; while others, such as Serra da Estrela, are made with sheep's milk or a blend, like Queijo Rabacal, a fresh cheese.

There is no doubt that, in the next few years, these wonderful Portuguese cheeses will become more readily available outside their country of origin.

São Jorge/Ilha de São Jorge

Region: *Azores*

Type: *Traditional, farmhouse, unpasteurized, hard cheese*

Source: *Cow's milk*

Description: *8–12kg/18–26lb cylinder. The hard, natural rind is yellowish-brown and slightly mottled*

Culinary uses: *Table cheese, grating, sauces*

São Jorge is a small island in the Azores. The high plateaux and craters, reminders of the island's violent volcanic past, give way to lush pastures, vibrant local flora and fertile soil.

A Flemish settlement was established on the nearby island of Faial in the fifteenth century. Isolation from the mainland made it necessary for the islanders to become self-sufficient. Cows were brought over and traditional cheesemaking was established both here and on neighbouring islands.

The Azores were the last stop for explorers *en route* to the New World, so the cheeses were much sought after. Like Gouda or Edam, São Jorge improves with age and keeps well, so it continues to prove popular with seafarers like the trans-atlantic yachtsmen who call at the Azores today for provisions. Over the centuries the recipe has been adapted to the local climate and conditions: the result is a unique cheese with the look of Gouda but the savoury tang of Cheddar.

Serra da Estrela

Region: *Beira*

Type: *Traditional, farmhouse, washed-rind cheese*

Source: *Sheep's milk*

Description: *900g/2lb flat round. The fine, leathery, washed rind is orange-brown and slightly sticky. When aged, it becomes smooth and firm*

Culinary use: *Table cheese*

Described as the king of Portuguese cheese, Serra da Estrela has been made for centuries by shepherds in the mountains of Serra da Estrela in the Beira region. Most is still made by small cheesemakers, who used the flowers or leaves of a wild thistle to coagulate the sheep's milk. This gives the cheese a subtle but distinct character, and is a contributing factor in the final texture. The curds are broken by hand rather than cut, and matured in caves for one to four months.

The cheese is so soft and voluptuous that it is almost spreadable. It has a rich, perfumed intensity as a result of the superb grazing, and the sweet, slightly burnt toffee character of the sheep's milk comes through on the finish, which is certainly discernible, but not as strong as you might expect.

When the cheese is allowed to age, the rind toughens and the interior becomes denser and more supple. It can then be sliced with ease.

Swiss Cheeses

Switzerland is a tiny country, whose success is largely due to the commitment of the Swiss to quality, hard work and co-operation. Other nations look with envy at their strong economy, efficiently run cities and excellent road system.

Originally known as Helvetia, Switzerland was home to a Celtic tribe, which in 58BC invaded the southern part of Gaul until the Romans forced them back. From the Romans they learnt the art of cheesemaking.

In the fifth century, Helvetia was invaded by tribes from northern Germany, who ruled the area until three of the cantons (provinces) joined forces in 1291 and defeated their foreign rulers. Eventually other cantons joined the battle and in the fifteenth century independence was won and the foundations for the Swiss Federation were laid.

Today Switzerland is a confederation consisting of 22 cantons, each with its own parliament, courts of law and education system. The people are very much involved in governing their own regions. This ability to work together is seen all over Switzerland, but nowhere is it more effective than in the dairy industry, where most of the cheese is made in mountain chalets or in small co-operatives owned by farmers or cheesemakers.

The primary objective of the Swiss agricultural policy is to uphold this system to ensure that the large number of meadows and pastures are maintained and the beauty of the countryside remains unchanged. This is essential in a country where tourism is a major source of revenue. With only 25 per cent of the land suitable for grazing, many of the cows, even in summer, are fed indoors so that the grass is not trampled down. Except in the relatively inaccessible mountain pastures, you will seldom see cows grazing in Switzerland; instead farmers cut and gather the fresh grass in a system known as zero grazing.

Early in its history, cheese was used as currency in Switzerland. Much of what was made was taken over the Alps to be exchanged with the Romans for rice, spices and wine.

Cheese is still a vital part of the Swiss economy, and the Swiss guard its quality fiercely. All hard cheeses have to be purchased by the Swiss Cheese Union. The price of the cheese is laid down by the government, as is the price of the milk. Although Swiss cheeses can be extremely expensive, their quality is guaranteed. None of the foreign copies can compare with the originals, which include some of the best-loved cheeses in the world.

BELOW: Tilsiter

ABOVE: Appenzeller

APPENZELLER

REGION: *Appenzell and St Gallen*
TYPE: *Traditional, farmhouse and creamery, unpasteurized, hard cheese*
SOURCE: *Cow's milk*
DESCRIPTION: *5–6.75kg/11–15lb convex wheel. The hard, brushed rind is pale yellow to burnt orange*
CULINARY USES: *Table cheese, melting, grilling*

One of Switzerland's oldest cheeses, Appenzeller dates back to the time of Charlemagne. As the name suggests, it originated in the Appenzell region, but today it is also made in the canton of St Gallen. Its quality and character are protected by rules similar to those operated by the AOC system in France, and it is at its best when made in mountain chalets from the milk of the summer pastures.

The dry, flat, pale yellow to orange rind derives its colour from being washed in a secret concoction of spices, white wine and salt. The aroma hints at spicy, fermenting fruit. If the cheese has been wrapped in plastic, it may sweat and develop a less than appealing, farmyard whiff. The cheese is firm and dense, yet retains a certain suppleness. A few peanut-sized holes are scattered throughout the yellow interior. At first, the taste is buttery, with fruity overtones. As it matures, the flavour becomes fuller and is reminiscent of hot toast and yeast extract. Appenzeller ripens in three to four months, with a fat content of 45 per cent.

BELOW: Emmental

EMMENTAL

REGION: *Central cantons*
TYPE: *Traditional, farmhouse, unpasteurized, hard cheese*
SOURCE: *Cow's milk*
DESCRIPTION: *60–130kg/132–286lb wheel with convex rim and slightly concave sides. The thin, hard, natural rind is a beige-yellow and is covered by paper identifying the producer*
CULINARY USES: *Table cheese, grilling, fondue*

The history of Emmental can be traced back to 1293, but it was first mentioned by name in 1542, when it was given to the people of Langehthal whose lives had been devastated by fire. It takes its name from the valley of the upper Emme River, but is now made throughout Switzerland, wherever there are high pastures.

Although Emmental resembles Gruyère, the aroma is sweeter, with hushed tones of fresh-cut hay. Squeeze the rind to savour the wine-like aroma. Smoother and more elastic than Gruyère, Emmental has holes the size of hazelnuts or even walnuts. The promise of the aroma is fulfilled in the flavour, which is very fruity, with a mouth-tingling acidity.

FRIBOURGEOIS

REGION: *Fribourg*
TYPE: *Traditional, farmhouse, hard cheese*
SOURCE: *Cow's milk*
DESCRIPTION: *8kg/18lb wheel. The dry, pale beige, natural rind is covered with a fine, orange, plastic coat*
CULINARY USES: *Table cheese, fondues, grilling*

Like most traditional Swiss cheeses, Fribourgeois can trace its family history back through the centuries to a significant event. According to local documents, it was served to the wife of Duke Sigismund of Austria in 1448. Firm but breakable, it has a very full-bodied, slightly cloying feel, a delicious, meaty quality and a lingering savoury tang. A traditional, hard, mountain cheese, it resembles a small Gruyère, with a spicy rather than nutty taste that intensifies when the cheese is grilled or melted. It is sometimes referred to as Fribourgeois Vacherin, but should not be confused with the better-known Vacherin Mont d'Or, which is much softer.

Fribourgeois is matured for at least three months.

FROMAGE À RACLETTE

REGION: *Various*
TYPE: *Traditional, farmhouse, hard cheese*
SOURCE: *Cow's milk*
DESCRIPTION: *8–11kg/18–24lb cylindrical wheel. The smooth, natural rind varies in colour from pale yellow to orange-brown and can be dry or slightly sticky and rough*
CULINARY USES: *Table cheese, grilling*

Until the nineteenth century, this wonderful melting cheese was known as Valais. It acquired its modern name from the French verb *racler*, meaning "to scrape". The cheese was traditionally cut in half and placed with the cut surface facing the fire. As the cheese started to bubble, it would be scraped on to boiled potatoes to make a delectable treat.

Raclette is very supple. The pale golden interior has a sweet, earthy taste and a pleasant, citrus tang that deepens to a savoury bite. When heated, the cheese bubbles, melts and intensifies in flavour. Also known as Bagnes or Conches, Fromage à Raclette (or simply Raclette) is available in both raw and pasteurized versions, and can be purchased ready-sliced for easy grilling. Some Raclette are made with peppercorns providing a hot, peppery finish to the cheese. It ripens in three to four months and has a fat content of 45 per cent.

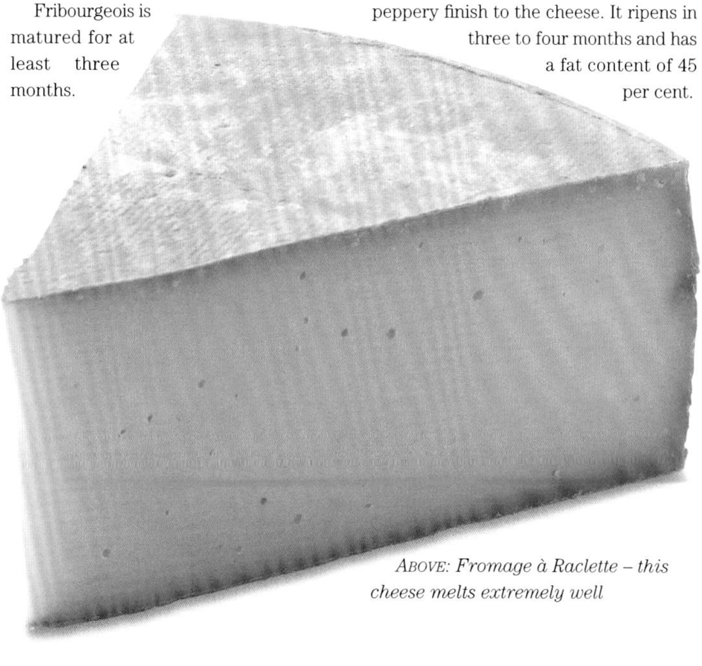

ABOVE: Fromage à Raclette – this cheese melts extremely well

Gruyère

Region: *Gruyère*
Type: *Traditional, co-operative and creamery, unpasteurized, hard cheese*
Source: *Cow's milk*
Description: *20–45kg/44–99lb wheel. The natural, rusty brown rind is hard, dry and pitted with tiny holes*
Culinary uses: *Table cheese, grilling, fondue*

Gruyère is part of the canton of Fribourg and Gruyère cheese has been made here for centuries. In 1115 a quantity of Gruyère was recorded as the tithe paid by local farmers to the monks of Rougement Abbey. Each of the enormous cheeses is made by a group of farmers or by a co-operative, since it takes 400 litres/88 gallons of milk to produce a single 35kg/80lb wheel.

The cheese is a darker yellow than Emmental and has a hint of brown in the colouring. The texture is dense and compact, yet flexible. It is this density that makes it stronger and less stringy than Emmental when heated, so it is better for gratins, grilling and in soups.

When Gruyère is first cut, the aroma suggests a million meadow flowers trapped in rich, creamy milk. Slightly grainy, the cheese has a wonderful complexity of flavours – at first fruity, then revealing more earthy, nutty characteristics that linger on the palate.

Royalp-Tilsiter

Region: *St Gallen*
Type: *Traditional, unpasteurized, hard cheese made in small creameries*
Source: *Cow's milk*
Description: *4kg/9lb wheel with smooth, polished, yellow, natural rind*
Culinary uses: *Table cheese, melting, grilling, breakfast*

Compared with Switzerland's ancient cheeses, this is a relative newcomer, having been introduced in the latter half of the nineteenth century by a Swiss cheesemaker who had learnt to make Tilsiter while in eastern Prussia after the Franco-Prussian war. The rich, creamy milk of the alpine pastures produced a cheese with a robust smooth texture and small, distinct holes, unlike the original Tilsiter, which had irregular cracks running through it.

Royalp-Tilsiter is smaller than other Swiss cheeses and has a fat content of 45 per cent. It is lightly pressed and ripened for at least two months, but is better after six months. To distinguish it from the other Tilsiter cheese, it is known as Royalp abroad.

Below: Royalp-Tilsiter

Above: Gruyère

Saanen

Region: *Fribourg*
Type: *Traditional, farmhouse, hard cheese*
Source: *Cow's milk*
Description: *20–40kg/44–88lb wheel. The natural, very tough rind is brushed and oiled*
Culinary use: *Cooking cheese*

Saanen is a very hard, brittle cheese, with a deep yellow interior that is intensely fruity. It resembles Parmesan or Sbrinz and is a good grating cheese that will keep almost indefinitely. Saanen was traditionally reserved for special occasions, when pieces of the cheese would be shaved off and served with a glass of fruity, local wine.

Sapsago

Region: *Glarus*
Type: *Traditional, farmhouse and creamery, hard cheese*
Source: *Cow's milk*
Description: *150g/5oz truncated cone. Pale green and rindless. Sold in foil*
Culinary uses: *Grating, as a condiment*

Sapsago owes its unusual, pale lime green colour to the addition of fenugreek. Very hard and gritty, it melts like Parmesan when heated. It is astringent, salty, sour – and mouthwatering. The aroma suggests warm cows and farmyards, with exotic, spicy overtones. Not a cheese to be taken lightly. Also known as Schabziger.

ABOVE: Tête-de-Moine

Sbrinz

REGION: *Various*
TYPE: *Traditional, farmhouse, hard cheese*
SOURCE: *Cow's milk*
DESCRIPTION: *Flat, cylindrical wheel, 60cm/24in in diameter*
CULINARY USES: *Table cheese, grating*

Sbrinz is thought to be the cheese Pliny the Elder referred to as *Caseus Helveticus* in his writings in the first century AD. The method of production is similar to that for Parmesan and the cheeses share similar traits. Sbrinz has the same fresh, pineapple taste and aroma. It has a lovely fruitiness, against a background of ground nuts, and a deliciously spicy finish. Not as potent as Parmesan, it makes a good and generally significantly cheaper alternative.

Sbrinz is matured for two to three years and has a fat content of 45 per cent.

Tête-de-Moine

REGION: *Bern*
TYPE: *Traditional, farmhouse and creamery, hard cheese*
SOURCE: *Cow's milk*
DESCRIPTION: *600g–2kg/1$\frac{1}{2}$–4$\frac{1}{2}$lb drum. The hard, ochre to terracotta rind tends to be smelly and sticky*
CULINARY USES: *Table cheese, also shaved over salads as a garnish*

It is often thought that the name of this cheese – which translates as "head of the monk" – derives from its shape, but there is a rather more prosaic explanation. The cheese was originally called Bellelay, after a monastery in the Jura Mountains. Following the French Revolution it was renamed Tête-de-Moine, after the monks who made it.

Tête-de-Moine has a strong, earthy flavour, like burnt toast with yeast extract. It is usually served in thick strips or ruffles, made by passing it through a special machine called a girolle. The ruffles are used to garnish salads, platters of cooked meats and other dishes.

Tête-de-Moine ripens in three months and has a fat content of 45 per cent.

Vacherin Mont d'Or

REGION: *Vaud*
TYPE: *Traditional, farmhouse and co-operative, washed-rind cheese*
SOURCE: *Cow's milk*
DESCRIPTION: *500g/1$\frac{1}{4}$lb or 3kg/6$\frac{1}{2}$lb round cheese. The supple, undulating, brownish-pink rind has a dusting of white mould. The cheese is girdled with a band of spruce bark and sold in a pine box*
CULINARY USE: *Table cheese*

During summer, the milk produced by the cows in the upper and lower reaches of the Jura Mountains is used to make Gruyère. When winter sets in, the animals are confined to their warm, cosy barns and fed on hay, and the richer, thicker milk is pasteurized and used to make Vacherin Mont d'Or. The same cheese, produced on the other side of the mountains in France, is simply called Mont d'Or and is made with raw milk.

When ripe, Vacherin Mont d'Or is so smooth and runny it can be eaten with a spoon. The aroma of resin from the bark girdle is absorbed by the cheese, and the taste is reminiscent of the flowers and herbs of the mountain pastures. The cheese ripens in four to six weeks.

If you can afford it, buy a whole Vacherin Mont d'Or. Enjoy the cheese with a bottle of full-bodied, fruity white wine or a smooth Pinot Noir.

ABOVE: Sbrinz can only be made in Switzerland

THE CHEESES OF HOLLAND

More than half the land in Holland is below sea level, and the sea is held back only by the intricate system of dykes and canals that was begun by the Romans. The superb grazing on this reclaimed land, known as the Polders, is the foundation on which the cheeses of Holland were built. Surprisingly, unlike other major cheese-producing countries of Europe, which produce a vast range of different cheeses, Holland concentrates on only two – Edam and Gouda – on which all the other Dutch cheeses are based.

Edam and Gouda played a major role in the economy of Holland in the Middle Ages, when their smooth texture and long-lasting qualities made them highly desirable. In 1621, the founding of the Dutch East India Company gave Holland a powerful trading base, as it held the monopoly on the spices from Indonesia. Cloves, aniseed, cumin and caraway were much sought after, and were soon incorporated into cheeses. Kruidkaas, which includes either caraway or cumin, is still made today, as is Nagelkaas (with cloves) and Leidsekaas (with cumin or aniseed).

By about the middle of the seventeenth century, Edam and Gouda were being exported to virtually every country in Europe. In France in the time of Louis XIV, the passion for Dutch cheese was so great that when the Treasury banned its importation on grounds of cost, the French started developing their own (the forerunner of Mimolette Française).

Artists of the day included cheeses in many masterpieces and it is rumoured that in 1841 the Uruguayan fleet, under American command, defeated the British by substituting Dutch Edams for cannonballs when their supply ran out.

With nearly a third of Holland dedicated to dairy farming, cheese plays a significant role in the economy and over 75 per cent of the annual production is exported. Most cheese is made in highly mechanized factories, a necessary development that has sadly led to a decline in the number of artisan cheesemakers. The few that remain largely make farmhouse Goudas, while some sheep's milk cheeses are produced on the island of Texel and in the province of Friesland, which gave the Friesian cow its name.

Copies of Gouda and Edam are now made all over the world, both in factories and by artisan cheesemakers, often Dutch emigrants seeking a better quality of life and a less regimented environment. To identify authentic Dutch cheeses – and ensure that their quality is maintained – production is governed by strict rules. Each cheese must carry a label that includes detailed information on origin, producer and fat content.

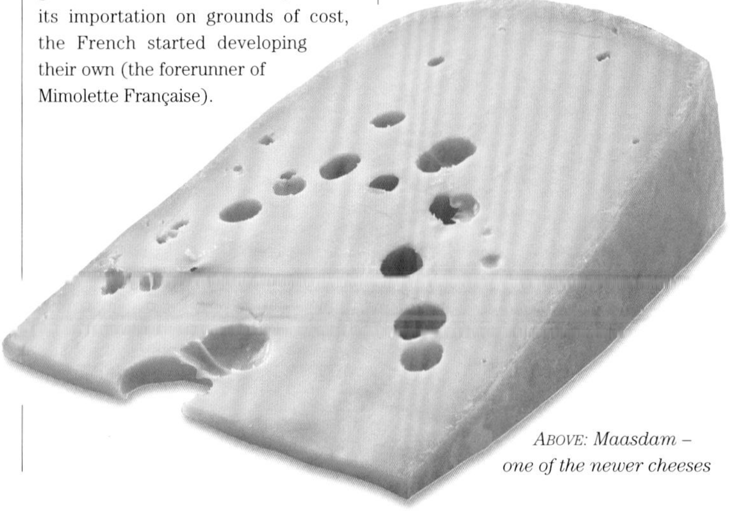

ABOVE: Maasdam – one of the newer cheeses

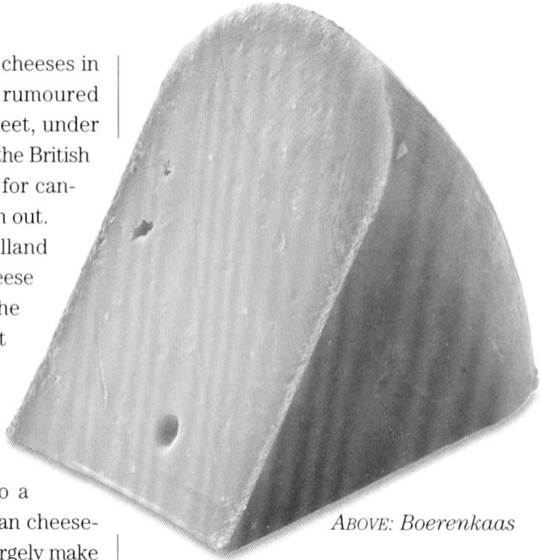

ABOVE: Boerenkaas

BOERENKAAS

REGION: *Various*

TYPE: *Traditional, farmhouse, unpasteurized, semi-hard cheese*

SOURCE: *Cow's milk*

DESCRIPTION: *8–40kg/18–88lb wheel with convex rim and glossy, brushed, natural rind*

CULINARY USES: *Table cheese, often sliced for breakfast; also melted in sandwiches*

Though most of Holland's cheese manufacture is highly mechanized, some farmhouse Gouda is still made by artisan cheesemakers using raw milk. This cheese gets its name – Boerenkaas – from the Dutch words for farmer (*boer*) and cheese (*kaas*). It is quite difficult to obtain in Holland today, due to the decline in the numbers of artisan cheesemakers, which in turn is linked to the scarcity and cost of agricultural land.

Boerenkaas is, however, made in the traditional way. The only modern touch is the porous plastic coating, which is "painted" on to the newly formed cheese to protect it during the months of slow ageing. When young, it is nutty and rich, with a dense, creamy texture and a fragrance reminiscent of meadow pastures and fresh hay. With age, its flavour intensifies, becoming strong and fruity. Tiny calcium crystals, like those in Parmesan, develop in well-aged cheeses.

BELOW: Gouda (left), and Edam (right), the majority of which is exported, because the Dutch prefer the stronger flavour of Gouda

FRIESEKAAS

REGION: *Various*
TYPE: *Traditional, creamery, semi-hard cheese*
SOURCE: *Cow's milk*
DESCRIPTION: *Large round, at least 10kg/22lb in weight, with waxed, natural rind*
CULINARY USES: *Table cheese, snacks, breakfast, grilling*

A spiced Dutch cheese, this is similar to Leyden, but is flavoured with a combination of cumin and cloves. It ripens in three to 12 months and has a fat content of 40 per cent.

GOUDA

REGION: *Various*
TYPE: *Traditional, creamery, hard cheese*
SOURCE: *Cow's milk*
DESCRIPTION: *5–10kg/11–22lb round with very smooth, yellow, waxed rind. Mature cheeses are hard and slightly granular, with a black wax coating*
CULINARY USES: *Table cheese, snacks, breakfast, grilling*

Gouda accounts for more than 60 per cent of the cheese produced in Holland. An ancient cheese, its history dates from the sixth century, when it was made on small farms around the village of Gouda. It has been exported since the thirteenth century and is now enjoyed worldwide.

Other European countries, notably Sweden, have adopted the Dutch style of cheesemaking, and produce cheeses that are similar to Gouda. Since the last century, Dutch immigrants in America and Australia have been making farmhouse versions by meticulously adhering to the old methods, although regulations prevent many of them from using raw milk.

When only a few months old, Gouda is firm, smooth and supple, with a scattering of small holes. The flavour is sweet and fruity. As time passes, the taste intensifies and becomes more complex. Mature Gouda (18 months plus) is coated in black wax, which provides a stark contrast to the deep yellow interior. At this age, the texture of the cheese is granular, and it can be grated. Gouda has a fat content of 40–45 per cent.

DUTCH MIMOLETTE/ COMMISSIEKAAS

REGION: *Various*
TYPE: *Traditional, farmhouse and creamery, hard cheese*
SOURCE: *Cow's milk*
DESCRIPTION: *3–4.5kg/6–9lb ball. The natural, pitted rind ranges from light brown to deep orange*
CULINARY USES: *Grating, in sauces and pastries, snacks*

Seldom seen outside northern Europe, this magnificent, fruity cheese looks like a giant orange with rough, pitted skin. Known as Commissiekaas in Holland and Dutch Mimolette everywhere else, the cheese is actually a matured Edam coloured with carrot juice.

At around five months Dutch Mimolette is firm, compact and slightly oily, with a fruity aroma and nutty flavour. The best is yet to come, however. When aged, the colour darkens to a deep orange, the texture becomes rock hard, granular and brittle and the flavour is pronounced. It is fruity, with a hint of orange zest (real or imagined). The nutty flavour intensifies to reach a mouth-watering crescendo.

This cheese ripens in six to 12 months and has a fat content of 45 per cent.

EDAM

REGION: *Various*
TYPE: *Traditional, creamery, semi-soft or hard cheese*
SOURCE: *Cow's milk*
DESCRIPTION: *1.5kg/3¼lb ball with barely perceptible rind covered in distinctive, red wax*
CULINARY USES: *Table cheese, popular for breakfast and in sandwiches, also grilled*

Named after the small port of Edam, just north of Amsterdam, this is a pressed, semi-soft or hard cheese in the shape of a ball. The red wax coat, first used in the fourteenth century, makes it a distinctive sight in delicatessens and supermarkets the world over. Most Edam is still produced from skimmed or semi-skimmed milk and has a fat content of between 30 and 40 per cent. Authentic Edam is mostly sold young, when the texture is still supple and elastic, and the flavour is mild, sweet and nutty. Imitations can be bland and rubbery.

A black wax coat indicates an Edam has been aged for at least 17 weeks. Some of the cheese is aged for up to 10 months, when it becomes strong, nutty and excellent for cooking.

Leyden/Leidsekaas

Region: *Leiden*
Type: *Traditional, farmhouse, hard cheese*
Source: *Cow's milk*
Description: *3–10kg/6½–22lb boulder-shaped cheese with brushed, natural rind which is either rubbed with annatto or "painted" with red plastic*
Culinary uses: *Table cheese, grilling*

Made on farms around Leiden, the famous university city, this cheese is similar in texture to Gouda, but because it is made with semi-skimmed milk it feels slightly drier. The curd is coloured with annatto and mixed with cumin seeds before being pressed and washed in brine. The cumin provides an aromatic flavour that contrasts well with the creamy, nutty character of the cheese.

A genuine Leyden will be identified as such by having the imprint of the city's emblem, the famous crossed keys, on the rind. To further distinguish the cheese, the rind is rubbed with annatto until it acquires a shiny reddish-orange colour.

The traditional custom of treading the spices into the curd has, needless to say, been replaced by machine.

Leyden is also called Komijnekaas.

Above: Leyden

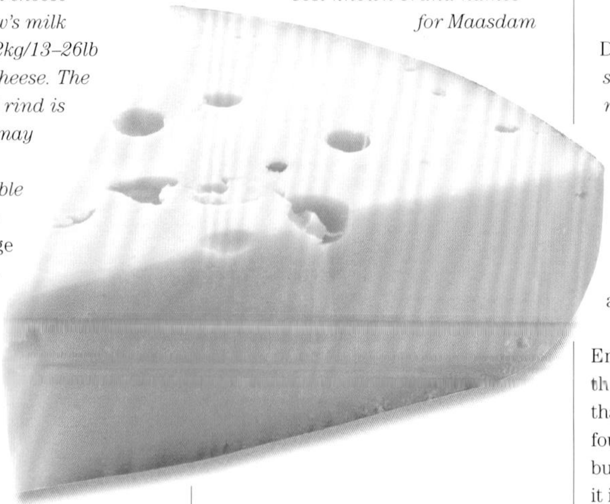

Below: Leerdammer is one of the best-known brand names for Maasdam

Leerdammer

Region: *Zuid-Holland*
Modern, creamery, semi-hard cheese
Source: *Cow's milk*
Description: *6–12kg/13–26lb boulder-shaped cheese. The smooth, natural rind is polished and may be waxed*
Culinary uses: *Table cheese, grilling*

Most of the large cheesemaking factories in Holland have begun to produce their own branded versions of Maasdam. Leerdammer is one of the better-known, along with Ronduer, Goyweter and Fricotal.

Maasdam

Region: *Various*
Type: *Modern, creamery, semi-hard cheese*
Source: *Cow's milk*
Description: *6–12kg/13–26lb boulder-shaped cheese. The smooth, natural rind is polished and may be waxed*
Culinary uses: *Table cheese, grilling*

Created in the early 1990s as an alternative to the more expensive Swiss cheese Emmental, Maasdam has attracted a large following. The market continues to increase, and it is already being copied in other countries.

Although there are similarities with Emmental, it is higher in moisture and therefore more supple. It ripens faster than other Dutch cheeses, being ready in four to 12 weeks. The flavour is sweet and buttery, with a fruity background, making it ideal for serving as a snack or breakfast cheese. It can also be grilled.

German Cheeses

The Germanic tribes, originally from Scandinavia and the Baltic, gradually expanded east of the Rhine and by 200BC were beginning to invade the Roman Empire. It was not, however, until the arrival of the Franks and the rule of Charlemagne that the cheeses of Germany began to emerge. Charlemagne's love of food is legendary, a fact that helped to shape German cuisine, which has a reputation for being both hearty and substantial.

Germany's dairy industry is huge, now rated fourth or fifth in the world, yet surprisingly its cheeses are far less well known beyond its borders than are its sausages, beers and breads. One of the main reasons for this is that many of the cheeses are either processed varieties, or copies of other European cheeses.

Quark is the notable exception. Now found all over Europe, it is a fresh curd cheese with a sharp, yogurt-like taste. Thought to have originated in the Iron Age, it led to the development of other types of *Sauermilchkäse* (sour milk cheese), which are often very pungent.

Limburger, adopted by the Germans from Belgium, is a Trappist-style cheese, as is Münster. Both have a strong, robust flavour that appeals to the German love of rich, spicy food.

As in Switzerland, the quality of German cheeses is very strictly controlled. Labelling must be precise, which is helpful for the informed local consumer, but not necessarily for the visitor.

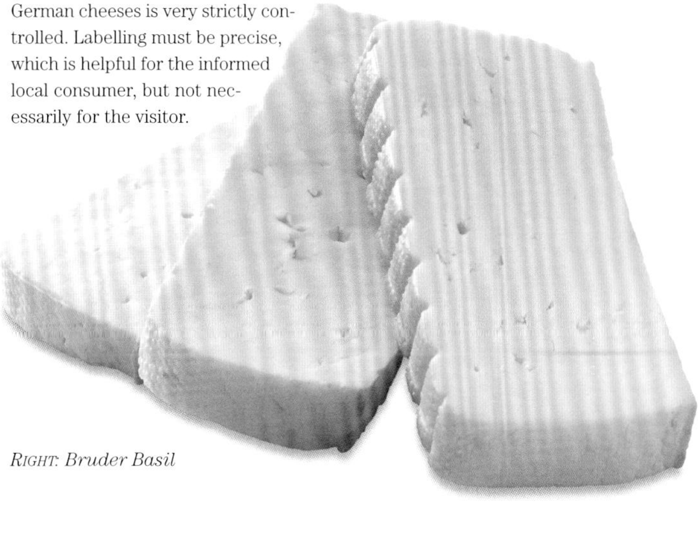

Right: Bruder Basil

Allgäuer Emmentaler

Region: *Bavaria*
Type: *Traditional, creamery and co-operative, hard cheese*
Source: *Cow's milk*
Description: *40–90kg/88–198lb wheel with smooth, waxed, natural rind*
Culinary uses: *Grilling, melting, snacks, breakfast*

The mountain pastures of Allgäu in southern Bavaria resemble those of their Swiss neighbours, and the cattle are similar, so it is not altogether surprising that the Bavarians produce a cheese that has much in common with that made on the other side of the mountains. Allgäuer Emmentaler is a sweet, fruity cheese, with holes the size of walnuts. It is less expensive than the Swiss original.

Since the end of the last century, when the makers of Allgäuer Emmentaler adopted the same stringent standards of quality maintained by the Swiss, it has been hard to tell the two cheeses apart, although lovers of Swiss Emmental would claim that their cheese has the edge in terms of flavour.

Determined to maintain their unique identity, the Swiss ensure that the rinds on their exported cheeses are completely covered with the words "Switzerland" and "Emmental", leaving the consumer in no doubt about where the cheese is made.

Bavarian Bergkäse

Region: *Bavaria*
Type: *Traditional, farmhouse and creamery, unpasteurized, hard cheese*
Source: *Cow's milk*
Description: *20–50kg/44–110lb wheel with natural rind, similar to but darker than Emmental*
Culinary uses: *Table cheese, grilling, melting*

Bergkäse simply means "mountain cheese" and is a smaller version of the popular Allgäuer Emmentaler. Firm but supple, and almost chewy, Bergkäse is a superb melting cheese. More aromatic than Emmental but still fruity, Bergkäse is made only in the summer months from the milk of cows grazing the mountain pastures, which explains why it is also known as Alpenkäse.

Control is less strict than for the Allgäuer Emmentaler and quality can vary from maker to maker, but it is nonetheless a good buy.

Bergkäse ripens in three to nine months and has a fat content of 45 per cent.

Bruder Basil

Region: *Bavaria*
Type: *Modern, creamery, semi-soft cheese*
Source: *Cow's milk*
Description: *1kg/2¼lb flattened brick with convex sides. The natural rind is dark mahogany in colour and is waxed*
Culinary uses: *Grilling; also used in snacks and sandwiches, often served with beer*

This is a traditionally made version of the Bavarian smoked cheese (Rauchkäse) found almost everywhere. The smooth, firm, yellow cheese has small holes. The taste is creamy and pleasantly smoky, but can be rather "plastic".

Bruder Basil ripens in one month and has a fat content of about 45 per cent. A version flavoured with chopped ham is also available.

ABOVE: Cambazola, which as the name implies, is based on Camembert and Gorgonzola, appeals to those who find other blue cheeses too ferocious. Bavarian Blue and Blue Brie are similar cheeses

BUTTERKÄSE

REGION: *Various*
TYPE: *Traditional, creamery, semi-soft cheese*
SOURCE: *Cow's milk*
DESCRIPTION: *1–4kg/2¼–9lb rectangular loaf or wheel with golden to red, natural rind*
CULINARY USES: *Snacks, breakfast*

Made in both Germany and Austria, this cheese lives up to its name and has a buttery taste and colour. Very supple, but odourless and rather bland, it needs pickles and beer to give it life.

Also called Damenkäse (ladies' cheese), Butterkäse ripens in one month and has a fat content of 50 per cent.

CAMBAZOLA

REGION: *Various*
TYPE: *Modern, creamery, blue cheese*
SOURCE: *Cow's milk*
DESCRIPTION: *2kg/4½lb flat round with penicillium rind*
CULINARY USES: *Table cheese, snacks*

Cambazola is a modern success story. Since its creation in the 1970s, others have tried to copy it, but few have achieved the consistency of quality and texture, which are responsible for Cambazola's success. The smooth, rich texture is achieved by adding cream to the milk, and the taste is mildly spicy and slightly sweet-sour.

LIMBURGER

REGION: *Various*
TYPE: *Traditional, creamery, washed-rind cheese*
SOURCE: *Cow's milk*
DESCRIPTION: *200–675g/7oz–1½lb brick. The smooth, sticky, washed rind is reddish-brown, with corrugated ridges*
CULINARY USES: *Table cheese, grilling, melting over potatoes*

The aroma is unmistakable – powerful, outspoken and impossible to ignore. The yellow interior hints at sweetness, but the overwhelming taste is spicy and aromatic, almost meaty. Despite its robust nature, Limburger has its limits and passes these if it is allowed to become runny, with a slimy rind. It is best when the texture is firm, yet yielding.

Limburger undoubtedly originated with the cheese-loving Trappist monks in Belgium, but was hijacked by German cheesemakers in the nineteenth century. It is now so popular that most Germans and even some Belgians believe it to be a German cheese.

The cheese ripens in six to 12 weeks and has a fat content that fluctuates between 20 and 50 per cent. A milder version is popular in the United States, having been introduced by German immigrants.

LEFT: Limburger has an unmistakable odour

AUSTRIAN CHEESES

BERGKÄSE

REGION: *Voralberg Massif*
TYPE: *Traditional, creamery, unpasteurized, hard cheese*
SOURCE: *Cow's milk*
DESCRIPTION: *6–30kg/13–65lb wheel with smooth, dark yellow, natural rind*
CULINARY USES: *Table cheese, melting, grilling, fondue*

Closely resembling the Bavarian Bergkäse, this has a creamy, fudge-like flavour with a hint of hazelnuts. The holes in the paste are smaller than those in the German cheese and the cheese is matured for six months or longer.

KUGELKÄSE

REGION: *Danube*
TYPE: *Traditional, creamery, fresh cheese*
SOURCE: *Cow's milk*
DESCRIPTION: *Speckled, white balls in various sizes*
CULINARY USES: *Added to local dishes; also served solo, with beer*

This is a simple local speciality. Once the fresh curd has formed – and while it is still warm – pepper, caraway seeds and paprika are added so that the curd becomes infused with their aroma and character. The cheese is then rolled into balls, which are salted and dried for weeks or even months.

MONDSEER

REGION: *Salzburg*
TYPE: *Traditional, creamery, semi-soft cheese*
SOURCE: *Cow's milk*
DESCRIPTION: *500g–1kg/1¼–2¼lb round. The soft, washed rind is deep orange, dusted with powdery, white mould*
CULINARY USES: *Grilling, snacks*

Firm yet moist, Mondseer is open-textured with a few irregular eyes. It has a slightly spicy aroma and a sweet-sour taste. Although it is related to other washed-rind cheeses, it tends to be milder and less pungent.

Mondseer ripens in about two to three months and has a fat content of 45 per cent.

MÜNSTER

REGION: *Schwarzwald*
TYPE: *Traditional, creamery, washed-rind cheese*
SOURCE: *Cow's milk*
DESCRIPTION: *125–500g/4½oz–1¼lb round cheese with sticky, orange, washed skin*
CULINARY USE: *Table cheese*

Münster is a smooth, fairly soft, yellow cheese with a thin, orange skin and a mildly piquant flavour that can become quite pungent with regular washings. In the Middle Ages the cheese was made by the monks at Munster Abbey in modern-day Alsace. When Alsace became part of Germany, the name of the cheese gained an umlaut, and it became Münster, after the Westphalian town. Ownership of Alsace switched from Germany to France several times after that, but the cheese continued to be made on both sides of the border. Today, it is also produced in the USA, where it is known as Muenster.

QUARK

REGION: *Various*
TYPE: *Traditional, creamery, vegetarian, fresh cheese*
SOURCE: *Cow's milk*
DESCRIPTION: *Moist, white cheese sold in pots*
CULINARY USES: *Cooking, spreading, in dips and cheesecakes, with fruit for breakfast*

Quark simply means "curd" in German, and the cheese is said to date from the Iron Age, when nomadic tribes discovered the means of fermenting milk without the use of rennet.

Quark can be made from whole, skimmed or semi-skimmed milk or even buttermilk. Soft and moist, like a cross between yogurt and fromage frais, it should taste lemon-fresh. Some versions have skimmed milk powder added and can be rather gritty. Quark ripens within a few days.

ROMADUR/ROMADURKÄSE

REGION: *Various*
TYPE: *Traditional, creamery, washed-rind cheese*
SOURCE: *Cow's milk*
DESCRIPTION: *200–500g/7oz–1¼lb rectangular loaf with yellowish-orange, washed rind*
CULINARY USE: *Table cheese*

Similar to Limburger, but milder and smaller, Romadur has a sweet-sour flavour with a hint of smoke. It can be made with whole or semi-skimmed milk and has a fat content between 20 and 60 per cent.

TILSIT

REGION: *Various*
TYPE: *Traditional, co-operative or creamery, semi-hard cheese*
SOURCE: *Cow's milk*
DESCRIPTION: *4.5kg/10lb wheel. The thin, dry, yellow-beige crust has some moulds*
CULINARY USES: *Table cheese, grilling, snacks*

The original Tilsit was apparently discovered accidentally by Dutch cheese-makers living in Tilsit, which was then in East Prussia. At the time, they were trying to make their beloved Gouda, but various factors combined to create a cheese that was markedly different, especially in relation to the rind.

The cheese is washed and brushed regularly for the first two months so that the crusty rind forms. This protects the smooth, supple interior, with its tiny, irregular holes, from drying out. The aroma is mildly pungent, while the taste is buttery and fruity, with a spicy tinge.

RIGHT: Quark

Belgian Cheeses

Belgium's cheeses are virtually unknown outside her borders, being overshadowed by those of her famous neighbour, France, yet the country produces over 250 varieties of cheese.

There is evidence that the Belgae, a Celtic people, had some knowledge of basic cheesemaking, and although the Romans introduced more sophisticated techniques, it was the Franks who were to have the most influence on cheesemaking in Belgium. Between AD771 and 800, their king, Charlemagne, developed an extensive empire, and encouraged the building of over 50 abbeys. The monks not only set about spreading the word of God, but also worked with the people to improve their herds and their cheesemaking skills.

The records kept by Charlemagne provide us with an insight into his world. At Aachen, his seat of power, cellars were dug to store and ripen his cheeses. As Charlemagne's empire faded, the country split into independent duchies and trade brought wealth and prosperity. Despite being governed in turn by the Austrians, Spanish and Dutch, Belgium emerged in 1831 as an independent kingdom, with its own culture and cuisine.

Respect for the past, and a determination not to allow the older varieties of cheese to become extinct, led several cheesemakers in 1960 to embark on a campaign to rediscover old recipes. Their research, in monasteries, farms and libraries, has revitalized the industry, creating a new identity for Belgian cheese, based on its rich and varied history.

Regrettably, the majority of cheeses produced in Belgium today are factory-made copies of traditional Belgian and other European cheeses, but those described here can be found and savoured in the many elegant restaurants and cafés for which Belgium is famous.

Left: Herve is Belgium's most famous cheese

Below: Beauvoorde

Beauvoorde

Region: *Various*
Type: *Traditional, creamery, semi-hard cheese*
Source: *Cow's milk*
Description: *3kg/6½lb or 6kg/13lb hexagonal cheese with grey, natural rind*
Culinary uses: *Table cheese, also used in snacks and sandwiches*

Beauvoorde cheese was created in the early 1900s by Arthur Djes, innkeeper of Beauvoorde village. His family continued to make the cheese until the Second World War forced them to abandon production. Recently revived, it is now made in creameries. Firm yet supple and open-textured, Beauvoorde has a mild flavour and a spicy aroma.

Brusselse Kaas/Fromage de Bruxelles

Region: *Brabant*
Type: *Traditional, creamery, washed-rind cheese*
Source: *Cow's milk*
Description: *150g/5oz flattened rounds, sold in tubs*
Culinary uses: *Spreading, snacks*

Made with skimmed milk, Brusselse Kaas is smooth, sharp and citric, with a bite that is surprisingly strong and salty. This is the result of the cheese having been regularly washed and dried over a period of at least three months. It is shaped into rough rounds and packed in tubs.

Herve

Region: *Liège*
Type: *Traditional, farmhouse and creamery, washed-rind cheese*
Source: *Cow's milk*
Description: *200g/7oz brick with glossy, orange-brown rind*
Culinary uses: *Table cheese, snacks*

Belgium's most famous cheese, Herve, has an autumn-coloured crust that is pungent and yeasty. Beneath it, the supple, tender interior ranges from sweet to powerful and spicy, depending on how long the cheese has been ripening. Small quantities of unpasteurized cheese are still made, and there is a double-cream version.

MAREDSOUS

REGION: *Various*
TYPE: *Traditional, farmhouse and creamery, washed-rind cheese*
SOURCE: *Cow's milk*
DESCRIPTION: *1kg/2¼lb or 2.5kg/5½lb loaf-shaped cheese. The firm, orange, washed rind sometimes has a fine dusting of white mould*
CULINARY USES: *Table cheese, grilling*

This is another of Belgium's Trappist-style cheeses and is made by the monks at Maredsous Abbey. It is lightly pressed, then washed in brine to create the firm, orange crust and pungent aroma. The supple, smooth interior is pale yellow with a slightly smoky tinge. Not as aggressive as Herve, it has perhaps more in common with France's Saint-Paulin.

PASSENDALE

REGION: *Flanders*
TYPE: *Modern, creamery, semi-soft cheese*
SOURCE: *Cow's milk*
DESCRIPTION: *3kg/6½lb round, shaped like a country loaf and with a dusting of fine, white mould that resembles flour*
CULINARY USES: *Table cheese, grilling, snacks, breakfast*

With its warm, brown crust lightly dusted with white mould, this looks like a loaf of country bread. A modern cheese, based on an old monastic recipe, it is firm, with small holes. The flavour is mild and creamy. The cheese takes its name from the Flemish village of Passchendaele, where thousands of British soldiers lost their lives in the First World War.

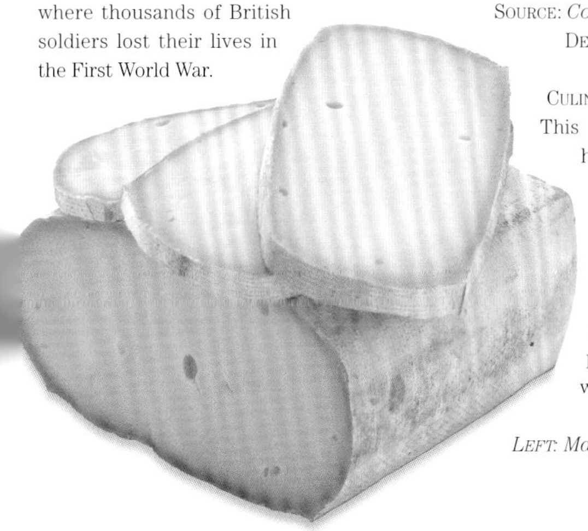

LEFT: Maredsous

PLATEAU DE HERVE

REGION: *Herve*
TYPE: *Traditional, creamery, washed-rind cheese*
SOURCE: *Cow's milk*
DESCRIPTION: *1.5kg/3¼lb dome with sticky, orange, washed rind wrapped in foil*
CULINARY USES: *Table cheese, snacks*

This lightly pressed cheese has a pale yellow interior with a creamy consistency. Washed regularly in brine, it has the flavour without the pervasive aroma of Herve. It ripens in two to three months.

POSTEL

REGION: *Various*
TYPE: *Traditional, farmhouse, washed-rind cheese*
SOURCE: *Cow's milk*
DESCRIPTION: *4kg/9lb rectangular cheese with orange, washed rind*
CULINARY USE: *Table cheese*

The monks at the Abbey of Postel resumed making this classic Trappist cheese in the 1960s, using the milk from their herd of 160 cows. Volume is small, but those who have discovered this cheese willingly travel to the abbey to buy it.

PRINC'JEAN

REGION: *Various*
TYPE: *Modern, creamery, fresh cheese*
SOURCE: *Cow's milk*
DESCRIPTION: *150g/5oz rindless round*
CULINARY USE: *Table cheese*

This triple cream cheese has a wonderfully rich texture. There is a peppercorn version as well as a softer type, which has a white rind and creamy flavour. The cheese is packed into small, wooden crates for sale.

REMEDOU

REGION: *Liège*
TYPE: *Traditional, farmhouse and creamery, washed-rind cheese*
SOURCE: *Cow's milk*
DESCRIPTION: *200–675g/7oz–1½lb square with shiny, moist, red-brown, washed rind*
CULINARY USE: *Table cheese*

Also known as Piquant, which is something of an understatement, this is a larger and particularly aggressive version of Herve. Its size means that it takes longer to ripen, which gives the surface bacteria time to exude the powerful aroma for which the cheese is famous. It is known locally as "stinking cheese" and is best eaten in the open air with a glass of robust, red wine or local beer.

The name of the cheese is said to come from *remoud,* which was an old Walloon word for the rich milk produced towards the end of a cow's lactation period.

ABOVE: Rubens

RUBENS

REGION: *Lo*
TYPE: *Traditional, farmhouse and creamery, semi-soft cheese*
SOURCE: *Cow's milk*
DESCRIPTION: *3kg/6½lb oval with firm, smooth, red-brown, washed rind*
CULINARY USE: *Table cheese*

A chubby, wholesome-looking cheese with a rich, smooth, subtle taste, Rubens is covered with a smooth, reddish-brown, protective coat. One of many old Belgian cheeses revived in the 1960s, it carries a label bearing a portrait of the Flemish painter after whom it is named.

Danish Cheeses

Denmark's maritime climate and flat meadowlands make it an ideal environment for the comfort-loving cow that becomes a familiar sight as you travel through the picturesque countryside.

Thanks to its geographical position and its Viking past, Denmark has always been a trading nation. The cheese industry was originally based upon varieties made in neighbouring Germany and Holland – cheeses like Gouda, valued for the way it withstood the rigours of sea travel, and Limburger. There are few original Danish cheeses: most are highly efficient copies, many of which now carry Danish names as a result of the Stresa Convention of 1951.

The classic example of Danish cheese is Samso, which was developed in the nineteenth century along the lines of a Swiss-style cheese. Outside Denmark, its best-known cheese is, however, Danish Blue (Danablu), which is based on the French blues.

Danish Feta, a popular cheese that is even exported to the Middle East, was recently at the centre of a controversy over the name. A fierce battle is now brewing between Greece and the European Parliament as to whether Greece should be allowed sole rights to use the name feta for its own cheese.

Over 60 per cent of all cheese made in Denmark is exported, and its Ministry of Agriculture is fiercely protective of the industry. It demands very high standards and has banned the production of raw milk cheeses. Although the cow is by far the most important dairy animal, some goat's milk cheese is made, but mainly for home consumption.

Bla Castello/Blue Castello

Region: *Various*

Type: *Modern, creamery, blue cheese*

Source: *Cow's milk*

Description: *150g/5oz and 1kg/2¼lb half-moon-shaped cheese. The moist, natural rind may develop some grey, brown or white moulds*

Culinary use: *Table cheese*

Developed in the 1960s to meet the growing demand for mild, creamy blues, Bla Castello has a Brie-like texture, with the the blue in fairly thick, horizontal lines. Enriched with cream, it has a fat content of 70 per cent. The aroma is of mushrooms and the taste is mildly spicy. A popular cheese, but one which some regard as rather bland.

Danablu/Danish Blue

Region: *Various*

Type: *Modern, creamery, blue cheese*

Source: Cow's milk

Description: *3kg/6½lb drum or block. The sticky, yellow, natural rind has some brownish-grey or blue moulds*

Culinary uses: *Table cheese, snacks, also crumbled in salads*

This cheese was invented in the early twentieth century by Marius Boel as an alternative to Roquefort, although the two cheeses are very different. It is now known throughout the western world and sales show no signs of abating. The name Danablu is protected by the Stresa Convention; Danish Blue, however, is not.

The appeal of the cheese lies in its sharp, almost metallic taste, salty bite and creamy feel in the mouth. The interior is very white and makes an attractive contrast to the blue-black mould, which is rather gritty and salty (additional salt is added to some exported cheeses).

Danablu ripens in two to three months and has a fat content of 50–60 per cent. It is also known as Marmora.

Left: Danish Blue (top) and Mycella

LEFT: Esrom

RIGHT: Havarti

DANBO
REGION: *Various*
TYPE: *Traditional, farmhouse and creamery, semi-soft cheese*
SOURCE: *Cow's milk*
DESCRIPTION: *Rectangular cheese with smooth, dry, yellow rind, sometimes covered in red or yellow wax*
CULINARY USES: *Snacks, breakfast, grilling*

One of the most popular Danish cheeses, it is similar to Samso. Mild and slightly aromatic, it has a pale, elastic interior with a few peanut-sized holes. Occasionally, the cheese contains caraway seeds.

Danbo ripens in six weeks to five months and has a fat content of 45 per cent. Similar cheeses include Fynbo, Elbo, Svenbo and Molbo. Danbo is also called King Christian or Christian IX, by which names it is known in the USA.

RIGHT: Danbo

ESROM
REGION: *Various*
TYPE: *Traditional, creamery, semi-soft cheese*
SOURCE: *Cow's milk*
DESCRIPTION: *200g–2kg/7oz–4½lb rectangular cheese with smooth, sticky, pale yellow, washed rind*
CULINARY USES: *Table cheese, snacks, open sandwiches*

Made from an old recipe that was rediscovered by the Danish Cheese Institute in 1951, this cheese is mild and buttery when young. As it ages, it develops a fuller, more robust flavour. The interior, which is scattered with small, irregular-shaped holes, is supple, elastic and generally quite sweet, although it can be pungent.

Esrom ripens in about three weeks and has a fat content of between 45 and 50 per cent. It is named after the ancient monastery of Esrom, and is protected by the Stresa Convention.

HAVARTI
REGION: *Various*
TYPE: *Traditional, creamery, semi-soft cheese*
SOURCE: *Cow's milk*
DESCRIPTION: *2–4.5kg/4½–10lb blocks or drums*
CULINARY USES: *Table cheese, slicing, grilling, snacks*

In the middle of the last century, Hanne Nielsen, a cheese "evangelist", undertook a one-woman crusade to learn about cheesemaking from some of Europe's best artisan cheesemakers. On her return to Denmark, she set about introducing new ideas and methods to the industry, which at that time was rather uninspired. Havarti, named after the farm where Hanne first made the cheese, was her greatest success.

It is a simple, washed-rind cheese with irregular holes throughout. Fairly full-flavoured and creamy at about three months old, it becomes more outspoken with age.

There is an enriched version, with added cream, which is softer and feels more luxurious in the mouth. There is also a version with caraway seeds.

Below: *Maribo*

Maribo

Region: *Various*
Type: *Traditional, creamery, semi-hard cheese*
Source: *Cow's milk*
Description: *9–14kg/20–31lb round or block. The natural rind has a pale yellow, wax coating*
Culinary uses: *Table cheese, grilling, breakfast*

Named after the town on the island of Lolland, Maribo is widely available in Denmark, but is seldom exported. More full-flavoured than Danbo, it resembles Gouda and has a firm, dry interior scattered with numerous irregular holes. It is usually coated with yellow wax and is sometimes flavoured with caraway seeds.

It ripens in four months and has a fat content of between 30 and 45 per cent.

Mycella

Region: *Various*
Type: *Traditional, creamery, blue cheese*
Source: *Cow's milk*
Description: *5kg/11lb drum with natural, pale orange-brown crust*
Culinary uses: *Table cheese, snacks, spreading, salads*

Once known as Danish Gorgonzola, this cheese takes its name from the mould that gives it its thin strands or streaks of greenish-blue: *Penicillium mycellium*. The veins in the cheese provide an attractive contrast to the very pale, creamy, almost buttery interior. The flavour of Mycella is relatively mild for a blue cheese.

Samsø

Region: *Various*
Type: *Traditional, creamery, semi-hard cheese*
Source: *Cow's milk*
Description: *14kg/31lb wheel or rectangle without rind*
Culinary uses: *Table cheese, grilling, grating, snacks, fondue*

In the early nineteenth century, the Danish king saw the potential for diversifying the cheesemaking in his country and invited a Swiss cheesemaker to advise the Danish farmers. The result was Samsø, named after the island of Samsø, and forefather of many Danish cheeses.

Looking rather like a pale Emmental, Samsø has a supple, elastic texture with a few irregular-sized holes. When young, it tastes mild and buttery. However, the Danes seem to prefer it aged, when it develops a definite sweet-sour pungency and a distinct, hazelnut flavour. It is the classic cheese to use for the Danish open sandwich.

Samsø ripens in two to three months and has a fat content of 45 per cent.

Below: *Samsø*

Norwegian Cheeses

Less than one per cent of the long, narrow strip of land bordering the Norwegian Sea is grazing land. Most of Norway consists of native forest and rugged mountains. In the north, the magnificent tundra is home to the reindeer, a few Laplanders and little else.

Yet the Vikings chose Norway as the base for their frequent forays across the sea. Around the ninth century, with the help and determination of Irish monks, they turned their ferocious energy to conquering the land and to making cheese. It would seem that some of the more eccentric cheeses the Norwegians have since created continue to reflect the intrepid sense of adventure of their ancestors!

Gammelost

Region: *Various*
Type: *Traditional, farmhouse and creamery, blue cheese*
Source: *Goat's milk*
Description: *3kg/6½lb drum. The hard, pitted, natural crust is greenish, brown, with some mould*
Culinary uses: *Table cheese, served after dinner with aquavit or gin; also grated*

Gammelost is extremely robust, sharp and aromatic. There is erratic blueing throughout the brownish-yellow paste. The texture starts soft, but is extremely hard, almost brittle, when the cheese is aged.

The name – Gammelost – means "old cheese" and stems from the fact that the rind grows a green-brown mould and looks old before its time. To encourage the mould, the young Gammelost was traditionally wrapped in straw soaked in gin and juniper berries, which added to the flavour.

Gammelost has a fat content of only 5 per cent.

Right: Gjetost

Gjetost

Region: *Various*
Type: *Traditional, farmhouse and creamery, semi-hard cheese*
Source: *Cow's and goat's milk*
Description: *250–500g/9oz–1¼lb block, deep honey-brown in colour, without rind*
Culinary uses: *Snacks; often served as a dessert, with coffee*

A fudge-coloured whey cheese, originally made entirely from goat's milk (*gjet* means goat), but is now more often made with a blend of goat's and cow's milk. It is sweet, with an unusual, aromatic quality.

Gjetost is not to everyone's taste, but Norwegians love it. It is their most popular cheese, available in various versions. When made from pure cow's milk it is called Mysost, while the pure goat's milk version is called Ekta Gjetost.

It is traditionally eaten for breakfast.

Jarlsberg

Region: *Various*
Type: *Traditional, creamery, hard cheese*
Source: *Cow's milk*
Description: *10kg/22lb wheel with smooth, yellow, waxed, natural rind*
Culinary uses: *Table cheese, melting, grilling, snacks*

This old Norwegian cheese, based on Emmental, was all but forgotten before its discovery in the mid-1900s. Today it is extremely popular and a great deal is exported, particularly to the USA.

Made from the rich milk of the high summer pastures, Jarlsberg is sweeter and less nutty than Emmental. Although it lacks the depth of that great cheese, Jarlsberg has a pleasant flavour. The paste is golden yellow, with holes of various sizes.

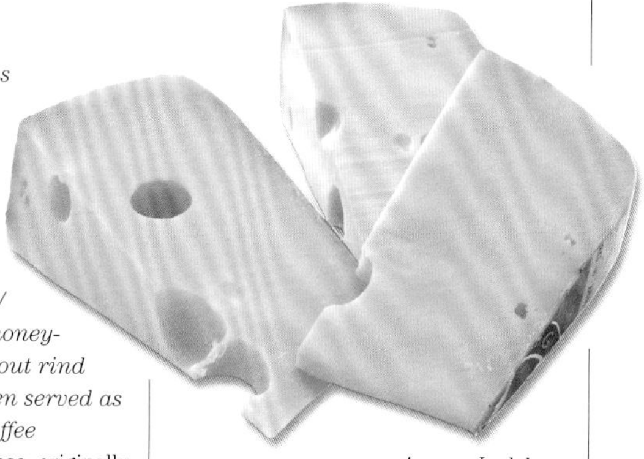

Above: Jarlsberg

Nökkelost

Region: *Various*
Type: *Traditional, creamery, semi-hard cheese*
Source: *Cow's milk*
Description: *5–12kg/11–26lb white wheel or block, flecked with cumin seeds and marked with the imprint of crossed keys*
Culinary uses: *Table cheese, grilling, melting over potatoes*

This mild, factory-made version of the Dutch cheese Leiden has been made in Norway since the seventeenth century. The crossed keys (*nökkel* in Norwegian) that appear on both Leiden and Nökkelost are the emblem of the city of Leiden. Nökkelost ripens in three months.

Ridder

Region: *Various*
Type: *Modern, creamery, semi-soft cheese*
Source: *Cow's milk*
Description: *3.25kg/7lb wheel with sticky, orange, washed rind*
Culinary use: *Table cheese*

Invented by Sven Fenelius, a Swedish cheesemaker, this cheese spread to Norway and is now made and copied the world over. It is open textured and elastic, not unlike the French Saint-Paulin, with a buttery feel and a sweet-savoury taste. The aroma can be quite pungent if the cheese is left wrapped in plastic for too long. Ridder ripens in three months.

Finnish Cheeses

Finland is a land of vast pine forests and thousands of lakes. One third of it lies within the Arctic Circle and the weather is often inhospitable. Despite these circumstances, dairy farming is the most important form of agriculture. Cows survive the winter in barns, and there is a tradition of cheesemaking dating back to the Middle Ages.

Many traditional cheeses share common ground with those made in neighbouring countries. More recently, with the help of Swiss cheesemakers, large, high-tech factories have created Finnish Swiss, a remarkably good copy of Emmental, which outsells all other types of Emmental in the United States.

Inside the Arctic Circle, some Laplanders still live the simple life of their ancestors, herding the reindeer that supply skins, meat and the milk from which Laplanders make their own unique cheese. Reindeer milk is exceptionally rich, containing nearly four times the amount of fat of cow's milk, and so coagulates easily. The cheese has a rather gamey, earthy flavour, which is said to intensify when it is dipped into hot coffee.

BELOW: *Juustoleipä*

Juustoleipä

REGION: *Various*
TYPE: *Traditional, farmhouse, fresh cheese*
SOURCE: *Cow's or reindeer's milk*
DESCRIPTION: *White, round cheeses in various sizes, charred from the fire*
CULINARY USES: *Generally served for breakfast or as a dessert with jam*

Juustoleipä is traditionally made on farms from cow's or reindeer's milk. The curds are drained and pressed into a flat, wooden platter with a rim. This is then held or placed in front of a fire until the outer layer is "toasted" – hence the name, which means "cheese bread". A speciality of Finland and Lapland, it is mild, creamy and smooth under the slightly charred, crusty surface. Today, most Juustoleipä is factory-made. It ripens in a few days.

Munajuusto/Ilves

REGION: *Various*
TYPE: *Traditional, farmhouse and creamery, fresh cheese*
SOURCE: *Cow's or reindeer's milk*
DESCRIPTION: *Pale yellow, flattened balls in various sizes, some with brownish pigments*
CULINARY USES: *Snacks, grilling*

This rather eccentric, farmhouse cheese is made by adding one or two eggs to milk, which is then heated until it curdles. The whey is drained off and the curd lightly pressed into hand-woven baskets. The result is a firm, moist, fresh cheese with a cheerful, sunshine-yellow colour. The surface becomes speckled with brown pigments. Like Juustoleipä, it can be roasted in front of a fire or grilled before being left to age. The factory version is called Ilves.

Tutunmaa

REGION: *Various*
TYPE: *Traditional, farmhouse and creamery, semi-hard cheese*
SOURCE: *Cow's milk*
DESCRIPTION: *6–10kg/13–22lb drum, pale yellow in colour, without rind*
CULINARY USE: *Table cheese*

A breakfast cheese, Tutunmaa was probably introduced in the sixteenth century and was first made in the great manor houses in Turku, Finland's ancient capital. The cheese is smooth and creamy, with a richness and depth of flavour that owes much to the excellent grazing. The texture is firm and open and the flavour is aromatic, with a slightly sharp tang on the finish.

Tutunmaa is matured for two months or more and has a fat content of 50 per cent. Korsholm is a similar cheese.

ABOVE: *Munajuusto/Ilves*

Swedish Cheeses

Unless you have been to Sweden in spring or summer, it is hard to imagine that this land of ancient glaciers and deep fjords could also be home to comfort-loving cows. Yet without them, and the hardy goats, survival would not have been possible during the long periods of winter isolation, when whole towns were cut off from supplies of fresh meat for months at a time.

Cheesemaking was introduced to Sweden in the ninth century AD by Benedictine monks, sent by Louis I, King of the Franks and Charlemagne's son, in an attempt to convert the warmongering Vikings to a more peaceful, God-fearing way of life. The monks set up dairies, encouraged the peasants to tend their goats and cows, and taught them how to make cheese. To avoid wasting the precious whey, still rich in milk sugars, minerals and protein, the Swedes came up with an ingenious way of converting it into a golden-brown, fudge-like cheese, which is known variously as Getost, Mesost and Getmesost.

Most cheesemaking in Sweden has now passed out of the hands of wives and families to become a national industry with stringent quality control. Sadly, much of the individuality and regional nature of the cheeses has been lost, although dairy products now represent a significant part of the Swedish economy.

Aria Ost, which is now one of the 10 largest cheesemakers in Europe, is a Swedish-based company producing more than 80,000 tonnes of cheese annually. Most of its output is semi soft cheese, which may help to explain why Swedes consume more semi-soft cheese than any other people in the world. Most of this is served and eaten either at breakfast or as part of a traditional smorgasbord.

Adelost

REGION: *Various*
TYPE: *Modern, creamery, blue cheese*
SOURCE: *Cow's milk*
DESCRIPTION: *2.5kg/5½lb drum with pale cream, natural rind lightly dusted with mould*
CULINARY USE: *Table cheese*

This moist, creamy cheese is not unlike Bleu d'Auvergne. The streaks of blue-grey mould are well distributed and it has a sharp, salty tang. Adelost ripens in two to three months and has a fat content of 50 per cent.

Gräddost

REGION: *Various*
TYPE: *Modern, creamery, semi-soft cheese*
SOURCE: *Cow's milk*
DESCRIPTION: *1kg/2¼lb truckle without rind*
CULINARY USES: *Table cheese, grilling, slicing*

This modern Swedish cheese was created in 1961 and soon became popular. Similar to Havarti, it is a firm cheese with small, evenly distributed holes. The flavour is mild and very creamy, with a fresh acidity. Gräddost has a fat content of about 60 per cent.

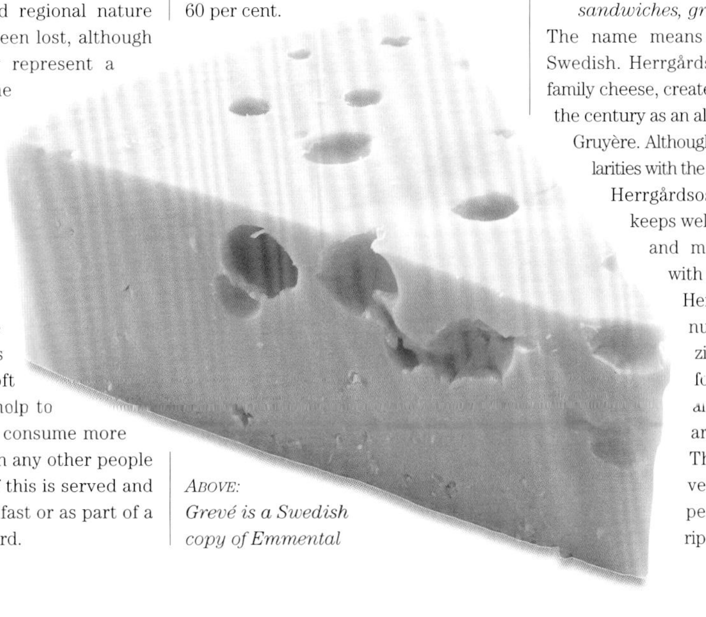

ABOVE: Grevé is a Swedish copy of Emmental

Grevéost/Grevé

REGION: *Various*
TYPE: *Modern, creamery, semi-hard cheese*
SOURCE: *Cow's milk*
DESCRIPTION: *14kg/30lb wheel with smooth, polished, pale yellow, natural rind*
CULINARY USES: *Table cheese, grating, melting*

A milder, more commercial copy of Swiss Emmental, Grevéost is supple and dense, with a few large holes. The pale interior is sweet and nutty, and feels very creamy. With age, the flavours become more pronounced, but it lacks the depth of flavour and character of genuine Emmental.

Grevéost ripens in 10 months and has a fat content of 45 per cent.

Herrgårdsost

REGION: *Various*
TYPE: *Traditional, creamery, semi-hard cheese*
SOURCE: *Cow's milk*
DESCRIPTION: *12–18kg/26–39lb round cheese. The smooth, pale yellow, natural rind is usually covered with yellow wax*
CULINARY USES: *Snacks, salads, sandwiches, grilling, breakfast*

The name means "manor house" in Swedish. Herrgårdsost is an all-round, family cheese, created at the beginning of the century as an alternative to imported Gruyère. Although there are some similarities with the original – like Gruyère, Herrgårdsost melts easily and keeps well – it is a much softer and more supple cheese, with smaller, round holes. Herrgårdsost has a mild nuttiness and fresh, zingy tang. It is ripened for up to seven months and has a fat content of around 45 per cent. There is also a low-fat version, which has 30 per cent fat. It is ripened for four months.

Hushållsost

Region: *Various*
Type: *Traditional, creamery, semi-soft cheese*
Source: *Cow's milk*
Description: *3kg/6½lb drum with natural rind*
Culinary uses: *Snacks, grilling, sandwiches*

The history of Hushållsost can be traced back over 700 years. The name simply means "household cheese", and its versatility has made it one of Sweden's best-known cheeses. The pale, straw-coloured interior has a smooth, open texture and small, irregular holes. The flavour is mild and creamy, with a lemon-fresh finish.

Unlike most Swedish cheeses, Hushållsost is made with whole milk, rather than skimmed. It has a fat content of 45 per cent and ripens in about one to three months.

Mesost

Region: *Various*
Type: *Traditional, farmhouse and creamery, whey cheese*
Source: *Cow's milk*
Description: *1–8kg/2¼–18lb block, smooth and pale tan to dark coffee in colour, without rind*
Culinary use: *Snacks*

Caramelized whey cheeses are peculiar to Scandinavia, and grew out of the need to utilize and preserve every element of the milk, a vital resource in a country where isolation is a way of life. The whey is heated, which causes the residual proteins and fat to separate out. Gradually the liquid evaporates to leave a sticky, toffee-like mass of caramelized milk sugars. This is poured into moulds and left to set, before being cut into blocks and wrapped in foil for sale.

The texture is dense and can be slightly brittle. Mesost looks like fudge and has a creamy, caramel flavour with a strangely bitter aftertaste. It is not as sweet as Norwegian Gjetost, which is made from whole milk.

Mesost has a fat content of between 10 and 20 per cent. The commercially made cheese usually has whole milk or cream added to ensure a greater yield and sweeter taste.

Prästost

Region: *Various*
Type: *Traditional, creamery, semi-hard cheese*
Source: *Cow's milk*
Description: *12–15kg/26–33lb wheel with a pale yellow rind covered in fine cloth and with a yellow wax coat*
Culinary use: *Table cheese*

The origin of Prästost ("priest's cheese") dates back to the sixteenth century, when farmers paid a tithe to the local pastor in milk. It was then his wife's lot to make it into cheese to be sold at the local market. Success at the marketplace was said to be as much a reflection of her husband's popularity as her cheesemaking skills.

Today, Prästost is made only in factories. The cheese is supple, with a slightly mushy texture and many irregular, rice-sized holes. It has a mellow to robust, sweet-sour, lactic flavour that leaves a sharp, fruity tingle on the palate. It is matured for at least two months and has a fat content of 45 per cent.

Prästost washed in whisky is called Saaland Pfarr and has the robust character of the French washed-rind cheeses.

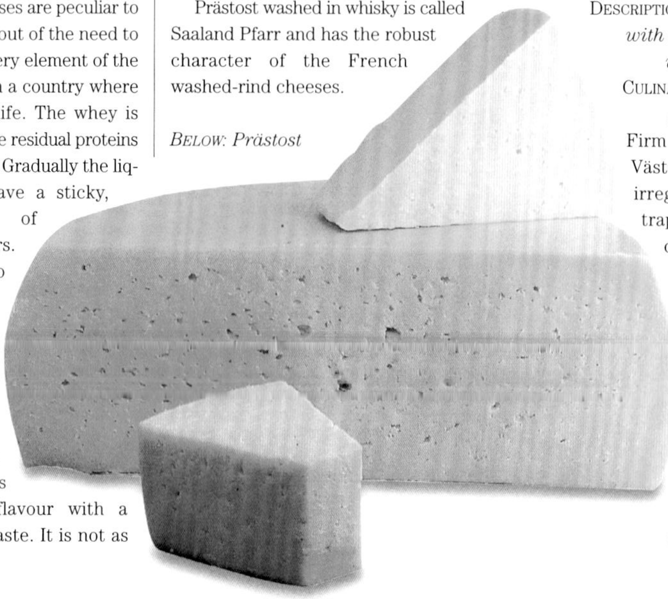

Below: *Prästost*

Sveciaost

Region: *Various*
Type: *Modern, creamery, semi-hard cheese*
Source: *Cow's milk*
Description: *12–16kg/26–35lb wheel without rind*
Culinary uses: *Table cheese, grating, grilling*

Svecia is the Latin name for Sweden and is here used to describe a range of cheeses in the traditional Swedish style which were introduced to compete on the international market with the cheeses of the Netherlands, such as Edam and Gouda. Available in different sizes and at different stages of maturity, the cheeses are frequently waxed and are sold in a variety of flavours, including cloves, cumin and caraway. Their fat content ranges from 30 to 45 per cent.

Semi-hard Sveciaost looks like Herrgårdsost, but is smaller. The texture is moist and supple and the cheese has a number of small holes. It has a pleasant, fresh acidity that matures to a more assertive piquancy.

Västerbottenost

Region: *Various*
Type: *Traditional, creamery, semi-hard cheese*
Source: *Cow's milk*
Description: *20kg/44lb wheel with smooth, orange, waxed rind*
Culinary uses: *Table cheese, grilling, grating*

Firm and very crumbly, Västerbottenost has small, irregular eyes and some trapped moisture. The cheese was invented in the mid-nineteenth century in West Bothnia and is still exclusive to the area. Excellent for grating and melting in sauces, this cheese has a biteable, somewhat granular texture and a very definite, sharply fruity bite.

GREEK CHEESES

The ancient Greeks regarded cheese as the food of the gods, as well as sustenance for mere mortals, and there are countless references to the subject in their literature. One of the earliest and most significant of these is in Homer's *Odyssey*, written around 700BC. In describing the meeting between Odysseus and the Cyclops Polyphemus in Sicily, Homer writes: "There it was that our human monster had his shelter. We entered into the caravan and looked around it: racks laden with cheese, lambs and kid goats in crowded pens – one stall for every age – metal pots, all filled with milk, earthenware vessels, buckets used for milking." Later, Homer describes Polyphemus making fresh cheese and turning "half his white milk into a curd, which he strained and placed in his rush basket". The baskets were called *formoi*, from which stems several modern words for cheese, such as the French *fromage* or the Italian *formaggio*.

In remote parts of Greece, women still weave by hand the reed baskets used for draining the cheese. Goats graze on wild, herb-scented hillsides, and the bray of the shepherd's donkey can be heard as flocks of sheep pass through the villages early in the morning on their way to new pastures.

A climate of strong contrasts, coupled with terrain that is inhospitable to all but the hardiest sheep and goats, has meant that meat has always been regarded as a luxury in Greece. Milk and its derivatives have therefore played a significant role in Greek cuisine.

The Greeks consume more cheese per head than even the French. For breakfast they enjoy semi-hard cheeses or bowls of fresh fruit covered with dollops of superb, creamy yogurt and wild honey. Lunch is the ubiquitous but unbeatable Greek salad of sun-ripened tomatoes, olives, cucumber, olive oil and feta. At other times of the day cheese appears in a wide range of guises – in pies, tarts, pastries, soups, bakes and toasted sandwiches.

Large modern factories and co-operatives are now established in the main dairy areas, producing Graviera, Kaseri and feta. Such is the demand for feta that much is now made from cow's milk or even imported from northern Europe.

Cheeses of all shapes and varieties are available in supermarkets and tiny cheese shops, but the best cheeses are often those the shepherds make themselves.

BELOW: The shape of feta is dictated by the containers used – pottery bowls, woven baskets or wooden trays

ANTHOTIRO/ANTHOTYROS

REGION: *Various*
TYPE: *Traditional, farmhouse, unpasteurized, whey cheese*
SOURCE: *Sheep's and goat's milk*
DESCRIPTION: *Made in various sizes and shapes, particularly balls and truncated cones. Dry and white, the cheese has no rind*
CULINARY USES: *For breakfast with honey or fruit; in desserts; in savoury dishes with oil and wild herbs*

Milk was, and still is, a valuable commodity to Greek shepherds and their families. It was important that none should be wasted, so the ancient Greeks – like the Romans in respect of ricotta – developed numerous ways of converting whey into delicious cheeses. Anthotiro has been made for centuries. The name means "flower cheese", so called because the aroma and flavour carry a hint of the wild flowers and herbs on which the animals graze. Smooth, hard and moist, the cheese has a fine, crumbly texture. The pure white interior is delicate, and the famed floral flavour has a smoky tinge.

Ripening between two and five days, the cheese has a fat content of between 20 and 30 per cent. Milk is sometimes added to the whey to make a slightly richer cheese.

FETA

REGION: *Various*
TYPE: *Traditional, farmhouse and creamery, unpasteurized, fresh (brined) cheese*
SOURCE: *Cow's, goat's and sheep's milk*
DESCRIPTION: *Made in various sizes, often as a loaf-shape, feta is smooth and white and has no rind*
CULINARY USES: *Baking, especially in pastries; also in salads*

One of the simplest forms of cheese, feta grew out of the necessity for shepherds long ago to preserve the milk of their nomadic herds. In the *Odyssey*, Homer gives a detailed description of how the cheese is made. Virtually the same recipe is used today: fresh milk is heated to about 35°C/95°F, the rennet is added and the mixture left to coagulate. Once the milk has curdled or separated, the curd is cut or broken and the whey drained off. The moist, lumpy curds are then put in a cloth bag, twisted or pressed, then hung for a few hours to dry out. When the curd is firm enough, it is cut into slices, liberally sprinkled with salt (the more salt added, the harder the cheese will be) and left to dry for about 24 hours before being packed in wooden barrels and covered with brine. The cheese is ready to eat in about a month and will keep almost indefinitely if submerged in salt or brine.

Feta is solid but crumbly, with some fissures. Pure white, it has a milky, fresh acidity. Today, most feta is made with pasteurized milk and tastes of little besides salt. In parts of Greece, Turkey and Bulgaria, however, it is still possible to find excellent feta that reflects the diversity and character of the rich, concentrated milk from animals that graze the wild and rocky mountain pastures.

Some people are put off by the strong salt content, but the salt is intended only as a preservative and is not supposed to overpower the taste of the cheese. Feta can be soaked in fresh, cold water or milk for a few minutes or longer, if necessary, to make it less salty.

Feta has a fat content of 40–50 per cent.

GRAVIERA

REGION: *Dodoni, Naxos and Crete*
TYPE: *Traditional, farmhouse and co-operative, unpasteurized, hard cheese*
SOURCE: *Cow's, goat's or sheep's milk*
DESCRIPTION: *2–8kg/4½–18lb wheel. The hard, cooked rind has a criss-cross pattern derived from the cloth in which the cheese was drained*
CULINARY USES: *Table cheese, snacks, pastries*

After feta, this is the most popular of the Greek cheeses, ideal for all occasions. Like many Greek cheeses, it can be made from cow's, goat's or sheep's milk, depending on the season, although the majority is today made from cow's milk. Much like Gruyère, from which it is copied, it is sweetish and fruity, with a firm yet supple texture, tiny holes and a rich, creamy feel. Graviera from Crete, made from sheep's milk, is much sought after for its delicate fragrance and burnt-caramel taste, which becomes richer and nuttier when the cheese is baked. The island of Naxos produces a wonderfully nutty, cow's milk Graviera in a small local co-operative.

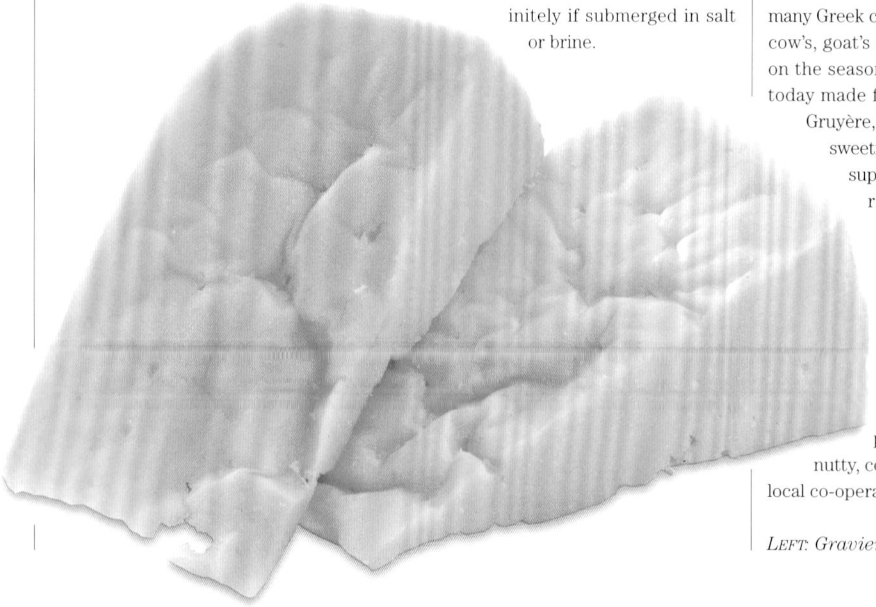

LEFT: Graviera

RIGHT: Kefalotiri is made from sheep's milk

KASERI

REGION: *Various*
TYPE: *Traditional, farmhouse and co-operative, unpasteurized, stretched curd cheese*
SOURCE: *Sheep's and goat's milk*
DESCRIPTION: *1–9kg/2¼–20lb wheel. There is no rind, but the white crust is smooth, creamy and springy*
CULINARY USES: *Table cheese, melting, grilling, baking (in pastries)*

Kaseri must be at least 80 per cent sheep's milk, with the remainder goat's milk. It is a young version of Kefalotiri, which has been immersed in hot brine to create the characteristic, rubbery, stringy texture. As such it resembles the Italian Provolone Dolce, but has a much stronger flavour. Quite salty and pungent, with a dry feel in the mouth, it has an underlying sweetness due to the sheep's milk. Kaseri is used in Greece in place of mozzarella and appears in numerous local dishes.

KEFALOTIRI/KEFALOTYRI

REGION: *Various*
TYPE: *Traditional, farmhouse and co-operative, unpasteurized, hard cheese*
SOURCE: *Sheep's milk*
DESCRIPTION: *6–8kg/13–18lb drum with thin, hard, natural rind ranging in colour from white to rich yellow*
CULINARY USES: *Breakfast cheese, grating, baking, snacks*

Kefalotiri was already well known and respected by the time of the Byzantine era. It is said to take its name from *kefalo*, a Greek hat. Historically, it was the first cheese to be made at the start of the new season. As soon as the young lambs were weaned, the sheep's milk was used to make this popular cheese. The colour varies from white to yellow, depending on the mix of milk and the grazing, and the firm, dry cheese has numerous irregular holes. The flavour is pleasantly fresh, with a distinct taste of sheep's milk and a slightly sharp finish, not unlike a very fruity, herbaceous olive oil.

Kefalotiri is described as a "male" or "first" cheese to indicate that it is made with full-cream milk; the more delicate whey cheeses (like Manouri, Myzithra or Anthotiro) are called "female" or "second" cheeses. The cheese ripens in two or three months and has a fat content of 40–55 per cent.

MANOURI

REGION: *Crete and Macedonia*
TYPE: *Traditional, farmhouse, unpasteurized, whey cheese*
SOURCE: *Sheep's or goat's milk*
DESCRIPTION: *Made in various sizes, in shapes ranging from large, tapered logs to truncated cones, this smooth, white cheese has no rind*
CULINARY USES: *Mainly used in pastries such as spanakopita or drizzled with honey and served for breakfast as a low-fat alternative to Greek yogurt*

An ancient cheese, made from the whey from feta or Kefalotiri, Manouri is creamy and white, with the texture of a light cheesecake. It melts in the mouth and has a fresh, milky, slightly citrus flavour. Firmer than Myzithra, it is also known as Manoypi.

MYZITHRA/MITZITHRA

REGION: *Various*
TYPE: *Traditional, farmhouse and co-operative, unpasteurized, whey cheese*
SOURCE: *Sheep's milk*
DESCRIPTION: *Rindless rounds of various sizes, showing the imprint of the cloth in which they were drained.*
CULINARY USES: *Baked in light pastries or with vegetables. Also eaten fresh*

Myzithra is a mild, refreshing cheese with a fine, crumbly texture. It was originally made with the whey from Kefalotiri or feta, to which some milk or cream was added. It can be eaten after a few days or ripened for several months. Where milk is abundant, Myzithra may be preserved in salt and dried as a firm, grating cheese. A sour form is sold as Xinomyzithira.

XYNOTYRO

REGION: *Various*
TYPE: *Traditional, farmhouse, unpasteurized, whey cheese*
SOURCE: *Sheep's and goat's milk cheese*
DESCRIPTION: *Made in various shapes and sizes and marked by the reed baskets in which they are drained, these cheeses do not have any rind*
CULINARY USES: *Baking, salads*

The name means "sour cheese", which is a rather inadequate description for a hard, flaky cheese that melts in the mouth to leave a distinct, sweet-sour sensation on the palate. The flavour of Xynotyro is a combination of sweet, burnt caramel, lanolin (typical of sheep's milk cheeses) and the sour taste of the whey. It ripens in a few days and has a fat content of 20 per cent.

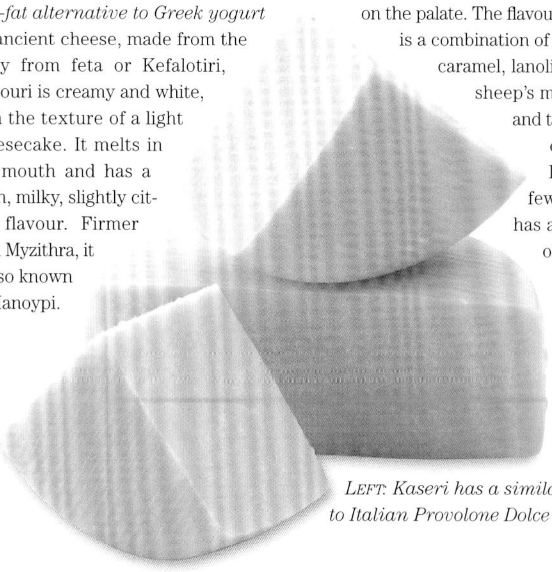

LEFT: Kaseri has a similar texture to Italian Provolone Dolce

Turkish Cheeses

The forefathers of the modern Turks migrated from Central Asia and arrived in Anatolia in the tenth century. Like many nomadic tribes, they travelled with the sheep on which they depended for their survival, and which provided them with wool for their clothing and rugs, meat and – most important – fresh milk for both their yogurt (*sivi tas*) and cheese (*peynir*).

In parts of Turkey, shepherds still wander the hills with their flocks and cheeses are still made from recipes handed down over many years from one generation to the next. Milking is done in ancient, stone enclosures, and cheeses can still be seen hanging over open fires, or draining in bags made from goat skins slung under the branches of trees.

In local markets, you may encounter the soft, white, sheep's milk feta (Beyaz Peynir) alongside Gravyer Peynir (Turkish Gruyère) and rustic cheeses, but the majority of cheese is now made in factories, from cow's, goat's or sheep's milk.

Other cheeses you may come across as you travel through this fascinating country include Taze Kaser (fresh cheese), which, despite its name, is a hard cheese, mainly used as a filling for the delicious Turkish-style toasted sandwiches. Another favourite is Eski Kaser (old cheese), which is rather like a Pecorino, though less salty. Firm, dry and white, it becomes softer and a turns a deep yellow with age. Eski Kaser is often served with honey for breakfast. Alternatively, it can be cut into blocks and preserved in brine.

Made from sheep's milk, Kasar Peynir is a hard, tangy cheese that is pale lemon in colour; Los Peynir is a light, creamy whey cheese, which resembles yogurt; Tulum is a cheese that is made and stored in the stomach or skin of a goat; Mihalic Peynir is a rich, unsalted sheep's milk cheese and Dil Peynir is a mild, stretched-curd cheese.

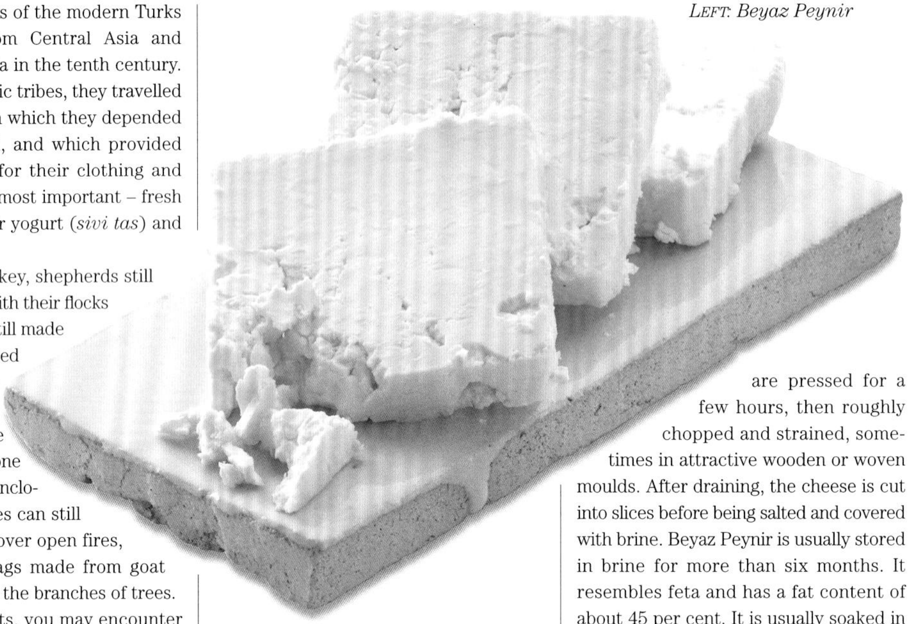

LEFT: *Beyaz Peynir*

One of the simplest cheeses, Koy Peynir, is made in village homes throughout Anatolia. Milk is warmed to blood heat, salt and rennet are stirred in, and the mixture is then pulled off the heat, covered and left overnight. Next morning, the coagulated milk is tipped into a cloth-lined sieve and left for six hours to drain. The cheese that remains in the sieve should be soft and creamy. It is either eaten as it is or used in cooking.

Beyaz Peynir

REGION: *Various*
TYPE: *Traditional, farmhouse and co-operative, unpasteurized, vegetarian, fresh cheese*
SOURCE: *Sheep's milk*
DESCRIPTION: *Pure white and rindless, the cheese has a grainy appearance. It is usually sold in blocks or slices*
CULINARY USES: *Fresh in salads, cooked in pastries and many local dishes*

The most popular Turkish cheese, Beyaz Peynir is made in factories and co-operatives and by shepherds. Vegetable rennet is used to clot the milk. The curds are pressed for a few hours, then roughly chopped and strained, sometimes in attractive wooden or woven moulds. After draining, the cheese is cut into slices before being salted and covered with brine. Beyaz Peynir is usually stored in brine for more than six months. It resembles feta and has a fat content of about 45 per cent. It is usually soaked in cold water or milk before use, to remove the excess salt.

Mihalic Peynir

REGION: *Bursa*
TYPE: *Traditional, farmhouse, unpasteurized, vegetarian, hard cheese*
SOURCE: *Sheep's milk*
DESCRIPTION: *Made in various sizes and shapes – often as balls or slices – the cheese is smooth and white with no rind*
CULINARY USES: *Fresh in salads, also used in baked dishes*

The fresh curd is divided into small portions, which are placed in hot water, which is then stirred. The curds are left in the water to harden and acquire a firm, slightly elastic texture, then they are tied in a cloth, which is twisted to force out the whey. Finally, the curds are rolled into small balls, or shaped and sliced, then salted and dried. Mihalic Peynir is stored in brine to preserve and protect the cheese until it is needed. It often goes by the name of the village where it is made.

The Cheeses of Cyprus

Traces of civilization dating back to the fifteenth century BC have been discovered in Cyprus. The modern city of Larnaca was once the centre of the Phoenician civilization and the island was for centuries an important trading post for the Aegean sea and the eastern Mediterranean. The discovery of rich copper deposits in the third century BC brought considerable wealth to the country and attracted often uninvited attention from a succession of invaders, including the Romans, the Byzantines and the Ottoman Turks.

Through all the centuries of conflict, the shepherds in the rugged interior continued to herd their goats and sheep, making cheese in the same way as their fathers and forefathers had before them. Feta, Kaskavali, which is similar to the Bulgarian Katschkawalj or the Italian Caciocavallo, and Halloumi are the most common varieties. Despite the on-going battle between the Greek and Turkish communities, Cyprus is an increasingly popular holiday destination.

Halloumi

Region: *Various*
Type: *Traditional, farmhouse and creamery, stretched curd cheese*
Source: *Sheep's, cow's or goat's milk*
Description: *Small, rectangular block or loaf shapes in various different sizes. The cheese is shiny, white and smooth, without rind*
Culinary uses: Frying, grilling, barbecuing

Originally a sheep's or goat's milk cheese, Halloumi is now more often produced from cow's milk. The curd is heated in hot water, then kneaded. Chopped mint is usually added and the elastic, squeaky curd is rolled out like pastry and cut into small blocks. These are stored in light brine until needed.

Halloumi has a fibrous, rubbery texture and its otherwise bland, milky taste is heightened by the herby flavour of the chopped fresh mint and the salt from the brine. Denser than mozzarella, it is fundamentally a cooking cheese, whose true character is only revealed when it is heated. Halloumi is one of the few cheeses that will hold its shape when it is fried or grilled. If thin slices of the cheese are placed in a hot, non-stick pan, the outside will rapidly become crisp and slightly charred, while the centre melts deliciously, rather like mozzarella.

In recent years Halloumi has become more popular, particularly amongst the young chefs of Australia, New Zealand and the West Coast of America. To respond to their demands, this traditional Cypriot cheese has begun to be made by cheesemakers in Australia where it is called Halloumy, and by Pelusso Cheese in California who call their version Haloumi.

Halloumi is also made in Romania and Lebanon.

Left: Halloumi is a cooking cheese similar to mozzarella

Eastern European Cheeses

Eastern Europe has been in turmoil since AD552, when the original settlers, the Slavs, were forced from what is now the Ukraine, by the tribesman of the Russian Steppes. The Slavs crossed into Romania and Bulgaria during the sixth century BC taking with them their knowledge of farming and how to preserve milk in the form of yogurt and Sirene (a cheese similar to feta). Later, Roman occupation lead to the introduction of the style of cheese preferred by the Roman forces, although the only obvious survivors today are Katschkawalj and Halloumi.

Hungary, too, has few indigenous cheeses, although Turkish invaders introduced Brynza, a soft feta-like sheep's milk cheese. In Poland in the tenth century BC Polish cheesemakers began producing and exporting copies of European cheeses. Tylzscki, based on Tilsit, is one of the few that is still made.

By the end of the Second World War artisan cheesemaking had all but died out and throughout Eastern Europe, huge factories were constructed to produce bland, industrial copies of European cheeses like Gouda, Cheddar, Camembert. Emmental, Tilsit and Limburger. However, in the late 1980s small cheese production began to flourish and artisan cheeses began to be made again.

Abertam

Country: *Czech Republic*
Type: *Traditional, farmhouse and co-operative, hard cheese*
Source: *Sheep's milk*
Description: *500g/1¼lb irregular ball with thin, yellow to orange, natural rind*
Culinary uses: *Table cheese, melting, grilling*

Abertam is made in Karlovy-Vary (formerly Carlsbad), the famous spa town. The natural pastures of this mountainous part of Bohemia provide the native sheep with a rich diet that is revealed in the robust flavour of the hard, pressed cheese. Abertam ripens in two months and has a fat content of 45 per cent.

Balaton

Country: *Hungary*
Type: *Traditional, farmhouse and creamery, hard cheese*
Source: *Cow's milk*
Description: *9–12kg/20–26lb loaf shape with thin, greasy, natural rind*
Culinary uses: *Table cheese, grilling*

Named after the beautiful Lake Balaton, this Hungarian cheese has a firm, compact texture with a scattering of small holes. The flavour is mild, with a pleasant acidity.

Brinza/Burduf Brinza

Country: *Romania*
Type: *Traditional, farmhouse and co-operative, fresh cheese*
Source: *Sheep's milk*
Description: *White, slightly grainy cheese made in blocks*
Culinary uses: *Cooking cheese*

Brinza is the local name for cheese in the Carpathian region. Its origins go back to Roman times and beyond, and similar cheeses have been made for centuries. It is mild, moist, creamy and crumbly. Usually eaten within a day or two of being made, it has a delicate, sweet, aromatic character. Some of it is also preserved in salt for use during winter, when it more closely resembles feta.

Bryndza

Country: *Slovakia*
Type: *Traditional, farmhouse and co-operative, fresh cheese*
Source: *Sheep's milk*
Description: *Stark, white cheeses in various shapes and sizes, without rind*
Culinary uses: *Spread on rye bread, used in salads, baking*

Made throughout Eastern Europe, particularly in the Carpathian Mountains, this is a subtly flavoured sheep's milk cheese, which is cut into cubes and stored in brine. Crumbly and moist, it resembles feta, but is not as salty.

Bryndza can also be made with cow's or goat's milk, either of which will result in a different consistency. The cheese can range from soft and spreadable to firm and crumbly. As the shepherds and their flocks are often some distance from the co-operatives, they turn their milk into simple curds, press these into cloth sacks and leave them to drain. They are then taken to the dairies, where the curds are broken up, salted, milled and remoulded into blocks. Bryndza is also sold in wooden barrels, packed with yet more salt.

Bryndza is matured for four weeks or more. It has a fat content of around 45 per cent. Similar cheeses include the Romanian Brinza, Hungarian Brynza, Sirene from Bulgaria and Greek feta.

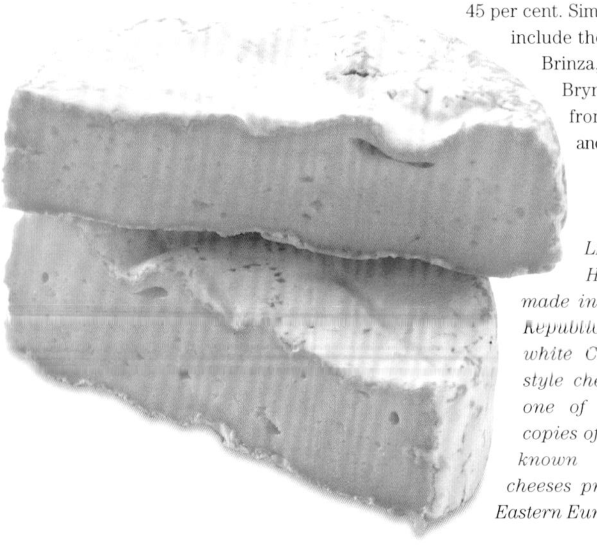

Left: Hermélin, made in the Czech Republic, is a soft-white Camembert-style cheese – just one of the many copies of the better-known European cheeses produced in Eastern Europe

HALLOUMI

COUNTRY: *Romania*
TYPE: *Traditional, farmhouse and creamery, stretched-curd cheese*
SOURCE: *Cow's milk*
DESCRIPTION: *300–675g/11oz–1½lb plaited cheese with smooth, shiny, pale yellow, natural rind*
CULINARY USES: *Frying, grilling, melting*

Like many Eastern European cheeses, Halloumi's origins are blurred by the migratory nature of the ancient peoples who once roamed this area. It seems likely that the Romans learned the stretched-curd technique from the Indo-Europeans who, before the Iron Age, spread over Europe from the Russian steppes. Their language and influence can be traced through Persia, Greece, Eastern Europe, the Middle East and down through Turkestan and northern India.

Halloumi is supple and stringy, becoming harder the longer it remains in the brine in which it is traditionally cured. It is also made in Cyprus and Lebanon.

KATSCHKAWALJ

COUNTRY: *Bulgaria*
TYPE: *Traditional, farmhouse and creamery, stretched-curd cheese*
SOURCE: *Sheep's milk*
DESCRIPTION: *6–9kg/13–20lb irregular round, with thin, pale yellow to yellowish-brown, natural rind*
CULINARY USES: *Table cheese, snacks, also fried or baked in local dishes*

Katschkawalj is a *pasta filata* (stretched-curd) cheese made from sheep's milk and found right across Eastern Europe and into Central Asia. It is thought to have originated before the days of the Roman Empire, and may have been the progenitor of the Italian Caciocavallo. Like all *pasta filata* cheeses, it is made by kneading and stretching the fresh curd before it is salted and aged. It keeps well and is valued for its versatility in cooking. Originally made principally by shepherds for their own consumption, it is now largely produced in factories.

Although the best Katschkawalj is made from sheep's milk, mixed milk and pure cow's milk versions are on the increase. The texture of the sheep's milk cheese is firm but flexible and crumbly. Underneath the pale yellow rind (which deepens in colour as the cheese matures), the cheese is salty, sharp and slightly bitter. The flavour has a hint of caramelized onion. Both eaten as a table cheese, and used extensively in cooking, Katschkawalj is sometimes referred to as the "Cheddar of the Balkans". It matures in two months and has a fat content of 45 per cent.

LAJTA

COUNTRY: *Hungary*
TYPE: *Traditional, farmhouse and co-operative, unpasteurized, semi-soft cheese*
SOURCE: *Cow's milk*
DESCRIPTION: *1kg/2¼lb rectangular cheese with moist, deep orange, washed rind*
CULINARY USE: *Table cheese*

This was undoubtedly introduced to Hungary by some order of intrepid monks, determined to convert the local populace, but missing the cheeses of Western Europe. The slightly sticky, washed rind covers a supple interior containing numerous small, irregular holes created as a result of the starter culture used and the ensuing vigorous fermentation process. Lajta has the robust aroma and taste characteristic of washed-rind cheeses. It ripens in four to six weeks and has a fat content of 50 per cent.

LIPTAUER

COUNTRY: *Hungary*
TYPE: *Traditional, farmhouse and co-operative, unpasteurized, fresh cheese*
SOURCE: *Sheep's or cow's milk*
DESCRIPTION: *Spiced, white cheese sold in pots*
CULINARY USE: *Forms the basis of numerous local dishes*

The Hungarians developed Liptauer from a simple, white, sheep's milk cheese called Liptoi, which was made by shepherds in their mountain huts. The curd was hung in cloth sacks for up to a week before being taken to a small dairy, where it was mixed with paprika and salt.

Each family has its own recipe for what has become known as Liptauer cheese. Onions, caraway seeds, capers, anchovies or other ingredients whose proportions are often secret are added to the curd, together with varying amounts of paprika. Hungarians have a great love of spicy food, so Liptauer can be exceedingly hot, even vicious. It has a fat content of around 50 per cent.

LIPTOI

COUNTRY: *Hungary*
TYPE: *Traditional, farmhouse and co-operative, unpasteurized, fresh cheese*
SOURCE: *Sheep's milk*
DESCRIPTION: *White, mousse-like cheese sold in pots*
CULINARY USES: *Snacks, hors d'oeuvres, salads*

For centuries, this simple cheese has been made by shepherds in the Tatra mountains. Fine and mousse-like, with the subtle, sweet taste of sheep's milk and rosemary, it is mixed with various spices and herbs. There are as many recipes for this cheese as there are makers, as the recipes are handed down from one generation to the next.

Liptoi is the basis for Liptauer, the best-known cheese of Eastern Europe, which combines paprika, caraway, onions and capers in a heady, sometimes wickedly hot spread. This is most often served as a dip, with celery – and copious amounts of the local beer.

MANUR/MANDUR

COUNTRY: *Serbia*
TYPE: *Traditional, farmhouse and creamery, unpasteurized, hard cheese*
SOURCE: *Sheep's or cow's milk*
Description: 2–3kg/4½–6½lb sphere with thin, white or straw-coloured, natural rind
CULINARY USES: *Grating – as a condiment or in soup*

This unusual cheese is unique to Serbia. The fresh milk (cow's or sheep's, depending on the season) is gradually heated until it boils. It is then cooled to hand hot and a mixture of buttermilk, fresh whey and rennet is added. Once set, the curd is drained in a cloth before being salted, shaped and dried. It ripens in a few days and has a fat content of 40 per cent.

Above: Koliba from the Czech Republic. Like this modern factory-made cheese, many of the traditional cheeses, which were made in what was once known as Czechoslovakia, had intricate designs carved into the moulds by the cheese-maker – giving each a unique pattern

Oschtjepka

Country: *Slovakia*
Type: *Traditional, farmhouse, unpasteurized, semi-hard cheese*
Source: *Cow's and sheep's milk*
Description: 500g/1¼lb round cheese with natural rind marked with slight indentations from the cloth used for draining and drying
Culinary uses: *Table cheese, grilling, melting*

Supple and elastic, Oschtjepka is similar to Bulgarian Katshkawalj. It has been made for centuries in the magnificent Carpathian Mountains, a mecca for sheep, with its fresh mountain streams and natural pastures.

Most of the cheese is still made by the shepherds themselves. The soured milk is pressed into balls, each the size of a small melon, and hung to dry from the ceilings of their mountain chalets. The sweet, aromatic smoke from the shepherds' fires gradually dries the cheese and adds to its flavour. Similar cheeses, which are also produced in Eastern Europe, include Parenica, which is made in Slovakia, and the Polish cheese, Oszczpek.

Oschtjepka ripens in about two to three months and has a fat content of around 45 per cent.

Oszczpek

Country: *Poland*
Type: *Traditional, farmhouse and co-operative, unpasteurized, semi-hard cheese*
Source: *Cow's and sheep's milk*
Description: *Made in various sizes and shapes (usually oval), with smooth, polished, pale lemon, natural rind which can be chocolate brown if the cheese is heavily smoked*
Culinary uses: *Table cheese, grilling, melting*

Oszczpek is one of the few remaining traditional cheeses to be found in Poland. Most of the other cheeses on sale there are factory-made imitations of the more popular European cheeses.Made in the Tatra Mountains, Oszczpek belongs to the same family as the Slovakian Oschtjepka.

The curd is kneaded, then pressed into hand-carved, wooden moulds. Once drained, the young cheeses are traditionally stored in the eaves of the house, where they gradually absorb the smoke from the fire.

Oszczpek ripens in one to four weeks and has a fat content of 45 per cent.

Podhalanski

Country: *Poland*
Type: *Traditional, farmhouse and creamery, unpasteurized, semi-hard cheese*
Source: *Cow's and sheep's milk*
Description: *500g/1¼lb brick or loaf shape with hard, pale yellow, natural rind that darkens to burnt orange if smoked*
Culinary uses: *Table cheese, grilling*

Firm, but supple, Podhalanski has tiny holes throughout the pale yellow interior. Some cheeses are lightly smoked in the style of earlier times. Podhalanski ripens in two months.

Siraz

Country: *Serbia*
Type: *Traditional, farmhouse, unpasteurized, semi-hard cheese*
Source: *Cow's milk*
Description: *200–400g/7–14oz flat disc. The rough, yellow, natural rind has some yeasts*
Culinary uses: *Table cheese, baking; often crumbled into local dishes*

To make this unusual Serbian cheese, the young curd is pressed into flat discs, about 15cm/6in in diameter. The cheese is then left in the sun to dry, often on a balcony wall, until the fat begins to ooze. The surface is rubbed and salted several times over the next few days until a crust forms, when the cheeses are stored in wooden containers of brine. The cheese ripens in a few weeks. It has a mellow, slightly sour, salty tang and a compact body.

Sirene

Country: *Bulgaria*
Type: *Traditional, farmhouse and creamery, unpasteurized, fresh cheese*
Source: *Sheep's and cow's milk*
Description: *White, slightly grainy cheese without rind, sold in blocks*
Culinary uses: *Salads, spreads, baking; also as a table cheese, with fresh herbs*

The most popular and most widely produced Bulgarian cheese. Moist, crumbly, fresh and lemony, it is stored in barrels or tins of brine. Sirene is richer and creamier than many similar cheeses, and has a fat content of 45–50 per cent.

The Cheeses of India and the Middle East

The culture and climate of India, and of many of her neighbours, have inadvertently conspired against the development of a dairy industry. The combination of high temperatures and humidity causes rapid growth of moulds, cracking of the cheese surface, excessive drying out and rapid putrefaction. Installation of equipment to alter the environment is expensive and inappropriate where the volume of available milk is low and the potential producers and customers widespread and isolated.

Such indigenous cheeses as do exist are generally very simple, and are dried over fires, often fuelled by cattle dung rather than wood, which is scarce, particularly in the Himalayas. Karut is a very dry, hard, skimmed-milk cheese made in Afghanistan and north-west India, while Krutt is made by the nomadic tribes in the middle Asiatic steppes, using skimmed milk from cows, goats, sheep or camels. The milk is coagulated by natural souring, and the curd is hung up in sacks to drain.

Elsewhere, milk is normally coagulated using rennet obtained from a young milk-fed calf, but this is not possible in India, where the cow is a sacred animal. Non-animal rennet can be used, but seldom is. Instead, the practice is to make simple, quick-ripening cheeses, which are coagulated by the action of the acid in milk, and not by bacteria or moulds.

In the mid-1990s, milk consumption in India has more than doubled; it is said to be the fastest-growing market in the world. Production of some of the popular cheeses of European origin is developing. Herds of cows and water buffalos are increasing, but the milk yield is still insufficient to meet the demand and it is necessary to import milk products.

Paneer, a simple cheese made in the home and eaten within a few days of being made, is very popular. It is used in various traditional Indian dishes, including meat and vegetable curries and spicy vegetable dishes.

To make your own paneer, bring 2 litres/3½ pints fresh whole milk to the boil. Stir in 30ml/2 tbsp vinegar or lemon juice and set aside. When the milk has curdled, pour it into a clean, scalded muslin cloth set in a strainer. Rinse with fresh water and drain well, then bring up the sides of the cloth to enclose the curd and shape it into a ball. Place under a heavy saucepan or similar weight and press for 10–15 minutes. This makes about 225g/8oz paneer.

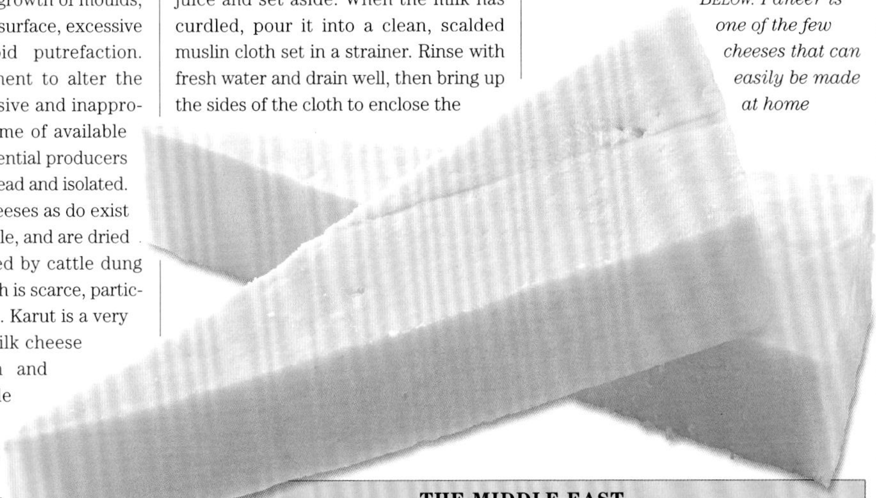

BELOW: Paneer is one of the few cheeses that can easily be made at home

THE MIDDLE EAST

Centuries ago in Iran, simple dried cheeses were produced, then, when milk was abundant, the people made a softer sheep's milk cheese, similar to feta, which was preserved in brine to last through the leaner months. The nomadic bedouins, too, made a soft cheese that was either eaten fresh or preserved in salt.

Nowadays, the most common cheese found in the region are small balls of fresh curd, sometimes rolled in herbs or spices, and served at breakfast time. They are called Lebneh in Lebanon and Israel, Lebney in Syria, Gibne in the Arabic countries and Labaneh in Jordan. A similar cheese, Serat, made in the high mountains of Iran and Afghanistan, is smoked and dipped in beeswax to help preserve it.

Although most exported Halloumi comes from Cyprus, this cheese was originally made by the Bedouin tribes from sheep's milk. It is still made today, popular because of its ability to hold its shape even when grilled on a skewer.

Kashakawan, found in the Lebanon and Syria, is similar to both Bulgarian Katshkawalj and Turkish Kasar Peynir. The name means "cheese on horseback", and is thought to originate from when the cheeses were tied in pairs and slung acrss a pole like saddle bags to dry. A kosher version of the cheese is made in Israel, where they also make the smaller, Smoked Basna.

Most other cheeses from Israel are copies of popular European cheeses. One of the most common, Bulgarian cheese, is actually feta, but is so-called because the best feta was considered to come from Bulgaria where the cheese is softer and less salty than the Greek varieties. Other cheeses include Bin-Gedi, a Camembert-type cheese; Galil, a sheep's milk cheese modelled on Roquefort; Golan, a hard Provolone-style cheese; Tal Ha'emek, a hard cheese with holes like Emmental; and Gilead, which is similar to mozzarella.

THE CHEESES OF THE USA

All too often, the prevailing attitude to cheese in the USA appears to be that it is something you have to cook, grate or melt for it to be useful. There is also a widely held belief that cheese is too fattening and too high in salt to indulge in more than occasionally. Unfortunately, the supermarket shelves reflect public opinion. They are laden with ready-to-go shredded or sliced Jack, Cheddar, Swiss or processed cheese, kept "fresh" with preservatives. Sanitized, sterilized and standardized – who can blame Americans for thinking cheese is just a commodity that you have to do something with?

How did this happen in a country where, by 1890, nearly a third of the population were European-born immigrants? Ironically, it was the enormous influx of immigrants that helped to create the situation. Mass production was seen as the only way to feed the soaring population. There was no time to invent new cheeses, and distribution of small-volume farmstead cheeses was impossible in such a huge country, so milk was processed, mainly into Cheddar, and "big" was the byword. By 1900, a thousand cheese factories had grown up along the East coast alone.

The first all-American cheese was Brick, set apart from European cheeses as much by name as by the process by which it was made. In 1877, John Jossi, a Wisconsin cheesemaker of Swiss extraction, discovered that if he squeezed fresh curd between two bricks, the result was a brick-shaped cheese similar to the popular German Limburger, but firmer and more rubbery. His cheese was ideal for cutting, and had a mild aroma and taste. Today, Brick is vacuum-packed in slices, strings or blocks and is sold right across the USA.

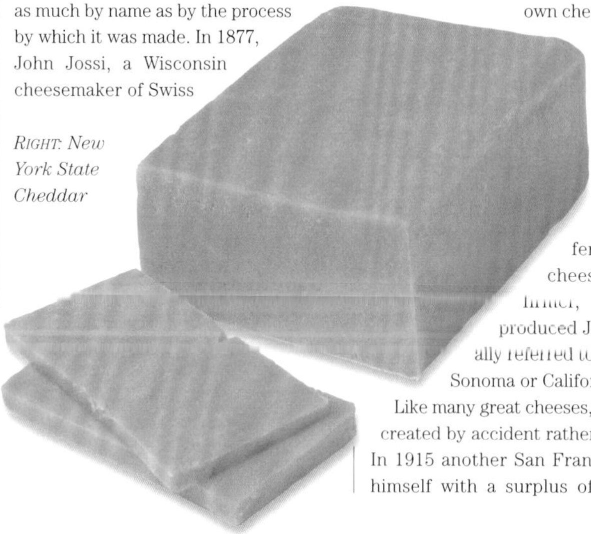

RIGHT: New York State Cheddar

Next (in 1882) came Colby, named after a town in Wisconsin. Similar to Cheddar, but softer and more elastic, it also matured more quickly and could be eaten within weeks rather than months. Sweet and bland, Colby was soon accepted as an all-purpose, family cheese. It remains a favourite.

The origin of Monterey Jack, although attributed to the Scot, David Jacks, can actually be traced back to the Spanish Franciscan monks who came north during the early days of the missions, when California was still part of Mexico. Finding themselves with surplus milk, they set about making *queso blanco*, a delicate, creamy cheese that originated in Spain and which had spread to South America.

David Jacks' contribution was to recognize its potential. He set up factories, and by the mid 1880s was producing his own cheese. To distinguish it from others on the market, it was known as Jack's cheese and ultimately Jack. To differentiate this cheese from the former, industrially produced Jack, it is usually referred to as Monterey, Sonoma or California Jack.

Like many great cheeses, Dry Jack was created by accident rather than design. In 1915 another San Franciscan found himself with a surplus of young Jack cheese. Needing the shelf space for other cheeses, he stored the Jack cheese on the floor, hand-salting each one in the hope that it would survive. Weeks later, he found that the Jack cheese had become fruity, rich and hard, not unlike Parmesan. Dry Jack proved instantly popular and has been a favourite ever since.

BELOW: Dry Jack

By 1930 most of the familiar European cheeses were being produced. However, the paranoia over raw milk in the 1950s closed down all but the most intrepid cheesemakers. The few remaining artisans relied on the loyalty of the local community to survive, while those in more isolated areas found success through mail-order sales.

The influence of the Vietnam War, coupled with the growth of the hippie movement, were just two of the catalysts that spawned a new generation of farmstead cheesemakers who had decided to embrace a different way of life.

By the late 1970s, production had moved into the hands of large companies. Small co-operatives disappeared as cheese became another commodity to be distributed as cheaply and efficiently as possible to the increasing number of supermarkets.

A new era of American cooking was emerging, with young chefs turning their backs on the imported cheeses in favour of seeking out regional produce. Mediterranean-style menus called for fresh mozzarella, ricotta and goat's milk cheeses. Delis and fancy food shops were on the increase and the wonderful farmers' markets, with their emphasis on quality rather than quantity, provided a showcase from California to New York for the American farmstead cheeses.

Many of the new generation of cheesemakers turned to goats or sheep. They were easier to handle, required less investment and there was a better return on their milk. The strict laws enforcing pasteurization had been relaxed, and raw cheese could be sold so long as it was matured for more than 60 days.

The consumers' attitude has also changed. When people buy farmstead cheeses, they feel they are supporting the old ways and encouraging those who practise sustainable farming methods. Today there are more than 80 producers of American farmstead cheeses. Seek them out, give them your support and enjoy them.

ABOVE: Monterey Jack

In addition to the smaller cheesemakers, the USA has large manufacturers producing different types of cheese, which are often versions of European varieties. In this section of the book, you will find entries for individual cheeses, as well as listings for companies whose entire range sets a standard that makes them worth looking out for.

BANDAGED CHEDDAR

REGION: *California*
TYPE: *Traditional, creamery, unpasteurized, vegetarian, hard cheese*
SOURCE: *Cow's milk*
DESCRIPTION: *27kg/60lb cylinder, clothbound with marks from the cloth creating an attractive pattern on the fine yellow rind*
CULINARY USE: *Various*

Fiscalini Bandaged Cheddar is the product of master craftsman Mariano Gonzalez, a versatile, innovative and passionate cheesemaker who perfected his craft at Vermont's Shelburne Farms where he developed one of the first American "clothbound" or bandage-wrapped cow's milk cheddars. Now in Modesto, California, at Fiscalini Farmstead, Mariano is making a raw milk Cheddar using milk from the huge Fiscalini dairy herd whose feed is strictly controlled and made up of a blend of silage, molasses, hay and corn. The result is a paler yellow interior but the flavour is certainly not pale. Available at 18 months and 24 months, it is firm and chewy with an intense fruity flavour and cheese and onion bite on the finish.

Mariano has also created an all-American cheese, San Joaquin Gold, inspired by the Italian classic Fontina, which is a washed cured cheese with a supple texture, nutty buttery taste and a salty finish.

BAYLEY HAZEN BLUE

REGION: *Vermont*
TYPE: *Modern, farmhouse, unpasteurized, traditional rennet, blue*
SOURCE: *Cow's milk (Ayrshire)*
DESCRIPTION: *3.2kg/7lb drum with thin, grey, finely ridged, crusty rind dusted with blues and grey*
CULINARY USE: *Various*

To get the sweetest milk from their Ayrshire cows, the Kehler brothers at Jasper Hill Farm use primarily morning milk that also tends to be lower in fat. Nevertheless it feels very buttery and dense in the mouth and has sweet spicy flavours with a salty tang, while the pale interior has well spread thick chunks and fine streaks of purple-blue *Penicillium roquefortii* mould. Named after an old military road built to carry troops to fight the English on a Canadian front, it is typically three to four months old and is certainly one of America's great blue cheeses. In addition, Jasper Hill also make a softer, creamier cheese, Constant Bliss, Aspenhurst, a variation of Red Leicester, and Winnimere.

BEL GIOIOSO CHEESES

REGION: *Wisconsin*
TYPE: *Range of unpasteurized, Italian cheeses*
SOURCE: *Cow's milk*
DESCRIPTION: *Various sizes and shapes, including bell, wheel, pear and wedge*
CULINARY USE: *Various*

Bel Gioioso is the name given to a range of Italian cheeses that have their origins in the Auricchio Cheese Company, which was founded near Naples in 1877. The company flourished and in 1979 they set up a factory in Wisconsin, using Italian equipment and cheesemakers.

Today, Bel Gioioso produces Fontina, Parmesan, Romano, Asiago and Gorgonzola as well as mascarpone and fresh mozzarella, plus the Provolone with which they began. Adherence to traditional Italian cheesemaking methods has given Bel Gioioso cheeses authenticity. However, the differences in climate and grazing have subtly altered the flavour and texture of the various cheeses, but fortunately, their fundamental character has not been lost.

BERGÈRE BLEUE

REGION: *New York State*
TYPE: *Modern, farmhouse, organic, blue cheese*
SOURCE: *Sheep's milk*
DESCRIPTION: *Cylindrical cheese, 16cm/6½in in diameter and 10cm/4in tall. The sticky, moist, natural rind has occasional blotches of natural yeasts and moulds*
CULINARY USE: *Various*

Bergère Bleue is a Roquefort-style cheese with a rich aroma of lanolin and yeast. It melts in the mouth like butter, releasing the flavour of burnt caramel. The blue-green streaks of mould give a spicy piquancy to the pale lemon-coloured cheese, which is moist and slightly crumbly.

The cheesemaker is Jane North, who learnt her craft in the French and Spanish Pyrenees. When she returned to the USA, she and her husband Karl built their farm at Freetown. Eight years later, they established Northland Sheep Dairy and started cheesemaking. In addition to Bergère Bleue, the dairy also produces Tomme Bergère and Folie Bergère.

Brier Run Cheeses

Region: *West Virginia*
Type: *Traditional, farmhouse, organic, fresh and aged cheeses*
Source: *Goat's milk (Nubian, Alpine and Saanen)*
Description: *Various sizes and shapes, ranging from 115g/4oz to 1kg/2¼lb in weight*
Culinary uses: *Table cheeses, salads, grilling*

Goats are hardy creatures, producing their best milk when conditions are tough and varied. The narrow valley, scrub-covered grey crags and herbaceous pastures of the Appalachian foothills provide Greg and Verena Sava's goats with the perfect environment. Their natural lifestyle also means that they breed at their own whim, not man's, so there are times when milk is in short supply and the cheese can be difficult to find. Greg and Verena handle the flavoursome milk with care, hand-ladling the curd to give a creamier, fuller flavour. Their goat's milk cheeses are among America's finest.

Bulk Farm Cheeses

Region: *California*
Type: *Various traditional, farmhouse, European-style cheeses*
Source: *Cow's milk*
Description: *Various*
Culinary uses: *Table cheese, grating, grilling*

Dutch cheesemakers are among the finest exports from Europe, adapting the traditional recipes of their native cheeses to their new climates. The Bulk family have been cheesemakers for generations, and Walter and Lenneke are doing a fine job of upholding the family tradition at their farm in California.

Those who have sampled the cheeses sold at their small retail store tend to come back, impressed by the quality. To ensure their Gouda has the authentic taste and texture, they import the traditional starter culture and rennet from Holland. This affects every stage of the cheesemaking process and has a direct bearing on the rich, nutty flavour of Gouda. Bulk Farm also produces its own Leyden, Edam and Quark.

Capriole Banon

Region: *Indiana*
Type: *Traditional, farmhouse, fresh cheese*
Source: *Goat's milk (Alpine)*
Description: *180g/6¼oz disc wrapped in marinated chestnut leaves*
Culinary use: *Table cheese*

Judy Schad's cheeses are exceptional in quality and character. Not only do the shapes and names reflect her wicked sense of humour – Wabash Cannonballs and Fromage à Trois are just two of the cheeses from her list – but her concentration on ageing the cheeses to the point of perfection demonstrates her belief that the American palate loves to experience new flavours.

Her Capriole Banon looks like an exquisitely wrapped gift, with its covering of interwoven chestnut leaves that have been marinated in brandy and white wine. Their aroma permeates the soft, creamy curd to devastating effect – a sensational blend of flavours.

Judy's company, Capriole Inc., also makes Mont St Francis, Old Kentucky Tomme and Festiva, which is a wonderful combination of a Jack-style goat's milk cheese with pine nuts, basil and flavoursome sun-dried tomatoes.

Chèvre de Provence

Region: *Alabama*
Type: *Modern, farmhouse, organic, fresh cheese*
Source: *Goat's milk (mixed breeds)*
Description: *Various shapes and sizes, without rind*
Culinary uses: *Table cheese, grilling or baking, spreading, salads*

Like great pastry chefs, some talented cheesemakers seem to possess an almost arcane touch. The judges at the 1994 and 1995 American Cheese Society conference certainly recognized Liz Parnell's many talents, awarding both her Chèvre de Provence and her fromage frais first place.

Liz's chèvre has been described as an American treasure. The subtle flavour of the tiny discs of fresh, lemony, goat's milk cheese is enhanced by the mixture of olive oil and fresh herbs in which it is packed.

Coach Farm Cheeses

Region: *New York State*
Type: *Modern, farmhouse, fresh and soft-white cheeses*
Source: *Goat's milk (French Alpine)*
Description: *Various shapes and sizes, textures and tastes*
Culinary uses: *Table cheeses, grilling, baking as filling for pastries, sauces and salads*

From fresh, mild and lemony to creamy, aromatic and mushroomy, Coach Farm Cheeses are of a consistently high quality. They set the standard by which many small farms match themselves, and it is not surprising that nowadays they are among the most widely distributed cheeses in America.

Miles, Lilian and Susan Cahn are perfectionists, taking as much trouble with the varied diet of their 800 goats as they do in finding a wrapping that will protect the cheese while allowing it to breathe.

Their fresh cheeses are ready to eat within days. The aged varieties grow a soft-white penicillium mould and are best eaten when still firm and flaky. Mild, but not bland, they dissolve like ice cream. Both types are available in a variety of flavours. One of their best-known cheeses is Pyramid, in which the young curd is flavoured with spicy and fragrant peppercorns.

Above: A young Capriole Banon

ABOVE: Cream cheese

COTTAGE CHEESE

REGION: *Various*
TYPE: *Modern, creamery, fresh cheese*
SOURCE: *Cow's milk*
DESCRIPTION: *Creamy, lumpy cheese sold in pots*
CULINARY USES: *Table cheese, snacks, salads, baking*

Americans have come to think of cottage cheese as their own invention, but it originated with the rural labourers of Europe, who had been making it for centuries before it crossed the Atlantic.

Cottage cheese is an acid curd cheese, relying on the natural tendency of warm milk to curdle, rather than requiring the addition of rennet. Once the soft, floppy curd has formed, it is cut into pea-sized cubes and heated gently in the whey until it reaches the desired texture and body. The whey is then drained off and the lumpy curd is rinsed in cold water to remove the excess whey and lactose. What remains is cottage cheese. Salt and a little milk or cream are routinely added, and many varieties are flavoured to lift what is essentially a bland and often rather boring flavour.

Cottage cheese accounts for nearly 25 per cent of all cheese consumed by weight-conscious Americans. It is produced in factories across the country, each fighting for their share of the market. The cheese ripens in one or two days and has a fat content of five to 15 per cent.

COUGAR GOLD

REGION: *Washington State*
TYPE: *Modern, creamery, semi-soft cheese*
SOURCE: *Cow's milk*
DESCRIPTION: *1kg/2¼lb round cheese without rind, packed in a can*
CULINARY USES: *Table cheese, snacks*

Established in 1948 by Washington State University to encourage the growth and quality of cheesemaking in the state, Cougar Gold remains popular – partly, no doubt, due to the novelty of buying a cheese that is packed in a can.

The university creamery, based in Pullman, Washington, is run largely by university students and sells eight different varieties of canned Cougar cheese, as well as many different flavours of ice cream. The milk used in the production of all of the creamery's products is supplied by the university's own herd of dairy cows.

Cougar Gold is creamy, smooth and rich, with a mellow cheese-and-onion-sauce aroma and taste. An enthusiast once sent the author two cans, one 12 months old and the other two years old, in order to prove that cheese in a can could be good and could be aged. The author was suitably impressed but not necessarily converted.

CREAM CHEESE

REGION: *Various*
TYPE: *Modern, creamery, fresh cheese*
SOURCE: *Cow's milk*
DESCRIPTION: *White, rindless cheese sold in pots*
CULINARY USES: *Spreads, baking, dips, cheesecakes*

Like cottage cheese, this is an acid curd cheese, but requires a starter culture to curdle the milk, which it does by turning the milk sugar (lactose) into lactic acid. Low-fat varieties may require the addition of a little rennet to help the milk to coagulate. The freshly formed, soft curd is poured into close-weave linen cloth (or a sack of woven plastic), the ends are knotted together and the bundle is left to drain. After two to three hours, the curd on the sides of the cloth is scraped into the centre, the cloth is re-tied and the bundle is placed on a draining tray under a weight and pressed for two to three hours. At this stage, salt is added. Theoretically, the cream cheese could now be packed into tubs for immediate use, but it is more often heated and extruded before being poured into moulds for sale.

Cream cheese is generally mild and velvety, with a fresh, lemony zing balanced by the buttery richness of the cream. Low-fat versions may contain whey powder, which gives them a slightly grainy feel. Cream cheese made at home must be eaten within a few days, but the commercially produced product can have a shelf life of up to 60 days depending on the method used to make and preserve it. Stabilizers are seldom used, but some manufacturers use a gum of sorts to hold the cheese together and improve its keeping qualities.

The Sierra Nevada Cheese Company, based in Willows, California, make the most perfect organic cream cheese, as well as a range of organic plain and flavoured Jack. Their cream cheese, whether plain or subtly flavoured with garlic, is delicately soft and spreadable, creamy and sweet from the milk, and wickedly rich.

Crowley

Region: *Vermont*
Type: *Traditional, farmhouse, semi-hard cheese*
Source: *Cow's milk*
Description: *Cylindrical or oblong cheeses in various sizes. The natural rind carries the imprint of the cheesecloth and has some natural mould*
Culinary uses: *Table cheese, grating, grilling*

This farmhouse cheese is made by washing the freshly cut curd with cool spring water. This removes much of the acidic whey, creating a cheese that is similar to but sweeter than Cheddar. The curd is then salted, loosely packed to allow the small holes to develop, then placed in wooden presses and hand-cranked for just long enough to ensure it develops a firm, yet moist texture. When aged for between three and six months, the cheese is magnificent; at around six months, while retaining some sweetness, it has the pungent, cheese-and-onion tang of mature Cheddar; at over 12 months and labelled "extra sharp" it is Crowley's best-seller.

The story of the cheese starts in the family kitchen, where Winfield and Nellie Crowley made cheese for friends and family. In 1882 they built their creamery. Demand soon grew for their cheese, which was made from a combination of recipes, modified repeatedly over the years to suit the preferences of individual family members.

Although officially designated as a Colby cheese, Crowley was actually made decades before Colby cheese existed. Nor is it a Cheddar, as the cheesemaking process is different.

In 1967 the factory was in serious danger of closing. Randolph Smith, who had come to Vermont to retire, heard the rumours, stepped in and rescued Crowley from extinction. His sons continue to produce the simple, farmhouse cheese by hand in the original wooden barn. They are often watched by some of the many thousands of tourists who visit the creamery every summer to watch the cheese being made.

Cypress Grove Chevre

Region: *California*
Type: *Modern and traditional, farmhouse, vegetarian, fresh and aged cheeses*
Source: *Goat's milk (Alpine)*
Description: *Various shapes and sizes*
Culinary uses: *Table cheese, salads, sauces, grilling and baking*

Consistent quality and distinctive tasteful packaging have spelt success for cheesemaker Mary Keehn and her daughter Malorie, who produce a range of highly successful goat's cheeses on their farm in Arcata, California.

Mary first made her name as an expert rearer of alpine goats, but with the expansion of her herd, and the surplus milk they produced, she turned her hand to cheese making in 1983.

Their fresh cheeses are made in the traditional, French, farmhouse style. Light and mousse-like, they have a pleasant acidity and herbaceous finish. When aged, the cheeses develop a white penicillium mould that forms a shell. The herbaceous character becomes more pronounced and the mushroom aroma of the rind penetrates the cheese. Although harder than the young cheeses, the aged cheeses melt in the mouth. Their other cheeses include Chèvre Log, Pee Wee Pyramid, Goat's Milk Cheddar, Tomme and feta.

Below: Dry Jack

Dry Jack

Region: *California*
Type: *Traditional, farmhouse, unpasteurized, vegetarian, hard cheese*
Source: *Cow's milk*
Description: *4kg/9lb square with rounded edges. The natural rind is hand-rubbed with oil, cocoa and pepper*
Culinary use: *Various*

As with many great cheeses, the creation of Dry Jack was a happy accident. In 1915 a San Francisco wholesaler found himself with an over-abundance of young Jack cheese. To clear shelf space for new arrivals, he reluctantly stacked the Jack on the floor, hand-salting each one in the hope that it would survive.

Weeks later, he found that the cheeses were fruity, rich and hard, not unlike the Pecorino and Parmesan he had run out of at the time. Necessity being the mother of invention, he coated each cheese with oil, pepper and cocoa, to imitate the lamp black being used on imported Italian cheeses at that time, and offered "Dry Jack" to his customers. A star was born.

Today the cheese, made by the Vella Cheese Company, is among the finest in the world. The rind looks like chocolate icing. Underneath, the deep yellow cheese is hard and when cut, the cheese shatters rather than breaks, releasing layer upon layer of flavour: sweet and fruity; sharp and mouth-watering; rich and full-bodied like a fine wine.

LEFT: Grafton Village Cheddar – an excellent uncoloured Cheddar made in Vermont using raw milk.

GRAFTON VILLAGE CHEDDAR

REGION: *Vermont*
TYPE: *Traditional, farmhouse, unpasteurized, hard cheese*
SOURCE: *Cow's milk*
DESCRIPTION: *Blocks of various sizes, without rind*
CULINARY USES: *Table cheese, grating, melting, grilling, in sauces*

By keeping to small-batch production and traditional methods, Grafton continues to produce excellent white (uncoloured) Cheddars, with the depth of flavour and character possible only with raw milk and long ageing.

The Grafton Village Cheese Company was established in 1890 in the village of Grafton, now meticulously restored. It draws its milk from local dairy farms, where cattle graze the rich grasslands of the southern Vermont mountains. The result is milk that is high in butterfat, with a consistent quality and texture, essential for the production of cheeses that develop character and real depth as they mature.

Grafton Village Cheddar ripens in six to 24 months and has a fat content of 50 per cent. The company makes several flavoured Cheddars (with sage, garlic or dill), plus a version that is smoked over corn cobs.

EWE'S BLUE

REGION: *New York State*
TYPE: *Modern, farmhouse, pasteurized, vegetarian, blue cheese*
SOURCE: *Ewe's milk*
DESCRIPTION: *1.8kg/4lb wheel with stark white sticky outside but no rind*
CULINARY USE: *Various*

Old Chatham Sheepherding have around 1200 sheep, which make this enormous herd the largest sheep dairy in the United States. They graze organic pastures in the upper Hudson River Valley and their superb milk is used to make this Roquefort-style blue, one of the best of its kind in the USA.

Moist yet crumbly with widely spaced shafts of blue-purple, it has a spicy tang that hints of caramelized onion, chocolate and pepper. It is best at around five months.

FRESH JACK

REGION: *California*
TYPE: *Traditional, farmhouse and creamery, semi-soft cheese*
SOURCE: *Cow's milk*
DESCRIPTION: *Rounds in various sizes. The straw-coloured, natural rind is fine and springy*
CULINARY USES: *Table cheese, snacks, melting, salads*

Another cheese from the famous Vella Cheese Company, Fresh Jack resembles Edam in texture, but is creamier and more springy. It has a distinctive taste: aromatic, with a hint of green-grass bitterness. Factory-made Jack tends to be bland, mild and milky, with a rubbery feel compared to this excellent cheese.

CANADIAN CHEESES

Canada's early settlers, from Britain and France, were mainly trappers, traders and foresters with little interest in either cheesemaking or farmsteading, so it is not surprising that cheesemaking was slow to develop in this beautiful, but often inhospitable land. When cattle were introduced, it was for meat, not milk. Cheese was hardly a consideration, since game and meat were plentiful sources of protein. Only in winter, when snow and isolation prevented fresh supplies from reaching large farms, were some rudimentary cheeses made.

It was the arrival of French Trappist monks that really began Canada's cheesemaking tradition. Their first monastery was in Quebec, and by 1881 they were producing a semi-soft, washed-rind cheese, Oka, which has been made commercially since 1960. The Benedictine monks at the abbey of Saint Benoit du Lac in Quebec created Canada's first blue cheese, Ermite (Hermit) in 1943. It, too, is still being made.

British immigrants gradually established dairy herds. They set up co-operatives to process the milk into Cheddar, as they have done in Australia, America and New Zealand.

Canadian Cheddar made its presence known in a big way when a 10-ton Cheddar was made in Ontario for the 1893 World Exhibition in Chicago. The cheese finally ended up in a London restaurant. As a marketing exercise, it was extremely successful, and Canadian Cheddar was placed firmly on the map – and in the minds of the British. It continues to sell well in supermarkets across Britain, industrially made but often aged to a mouth-puckering degree of acidity, a taste staunch supporters insist is the mark of the perfect Cheddar. Epicures who prize the firm, rich nuttiness of traditional British Cheddar, with its final savoury bite, might disagree, however.

Cheddar continues to dominate the Canadian cheese market, although the growth of tourism has brought about a dramatic increase in sales of Canadian Raclette and Oka. So far, the revival of artisan cheesemaking, which has had such a beneficial affect in America and Great Britain, has scarcely begun in Canada, but cannot be too far away, as a few small cheesemakers scattered across the provinces are already finding a market for their hand-made cheeses.

LEFT: Canadian Cheddar

ABOVE: *Harley Farm's Chevre Logs.*

GRAYSON

REGION: *Virginia*
TYPE: *Modern, farmhouse, unpasteurized, vegetarian, semi-soft cheese*
SOURCE: *Cow's milk (Jersey)*
DESCRIPTION: *2.3kg/5lb cube with rounded corners and thin crosshatch ridges in the sticky orange rind*
CULINARY USE: *Various*

Based on one of Italy's best-loved washed rind cheeses, Taleggio, Grayson is made near the Appalachian Mountains by Helen Feete with the milk of her magnificent herd of Jersey cows whose grazing of meadow flowers, lush grass and clean, crisp mountain water ensures their milk is fresh, sweet and untainted. The result is a rich, creamily smooth cheese with a very meaty flavour and back notes of smoky bacon yet still hinting of lovely floral flavours. It is best aged for between four and five months.

HARLEY FARM GOAT CHEESES

REGION: *California*
TYPE: *Modern, farmhouse, fresh cheeses*
SOURCE: *Goat's milk (Alpine)*
DESCRIPTION: *Small rounds and logs, garnished with edible flowers*
CULINARY USE: *Table cheese*

Nancy Gaffney fell in love with goats 30 years ago, established Sea Stars Goat's Cheese and quickly earned a following for her delicious and unusual goat's cheeses. Nancy retired in 2007 and sold Sea Stars to Yorkshire-born Dee Harley, who renamed the business Harley Farms.

Dee's beautiful cheeses are gentle, moist and lemon-fresh. Soft and spreadable, they are garnished with nasturtiums, marigolds and other edible flowers. The range includes several chèvre tortas, one with layers of sun-dried tomatoes and basil and another with layers of pistachio and dried apricots. The cheeses have won first place at the American Cheese Society's conferences, and are found in all the best places up and down America's West Coast.

HUBBARDSTON BLUE COW

REGION: *Massachusetts*
TYPE: *Modern, farmhouse, fresh cheese*
SOURCE: *Cow's milk*
DESCRIPTION: *Small round with natural rind covered in blue-grey mould*
CULINARY USE: *Table cheese*

Not a conventional blue, this is so called because of the soft, fuzzy rind of blue-grey mould that helps to speed up the ripening process, softening the cheese close to the rind to the point where it almost runs. The flavour is gentle and aromatic, with a hint of almonds.

Hubbardston Blue Cow is made by Westfield Farm, who also make some goat's milk cheeses.

IDAHO GOATSTER

REGION: *Idaho*
TYPE: *Modern, farmhouse, hard cheese*
SOURCE: *Goat's milk (Saanen)*
DESCRIPTION: *2kg/4½lb wheel with natural, waxed rind*
CULINARY USES: *Table cheese, grating, grilling*

Exchanging their potters' wheels and artists brushes for milking machines and curd cutters seems to have been a natural progression for Charles (Chuck) and Karen Evans, who have turned cheese-making into almost an art form. Their Idaho Goatster looks very attractive, with its annatto-rubbed and waxed rind. The hard, almost dry texture of the cheese is similar to that of an Italian Pecorino, while the flavour of the goat's milk gives it a nutty, almond-like quality.

Chuck and Karen also make Bleu Age, a surface-ripened cheese with the blue mould on the outside. Here it differs from traditional blue cheeses, which blue from the inside out. Bleu Age is creamy and quite sharp, with a spicy quality not unlike Stilton's. At the American Cheese Society's 1990 conference it was judged Best of Show and also took a gold award.

Cranberry Torta consists of alternate layers of plain chèvre and chèvre mixed with cranberries and lemon zest, liberally sprinkled with walnuts. The company also makes Idaho Goatster with Porcini.

Laura Chenel's Chèvre

Region: *California*
Type: *Various fresh and aged, traditional, farmhouse cheeses*
Source: *Goat's milk*
Description: *Various sizes and shapes*
Culinary uses: *Table cheese, salads*

Laura Chenel is to chèvre what Pavarotti was to opera. She has brought these simple yet complex cheeses to the attention of the people of America, and in doing so she has destroyed the myth that goat's cheese is harsh and only for sophisticated palates. Her cheeses are hand-made and matured to the point where the subtlety of the milk is at its most revealing. Inspired by the French artisan cheesemakers she worked with in 1979, Laura adheres to the ancient traditions while allowing the vagaries of the Sonoma climate, the soil and her goats to influence each cheese.

She makes a range of shapes, from the tiny Cabecou in oil to the aged Tomme. All are sought after, not only by the thousands of visitors to the region of Mendocino, but also by chefs and restaurateurs. When Alice Waters of the famous Chez Panisse restaurant put the cheeses on her menu it was like receiving the royal seal of approval.

Lincoln Log

Region: *Michigan*
Type: *Traditional, farmhouse, pasteurized, soft-white cheese*
Source: *Goat's milk*
Description: *1kg/2lb log with a sprig of myrtle on the fine, ridged white rind*
Culinary uses: *Table cheese, grilling or baking*

Zingerman's delicatessens have always been innovative in their approach to retailing and were one of the very first to dedicate space and support to the new generation of artisan American cheeses. It was therefore almost inevitable that they would create their own cheese, Lincoln Log. Based on the traditional French Boucheron Log, it is made by award-winning cheesemaker, John Loomis, using organic milk from Southeast Michigan. The thin white rind has a subtle mushroom aroma, the silky smooth texture feels like ice cream and it has a lemony fresh tang like crisp white wine, with a gentle goaty flavour.

Maytag Blue

Region: *Iowa*
Description: *Traditional, farmhouse, unpasteurized, vegetarian, blue cheese*
Source: *Cow's milk*
Description: *2kg/4½lb cylinder. The ivory-coloured, natural rind has some grey, blue and white moulds*
Culinary uses: *Table cheese, blue cheese dressing, dips, salads*

Since 1941 the name Maytag has become synonymous in America with the unlikely combination of washing machines and blue cheese. The link began in the 1920s when the sons of the founder of Maytag Appliances decided to demonstrate their own entrepreneurial skills and started the family farm. They gradually built up a pedigree herd of black and white Holstein/Friesian cows. Selling milk proved to be high in effort and low in profit, so they turned to cheesemaking. Since then they have not looked back, thanks largely to their recognizing the potential of the mail-order business: today, close to 50 per cent of their cheese is sold that way.

You might expect that a cheese that is as well known as Maytag Blue would be produced in huge volumes, but the makers have kept production small to ensure that they retain the quality only achievable when the cheese is made by hand. Maytag Blue has a dense, crumbly texture. Like Roquefort, it melts in the mouth, revealing a very spicy flavour from the fine streaks of blue-grey mould that are scattered throughout the creamy, moist cheese. The finish is hot, with a delicious bite that tempts you to try another piece.

Part of Maytag Blue's success is due to the company's "caves" or cellars, built into the side of a hill. Here the natural moulds and yeasts reside. The temperature and humidity are controlled by nature rather than pure technology, and the cheeses are permitted to ripen slowly over six months. This ensures a creamy texture and a depth of flavour comparable to that achieved by some of the famous European blues.

In addition to Maytag Blue, Maytag Dairy Farms also make varieties of White Cheddar and Edam.

Above: Maytag Blue

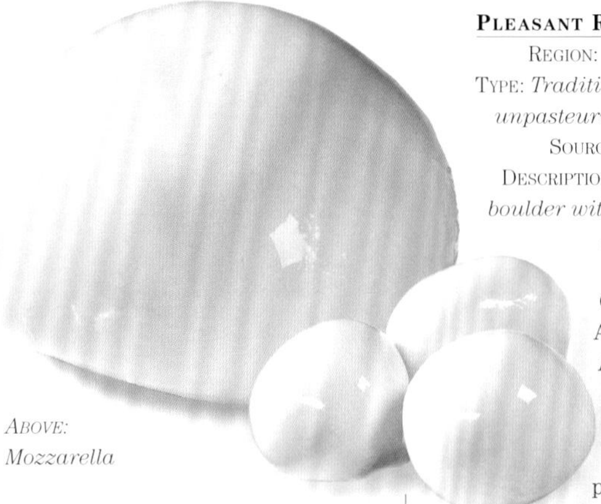

ABOVE: Mozzarella

MOZZARELLA

REGION: *Texas*
TYPE: *Traditional, creamery, vegetarian, stretched-curd cheese*
SOURCE: *Cow's and goat's milk*
DESCRIPTION: *Small, irregularly shaped balls in various sizes*
CULINARY USES: *Salads, baking, pizzas, pastries*

Paula Lambert started the Mozzarella Company when she returned to America after living in Italy and really missed the cheeses she left behind. Undaunted, she set out to make her own. That was in 1982. Today she produces over 20 different cheeses. In addition to Italian specialities, she makes classic French and Mexican-style, soft and semi-soft cheeses. At the annual conferences of the American Cheese Society in 1992, 1994 and 1995, her Scamorza was voted number one in its category.

Paula's mozzarella di bufala was virtually indistinguishable from the classic Italian cheese, but the supply of buffalo's milk dried up and another source has not yet been found. Fortunately, both the cow's milk mozzarella and Capriella (made from a mixture of cow's and goat's milk) are equally delicious.

PLEASANT RIDGE RESERVE

REGION: *Wisconsin*
TYPE: *Traditional, farmhouse, unpasteurized, hard cheese*
SOURCE: *Cow's milk*
DESCRIPTION: *4.5kg/10lb small boulder with a thin red-brown, crusty, dry and leathery rind*
CULINARY USE: *Various*

A true classic modern American cheese, this won Best in Show at the American Cheese Society's annual competition in both 2001 and 2005. Made in the style of Beaufort, a French mountain cheese, by Mike and Carol Gingrich on their farm, where the cows are free range, ensuring the milk has a sweet freshness. Firm yet supple with some crunchy crystals, the interior is a pale butter yellow that darkens towards the edge while the cheese is creamy with a fermenting fruit tang and hints of smoky bacon, yeast and meadow flowers. It is best when two to six months old.

BELOW: Pleasant Ridge Reserve

PONDHOPPER

REGION: *Oregon*
TYPE: *Modern, farmhouse, pasteurized, vegetarian, hard cheese*
SOURCE: *Goat's milk*
DESCRIPTION: *4kg/9lb smooth, yellow waxed rind cheese*
CULINARY USE: *Various*

The lush alpine pastures and sunny climate at Tumalo Farms, situated 1,000 metres (3,500 feet) above sea level in the Cascade Mountains, provide the ideal environment for the contented goats to produce lots of flavoursome milk that cheesemakers Flavio and Marguie DeCastilhos convert into their own unique cheeses using traditional Dutch and Italian cheesemaking methods. Pondhopper is a bold, appealing looking cheese with a pale yellow-white interior with a few tiny eyes and smooth, creamily supple feel. It is washed with a local beer giving it a slightly bitter, hoppy taste, which is balanced by the smooth, creamy texture and nutty tang of the goat's milk. It is best eaten at around 10–12 weeks.

RED HAWK

REGION: *California*
TYPE: *Modern, pasteurized, vegetarian, organic, washed-rind cheese*
SOURCE: *Cow's milk*
DESCRIPTION: *350g/12oz flattened ball with pale sunset red-orange rind that is marked by the mould*
CULINARY USE: *Various*

A triple cream cheese, Red Hawk is a pale ivory-white with the taste of double cream and a delicate tang on the finish. Surprisingly mild, it is soft and almost gooey around the edges while the centre has not yet broken down so is still slightly grainy. It melts in the mouth and the rind is very edible – neither too strong nor too gritty.

Created by Cowgirl Creamery using organic cow's milk from the Straus Family Dairy, it captures the essence of West Marin county and won Best In Show at the American Cheese Society's Annual Conference in 2003.

ABOVE: Red Hawk

ROGUE RIVER BLUE

REGION: *Oregon*
TYPE: *Modern, farmhouse, unpasteurized, vegetarian, blue cheese*
SOURCE: *Cow's milk*
DESCRIPTION: *2.3kg/5lb drum wrapped in deep forest green vine leaves*
CULINARY USE: *Various*

Rogue Creamery was set up in the 1930s by Tom Vella, grandfather to renowned cheesemaker Ig Vella. Today's owners, David Gremmels and Cary Bryant, continue to respect the principles set out by the Vellas. The leaves of this unusual and attractive blue are seeped in Clear Creek pear brandy, which turns them a deep and appealing forest green and imparts a heady mix of fermenting pears and wild yeast. Dense, moist and crumbly, rather than creamy, with thin blue-grey steaks and broken lines through the pale yellow interior, it has a fruit tang and a real salty bite. Aged for a surprising eight months – most blues are only three to four months old.

RIGHT: One of Sally Jackson's goat's milk cheeses

ST. GEORGE

REGION: *California*
TYPE: *Traditional, farmhouse, pasteurized, vegetarian, hard cheese*
SOURCE: *Cow's milk*
DESCRIPTION: *4.5–11kg/10–21lb drum with thin reddish brown crust that looks like paper and is dusted with white moulds*
CULINARY USE: *Various*

Joe and Mary Matos grew up on the little-known, windswept, volcanic island of Sao Jorge in the Portuguese Azores, where the local cheese is based on a Cheddar recipe. So when they moved to Santa Rosa California, they decided to recreate the cheese of their childhood. Since first tasting this cheese in 2001 it has gone from strength to strength and is now up there with the best. It has a very sweet, floral aroma, a hard, dense texture that feels chewy like Cheddar but less compact and tastes like cream caramel – all flavours more typically associated with ewe's milk cheese rather than cow's, the result of the unique recipe and superior grazing. It is best when aged for up to seven months.

ABOVE: One of Sally Jackson's sheep's milk cheeses, wrapped in brandy-soaked chestnut leaves

SALLY JACKSON CHEESES

REGION: *Washington State*
TYPE: *Modern, farmhouse, unpasteurized, aged cheeses*
SOURCE: *Cow's, goat's and sheep's milk*
DESCRIPTION: *Various shapes and sizes*
CULINARY USES: *Table cheeses, cooking*

Sheep's milk cheeses seem to be emerging as the new stars of the cheese world, and Sally Jackson makes some of the best. The Jackson farm is based on 55 hectares/140 acres in the Okanogan Highlands of eastern Washington State and Sally custom-makes her cheeses to her customers' requirements.

Sally's mild, nutty, sheep's milk cheese snugly wrapped in brandy-soaked chestnut leaves has a wonderful texture – it glides like fine silk across the palate, and the chestnut leaf wrap gives a vegetal, earthy and vaguely alcoholic subtlety to the final flavour.

San Andreas

Region: *California*
Type: *Modern, unpasteurized, vegetarian, hard cheese*
Source: *Sheep's milk*
Description: *1.4kg/3lb fat round, with caramel-coloured rind and rows of tiny holes*
Culinary use: *Various*

This is a squat round cheese made by the Callahans at Bellwether Farm and named after the California fault line that runs past the farm in Sonoma County. Inspired by the Pecorino cheeses of Tuscany, it looks like it has sat on a bed of nails as it is covered in tiny holes dusted with white and blue moulds. Lemon yellow with a slightly dry, crumbly texture, it has a gentle, undemanding but rather addictive flavour and is typically aged for around three to four months.

Bellwether also makes Ricotta, Crescenza and Carmody, a semi-soft 1.4kg/3lb wheel with a myriad of tiny holes through the pale interior that smells and tastes of sweet butter with a slight sharpness on the finish but becomes sweeter with age.

Above: Silver Mountain

Shelburne Cheddar

Region: *Vermont*
Type: *Traditional, farmhouse, unpasteurized, vegetarian, hard cheese*
Source: *Cow's milk (Brown Swiss)*
Description: *Block cheese without rind*
Culinary uses: *Table cheese, also widely used in cooking*

Mariano Gonzales uses the traditional cheddaring process to make this prize-winning cheese for Shelburne Farms. The cheese has a firm, biteable texture, and the milk yielded by Brown Swiss cows gives the flavour a rich complexity.

Shelburne Cheddar is matured for between 18 and 24 months and has a fat content of 51 per cent. At the annual conference of the American Cheese Society in 1990, it was declared Best In Show. Four years later, it won the Best Farmhouse Cheese category.

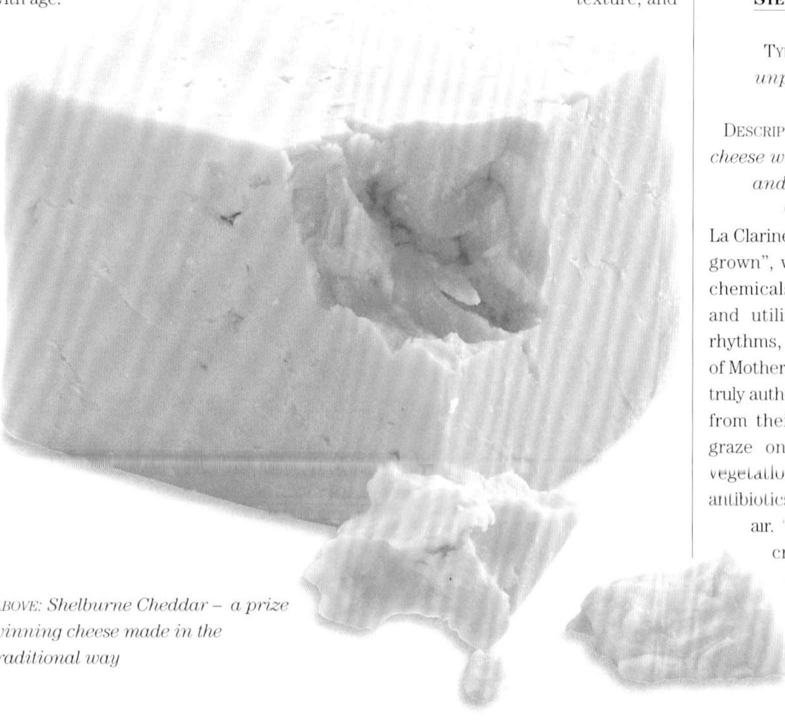

Above: Shelburne Cheddar – a prize winning cheese made in the traditional way

Sierra Mountain Tomme

Region: *California*
Type: *Modern, farmhouse, unpasteurized, hard cheese*
Source: *Goat's milk*
Description: *1.4kg/3lb drum shaped cheese with a thick coat of grey mould and sparse blotches of white*
Culinary use: *Various*

La Clarine Farm is certified "wholistically grown", which means thet they use no chemicals, no poisons and no GMOs and utilize and respects the natural rhythms, energies and seasonal changes of Mother Nature. As a result they make a truly authentic farmstead cheese with milk from their American alpine goats that graze on big pastures full of native vegetation, no pesticide residues, no antibiotics, and plenty of fresh, mountain air. The resulting milk makes a lovely creamy smooth and supple yet dense cheese with the subtle aromatic character typical of goat's milk with a spicy, peppery tang on the finish.

Below: Teleme develops a wonderful aroma when it is left to ripen

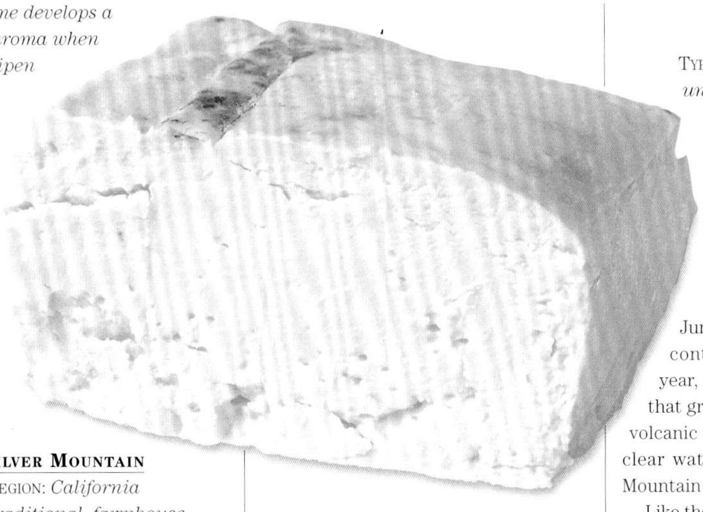

Silver Mountain

Region: *California*
Type: *Traditional, farmhouse, unpasteurized, vegetarian, hard cheese*
Source: *Cow's milk*
Description: *2.3kg/5lb cloth-wrapped cylinder*
Culinary use: *Various*

When Pat and Bill Boersma started Bravo Farms dairy in 1979 they became one of the pioneers in the new wave of farmstead cheesemakers. Inspired, like so many of the American cheesemakers, by the great cheeses of Europe, they decided to make a hard cloth-bound cheese. In 2006 they sold their cows to a nearby farmer so they could concentrate on cheesemaking but still use milk from their own herd. It is at its best around nine months, when it has a full, well-rounded flavor with the sharpness or acidity of a classic Cheddar with a raw onion bite.

Below: Sierra Mountain Tomme

Teleme

Region: *California*
Type: *Traditional, farmhouse, vegetarian, semi-soft cheese*
Source: *Cow's milk*
Description: *5kg/11lb square, 30cm/12in across. The pale pinkish-orange rind is dusted with rice flour*
Culinary use: *Various*

The Peluso family have been making Teleme for three generations, but in 2007 sold the rights to the Peluso family name and started producing their famous cheese under the new name of Franklin's Teleme.

Delicious when young, it really comes into its own when ripened. The pale pinkish rind, mottled with moulds and yeasts, bursts at the seams, and the aroma is utterly compelling. The taste conjures up conflicting images – meadow flowers, wild game and sour cream – and the cheese has a yeasty finish.

Teleme was introduced to America by Greek immigrants over a century ago. It is based on Touloumotyri or Touloumi, a goat's milk cheese similar to feta but not as salty. The immigrants did not have access to goat's milk, so used cow's milk instead. Italian cheesemakers found the cheese to their liking, made a few adjustments, and Teleme was born.

Franklin's Cheese also make a Pepper Teleme, with coarsely ground black peppercorns through the creamy interior.

Tumalo Tomme

Region: *Oregon*
Type: *Modern, farmstead, unpasteurized, semi-soft cheese*
Source: *Goat's milk*
Description: *1.8kg/4lb wheel with a greyish rind dusted with a multitude of red, blue, grey and white moulds of various sizes and shapes*
Culinary use: *Various*

Juniper Grove Farm's herd of 110 contented goats live outside all year, grazing on the abundant alfalfa that grows in the area's mineral-rich, volcanic soil, which is fed with crystal-clear water from the nearby Cascade Mountain snowpack.

Like the area where it is made, Tumalo Tomme's washed rind has a wild ruggedness about it and an aroma reminiscent of camping in the woods or walking through Alpine pastures. Made by Pierre Kolisch, it was inspired by the mountain-style cheeses of France, where Pierre received his education in cheesemaking in 1985. It is chewy yet dry, rather than oily, with a crunch from the calcium crystals that occur in some hard aged cheeses. Aromatic yet sweet with a nuttiness on the finish, it is a well-balanced goat's cheese and best around three months.

Vermont Cheddar

Region: *Vermont*
Type: *Traditional, creamery, hard cheese*
Source: *Cow's milk (Friesian and Jersey)*
Description: *Cylinders and truckles in various sizes, with waxed rind*
Culinary uses: *Table cheese, grating, cooking*

Despite the time, money and space it takes to make a good Cheddar, the Cabot Farmers Co-operative Creamery has never faltered. Founded in 1919, the creamery is now owned by over 500 farmers, and produces both hard and soft cheeses. Once tasted, the rich, robust flavour, smooth texture and mouth-watering, tart finish of the Extra Sharp or Private Stock Cheddars are unforgettable.

Above: Wabash Cannonball

Wabash Cannonball

Region: *Indiana*
Type: *Modern, farmhouse, pasteurized, soft-white cheese*
Source: Goat's milk
Description: *85g/3oz small flattened cannonball-shaped cheese with a white rind dusted with charcoal*
Culinary use: *Various*

Another great cheese from Judy Schad and her herd of 400 Alpine, Saanen, and Nubian goats. It looks like a squashed ball with a layer of ash under the fine white rind. At around 10 days it has a subtle goaty taste, very light mousse texture, and delicate lemony tang. At three to four weeks it becomes creamier and dense, the distinct goaty flavour intensifies and there is a salty tang on the finish.

Winnimere

Region: *Vermont*
Type: *Traditional, farmhouse, unpasteurized, washed-rind cheese*
Source: Cow's milk (Ayrshire)
Description: *225g/8oz thick orange-pink rind, dusted with moulds and encircled with a strip of pine bark*
Culinary use: *Table cheese*

Once tasted you cannot doubt the passion and expertise that has gone into the creation and making of this wonderful cheese. Smooth and voluptuous, it is held in place with a strip of freshly cut spruce bark, which imparts it own unique "woodsy" aroma and flavour. Washed with local beer, it is made with winter milk, like Vacherin Mont d'Or on which it is modelled, from November to April. It is ripe after 60 days.

THE CHEESES OF CENTRAL AND SOUTHERN AMERICA

The Altiplano or High Andes, the backbone and natural border dividing Chile from Argentina and running north through Bolivia and into Peru, is the home of the indigenous llama, alpaca and vicuna. The native Indians domesticated these fascinating creatures, relying on them not only as beasts of burden but also as a source of meat, milk, wool and hides. Cheese, however, was unknown until the Spanish and Portuguese missionaries arrived in the sixteenth and seventeenth centuries.

Even then, there was no instant conversion to cheesemaking. The High Andes were a hostile territory to all but the native beasts, and the lowlands were too humid for cows or goats. Only in the cooler areas in between did cows thrive.

As cheesemaking became established, it was the mild, fresh *queso blanco* that proved most popular, partly because it suited the diet of the people and partly because the cooler temperatures made it less important to mature the cheese. In Peru, where a few hardy goats survive the rigorous climate, the locals suspended sacks or skins containing the curd over slow-burning wood fires to speed up the draining process. More recently, in Chile, there has been a move to imitate the sheep's milk cheese of the Pyrenees.

Argentina is famous the world over for the quality of its beef, but was never a great cheese producer. The greatest influence on the cheese industry, such as it is, was the immigration of large numbers of Italians in the middle of the nineteenth century. Unable to survive without their cheese – and too far away to rely totally on imports – they started making a Parmesan equivalent, Treboligiano, together with a mozzarella-type cheese called Moliterno.

In Brazil, too, cattle are regarded principally as a source of meat. The humid conditions make cheesemaking extremely difficult, so cheese has never really caught the imagination – or the palates – of the people. Most of the cheese that is consumed is imported, but some local cheese is made in the Minas Gerais region, north of Rio de Janeiro. Minas Frescal (fresh cheese) and Minas Prensado (a stretched curd cheese) are no doubt based on recipes introduced by the early missionaries.

Yerba Santa Shepherd's Cheese

Region: *California*
Type: *Modern, farmhouse, unpasteurized, hard cheese*
Source: *Goat's milk (Alpine)*
Description: *1.6kg/3½lb oval. The thick, beige to yellow, natural rind is hard and slightly oily*
Culinary uses: *Table cheese, cooking*

Easily as good as any of the hard, artisan, goat's milk cheeses of Spain, Yerba Santa Shepherd's Cheese is very hard, dry and flaky, with small holes. The intensity and diversity of flavour is magnificent: at first the cheese has an almost minty freshness that tingles on the palate, then its more powerful, aromatic character, suggesting toffee, herbs and almonds, kicks in.

A consistent winner in the hard aged section at the annual conference of the American Cheese Society, Yerba Santa Shepherds Cheese is made by Chris and Jan Twohy at their farm near Clear Lake. They take pride in the quality of their milk and use no pesticides, artificial feed supplements or stabilizers.

Below: Yerba Santa Shepherd's Cheese

Mexican Cheeses

Although Mexican civilization dates back to at least 2000BC, it wasn't until the Spanish conquest of 1521 that cheeses were first introduced to Mexico. The Spanish brought with them chickens, pigs, cattle, goats and a few sheep. They established huge estates for themselves. Trade with the Old World created considerable wealth, not only from precious metals, but also from the export of the hitherto unknown tomatoes, peppers, chillies, potatoes and cocoa beans. The intrepid monks who travelled with the conquerors introduced cheesemaking. Pecorino, Manchego, fresh cheeses and hard cow's milk cheeses were welcome reminders of home.

Maize (corn), the main crop of Mexico, played an integral part in the national cuisine, especially in the form of tortillas. In addition, the ubiquitous beans ensured the diet was rich in fibre. These staples, plus tomatoes, chillies and peppers, along with cheese, have created some of Mexico's most famous dishes.

Queso blanco – a crumbly, soft, white cheese – is famously used in enchiladas, when it is mixed with raw onion and wrapped in a hot tortilla, which is then covered with a tomato and chilli sauce. Queso anejo, a clothbound goat's or cow's milk cheese, is crumbled into numerous dishes, while the stretched-curd cheese Asadero is popular as a melting cheese.

In the last 20 years, travel and the influence of a growing multinational community have created new markets for cheese in Mexico. Local producers now make versions of Gruyère, Camembert and Port Salut. Cream cheese is also produced, often with a flavouring of jalapeños or other chillies.

Asadero

Region: *Various*
Type: *Traditional, creamery, stretched curd cheese*
Source: *Cow's milk*
Description: *Various shapes, ranging in weight from 225g–5kg/8oz–11lb. The rind is smooth and polished*
Culinary uses: *Grilling or baking*

The name of this cheese means "fit for roasting". It melts superbly and is used in numerous dishes. Originally from Oaxaca – and sometimes referred to as queso Oaxaca – it is similar to Provolone. The curd is stretched, then shaped into balls, loaves or plaits (braids). White and supple, it ranges from bland to buttery and sweet.

Queso Anejo

Region: *Various*
Type: *Traditional, farmhouse and creamery, hard cheese*
Source: *Cow's and goat's milk*
Description: *5–10kg/11–22lb rounds or blocks, without rind*
Culinary uses: *Grilling or baking*

Queso anejo (aged cheese) was originally made with goat's milk, but today cow's milk is often used. Crumbly and salty, it resembles feta when fresh. When dried, it acquires a texture not unlike that of Parmesan.

Left: *Asadero, which is also known as queso Oaxaca*

Above: *Queso anejo*

Queso Blanco

Region: *Various*
Type: *Traditional, creamery, fresh cheese*
Source: *Cow's milk*
Description: *Various shapes and sizes, often in block form*
Culinary uses: *Grilling, pan-frying, baking, salads*

The name simply means "white cheese". Queso blanco is made in most Latin American countries, and resembles a cross between mozzarella and salty cottage cheese. Traditionally, it is produced from skimmed milk or whey, coagulated with lemon juice, although recently some creameries have begun making it with full-cream milk coagulated with rennet. The curd is scalded and pressed to create an elastic texture which holds its shape when heated. Like Halloumi, it can be sliced and fried. The flavour is mild, creamy and lemon-fresh.

Queso Fresco

Region: *Various*
Type: *Traditional, farmhouse and creamery, fresh cheese*
Source: *Cow's or goat's milk*
Description: *Various sizes and shapes, often round*
Culinary uses: *Grilling and baking, also used fresh in salads*

Based on the Spanish cheese Burgos, queso fresco (fresh cheese) is normally eaten within a few days of making. Soft and breakable, rather than crumbly, it has a grainy feel and very mild, fresh acidity. It holds its shape when heated.

Australian Cheeses

Australia's often inhospitable climate, extraordinary marsupials and abundant wildlife did not exactly inspire the nomadic Aborigines to set up homesteads, domesticate their animals and start cheesemaking, unlike their counterparts in the Northern Hemisphere. Instead, cheesemaking had to wait until the first European settlers arrived in the late 1700s, bringing with them cows, goats and sheep.

At first, cheese was made in kitchens on the isolated farms with tree stumps and boulders as presses, but gradually, as herds grew, the dairy farmers formed co-operatives.

Until the late 1960s, however, butter and Cheddar or variations on those themes were virtually the only dairy products being made, for it was largely the British and Irish who colonized Australia, and much of their production was exported back to the "home country".

The cheese revolution was fired by immigrants from Italy, Greece, Yugoslavia, Holland and Germany, who arrived in droves after the Second World War. Cheese was an integral part of their culture, and before long European cheesemakers were setting up factories. Most notable of these was Czech-born Milan Vyhnalek, who established Lactos in 1955 to make Brie, Camembert, Gouda and Edam. Kraft followed suit, developing a Pecorino-style cow's milk cheese and a Parmesan.

Above: Gabriella Kervella, one of Australia's new breed of artisan cheesemakers with her herd of goats

In the 1980s, when soft, smelly, flavoursome cheeses were first airfreighted in by Bill Studd, rather than being shipped, the large dairy companies and wholesalers watched in disbelief as chefs responded with almost indecent haste, snapping up the new arrivals as fast as they became available, despite the high prices and the availability of indigenous (if bland) copies.

It took about another 10 years before the number of modern, Australian, farmhouse cheeses could be counted on more than one hand, but things were changing. A new breed of Australian cheesemaker was emerging.

Despite the revolution, farmhouse production remains small and industrial Cheddar dominates the market. However, as with wines, the best cheeses are made by individuals striving to perfect their craft. Unlike Europe, where land is scarce and cattle must often live in barns, having their fodder delivered on the back of a tractor, the majority of Australian cows graze on natural pastures – clean, pure and healthy. Regrettably, regulations in Australia ban the production of unpasteurized cheese, a ban shared by New Zealand and South Africa, so much of the character and flavour of the milk is lost.

Unlike their European counterparts, Australian cheeses tend to be made by one cheesemaker in an area, rather than several. This section therefore lists the makers to look out for, and highlights one or two examples of their cheeses. Also included is the occasional exception from a large creamery that has proved to be particularly good.

Other names to look out for are Elgaar Farm Cheddar from Tasmania, which also makes the herb- and spice-flavoured Meadow cheeses, and Faudel Farm in South Gippsland, whose goats yield fine fromage frais and curd cheese.

Below: Surprise Bay Cheddar

Above: Meredith Blue (left), Bass Straight Blue (right) and Gippsland Blue (front)

Gippsland Blue

Region: *Victoria*
Type: *Modern, farmhouse, blue cheese*
Source: *Cow's milk (Friesian)*
Description: *5kg/11lb round with natural, orange crust covered with a dusting of white and blue-grey moulds*
Culinary uses: *Table cheese, grilling, salads*

Gippsland Blue is produced by the Tarago River Cheese Company, a joint venture begun in 1982 by Laurie Jensen, Richard Thomas and Robert Johnson, cheese lovers with a pioneering spirit that led them to make one of Australia's finest and best-known blue cheeses. Using milk from their own herd (and occasionally making their own starter cultures), they have adapted methods learnt in Europe to their own climatic and grazing conditions.

Gippsland Blue was probably the first genuine farmhouse cheese to be made in Australia. It resembles traditional Dolcelatte: sharp, yet sweet and buttery, with a spicy, lingering, blue-cheese tang. The chunky veins of blue mould spread unevenly through the dense, rich cheese, which ripens in eight to 10 weeks.

Learning from the marketplace and continuing to build on their own experience, the cheesemakers have created a variety of other blues as well as softer Camembert and Brie-style cheeses, using Jersey milk to obtain a deeper yellow colour and a more velvety, smooth texture. Committed to both good quality and consistency while acknowledging the seasonal nature of milk, they have successfully introduced numerous other cheeses, the more eclectic being Tarago Lavender, whose unusual additive has inspired local chefs to create some interesting dishes.

Shadows of Blue is milder than Gippsland Blue, with a Brie-like texture and taste, whereas Blue Orchid has a somewhat more vicious, intense nature and should not be treated lightly. Thanks to the richness of the Jersey milk, Gippsland Brie is in the Double Brie category, with a buttery texture softened by the white moulds, which also help create the mild, milky flavour with its mushroomy overtones.

Grabetto

Region: *Victoria*
Type: *Modern, farmhouse, cheese (fresh and aged)*
Source: *Goat's milk*
Description: *25g/1oz thimble-like cheese. The fine, crusty, natural rind has touches of white and grey*
Culinary use: *Table cheese*

When young, Grabetto has a taste not unlike crushed Brazil nut ice cream with a tingle of lemon sorbet. With age, the cheese becomes very hard and flaky in texture. It develops a sharp, mouthwatering flavour with more than just a hint of the goat's milk. Grabetto is produced by Yarra Valley Cheese. It ripens in three to six weeks.

ABOVE: Two of the many different Kervella goat's cheeses – Affine (back) and Chèvre Frais log (front)

HEIDI GRUYÈRE

REGION: *Tasmania*
TYPE: *Traditional, farmhouse, vegetarian, hard cheese*
SOURCE: *Cow's milk (Friesian)*
DESCRIPTION: *20–35kg/44–80lb wheel. The classic, crusty, Beaufort-type, natural rind looks almost polished*
CULINARY USES: *Table cheese, grilling, fondue*

Experienced in the traditional cheese-making techniques of his native country, Switzerland, Frank Marchand was brought out to Tasmania by Lactos in the 1970s. Like so many others, he fell in love with his adopted country. In 1985, with a small herd of 100 Friesians, he started Heidi Farm in order to make the cheeses of his childhood: Tilsit, Gruyère and Raclette.

Frank is fascinated by cheese and loves developing new varieties. Heidi Gruyère has a firm yet supple texture, similar to French Beaufort, with tiny, crunchy crystals and a profusion of flavours. The sweet, fruity taste initially suggests pineapple, then becomes nutty. The more mature the cheese, the better it tastes.

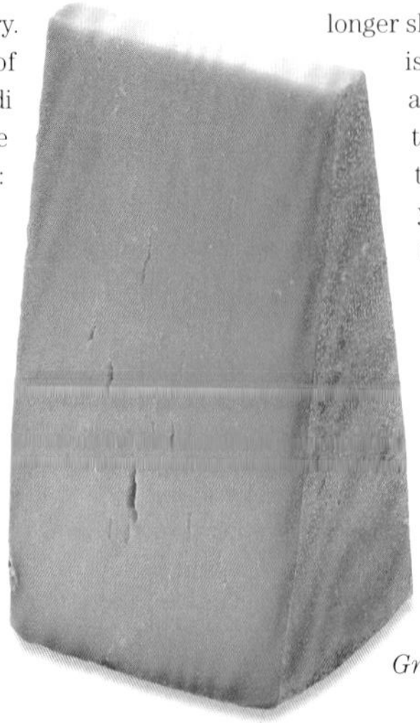

LEFT: Heidi Gruyère

JINDI BRIE

REGION: *Victoria*
TYPE: *Modern, farmhouse, soft-white cheese*
SOURCE: *Cow's milk (Shorthorn/Jersey)*
DESCRIPTION: *2.75kg/6lb round with smooth, velvety, white penicillium rind*
CULINARY USES: *Table cheese, also used in salads*

George Ronalds has been farming in Gippsland since the early 1980s. He saw the opportunities for European-style cheeses in Australia and he and his team have concentrated on Camembert- and Brie-style cheeses.

Jindi Brie is semi-stabilized to give it a longer shelf life. The texture is rich and buttery and has slightly sweet tones. The flavour of the cheese resembles young mushrooms in melted butter. It ripens in four to five weeks.

Other cheeses made by George Ronalds include Jindi Camembert and a triple cream cheese.

KANGAROO ISLAND BRIE

REGION: *Adelaide*
TYPE: *Traditional, farmhouse, soft-white cheese*
SOURCE: *Cow's milk*
DESCRIPTION: *20cm/8in wheel with a smooth, velvety, white penicillium rind*
CULINARY USE: *Table cheese*

Mos and Liz Howard have been making cheese at the family farm on Kangaroo Island for the past five years, using only milk from their own cows. Each cheese is made by hand, the curd being gently ladled into the moulds or hoops.

The young curd is drained and turned; after about 12 hours it will reduce to about half the original volume. Some four to six weeks later, each batch is tasted, tested and checked, then labelled and sent to the mainland.

Kangaroo Island Brie is smooth and voluptuous, with the sweet, creamy taste of fine mushroom soup. It melts like butter in the mouth, with just a hint of lush, green grass and a whisper of sea breezes. As the cheese is made all year round, and the curd is not stabilized, it is subject to subtle seasonal changes – the mark of a true hand-made cheese.

Like all cheeses, Kangaroo Island Brie is at its best when eaten at room temperature. It has a fat content of 55 per cent.

KERVELLA AFFINE

REGION: *Western Australia*
TYPE: *Modern, farmhouse, organic, soft-white cheese*
SOURCE: *Goat's milk*
DESCRIPTION: *100g/3¾oz round or log with soft, fine, white rind*
CULINARY USE: *Table cheese*

Named for the cheesemaker, Gabrielle Kervella of Fromage Fermier, this goat's milk cheese can be eaten at two weeks, when it has a mild, sweet taste. More often, though, it is allowed to mature to eight weeks, when the soft curd becomes hard and flaky and the aromatic character of the goat's milk intensifies. The distinct, lingering taste of this more mature cheese suggests crushed, salty macadamia nuts.

Kervella Chèvre Frais

Region: *Western Australia*
Type: *Modern, farmhouse, organic, fresh cheese*
Source: *Goat's milk*
Description: *Round or log-shaped cheese, made in various sizes*
Culinary uses: *Table cheese, grilling, spreading, soufflés*

Gabrielle Kervella has become synonymous with Australian cheese, yet she only started making her traditional French-style goat's cheese in Gidgegannup around the mid-1980s. In the years that followed, she worked alongside French artisan cheesemakers, returning to Australia to adapt the recipes to prevailing conditions that were very different from those she encountered in Europe. Heat, dust and significant seasonal variations in the pastures were just some of the difficulties she had to contend with, but she has produced a range of delicious cheeses.

Kervella Chèvre Frais is a classic, French-style, fresh chèvre. It ripens in a few days, has no rind and has a light mousse-like texture. Smooth and lemon-fresh, it melts in the mouth with a hint of almonds and just a suggestion of goat's milk. The finish is slightly sweet. It is sometimes dusted with ash or herbs.

King Island Cape Wickham Brie

Region: *Tasmania*
Type: *Modern, creamery, soft-white cheese*
Source: *Cow's milk*
Description: *1kg/2¼lb wheel with thick, velvety, soft rind*
Culinary use: *Table cheese*

Small and exposed, King Island guards the western entrance to Bass Strait, which separates Tasmania from the Australian mainland. The winds that buffet the island are legendary, and flotsam and jetsam from wrecked ships have often fetched up on these shores.

Straw from shipwrecked sailors' mattresses is thought to have been responsible for the unusual and varied grasses on which the King Island cattle graze all year round, contributing to the unique character of the island cheeses.

Founded in 1902, King Island Dairy became a co-operative in 1939, but it was not until 1988 that the company started producing the cheeses that have made it a household name – rich, sweet-tasting cream cheeses, spicy, aromatic blue cheeses, the famous Cape Wickham Brie and the rich, full-flavoured, hand-made Surprise Bay Cheddar.

King Island Cape Wickham Brie is a stabilized cheese, with cream added. It ripens in 20–45 days and is covered in a soft-white rind with a mushroomy aroma and taste. The creamy yellow interior melts like butter in the mouth and the flavour hints of sea breezes and sweet pastures.

Below: Cape Wickham Brie (front) and Jindi Brie (back)

King River Gold

Region: *Victoria*
Type: *Modern, farmhouse, semi-soft cheese*
Source: *Cow's milk (Jersey/Friesian)*
Description: *600g/1½lb round. The washed, natural rind is pinkish-orange, with a dusting of grey mould*
Culinary uses: *Table cheese; also good if the rind is removed and the cheese sliced and melted over vegetables*

David and Anne Brown have come a long way since they stumbled across an old butter factory in Milawa, 200km/125 miles north of Melbourne. With the help of Richard Thomas for the first two years, they developed the Gorgonzola-style Milawa Blue. As David's expertise increased, they gradually widened their repertoire, and today they produce a wide range of excellent cheeses, including several made from Sheep's and goat's milk.

A pilgrimage by one of their cheesemakers to France to work alongside the artisan makers of Reblochon, Chevrotin des Aravis, Cabicou and Beaufort has obviously influenced the quality and flavour of cheeses like Oxley Traditional Blue, Milawa White (a fresh, acid cheese) and their two washed-rind cheeses, King River Gold and Milawa Gold.

The rind of King River Gold is washed and rubbed to encourage the pinkish-orange bacteria to spread over the cheese, sealing in the flavour and creating a smooth, dense, voluptuous interior with random small holes. The flavour hints at warm cow's milk and the cheese has a slightly sharp, green-grass finish. Milawa Gold is a stronger, more piquant version of the same cheese. Inspired by the Trappist-style cheeses of Europe, it has a distinctive, red-gold rind and a supple, smooth texture.

Meredith Blue

Region: *Victoria*
Type: *Modern, farmhouse, blue, cheese*
Source: *Cow's milk*
Description: *1.5–2kg/3–4½lb round. The crusty, natural rind is orange, covered with grey, white and blue moulds*
Culinary use: *Table cheese*

Now in her fifth year at Meredith Dairy, Julie Cameron, the cheesemaker, is producing a number of different types of cheeses using sheep's milk, including a version of the fresh French cheese, fromage blanc. She also makes a delicious, sweet, caramel-tasting yogurt that has just a hint of fresh rosemary and eucalyptus flavours. More recently, she has been experimenting with goat's milk and makes a lovely, fresh chèvre and a goat's milk fromage frais.

Although described as Roquefort-style, Meredith Blue is a mild and creamy blue cheese with its own unique character. The sweetness of the sheep's milk comes through the distinct and spicy, but not overly strong finish.

Meredith Blue ripens in two months and, because it is made using sheep's milk, is a seasonal cheese.

The dairy also produces Woodburne, which is a small moulded, white, sheep's milk cheese.

Above: Purrumbete Mozzarella – Australia's first true buffalo's milk cheese

Milawa Blue

Region: *Victoria*
Type: *Modern, farmhouse, blue cheese*
Source: *Cow's milk*
Description: *6kg/13lb squat cylinder. The rugged, wrinkled, natural rind is grey or pink, with various shadings of mould*
Culinary use: *Table cheese*

Made by David and Anne Brown of the Milawa Cheese Company. The streaks of blue invade a rich, buttery interior that melts in the mouth. Milawa Blue has a lovely, vegetal taste, with undertones of bitter chocolate. Matured for eight to 12 weeks, it ranges from the sublime to the slightly disappointing.

Polkolbin

Region: *New South Wales*
Type: *Modern, farmhouse, semi-soft cheese*
Source: *Cow's milk*
Description: *250g/9oz square. The fine, slightly wrinkled, orange rind tends to be sticky*
Culinary uses: *Table cheese; grilling*

At the Hunter Valley Cheese Company, set up in 1995 by David Brown of Milawa, cheesemaker Peter Curtis produces the popular Polkolbin. Similar to the French cheese Pont l'Evêque, it has the aroma of damp washing or a farmyard. Sharp and spicy, it has a lingering, piquant, almost meaty taste.

Left: Woodburne is a moulded, white sheep's milk cheese made by Meredith Dairy

Purrumbete Mozzarella

Region: *Victoria*
Type: *Traditional, farmhouse, stretched-curd cheese*
Source: *Water buffalo's milk*
Description: *200g/7oz ball*
Culinary uses: *Melting, grilling, in salads*

The water buffalo grazing at the edge of beautiful Purrumbete Lake look as though they have been there for ever, yet it took a man with determination and a dream to make it happen. Roger Haldane's fascination with the animal kingdom began when he introduced alpacas into Australia, but it was the magnificent water buffalos of southern Italy that really captured his imagination and drove him through red tape to import 55 of the animals in 1996.

Roger's imposing blue-stone homestead overlooks the meadows running down to the lake. The milking parlour has been upgraded to house the buffalo (which demand more tranquil surroundings and more privacy than their bovine cousins) and, with the help of confirmed cheese addict Nick Haddow, Roger has developed Australia's first buffalo's milk mozzarella.

Purrumbete Mozzarella has the authentic perfume and nutty taste of Italian mozzarella and is a tribute to the months Nick spent in Italy learning the process from artisan producers. The porcelain-white colour is equally accurate, but most importantly, the texture – springy, stringy and wet – is entirely right.

The company also produces Dancing Brolgo, a washed-curd cheese named after a native bird famous for its weird dance.

PYENGANA CHEDDAR

REGION: *Tasmania*
TYPE: *Modern, farmhouse, hard cheese*
Source: Cow's milk
DESCRIPTION: *8kg/18lb and 18kg/40lb truckles. The natural rind has the imprint of the cloth, with some moulding*
CULINARY USES: *Table cheese, grilling, grating*

Firm, but neither as hard nor as smooth as traditional Cheddar, this cheese has a slightly granular feel to it. After about 12 months, the natural bacteria in the milk produce a rich, nutty cheese with a real depth of flavour. The cheesemaker is John Healey, who took over the old Pyengana cheese factory in the mid 1990s. He uses pasteurized milk from his own farm and continues to follow the old Pyengana methods, which are often labour-intensive but produce wonderful results.

RACLETTE

REGION: *Tasmania*
TYPE: *Traditional, farmhouse, vegetarian, semi-soft cheese*
SOURCE: *Cow's milk (Friesian)*
DESCRIPTION: *5kg/11lb flat wheel. The brown, leathery rind is drier than that of traditional Raclette and can be somewhat sticky*
CULINARY USES: *Table cheese; also marvellous if sliced and grilled*

Frank Marchand's Raclette comes close to the original French cheese, and is elastic and supple, yet dense. Small holes, spread through the paste, give it a slightly open texture. There is a hint of sweetness, but the overriding taste is savoury, meaty and yeasty. Made by Heidi Farm, the cheese is produced only in spring and summer, and it matures in two months.

ROMNEY MATURE

REGION: *Victoria*
TYPE: *Traditional and modern, farmhouse, semi-soft cheese*
SOURCE: *Sheep's milk (Romney)*
DESCRIPTION: *1.5kg/3¼lb cylinder with natural rind imprinted with the marks of the cheesecloth, and some light grey mould*
CULINARY USES: *Table cheese; also used for cooking*

Robert Manifold's family have been in this area for so long that you expect to find mountains or rivers bearing the names of his ancestors. He bases his cheesemaking at the Mount Emu Creek Dairy in Camperdown and uses the milk from two or three local farms. Romney (named for the breed of sheep) is a washed-curd cheese and comes in two different forms. For the waxed version, the young curd is shaped and drained in a mould, then waxed while still moist. As a result, the finished cheese is fresh, moist and springy, with tiny holes and a mild, sweet flavour.

For Romney Mature, the curd is bound in cloth and allowed to mature for up to six months. The sweet, caramel taste of the sheep's milk intensifies and the cheese develops a more nutty flavour and a hard, flaky texture.

Mount Emu Creek Dairy also makes Romney Fresca, as well as its own feta.

BELOW: Pyengana Cheddar is not as hard as some traditional Cheddars

ABOVE: Romney Mature

ST CLAIRE

REGION: *Tasmania*
TYPE: *Traditional, creamery, hard cheese*
SOURCE: *Cow's milk*
DESCRIPTION: *9kg/20lb wheel with fine, leathery, waxed, yellow rind*
CULINARY USES: *Table cheese, grating, grilling*

Made in the style of a traditional Gruyère, the deep yellow St Claire is smooth and firm (and a little too rubbery for the author's taste). Sweeter and milder than traditional Gruyère, it has a fairly mellow, fruity finish.

It is made by one of Australia's oldest manufacturers of Continental-style cheeses, Lactos, which was founded by Milan Vyhnalek in 1955. Bongrain, the huge French cheese company, soon realized its potential and bought Lactos in 1981. Now highly successful, with plants in several locations, Lactos makes a range of cheeses and consistently wins prizes around the world for their quality. Although best known for its Brie- and Camembert-style cheeses, it also makes Edam, Gouda, Neufchâtel and several blues in addition to cream and processed cheeses. St Claire is its only Gruyère-style cheese.

TASMANIA HIGHLAND CHÈVRE LOG

REGION: *Tasmania*
TYPE: *Modern, farmhouse, fresh cheese*
SOURCE: *Goat's milk (Toggenberg/Saanen)*
DESCRIPTION: *150g/5oz log*
CULINARY USES: *Table cheese, grilling*

John Bignell's chèvre is fresh and lemony, with a moist, cheesecake texture. It has a distinct, but not overpowering, goat taste, redolent of thyme and white wine. Both plain and ash-covered versions are available. They mature in one to three weeks and have a fat content of 35 per cent.

John and Jill Bignell also make sheep's milk cheeses, both fresh and aged. Their semi-hard Sheep's cheese has a natural rind, a spongy, Havarti texture and a sweet, fruity finish. The author has yet to track this cheese down, but had it described to her by Bill Studd, joint owner of the Richmond Hill Cafe and Larder in Melbourne, who stocks a marvellous selection of Australian artisan cheeses.

The Bignells' newest venture, is a wickedly rich, triple cream cheese based on the French Brillat-Savarin.

TIMBOON BRIE

REGION: *Victoria*
TYPE: *Traditional and modern, soft white, organic cheese*
SOURCE: *Cow's milk*
DESCRIPTION: *1kg/2¼lb round with soft-white, velvety penicillium crust*
CULINARY USE: *Table cheese*

Herman Schultz and his family must have felt like pioneers when they started making cheese in 1984. Today there are more than 30 farmhouse dairies in Australia, but Herman is still an innovator. His cheeses are made using only bio-dynamic milk (a type of organic milk).

Timboon Brie ripens in 45–60 days. It is not stabilized, and therefore has a more tempestuous nature and a greater depth of flavour than many cheeses of the same type. Because the milk is pasteurized, the rind does not develop the wild yeasts and pigments that would give Timboon the authenticity of a traditional Brie, but it comes closer than most.

Other Timboon Farmhouse Cheeses include Buetten and Fleurie.

ABOVE: Washed Rind (back) and Timboon Brie (front)

TOMME DE CHÈVRE

REGION: *New South Wales*
TYPE: *Modern, farmhouse, semi-soft cheese*
SOURCE: *Goat's milk*
DESCRIPTION: *1kg/2¼lb cylinder with orange, natural rind patched with blue and white moulds*
CULINARY USES: *Table cheese, grilling, baking, salads*

Hunter Valley Cheese Company's Tomme is smooth and dense, with a slightly salty tang and the subtle background flavour of tarragon and white wine that is characteristic of goat's milk cheese. It is slightly firmer than an unpasteurized French Tomme, and does not have quite the same depth of flavour.

Cheesemaker Peter Curtis also produces Chèvre Brie, which is based on an old French recipe for Brie de Melun. The fresh curd is dusted with vine ash and salt.

WASHED RIND

REGION: *Victoria*
TYPE: *Modern, farmhouse, semi-soft cheese*
SOURCE: *Cow's milk (Red Shorthorn)*
DESCRIPTION: *3kg/6½lb flat wheel. The sticky, orange, washed rind is dusted with blue, grey and white moulds*
CULINARY USE: *Table cheese*

Fred Leppin entered the world of cheesemaking in the late 1980s. His English and French-style cheeses are not mere copies of the originals. Instead, he creates new world versions. His semi-soft, washed-rind cheese, while made in the Trappist style, has different qualities from the original. The cheese has a meaty, pungent aroma with a soft, springy texture, and the flavour seems to have absorbed the warm, minty aroma of the eucalyptus trees.

Fred Leppin's washed rind cheeses – Whitelaw, Bass River Red, Wine Washed Rind, Cronwell, Ranceby, Loch and Kardella – have been greeted with great enthusiasm in Australia.

WOODSIDE CABECOU

REGION: *Adelaide*
TYPE: *Traditional, farmhouse, fresh and aged cheeses*
SOURCE: *Goat's milk*
DESCRIPTION: *30g/1¼oz disc. The thin, natural crust is yellowish and wrinkled. It may develop rogue moulds, but these can easily be brushed off*
CULINARY USE: *Table cheese*

Paula Jenkins has a passion and an innate talent for cheesemaking. Much of her knowledge was acquired through working alongside artisan cheesemakers in France and Britain, and she is skilled at adapting their recipes and methods for the Australian climatic conditions and milk.

Along with chef Simon Burr, Paula has been running Woodside Cheese Wrights for just over two years. The cheesery is located in the old Farmers' Union factory at Heritage Park in Woodside, where Paula makes a variety of cheeses from both goat's and cow's milk.

Woodside Cabecou is ivory-white, soft and mousse-like when young, with a fresh acidity. After a few days, it develops a fine surface skin which blossoms into a delicate, white mould. This helps to ripen the fresh curd. With age, the cheese hardens, the herbaceous, mushroomy flavour and aroma become more obvious and some furry, grey mould may appear.

The fresh chèvre curd makes an excellent alternative to cream cheese, adding an extra dimension to salads, grilled vegetable dishes and snacks.

Edith takes its name from an artisan cheesemaker with whom Paula worked in Burgundy. A soft cheese with a luxurious texture, it is encouraged to grow its velvet coat before being rolled in vine ash and aged for a few weeks. The texture is the result of the laborious task of hand-ladling the curd into the moulds. This, together with the lingering goaty flavour, is ensuring its success.

The company also produce Capricorn and Charleston, a cloth-matured Cheddar.

LEFT: *Yarra Valley Feta*

SOUTH AFRICAN CHEESES

Most cheeses sold in South Africa today are factory-made copies of Gouda and Cheddar, which is not surprising, given that the majority of European immigrants who first settled in this country came from Holland and Great Britain. Small amounts of feta, Edam and Brie are produced locally, and it is possible to obtain industrial imports of European cheeses, but cheeses that are uniquely South African are difficult to come by.

Cheesemakers like Christine Briscoe are doing their best to change the situation, however. Christine farms Ayrshires in Natal, some 3,000 miles from her main market, Cape Town. This does not prevent her from ensuring her cheeses are delivered in peak condition to the wine farms where they sell extremely well. She simply air freights them in from Durban. Her range, sold under the name Galtee Mare, consists mainly of English-style territorials like Sage Derby, Leicester and Cheddar, and she even makes two blues. All her cheeses are hand-made.

The Harris family also farm in Natal, but their herd consists of Jerseys, not Ayrshires. They make small volumes of several cheeses under the name Bellavigne. These include Saint-Paulin, Tilsit and a soft, creamy, sweet cheese that looks like Edam.

Fairview Estate, a wine farm near Paarl, in the Cape Province, has been producing a soft, Brie-style blue since the early 1980s. It can be found in supermarkets and speciality shops.

The booming tourist industry will undoubtedly lead to a demand for more locally produced cheeses, as has happened elsewhere in the world. When it does, South African cheesemakers – as determined and dedicated as any of their international colleagues – will come into their own.

YARRA VALLEY PYRAMID

REGION: *Victoria*
TYPE: *Modern, farmhouse, fresh cheese*
SOURCE: *Goat's milk*
DESCRIPTION: *Small pyramid, plain or ash-covered*
CULINARY USES: *Table cheese, grilling*

Firm, yet light in texture, Yarra Valley Pyramid resembles Sainte-Maure. Creamy, lemon-fresh and slightly salty, it melts in the mouth like ice cream. If left to age, the cheese becomes firmer and may develop some mould.

The cheese is produced by Richard Thomas, a man who is in danger of becoming a living legend in the Australian cheese world. His name first appeared when, in partnership with David Brown, he started the Milawa Cheese Company. Next, he helped to set up Meredith Dairy. Yarra Valley is his first venture with goat's milk cheese, but looks like becoming another Australian success story.

They also make Yarra Valley Feta. This cheese is sold packed into small cans. The little balls of refreshingly salty, moist cheese are immersed in olive oil and fresh herbs to give extra flavour to the cheese.

The Cheeses of New Zealand

It is thought that the Maoris, travelling in canoes from Polynesia, were the first to settle New Zealand, around the first century AD. Some historians say that the red-headed Morioris arrived first, but were wiped out by the Maoris. In any event, the early settlers found no indigenous mammals to provide milk or meat, and their diet consisted mainly of ferns, roots, birds, fish and shellfish.

The absence of indigenous mammals meant that when the first British settlers arrived in the late eighteenth century, they had to bring their cattle with them. To provide grazing for their Friesian, Jersey and Guernsey cows, they hacked and burned vast areas of primeval forest. The sheep were chosen for their meat and wool rather than for milking, and the few goats that survived the treacherous sea voyages were mainly for domestic use.

Co-operative dairies, owned by the farmers, were established throughout New Zealand to process milk from the many small and isolated farms. From the late 1840s Cheddar became a major export to the home country. Blue cheese was also being made in small quantities by the middle of the nineteenthth century.

During the Second World War, Cheddar from New Zealand was welcomed in a Britain enduring rationing. Customer loyalty and consistency of quality have kept it on British tables, although the volume has been cut back considerably since Britain's entry into the Common Market.

New Zealand has been forced to look elsewhere for trading partners, and today large volumes of cheese and other dairy products are exported to North America, the Middle East, Russia and Japan.

Over the past 30 years or so, the small co-operatives have merged, and New Zealand now has some of the largest and most efficient milk-processing factories in the world. However, much of the cheese is being made to meet the requirements of large overseas customers. Consistency is important and regional characteristics are quashed so that a buyer can purchase cheese with an identical profile – good news for buyers looking for uniformity, but disappointing for those seeking subtle nuances of flavour.

In a country the size of Britain, but with a population of just over 3.5 million, it is a challenge for the large co-operatives to produce a variety of cheeses and yet remain profitable. Blue cheese was introduced commercially in the 1950s by the New Zealand Rennet Company, now Ferndale Dairies, who are the country's largest producer of speciality cheeses, especially blue cheeses.

The redoubtable Ross McCallum saw the potential for more specialized cheeses, and started his own company – Kapiti Cheese – in 1985. His aim was to produce New Zealand cheeses rather than European imitations, and he set about developing a range of cheeses with Maori names. Equally important, he created an image that would encourage New Zealanders to buy the local cheese by choice and not just because there was nothing else. His strategy has worked, and Kapiti Cheese now produces over 50 different cheeses.

Several resourceful Dutch cheesemakers emigrated to New Zealand in the 1980s. Combining traditional methods with modern practices, they recreated the traditional cheeses of their homeland – Gouda, Leiden, Edam and Maasdam, many of which are delicious when aged.

Change was afoot. Large factories started to mass-produce Camembert and Brie, and a few took courage and introduced New Zealanders to chèvre, but it was not until Kapiti's small, feta-like, sheep's milk cheese, *hipi iti* (which means "little sheep" in Maori) hit the market in 1990 that New Zealand could boast a commercially produced sheep's milk cheese. Considering that at the time there were over 40 million sheep in New Zealand, this seems quite extraordinary.

Today there are around 14 factories and 19 independent or artisan cheesemakers, producing over 300 different cheeses. Many are uniquely New Zealand discoveries, bearing local names and exhibiting distinct characteristics and considerable charm. Because it would be impossible to list them all, they have been selected on the basis of their success at the New Zealand Cheese Awards.

BELOW: A cheesemaker at Kapiti turning Aorangi cheeses to ensure the white mould coats the entire cheese

Airedale

Region: *Oamaru*
Type: *Modern, farmhouse, vegetarian, semi-hard cheese*
Source: *Cow's milk*
Description: *2kg/4½lb straight-sided round. The thin, natural crust has a coating of red cheese "paint"*
Culinary uses: *Table cheese, grating, grilling*

Made by Bob Berry for Whitestone Cheese, Airedale is compact, rather than elastic. Its texture is on the borderline between semi-soft and hard. Special red cheese "paint" conceals its deep sun-yellow centre and encourages the cheese to develop a real depth of flavour. Fruity when young, it becomes full-bodied, with an onion aroma and memorable savoury aftertaste.

Barry's Bay Cheddar

Region: *Banks Peninsula*
Type: *Traditional, creamery, hard cheese*
Source: *Cow's milk*
Description: *35kg/80lb cylinder, waxed and clothbound*
Culinary uses: *Table cheese, grating, grilling*

Cheesemaking was first introduced to the Banks Peninsula around 1844 by English and Scottish settlers. By the late 1890s there were at least nine factories, producing butter, Cheddar and other cheeses; today Barry's Bay is the only one left. Here cheesemaker Don Walker and his team successfully combine modern technology and traditional cheesemaking methods to produce a range of European cheeses, which consistently win medals at the New Zealand Cheese Awards. Their rinded Cheddar is the only traditional, clothbound Cheddar in New Zealand. It is made in large cylinders, which are first waxed and then left to mature for six to 36 months. This results in a firmer texture than that of Cheddars that are made in blocks and matured in plastic. At around 18 months, the flavour intensifies and the cheese seems to develop a mind and style of its own. Barry's Bay Cheddar is a past gold medal winner at the New Zealand Cheese Awards.

Bleu de Montagne

Region: *Various*
Type: *Modern, creamery, blue cheese*
Source: *Cow's milk*
Description: *200g/7oz and 1.8kg/4lb tall cylinders. The fine, straw-coloured rind has a dusting of white, pale blue and sometimes red moulds*
Culinary use: *Table cheese*

Made by Ferndale Dairies, Bleu de Montagne is smooth and quite creamy, with a spicy, blue tang that becomes more pronounced with age. A few weeks after the cheese is made, the natural crust is rubbed with salt, then pierced with stainless-steel rods. This allows the blue mould already present in the cheese to breathe in the oxygen and weave the threads and patches of blue-grey mould through the open-textured, creamy interior. Bleu de Montagne ripens in 60 days. It won a gold medal at the 1997 New Zealand Cheese Awards.

Brick

Region: *Wellington*
Type: *Modern, small, creamery, semi-soft, vegetarian cheese*
Source: *Cow's milk*
Description: *2kg/4½lb brick with sticky, burnt-orange, washed rind*
Culinary use: *Table cheese*

Brick was first made in America in the early nineteenth century, based upon the traditional, monastery-style cheeses of Europe. Kapiti Cheese began experimenting with Brick in the 1990s. Having tried it in America, they tested it in New Zealand by entering it for the 1994 Cheese Awards. It won a gold medal that year and the Cheese Lover's Cheese Award in 1995.

The rind has a marvellous, pungent aroma with overtones of yeast and roast lamb. The pale yellow interior is velvety-smooth and dense – typical of a washed-rind cheese. It has a sweet and savoury taste, with a spicy tang.

The sticky orange rind has, however, not responded well to being entombed in plastic film – a prerequisite in New Zealand supermarkets. This factor, combined with the pungent aroma, has caused retailers some concern. Sadly, Kapiti have either withdraw it or sold a younger, less exciting version. Fortunately the young chefs of New Zealand love Brick and it continues to find its way on to numerous cheeseboards. Hopefully, it is the first of many washed rind cheeses to be made in New Zealand.

Brie

Region: *Various*
Type: *Modern, creamery, soft-white cheese*
Source: *Cow's milk*
Description: *Various sizes and shapes, with thick, white penicillium rind*
Culinary use: *Table cheese*

Numerous Brie- and Camembert-style cheeses are made in New Zealand. The quality is uniform and consistent. Because most of these soft-white cheeses are stabilized, there is little variation in taste. Stabilization means that once the curd has broken down and the cheese has a dense but creamy consistency, it will remain in that state rather than continuing to ripen.

It is becoming more usual for the locally produced cheeses to be given Maori names. Kapiti's Aorangi, for instance, is a Brie-style cheese whose Maori name means "white cloud".

Below: Brick

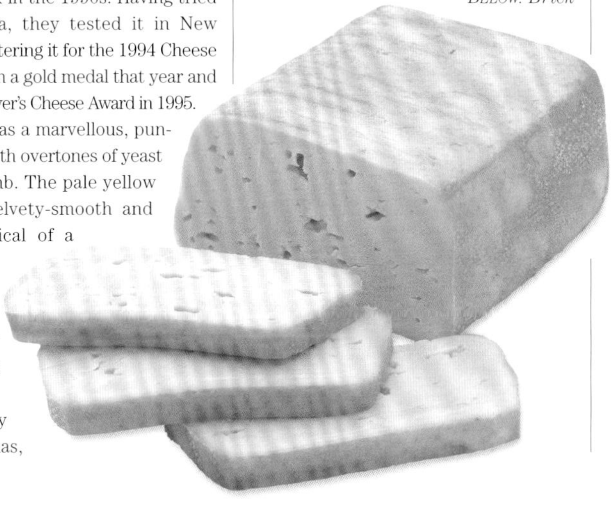

CHEDDAR

REGION: *Various*
TYPE: *Traditional, creamery, hard cheese*
SOURCE: *Cow's milk*
DESCRIPTION: *Sizes vary, but they are typically block-shaped and free of rind*
CULINARY USES: *Table cheese, grating, in salads and sauces, baking*

Block Cheddars are never as hard as those matured in cloth, but when aged for 18 months or more, they develop a firm, bite-able texture and a delicious cheese-and-onion tang that intensifies when the cheese is cooked. The natural carotene in the grass gives New Zealand Cheddar extra depth of colour and strict controls imposed by the dairy boards ensure that Cheddars of the same age will have a virtually identical profile, no matter where in New Zealand they are produced.

It is this predictable uniformity, regardless of season or place of origin, that has made New Zealand Cheddar the popular choice of buyers the world over. However, because the grazing and climate are so diverse, there is a move by smaller producers to produce Cheddar-style cheeses that celebrate these differences.

A recent development (presumably a marketing initiative) has seen the word Cheddar disappearing from the labelling on some pre-packed cheeses, leaving only the strength of flavour to identify the cheese. Degrees of strength are as follows: Mild, Medium, Mature, Tasty, Extra Mature and Vintage.

There are so many New Zealand Cheddars it would be impossible to name them all or say which were the best. However, in recent years Duke of Marlborough, Marlborough Tasty Cheddar and Tararua BONZ Cheddar and have each been declared to be Champion Cheddar at the New Zealand Cheese Awards. One of the "Best Cheddars up to 12 months" is Anchor Mild Cheddar, which is made by Anchor Products.

COLBY

REGION: *Various*
TYPE: *Traditional, creamery, semi-soft cheese*
SOURCE: *Cow's milk*
DESCRIPTION: *Sizes vary, but they are generally block-shaped and free of rind*
CULINARY USES: *Table cheese, grating, grilling, snacks and salads*

Colby was named after the town in Wisconsin, USA, where it was first made. It came to New Zealand in 1882 and is still one of the most popular cheeses.

It is a washed-curd cheese, which means that the curds are thoroughly rinsed in fresh water to remove all excess whey and any stray lactose. This prevents the acidity in the curd from rising, so the cheese remains soft and springy, with a sweet and mild flavour.

Colby has a higher moisture content than Cheddar and feels more elastic. It is also sweet, rather than savoury, thus lacking the depth of flavour acquired by a good Cheddar. For this reason, it is seldom cooked; if it is used in recipes, it is for reasons of texture rather than flavour.

Colby ripens in four months.

EVANSDALE FARMHOUSE BRIE

REGION: *South Island*
TYPE: *Modern, farmhouse, vegetarian, soft-white cheese*
SOURCE: *Cow's milk*
DESCRIPTION: *Thick rounds in various sizes, with soft, fine, white rind*
CULINARY USE: *Table cheese*

Colin Dennison seems to make the impossible look easy. A school teacher, he makes cheese in his "spare time", helped by members of his family. Self-taught, he has a zealous desire for perfection and a strong dose of the New Zealand attitude that if you need something doing you do it yourself.

He had not planned to become a cheesemaker, but when Daffodil, their house cow, produced more milk than the family could consume, Colin entered the challenging cheese world. His first attempt, Monterey Jack, was not a great success, but Colin persevered. The result was Evansdale Farmhouse Brie, still his most popular cheese.

Deeper in hieght than traditional Brie, Evansdale Farmhouse has a soft-white rind and a smooth, creamy texture that melts in the mouth, gradually releasing its flavour of mushrooms, melted butter and green grass. The cheese ripens in six weeks. Seldom found outside Dunedin, it is available by mail order from Colin at Evansdale Cheese, who also make Caerphilly, Komene Kaas, Sage Derby, Wensleydale, ricotta and feta.

FOUR HERB GOUDA

REGION: *Christchurch*
TYPE: *Traditional, farmhouse, organic, vegetarian, hard cheese*
SOURCE: *Cow's milk*
DESCRIPTION: *5kg/11lb boulder-shaped cheese with waxed, natural rind*
CULINARY USES: *Table cheese*

Rients Rympa grew up in Holland, close to a cheese factory. When he and his wife Karen decided to emigrate to New Zealand, they first spent a year studying and learning about cheese in Holland. Nearly 15 years later, they have a thriving business and the Karikaas brand is familiar throughout South Island.

Their Four Herb Gouda is made from organic milk from a nearby farm's herd of Friesian/Holstein cows, the same breed that is used in Holland to make the traditional cheese. The creamy, rich and nutty taste of the cheese marries well with the flavour of the fresh, finely cut herbs that are distributed through it. Four Herb Gouda is matured for three to six months.

They also produce Leyden, Maasdam, plain Gouda and Kwark (Quark).

BELOW: New Zealand Cheddar

HIPI ITI

REGION: *Wellington*
TYPE: *Modern, creamery, vegetarian, fresh cheese*
SOURCE: *Sheep's milk*
DESCRIPTION: *90g/3½oz cylinder*
CULINARY USES: *Table cheese, grilling, baking, salads*

In a country where sheep vastly outnumber people, it is perhaps surprising that New Zealand had to wait until 1990 for its first sheep's milk cheese to appear. Using the milk from an experimental herd, Kapiti created a fresh cheese similar to feta. It is called Hipi Iti, from the Maori meaning "little sheep", and is packed with herbs in jars of oil.

Fresh and lemony, with the characteristic sweet, caramel taste of sheep's milk, Hipi Iti is crumbly like feta but is only slightly salty. It gradually absorbs the subtle taste of the herbs in the oil in which it is stored.

Hipi Iti ripens in two months and has a fat content of 52 per cent. It won silver medals at the New Zealand Cheese Awards of 1996 and 1997.

JUBILEE BLUE

REGION: *Various*
TYPE: *Modern, creamery, blue cheese*
SOURCE: *Cow's milk*
DESCRIPTION: *250g/9oz log with smooth, velvety-soft-white rind*
CULINARY USES: *Table cheese, salads*

The first New Zealand blue cheese, Blue Vein, was launched in 1951 by the NZ Rennet Company. Jubilee Blue was created to celebrate Blue Vein's 40th anniversary and the 75th anniversary of the founding of the company. Smooth, creamy and Brie-like, it has small blotches of blue mould scattered throughout the white paste. There is a delicate aroma of mushrooms, and the taste suggests melted butter with rather spicy, slightly bitter overtones, reminiscent of rocket (arugula) or radiccio. Jubilee Blue ripens in 40 days.

RIGHT: Hipi Iti (front) and Aorangi, a Brie-type cheese (back), are just two of the many excellent cheeses made by Kapiti Cheese in Wellington on the North Island

KIKORANGI

REGION: *Wellington*
TYPE: *Modern, creamery, vegetarian, blue cheese*
SOURCE: *Cow's milk*
DESCRIPTION: *2kg/4½lb cylinder. The slightly moist, natural rind is cream in colour, with grey and blue moulds*
CULINARY USE: *Table cheese*

Another fine cheese from Kapiti, Kikorangi is superbly creamy, almost buttery, with a slightly gritty texture. The distinct, blue veins give the cheese a very strong, piquant, blue taste. Vibrant rather than vicious, it makes the tastebuds hum.

MAHOE AGED GOUDA

REGION: *Kerikeri*
TYPE: *Traditional, farmhouse, vegetarian, speciality cheese*
SOURCE: *Cow's milk*
DESCRIPTION: *6kg/13lb millstone. The smooth, pale yellow, natural rind is coated in yellow wax*
CULINARY USES: *Table cheese, grilling, grating*

Mahoe Cheese began as an experiment in the kitchen. When Anne and Bob Roastrevear decided to make cheese, they originally made varieties from their native Holland – Edam and Gouda – but demand and the desire for experimentaition led to the production of other cheeses, including feta, ricotta and Mahoe Aged Gouda.

Mahoe Aged Gouda is a very firm, smooth cheese with a slightly pliable texture that is almost chewy. It has a fruity, fresh tang and is rich and buttery in the mouth. The finish suggests caramel. The cheese is matured for 15 months and is a consistent medal winner at the New Zealand Cheese Awards.

MERCER GOUDA

REGION: *Hamilton*
TYPE: *Traditional, farmhouse, hard cheese*
SOURCE: *Cow's milk*
DESCRIPTION: *10–12kg/22–26lb boulder-shape. The smooth, pale yellow, natural rind is waxed*
CULINARY USES: *Table cheese (enjoyed for breakfast), grilling, snacks*

Like many artisan cheesemakers, Albert Alfernick believes that the best cheeses are made with unpasteurized milk, which gives them a deeper, more complex flavour. Regulations in New Zealand do not permit either the production or the importation of cheeses made with raw milk, but this does not stop Albert from producing a range of wonderful cheeses.

Enter Albert and Enika's tiny shop in Mercer, just off the main Auckland to Hamilton road, and you will be faced with shelves groaning with golden orbs of cheese, just begging to be tasted: Goudas of all ages, some with cumin, cracked pepper, garlic or herbs; delicious aged Edam; and sweet, fruity Maasdam.

Meyer Vintage Gouda

Region: *Hamilton*
Type: *Traditional, farmhouse, semi-hard cheese*
Source: *Cow's milk*
Description: *10–12kg/22–26lb boulder-shape with smooth, mellow yellow, waxed rind*
Culinary use: *Table cheese*

Declared Supreme Champion at the New Zealand Cheese Awards of 1994, Meyer Vintage Gouda is firm, smooth, dense and creamy. The peach-coloured interior won the hearts and palates of the judges with its aroma of almonds and rich, nutty flavour. Phrases like "sweet and fruity"; "hard, granular and crunchy" and "wonderful depth of character" were bandied about. The pronounced tang and lingering, fruity finish were also lovingly described.

It is therefore not surprising that demand has grown steadily for Ben and Fieke Meyer's Vintage Gouda, which takes about 12 months to develop its full potential. The price reflects the time and labour involved in its production, but it is definitely value for money.

Ben and Fieke emigrated to New Zealand in 1994 and set up a small dairy near Hamilton. They brought with them a passion for cheese and a belief in the traditional methods of their native Holland. What they had not encountered before, however, was the way the composition of milk could alter with the seasons when animals had natural grazing. Their first cheese, made with rich, spring milk, was "very hard indeed", according to Fieke. With the help of Albert Alfernik, another Dutch cheesemaker, they tried again and this time met with success.

Their shelves are now filled with wonderful, round, yellow cheeses – over 3,000 at the last count – each one turned and brushed by hand as they slowly reach maturity. The Meyers produce Gouda at various stages of maturity, some plain, others flavoured with cumin, cloves or pepper.

Left: Sainte Maure

Port Nicholson

Region: *Wellington*
Type: *Modern, creamery, vegetarian, semi-soft cheese*
Source: *Cow's milk*
Description: *1.8kg/4lb round with smooth, bright orange, washed rind*
Culinary uses: *Table cheese, grilling, melting*

Port Nicholson has the characteristic, sweet-sour, slightly smoked aroma and taste of the Trappist-style cheese Port-Salut, upon which it is based, but is more supple and open textured. The producers, Kapiti, named the cheese after the magnificent harbour of New Zealand's capital city, Wellington.

Below: Port Nicholson

Sainte-Maure

Region: *Wellington*
Type: *Modern, creamery, vegetarian, soft-white cheese*
Source: *Goat's milk*
Description: *200g/7oz log with thick, white penicillium rind*
Culinary uses: *Table cheese, grilling, salads*

Ross McCallum and his wife Glenys founded Kapiti Cheese in 1985 and rapidly made their mark on the gourmet world with an impressive range of quality speciality cheeses. Their meteoric rise is due to the passion Ross has for cheese, his vision and uncompromising attitude to quality and his desire to create cheeses with a unique New Zealand identity. Using names inspired by the Maori language, traditional cheesemaking methods and elegant and informative packaging, he set out to conquer the local market.

In the early 1990s, Kapiti began working alongside young chefs excited at the possibilities of their wonderful range of cheeses. Sainte-Maure, was Supreme Champion at the 1997 New Zealand Cheese Awards. It is firm yet velvety-smooth and melts in the mouth to release a medley of flavours – aromatic, distinctly nutty and deliciously sweet.

Saratoga

Region: *Masterton*
Type: *Modern, farmhouse, vegetarian, fresh cheese*
Source: *Goat's milk*
Description: *100–150g/3¾–5oz rounds, waxed in various colours*
Culinary uses: *Table cheese, grilling, salads and pastries*

Dee Lever is a woman of extraordinary courage. Before a serious car accident left her severely disabled, she had never made cheese. A few years ago her tiny, fresh, goat's milk cheese, Saratoga, won two of the top New Zealand Cheese Awards. Not only was it declared Best Fresh Cheese, but it also scooped the Cheese Lover's Cheese Award.

Saratoga has a moist, almost mousse-like texture. Lemon-fresh, it has just a hint of almonds, tarragon and white wine, characteristics of good goat's milk. Each cheese is carefully dipped in wax to protect it and prevent it from drying out.

Production at Saratoga Dairy Goats is small, but the cheeses improve from year to year. The latest additions – Piccolo, Encore, Sonata, Minuet and Opus – have a delicate, aromatic flavour, achieved not merely through careful handling of the curd, but also through good feeding and care of the goats and a commitment to consistent quality. Piccolo was declared Best New and Experimental Cheese at the 1997 New Zealand Cheese Awards.

Waimata Farmhouse Blue

Region: *Gisbourne*
Type: *Modern, farmhouse, vegetarian, blue cheese*
Source: *Cow's milk*
Description: *2.5kg/5½lb cylinder with sticky, natural rind blotched with some grey and blue mould*
Culinary uses: *Table cheese, salads and sauces*

Unanimously chosen Best Blue at the 1997 New Zealand Cheese Awards, where it was also declared to be Best Vegetarian Cheese, Waimata Farmhouse Blue is creamy without being rich, spicy without being vicious: in short, it is everything a blue should be.

Cheesemaker Carol Thorpe is a relative newcomer to the New Zealand cheese scene. She and her husband Rick first became interested in cheesemaking when they visited Wales in the late 1970s to further their knowledge and experience of self-sufficiency, but it was only in 1992, when the kiwifruit industry looked rather gloomy, that Carol examined the prospect of making cheese on a commercial basis.

By late 1994, Carol felt that her cheeses were ready for the market. Making blue and white moulded cheeses at the same location proved a challenge, but less than a year later, her success at the New Zealand Cheese Awards proved she was a master of the moulds.

Her company, Waimata Cheese, now makes various Brie-style blues, plus both a traditional Camembert and a version made with double cream. Also on the list are Port Gisborne, Vine Ash and feta.

Whitestone Farmhouse

Region: *Oamaru*
Type: *Modern, farmhouse, vegetarian, soft-white cheese*
Source: *Cow's milk*
Description: *800g/1¾lb or 1.5kg/3¼lb cylinder with a fine powdering of penicillium mould*
Culinary use: *Table cheese*

This is one of a handful of cheeses that are uniquely New Zealand. Produced from Friesian cows grazing the North Otago limestone country, it is made in an open vat. Covered in a fine, penicillium rind, it has the fragrance of grass and an elasticity, rather like a young Caerphilly. The curd remains moist and crumbly in the centre, becoming softer towards the rind, and there is a slight fruity tang, reminiscent of feijoa (pineapple guava), on the finish.

Unlike many New Zealand cheeses, which are stabilized to improve their shelf life, Whitestone Farmhouse is allowed to continue to ripen, developing more character as it does so. At the 1995 New Zealand Cheese Awards, it was declared Best Original New Zealand Cheese.

Whitestone Cheeses, owned by Bob Berry also produces Airedale, Mt Dasher, Monte Cristo and Windsor Blue.

CANTERBURY CHEESEMONGERS

Affinage, or the art of maturing cheese, is not something that can be learnt in a few weeks or even a few months, as each cheese has its own unique timetable for development and can be influenced by the weather, the grazing, the breed of animal and a myriad of other small, even microscopic elements. New Zealand's first and currently only affineurs, Martin and Sarah Aspinwall, began Canterbury Cheesemongers in 2000, selling their cheese from the back of a French Simca after more than seven years in Britain working alongside experts and cheesemakers at Neals Yard Dairy in London.

In 2002 they opened their delightful shop with its glass-fronted ripening room that attracts thousands of cheese-lovers every year. Their timing was perfect as New Zealanders were just discovering a passion and curiosity for unusual and beautifully made artisan cheeses.

Most of their cheeses are handmade, the result of endless tweaking of recipes by people who are both skilled and passionate about what they produce. Each cheese is cared for lovingly and receives the same level of treatment a guest would expect at a luxury spa. They are turned, rubbed down, washed in brine, wine or olive oil, wrapped in cloth or walnut leaves, and only leave when Martin or Sarah are sure they are at their very peak of perfection.

Martin, who is also an exceptional baker, makes a delicious range of preserves, breads and traditional English pastries to perfectly complement the cheeses. If you are a New Zealander, but are not lucky enough to not live nearby their cheeses are available to buy via Mail Order.

Full address and contact details for Canterbury Cheese are available at the back of this book.

The Recipes

Cheese is such a wonderful ingredient that there is little to beat it as a food on its own and most cheeses are best eaten simply with bread or fruit. However, there are some excellent cooking cheeses. A few, especially some fresh cheeses, are even better cooked than uncooked as their flavour and texture act as a foil for other ingredients to shine. The recipes that follow are mainly quick and simple, they include some wonderful, classic dishes that have stood the test of time and other more up-tempo dishes, which are appropriate for modern life-styles.

Soups, Savouries and Snacks

Place cheese between slices of fresh bread for sandwiches, crumble it on top of soup, stuff cubes of it into hot baked potatoes, and you have some idea of how you can use a wonderful food quickly and elegantly. These recipes are great for many simple meals such as brunches and suppers, picnics and even easy entertaining.

Broccoli and Maytag Blue Soup

Broccoli is such a flavoursome vegetable that it needs little by way of additional ingredients to make a tasty soup. However, the creamy tang of a blue cheese makes it quite special.

25g/1oz/2 tbsp butter
1 onion, chopped
1 potato, peeled and chopped
500g/1¼lb/2 heads of broccoli, or purple sprouting broccoli, chopped
1 litre/1¾ pints/4 cups water
100g/3¾oz Maytag Blue cheese, rind removed, and cubed
freshly grated nutmeg
salt and ground black pepper
a little walnut oil, to serve

Serves 4

VARIATION
Use Stilton or a milder blue cheese such as Dolcelatte or Bleu d'Causses.

1 Heat the butter in a large saucepan and stir in the onion and potato. Cover and cook gently for 5 minutes, then add the broccoli and cook for another 5 minutes. Add the water, bring to the boil, season and simmer for 15 minutes.

2 Strain, reserving the liquid. Put the cooked vegetables in a food processor and moisten with a little of the cooking liquid. Process until very silky and smooth. With the motor running, gradually add the remaining cooking liquid through the feeder tube.

3 Strain the soup back into the clean saucepan. Reheat until nearly boiling, then remove from the heat.

4 Stir in the cheese until melted. Add nutmeg, salt and pepper to taste. Serve in four warmed bowls with a trickle of walnut oil in each.

French Onion Soup

Bread and cheese soups are popular in many countries. One of the great classics is the soup made famous in Les Halles in Paris. It is sold there today, although sadly the market itself has moved on. It is always served with a lightly chewy topping of melted Gruyère.

50g/2oz/¼ cup butter
2 onions, about 250g/9oz, sliced
10ml/2 tsp plain flour
1 litre/1¾ pints/4 cups vegetable or chicken stock
60ml/4 tbsp dry white wine or 30ml/2 tbsp dry sherry
4 slices crusty white bread
150g/5oz Gruyère or Emmental cheese, grated
salt and ground black pepper

Serves 4

COOK'S TIPS
To give the soup a good colour, make sure the onions are lightly browned before you add the stock.
Cheddar could be substituted for Gruyère or Emmental, but the soup would no longer be strictly authentic.

1 Melt the butter in a large saucepan. Add the onions and cook for about 12 minutes or until lightly browned. Stir in the flour and continue to cook until the flour turns a sandy colour.

2 Pour in the stock and wine or sherry and bring to the boil, stirring. Season, cover and simmer for 15 minutes.

3 Meanwhile, preheat the grill. Lightly toast the bread. Divide the cheese among them. Return to the grill and heat until the cheese is bubbling. Place in four warmed, heatproof bowls.

4 Remove the onions from the stock and divide them among the bowls. Pour over the stock, then serve immediately.

Welsh Rarebit

Popularly called Welsh Rabbit, this has been a favourite snack for generations and is made in a wide variety of ways. Use a good melting cheese, such as Cheddar, Lancashire, Monterey Jack, Cheshire or Caerphilly.

2 thick slices of bread
a little unsalted butter, for spreading
100g/3¾oz Cheddar or similar cheese, sliced
10ml/2 tsp spicy or mild mustard or good pinch of paprika or cayenne pepper
ground black pepper

Serves 2

Cheddar is an excellent cheese for melting.

1 Preheat the grill and lightly toast the bread on both sides. Spread sparingly with butter, then top with the cheese, leaving a narrow border around the edges. Heat under the grill until the cheese melts and starts to brown.

2 Spread the cheese quickly with some mustard or sprinkle with a little paprika or cayenne. Add a grinding of pepper. Cut in half diagonally and serve at once.

Traditional Welsh Rarebit

Toasted bread can also be topped with a deliciously rich, creamy cheese sauce, which can be made with either beer or milk. Beer gives the sauce a mellow, hoppy taste and a wonderful country flavour.

130g/4½oz Cheddar or similar cheese, grated
10ml/2 tsp plain flour
10ml/2 tsp mild mustard
60ml/4 tbsp beer or milk
4 thick slices of country-style bread
good pinch of paprika or cayenne pepper
fresh basil leaves and tomato wedges, to garnish

Serves 4

VARIATIONS

For Buck Rarebit, top Traditional Welsh Rarebit with a poached egg and perhaps a rasher or two of grilled bacon. For a more upbeat presentation, top plain Welsh Rarebit with grilled roasted peppers or plum tomatoes, or caramelized red onions. Serve with a mixed herb and green leaf salad.

1 Mix the cheese, flour and mustard in a small saucepan. Pour in the beer or milk and stir well.

2 Heat gently, stirring until thick and creamy. Do not allow it to boil. Toast the bread lightly under the grill. Pour the melted cheese on to the toast and spread to the edges. Return to the grill and cook until the cheese is browned.

3 Sprinkle the grilled cheese with paprika or cayenne and serve at once, garnished with basil and tomatoes.

Croque Monsieur

A popular French snack that literally translated means "crunch (or munch) gentleman". This is an easy dish for children to prepare, especially when a sandwich toaster is used.

a little butter, for spreading
4 thin slices of country-style bread
75g/3oz Gruyère or Cheddar cheese, sliced
2 lean honey roast ham slices
ground black pepper
flat leaf parsley, to garnish

Serves 2

1 Preheat a sandwich toaster or the grill. Lightly butter the bread and lay the cheese and ham on two of the slices (*left*). Top with the other slices of bread and press firmly together.

2 Cook in the sandwich toaster, following the manufacturer's instructions, or grill until browned on both sides. Serve hot, garnished with parsley.

Below: Traditional Welsh Rarebit (left) and Croque Monsieur (right).

MEXICAN TACOS

Ready-made taco shells make perfect edible containers for shredded salad, meat fillings, grated cheese and soured cream. For an authentic touch, use Mexican queso blanco or queso anejado.

15ml/1 tbsp olive oil
250g/9oz lean minced beef or turkey
2 garlic cloves, crushed
5ml/1 tsp ground cumin
5–10ml/1–2 tsp mild chilli powder
8 ready-made taco shells
½ small iceberg lettuce, shredded
1 small onion, thinly sliced
2 tomatoes, chopped in chunks
1 avocado, halved, stoned and sliced
60ml/4 tbsp soured cream
125g/4oz/1 cup crumbled queso blanco or anejado, or grated Cheddar or Monterey Jack cheese
salt and ground black pepper

SERVES 4

1 Heat the oil in a frying pan. Add the meat, with the garlic and spices, and brown over a medium heat, stirring frequently to break up any lumps. Season, cook for 5 minutes, then set aside to cool slightly.

2 Meanwhile, warm the taco shells according to the instructions on the packet. Do not let them get too crisp. Spoon the lettuce, onion, tomatoes and avocado slices into the taco shells. Top with the soured cream followed by the minced beef or turkey mixture.

3 Sprinkle the crumbled or grated cheese into the tacos and serve immediately. Tacos are eaten with the fingers, so have plenty of paper napkins handy.

FONTINA PAN BAGNA

When the weather is hot, a crusty flute or baguette filled with juicy tomatoes, crisp red onion, green pepper, thinly sliced Fontina and sliced black olives makes a refreshing snack.

1 small red onion, thinly sliced
1 fresh flute or baguette
extra virgin olive oil
3 ripe plum tomatoes, thinly sliced
1 small green pepper, cored, halved and thinly sliced
200g/7oz Fontina cheese, thinly sliced
about 12 stoned black olives, sliced
a handful of flat leaf parsley or basil leaves
salt and ground black pepper

SERVES 2–4

VARIATIONS

Instead of Fontina, try Havarti, or Taleggio. Use chopped canned anchovies instead of olives.

1 Soak the red onion in plenty of cold water for at least an hour, then drain well in a colander, tip on to kitchen paper and pat dry.

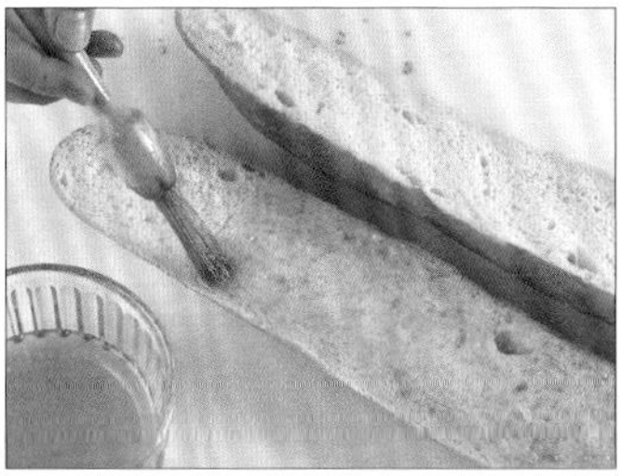

2 Slice the flute or baguette in half lengthways and brush the cut sides well with olive oil. Lay the tomato slices down one side and season well.

3 Top with the pepper slices followed by the onion slices, then add the cheese and olives. Scatter over the parsley or basil leaves and season again.

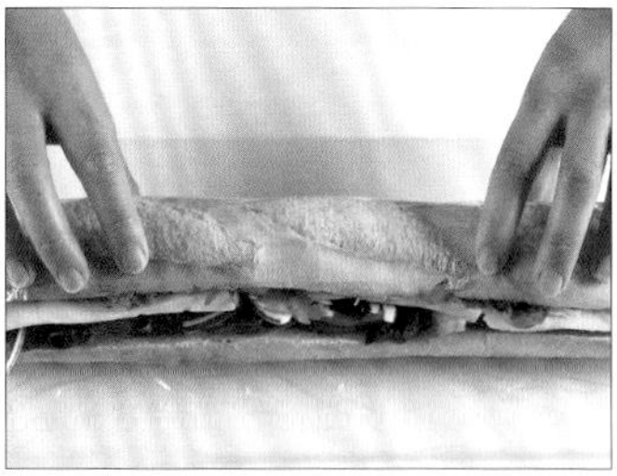

4 Press the halves together, then wrap tightly in clear film to compress. Chill for at least 1 hour. Unwrap and cut diagonally in thick slices to serve.

Mozzarella in Carozza with Fresh Tomato Salsa

The title of this delectable Italian snack translates as cheese "in a carriage". The recipe is similar to Croque Monsieur except that it contains mozzarella and is dipped in beaten egg and fried like French toast.

200g/7oz mozzarella cheese, thinly sliced
8 thin slices of bread, crusts removed
a little dried oregano
30ml/2 tbsp freshly grated Parmesan cheese
3 eggs, beaten
olive oil, for frying
salt and ground black pepper
fresh herbs, to garnish

For the Salsa

4 ripe plum tomatoes, peeled, seeded and finely chopped
15ml/1 tbsp chopped fresh parsley
5ml/1 tsp balsamic vinegar
15ml/1 tbsp extra virgin olive oil

Serves 4

1 Arrange the mozzarella on four slices of the bread. Season with salt and pepper and sprinkle with a little dried oregano and the Parmesan. Top with the other bread slices and press them firmly together.

2 Pour the beaten eggs into a large shallow dish and season with salt and pepper. Add the cheese sandwiches, two at a time, pressing them into the egg with a fish slice until they are well coated. Repeat with the remaining sandwiches, then leave them to stand for 10 minutes.

3 To make the salsa, put the chopped tomatoes in a bowl and add the parsley. Stir in the vinegar and the extra virgin olive oil. Season well with salt and pepper and set aside.

4 Heat olive oil to a depth of 5mm/¼in in a large frying pan. Carefully add the sandwiches in batches and cook for about 2 minutes on each side until golden and crisp. Drain well on kitchen paper. Cut in half and serve garnished with fresh herbs and accompanied by the salsa.

Cheese Aigrettes

These choux buns, flavoured with mature Gruyère and dusted with grated Parmesan, are a bit fiddly to make, but the dough can be prepared ahead and then deep fried to serve. They make a wonderful party snack.

100g/3¾oz/scant 1 cup strong plain flour
2.5ml/½ tsp paprika
2.5ml/½ tsp salt
75g/3oz/6 tbsp cold butter, diced
200ml/7fl oz/scant 1 cup water
3 eggs, beaten
75g/3oz/¾ cup coarsely grated mature Gruyère cheese
corn or vegetable oil, for deep frying
50g/2oz piece of Parmesan cheese, finely grated
ground black pepper
sprigs of flat leaf parsley, to garnish

Makes 30

VARIATION

Make slightly larger aigrettes, slit them open and scoop out any soft paste. Fill the centres with taramasalata or crumbled Roquefort mixed with a little fromage frais.

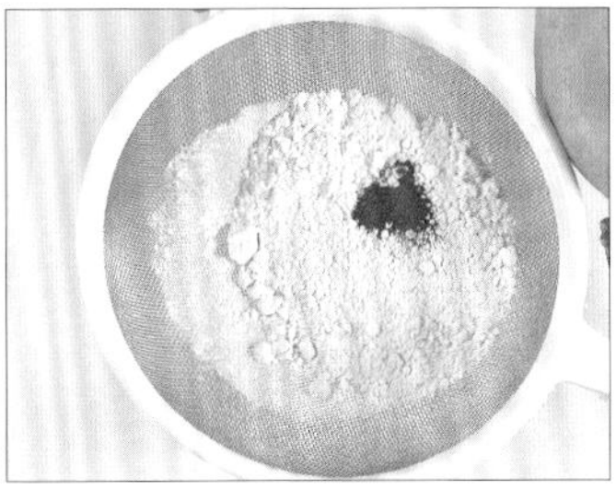

1 Sift the flour, paprika and salt on to a sheet of greaseproof paper. Add a generous grinding of black pepper.

2 Put the butter and water into a medium saucepan and heat gently. As soon as the butter has melted and the liquid starts to boil, tip in all the seasoned flour at once and beat hard with a wooden spoon until the dough comes away from the sides of the pan.

3 Remove the saucepan from the heat and cool the paste for 5 minutes. This step is important if the aigrettes are to rise well. Gradually beat in enough of the beaten egg to give a stiff dropping consistency that still holds a shape on the spoon. Mix in the Gruyère.

4 Heat the oil for deep frying to 180°C/350°F. Take a teaspoonful of the choux paste and use a second spoon to slide it into the oil. Make more aigrettes in the same way. Fry for 3–4 minutes until golden brown. Drain on kitchen paper and keep warm while cooking successive batches. To serve, pile the aigrettes on a warmed serving dish, sprinkle with Parmesan and garnish with sprigs of parsley.

Raclette with New Potatoes

Made in both Switzerland and France, raclette melts to a velvety creaminess and warm golden colour. Melted over hot new potatoes and served with cold meats and red onion pickle, it makes the ideal quick meal.

2 red onions, sliced
5ml/1 tsp sugar
90ml/6 tbsp red wine vinegar
2.5ml/½ tsp salt
generous pinch of dried dill
500g/1¼lb new potatoes, halved if large, scrubbed
250g/9oz raclette cheese slices
salt and ground black pepper
selection of salamis, garlic sausages or country-style ham, to serve

Serves 4

COOK'S TIP
Look for ready-sliced raclette for this dish – it is available from most large supermarkets and specialist cheese shops.

1 First, make the pickle. Spread out the onions in a dish, pour over boiling water to cover and leave to soak until cold. Meanwhile, mix the sugar, vinegar, salt and dill in a small pan. Heat gently, stirring until the sugar has dissolved, then cool. Drain the onions, pour the vinegar mixture over, cover and leave for at least 1 hour, preferably overnight.

2 Boil the potatoes in their skins, then drain and place in a roasting tin. Preheat the grill. Season the potatoes and arrange the raclette on top. Place under the heat until the cheese melts. Serve hot with sliced cold meats. Drain the excess vinegar from the pickled red onion and serve the pickle with the potatoes.

Tuna Melt Muffins

Take a tip from the Americans and try this delicious and nutritious snack consisting of wholemeal muffins topped with tuna and hot bubbling cheese. Use wholemeal toast in place of the muffins, if you like.

200g/7oz can tuna, drained and flaked
1 spring onion, chopped
1 small celery stick, chopped
15ml/1 tbsp chopped canned pimiento or 1 medium tomato, chopped
30ml/2 tbsp mayonnaise
generous pinch of dried oregano or marjoram
2 wholemeal muffins, split
65g/2½oz mature Monterey Jack or Cheddar cheese, coarsely grated or sliced
8 pimiento- or anchovy-stuffed olives, sliced
salt and ground black pepper

Serves 2

1 Mix the tuna with the spring onion, celery, pimiento or tomato, mayonnaise and oregano or marjoram. Stir in salt and pepper to taste, then set aside.

2 Preheat the grill and toast the cut side of the muffins until golden.

3 Spoon a quarter of the tuna mixture on to each muffin half, then top with the cheese and stuffed olive slices. Grill until the cheese has melted and is bubbling. There is no need to brown the cheese. Serve hot, sprinkled with more black pepper.

Salads and Vegetable Dishes

Cheese has an affinity with vegetables. Many cheeses taste best uncooked and at room temperature, so they are ideal for using in salads and look sensational tossed into crisp green leaves and colourful salad vegetables. However, cheeses can also be turned into satisfying hot main dishes, stirred into simple sauces and used to coat lightly cooked vegetables.

Caesar Salad

Not a classic dish of ancient Roman times, but a salad created in America in the 1920s by a restaurateur called Caesar Cardini. Fresh Parmesan is an essential ingredient, as is ice-cold cos, Romaine or Little Gem lettuce.

2 large garlic cloves, halved
45ml/3 tbsp extra virgin olive oil
4 slices of wholemeal bread
1 small cos or 2 Romaine or Little Gem lettuces
50g/2oz piece of Parmesan cheese, shaved or coarsely grated

For the Dressing
1 egg
10ml/2 tsp French mustard
5ml/1 tsp Worcestershire sauce
30ml/2 tbsp fresh lemon juice
30ml/2 tbsp extra virgin olive oil
salt and ground black pepper

Serves 4

VARIATIONS

Anchovies could be added to the salad. Drain a 50g/2oz can and cut the anchovies into long, thin strips. Pat dry using kitchen paper. Instead of adding a semi-raw egg to the dressing, hard-boil 2 eggs, peel and quarter them and use in the salad itself.

1 Preheat the oven to 190°C/375°F/ Gas 5. Rub the inside of a salad bowl with one of the half cloves of garlic. Mix the oil with the remaining garlic in a small pan and heat for 5 minutes, then remove the garlic.

2 Remove the crusts from the bread and cut the slices into small cubes. Toss these in the garlic-flavoured oil, making sure that they are well coated. Spread out the bread cubes on a baking sheet, bake for about 10 minutes until crisp, then leave to cool.

3 Separate the lettuce leaves, wash and dry them and arrange in a shallow salad bowl.

4 To make the dressing, boil the egg for 1 minute only. Crack it into a bowl, using a teaspoon to scoop out any softly set white. Using a balloon whisk beat in the mustard, Worcestershire sauce, lemon juice, olive oil and salt and pepper. Sprinkle the Parmesan over the salad and drizzle the dressing over. Scatter with the croûtons. Take the salad to the table, toss lightly and serve immediately.

TRICOLOUR SALAD

A popular salad, this dish depends for its success on the quality of its ingredients. Mozzarella di bufala is the best cheese to serve uncooked. Whole ripe plum tomatoes give up their juice to blend with extra virgin olive oil for a natural dressing.

150g/5oz mozzarella di bufala cheese, thinly sliced
4 large plum tomatoes, sliced
sea salt flakes, to season
1 large avocado
about 12 basil leaves or a small handful of flat leaf parsley leaves
45–60ml/3–4 tbsp extra virgin olive oil
ground black pepper

SERVES 2

1 Arrange the sliced cheese and tomatoes randomly on two salad plates. Crush over a few good pinches of sea salt flakes. This will help to draw out some of the juices from the tomatoes. Set aside in a cool place to marinate for about 30 minutes.

2 Just before serving, cut the avocado in half using a large sharp knife and twist to separate. Lift out the stone and remove the peel.

3 Slice the avocado flesh crossways into half moons, or cut it into large chunks if that is easier.

4 Place the avocado on the salad, then sprinkle with the basil or parsley. Drizzle over the olive oil, add a little more salt if liked and some black pepper. Serve at room temperature, with chunks of crusty Italian ciabatta.

VARIATIONS

A light sprinkling of balsamic vinegar added just before serving gives the salad a refreshing tang, while a few thinly sliced red onion rings would add extra colour and flavour.

ROQUEFORT AND FLAGEOLET BEAN SALAD WITH HONEY DRESSING

Pungent and creamy, classic sheep's milk Roquefort from the Massif Centrale of France makes an excellent salad cheese. It goes particularly well with pale green flageolet beans and a light sweet-sour dressing.

150g/5oz/scant 1 cup dried flageolet beans, soaked overnight in water to cover
1 bay leaf
1 sprig of thyme
1 small onion, sliced
30ml/2 tbsp chopped fresh parsley
30ml/2 tbsp chopped walnuts
200g/7oz Roquefort cheese, lightly crumbled
salt and ground black pepper
red and green salad leaves, to serve

FOR THE DRESSING
60ml/4 tbsp extra virgin olive oil
30ml/2 tbsp rice wine vinegar or half wine vinegar and half water
5ml/1 tsp French mustard
10ml/2 tsp clear honey

SERVES 4

1 Drain the beans and put them in a saucepan. Pour in cold water to cover. Bring to the boil. Cook over a medium heat for 10 minutes, then reduce the heat. Add the bay leaf, thyme and onion and simmer for about 20–25 minutes or until the beans are tender.

2 Drain the beans, discarding the herbs but not the onion. Tip into a bowl, season and leave until just warm.

3 Make the dressing. Mix the oil, vinegar or vinegar and water, mustard and honey in a small bowl. Add salt to taste and a generous grinding of pepper. Pour over the beans. Add the parsley and walnuts.

4 Gently mix the crumbled Roquefort into the salad. Serve the salad at room temperature accompanied by red and green salad leaves.

VARIATIONS

Any other sheep's milk blue cheese could be used instead of Roquefort. The salad is also delicious with either cooked green or Puy lentils instead of the beans.

Toasted Crottins with Beetroot Salad

Crottins grill to a delicious, nutty creaminess in a matter of minutes for serving on thinly sliced walnut bread toast. A salad of grated raw beetroot makes a colourful accompaniment.

2 raw beetroots, about 200g/7oz total weight
1 celery stick
2 spring onions
60ml/4 tbsp French dressing
generous pinch of ground cumin
4 small slices of walnut bread
a little butter, for spreading
4 crottins (small goat's milk cheeses), about 60g/2¼oz each
salt and ground black pepper
rocket or watercress leaves, to serve

Serves 4

1 Peel the beetroots and grate coarsely. Ideally, the beetroot should be served raw, but, if you prefer, blanch it in boiling water for 3 minutes, then drain, refresh under cold running water and drain again. Put the beetroot in a bowl.

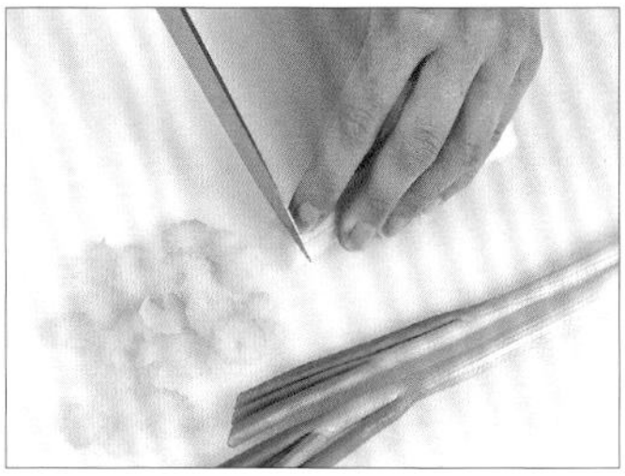

2 Slice the celery and spring onions finely and toss with the beetroot, dressing and cumin. Add salt and pepper to taste. Leave to marinate for an hour or so, if possible, then mound on to four salad plates.

3 Preheat the grill. Toast the walnut bread lightly on each side. Keep warm. Place a sheet of foil on the rack, add the crottins and grill for 3–5 minutes until they turn golden brown on top and just start to melt.

4 Meanwhile, butter the toast lightly. Place on the plates, then, using a palette knife, transfer the crottins to the toast and serve immediately, accompanied by the beetroot salad and the rocket or watercress leaves.

HOT HALLOUMI WITH ROASTED PEPPERS

The best-known cheese from Cyprus is the salty, hard Halloumi. Delicious served simply sliced or cubed, it takes on a wonderful texture when grilled or fried. A tumble of roasted sweet peppers makes a fine accompaniment.

selection of 6 peppers, red, green or yellow
olive oil
30ml/2 tbsp balsamic or red wine vinegar
small handful of raisins (optional)
300g/11oz Halloumi cheese, thickly sliced
salt and ground black pepper
flat leaf parsley, to garnish
sesame seed bread, to serve (optional)

SERVES 4

COOK'S TIPS

For a crisp coating on the Halloumi, toss the slices in plain flour before frying them. Plain Halloumi can be grilled instead of fried. Simply preheat a grill or ridged grilling pan, add the cheese slices and cook until golden brown, turning once. They are good grilled on a barbecue, too.

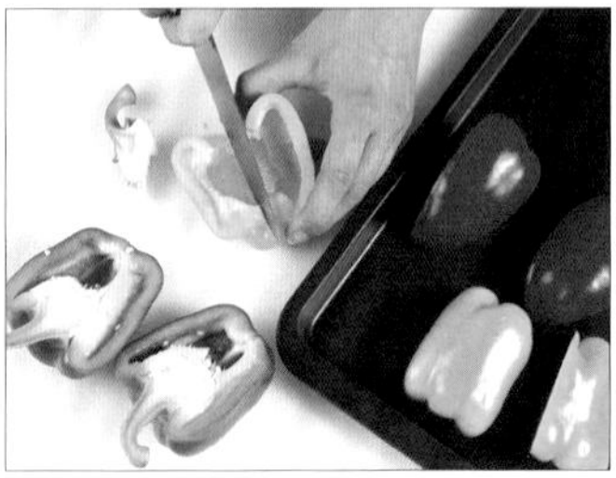

1 Preheat the oven to 220°C/425°F/Gas 7. Cut the peppers in quarters, discard the cores and seeds, then place cut side down on a non-stick baking sheet. Roast for 15–20 minutes until the skins start to blacken and blister. Remove and cover with several layers of kitchen paper. Set aside for 30 minutes, then peel off the skins. Slice the flesh into a bowl. Save any roasting juices and mix these with the peppers.

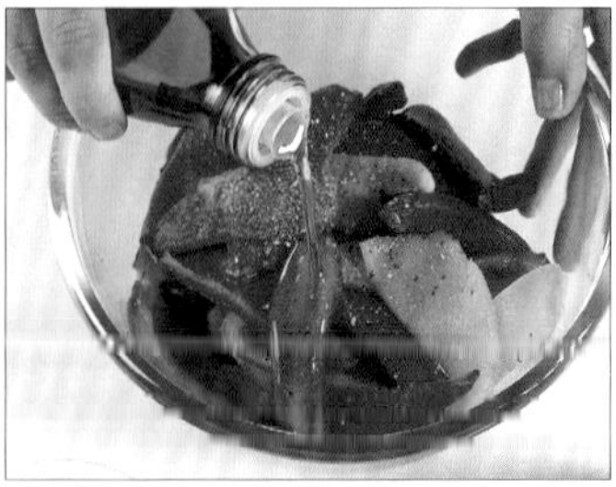

2 Pour a little olive oil over the peppers. Add the vinegar and raisins, if used, with salt and pepper to taste. Toss lightly and leave to cool.

3 When ready to serve, divide the pepper salad among four plates. Heat olive oil to a depth of about 5mm/¼in in a large heavy-based frying pan. Fry the Halloumi slices over a medium-high heat for about 2–3 minutes, turning them halfway through cooking until golden brown on both sides.

4 Drain the Halloumi thoroughly on kitchen paper and serve with the roasted peppers and a parsley garnish. Offer chunks of sesame seed bread, if you like.

LENTIL, TOMATO AND CHEESE SALAD

Lentils and cheese are a natural combination. The small blue-green Puy lentils from France are perfect for salads; flat green Continental lentils or massor dhal lentils from India are also good. Chunks of crumbly feta or a mild goat's milk cheese provide a colour and flavour contrast, but cubes of hard cheese are also inviting.

200g/7oz/scant 1 cup lentils (preferably Puy lentils), soaked for about 3 hours in cold water to cover
1 red onion, chopped
1 bay leaf
60ml/4 tbsp extra virgin olive oil
45ml/3 tbsp chopped fresh parsley
30ml/2 tbsp chopped fresh oregano or marjoram
250g/9oz cherry tomatoes, halved
250g/9oz feta, goat's milk cheese or Caerphilly cheese, crumbled
salt and ground black pepper
leaves of chicory or frisée and fresh herbs, to garnish
30–45ml/2–3 tbsp lightly toasted pine nuts, to serve

SERVES 6

1 Drain the lentils and place them in a large saucepan. Pour in plenty of cold water and add the onion and bay leaf. Bring to the boil, boil hard for 10 minutes, then lower the heat and simmer for 20 minutes or according to the instructions on the packet.

2 Drain the lentils, discard the bay leaf and tip them into a bowl. Add salt and pepper to taste. Toss with the olive oil. Set aside to cool, then mix with the fresh parsley, oregano or marjoram and cherry tomatoes.

3 Add the cheese. Line a serving dish with chicory or frisée leaves and pile the salad in the centre. Scatter over the pine nuts and garnish with fresh herbs.

WALDORF SALAD WITH CHEESE

A multi-purpose salad that can serve as a side dish or a vegetarian main course. The salad is best made the night before, so that it can marinate and soften before serving.

3 celery sticks, thinly sliced
1 small onion, thinly sliced
1 carrot, coarsely grated
400g/14oz white cabbage
1 sharp apple
2.5ml/½ tsp caraway seeds
50g/2oz/½ cup chopped walnuts
200g/7oz Cheddar or other hard cheese, cut into small cubes

For the Dressing
45ml/3 tbsp olive oil
30ml/2 tbsp sunflower oil
45ml/3 tbsp cider vinegar or white wine vinegar
generous pinch of sugar
generous pinch of mustard powder
generous pinch of dried tarragon
salt and ground black pepper

Serves 6

1 Put the celery, onion and carrot in a bowl. Cut the cabbage in quarters, remove and discard the core, then shred each piece finely. Add the cabbage to the bowl. Grate the apple coarsely and add it to the bowl along with the caraway seeds and walnuts. Toss well.

2 Whisk the dressing ingredients in a jug and season well with salt and pepper. Stir the dressing into the vegetable mixture and leave for at least 1 hour, preferably overnight, to allow the flavours to blend together. Mix in the cubes of cheese, then spoon into a dish and serve at once.

VARIATIONS

For a colour contrast, try making this salad with red cabbage or a mixture of red and white cabbage. Substitute toasted hazelnuts for the walnuts, if you like.

PEAR AND PARMESAN SALAD WITH POPPY SEED DRESSING

This is a good starter when pears are at their seasonal best. Try Packhams or Comice when plentiful, drizzled with a poppy-seed dressing and topped with shavings of Parmesan.

4 just-ripe dessert pears
50g/2oz piece of Parmesan cheese
watercress, to garnish
water biscuits or rye bread, to serve (optional)

For the Dressing
30ml/2 tbsp extra virgin olive oil
15ml/1 tbsp sunflower oil
30ml/2 tbsp cider vinegar or white wine vinegar
2.5ml/½ tsp soft light brown sugar
good pinch of dried thyme
15ml/1 tbsp poppy seeds
salt and ground black pepper

Serves 4

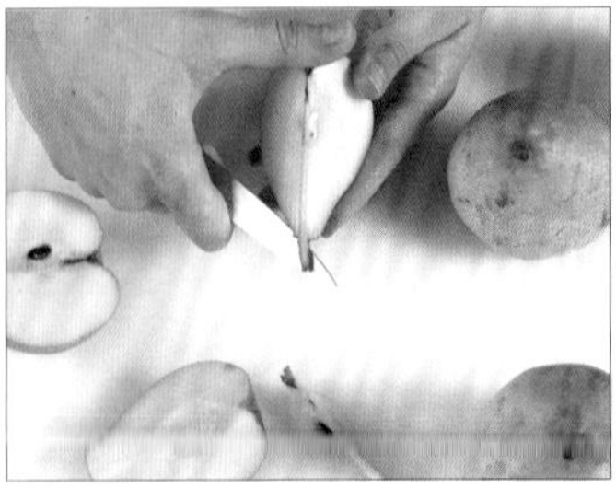

1 Cut the pears in quarters and remove the cores. Cut each pear quarter in half lengthways and arrange them on four small serving plates. Peel the pears if you wish, though they look more attractive unpeeled.

2 Make the dressing. Mix the oils, vinegar, sugar, thyme and seasoning in a jug. Whisk well, then tip in the poppy seeds. Trickle the dressing over the pears. Garnish with watercress and shave Parmesan over the top. Serve with water biscuits or thinly sliced rye bread, if you like.

VARIATION

Blue cheeses and pears also have a natural affinity. Stilton, Dolcelatte, Gorgonzola or Danish Blue (Danablu) are good substitutes. Allow about 200g/7oz and cut into wedges or cubes.

Potato Gratin with Munster Cheese

Munster melted in cream creates a superb topping for layered potatoes.

500g/1¼lb potatoes
150g/5oz Munster cheese, rind removed, and diced
60ml/4 tbsp double cream
150ml/¼ pint/⅔ cup milk
30ml/2 tbsp snipped fresh chives or chopped fresh parsley
freshly grated nutmeg
salt and ground black pepper

Serves 4

VARIATION
Any semi-soft or washed rinded French cheese can be used for this dish. Reblochon gives excellent results. For an extra-punchy flavour try Langes or Epoisses.

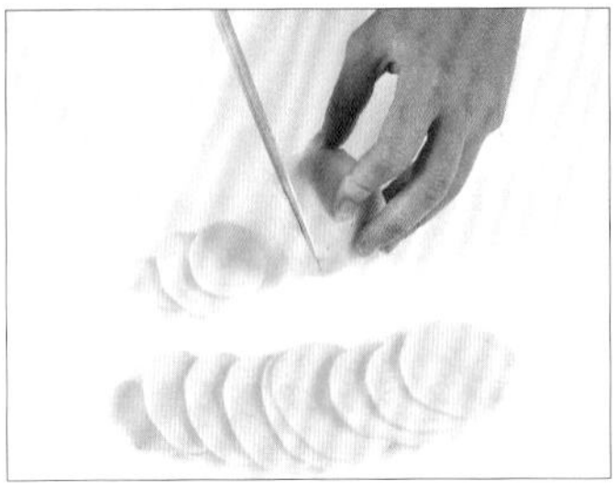

1 Peel the potatoes and slice them thinly. Cook the slices in boiling lightly salted water for about 10 minutes until tender. Drain and place in a gratin dish. Preheat the grill.

2 Mix the cheese, cream and milk in a small saucepan. Heat gently until the cheese has melted. Do not allow to boil. Remove from the heat, stir in the chives or parsley, add nutmeg to taste and season lightly. Pour the mixture over the potatoes. Grill until the topping is golden brown and serve.

Parsnip, Carrot and Goat's Milk Cheese Fricassée

This excellent vegetarian main course also makes a fine accompaniment for roast or grilled meats or fish. Serve it with roast potatoes.

4 parsnips
4 carrots
1 red onion, sliced
30ml/2 tbsp pine nuts or flaked almonds, lightly toasted
sprigs of tarragon, to garnish

For the Sauce
40g/1½oz/3 tbsp butter
40g/1½oz/⅓ cup plain flour
300ml/½ pint/1¼ cups milk
130g/4½oz chèvre (goat's milk cheese)
15ml/1 tbsp chopped fresh or 2.5ml/½ tsp dried tarragon
salt and ground black pepper

Serves 4–6

1 Cut the parsnips and carrots into sticks. Put them in a saucepan and add the onion. Season, cover with cold water and bring to the boil. Lower the heat and simmer for 10 minutes or until the vegetables are just tender. Drain, reserving 200ml/7fl oz/scant 1 cup of the cooking water. Put the vegetables in a dish and keep hot.

2 Make the sauce. Melt the butter in a clean pan and stir in the flour. Cook for 1 minute, stirring, then gradually whisk in the reserved vegetable water and the milk. Heat, whisking, until the sauce boils and thickens. Simmer gently for 2 minutes.

3 Remove from the heat and stir in the chèvre, tarragon and salt and pepper. Pour the sauce over the vegetables and sprinkle with the pine nuts or almonds. Garnish with tarragon and serve.

Try other goat's milk cheeses, such as Chevrotin or chèvre-fevrille.

Roast Mediterranean Vegetables with Pecorino

Aubergines, courgettes, peppers and tomatoes make a marvellous medley when roasted and served drizzled with fragrant olive oil. Shavings of sheep's milk Pecorino add the perfect finishing touch.

1 aubergine, sliced
2 courgettes, sliced
2 peppers (red or yellow or one of each), cored and quartered
1 large onion, thickly sliced
2 large carrots, cut in sticks
4 firm plum tomatoes, halved
extra virgin olive oil
45ml/3 tbsp chopped fresh parsley
45ml/3 tbsp pine nuts, lightly toasted
125g/4oz piece of Pecorino cheese
salt and ground black pepper
crusty bread, to serve (optional)

SERVES 4–6

VARIATION

Any hard sheep's milk cheese can be used for the topping. Try Spanish Manchego or British Malvern.

1 Layer the aubergine slices in a colander, sprinkling each layer with a little salt. Leave to drain over a sink or plate for about 20 minutes, then rinse thoroughly, drain well and pat dry with kitchen paper. Preheat the oven to 220°C/425°F/Gas 7.

2 Spread out the vegetables in one or two large roasting tins. Brush the vegetables lightly with olive oil and roast them in the oven for about 20 minutes or until they are lightly browned and the skins on the peppers have begun to blister.

3 Transfer the vegetables to a large serving platter. If you like, peel the peppers. Trickle over any vegetable juices from the pan and season with salt and pepper. As the vegetables cool, sprinkle them with more oil (preferably extra virgin olive oil). When they are at room temperature, mix in the parsley and pine nuts.

4 Using a vegetable peeler, shave the Pecorino and scatter the shavings over the vegetables. Serve with crusty bread as a starter or an accompaniment for a buffet or barbecue.

Cauliflower and Broccoli Mornay

As we become more aware of the value of simple, honest flavours, this nursery favourite is enjoying a revival. The secret of a good cheese sauce is not to make it too thick and to stir in the cheese off the heat so that it melts gently.

1 medium cauliflower
2 heads of broccoli
1 onion, sliced
3 hard-boiled eggs, quartered
6 cherry tomatoes, halved (optional)
30–45ml/2–3 tbsp natural-coloured dried breadcrumbs

For the Sauce

40g/1½oz/3 tbsp butter
40g/1½oz/⅓ cup plain flour
600ml/1 pint/2½ cups milk or a mixture of milk and vegetable water
150g/5oz/1¼ cups grated mature Cheddar cheese
freshly grated nutmeg
salt and ground black pepper

Serves 4–6

VARIATIONS

The sauce can also be used for Macaroni Cheese. Cook 200g/7oz/1¾ cups dried macaroni or pasta shapes according to the package instructions. Add 1 sliced onion when boiling the macaroni, if you like. Drain and mix with the sauce, quartered hard-boiled eggs and tomato halves.

Use any mature hard cheese suitable for cooking. Red Leicester gives the sauce a deep golden colour. For a more pungent flavour, try a Munster.

To make a quick cheese sauce, melt 250g/9oz/2¼ cups grated mature Cheddar into 475ml/16fl oz/2 cups scalded single cream. Season. Flavour with freshly grated nutmeg.

1 Trim the cauliflower and broccoli and cut them into even-size florets, slicing the thinner parts of the stalks if you prefer. Bring a large saucepan of lightly salted water to the boil and cook the cauliflower, broccoli and onion slices for 5–7 minutes or until just tender. Do not over-cook.

2 Drain, reserving some of the vegetable water if you intend using it for the sauce. Place the vegetables in a shallow heatproof dish and add the quartered eggs.

3 To make the sauce, melt the butter in a saucepan and stir in the flour. Cook for 1 minute.

4 Gradually add the milk, or milk and vegetable water, whisking constantly until the mixture boils and thickens to a smooth sauce. Lower the heat and simmer for 2 minutes until glossy. Whisk three-quarters of the cheese into the sauce and season with nutmeg, salt and pepper.

5 Preheat the grill. Pour the sauce over the vegetables and dot with the tomato halves, if using. Mix the remaining cheese with the dried breadcrumbs. Sprinkle the cheese and breadcrumb mixture over the vegetables, and grill until the top is bubbling and golden brown, then serve immediately.

Main Meal Dishes

There are meals when cheese is a good complementary ingredient to meat or fish. In the main, it is a good idea to use cheese that does not overpower the rest of the ingredients, but sometimes a strong cheese works very well: for instance, a piquant blue cheese is delicious with veal, and a full-flavoured Greek cheese with aubergines and a meat sauce makes a memorable moussaka.

Veal Escalopes with Smoked Cheese Sauce

Sheep's milk cheeses melted with cream make a simple and luxurious sauce for serving with pan-fried veal escalopes or chops. The escalopes are used as purchased, not beaten thin as for schnitzel.

25g/1oz/2 tbsp butter
15ml/1 tbsp extra virgin olive oil
8 small veal escalopes
2 garlic cloves, crushed
250g/9oz/2¼ cups button mushrooms or closed cup mushrooms, sliced
125g/4oz/1 cup frozen peas, thawed
60ml/4 tbsp brandy
250ml/8fl oz/1 cup whipping cream
150g/5oz Idiazabal (smoked sheep's milk cheese), diced
salt and ground black pepper
sprigs of flat leaf parsley, to garnish

Serves 4

VARIATION

This dish would also work well with lean pork steaks. However, as it is important to ensure that pork is well cooked right through, they will need a longer frying time.

1 Melt half the butter with the oil in a large heavy based frying pan. Season the escalopes with plenty of pepper and brown them in batches on each side over a high heat. Reduce the heat and cook for about 5 minutes on each side until just done. The escalopes should feel firm to the touch, with a very light springiness.

2 Lift the escalopes on to a serving dish and keep hot. Add the remaining butter to the pan. When it melts, stir-fry the garlic and mushrooms for about 3 minutes.

3 Add the peas, pour in the brandy and cook until all the pan juices have been absorbed. Season lightly.

4 Using a slotted spoon, remove the mushrooms and peas and place on top of the escalopes. Pour the cream into the pan and stir in the diced cheese. Heat gently until the cheese has melted. Season with pepper only and pour over the escalopes and vegetables. Serve immediately, garnished with sprigs of flat leaf parsley.

Polpettini with Fontina

Meatballs are easy to stuff with nuggets of creamy cheese that melt during cooking. In this Italian dish, the meatballs are filled with Fontina cubes and then rolled in crumbs and fried.

500g/1¼lb lean minced beef
500g/1¼lb lean minced pork
3 garlic cloves, crushed
grated rind and juice of 1 lemon
2 slices of day-old bread, crumbed
40g/1½oz/½ cup freshly grated Parmesan cheese
2.5ml/½ tsp ground cinnamon
5ml/1 tsp dried oregano
2 eggs, beaten
5ml/1 tsp salt
150g/5oz Fontina cheese, cut into 16 cubes
115–150g/4–5oz/1–1¼ cups natural-coloured dried breadcrumbs
olive oil, for shallow frying
ground black pepper
fresh herbs and freshly grated Parmesan cheese, to garnish
cooked pasta, a mixed leaf salad and tomato sauce, to serve

SERVES 6–8

VARIATION
Use cubes of raclette, Gouda or Monterey Jack instead of Fontina.

1 Preheat the oven to 180°C/350°F/Gas 4. Put the minced beef and pork with the garlic, lemon rind and juice, fresh breadcrumbs, Parmesan, cinnamon and oregano in a bowl. Stir in the beaten eggs and beat well. Add the salt and a generous grinding of black pepper.

2 Using clean hands occasionally dipped into cold water, knead the mixture to ensure all the ingredients are well distributed, then shape it into 16 balls. Cup each ball in turn in your hand and press a piece of Fontina into the centre. Reshape the ball, making sure the cheese is well covered.

3 Roll the meatballs in the dried crumbs. Heat the olive oil in a large frying pan. Add the meatballs in batches and cook them quickly all over until lightly browned and sealed. Transfer them to a roasting tin and bake for 20 minutes or until cooked through. Garnish with fresh herbs and Parmesan and serve with pasta, salad and tomato sauce.

Moussaka

Although feta is perhaps their best-known cheese, the Greeks have a number of others that can be used in cooking. Kefalotiri, a hard cheese made with sheep's or goat's milk, makes the perfect topping for a classic Moussaka.

2 large aubergines, thinly sliced
45ml/3 tbsp olive oil
675g/1½lb lean minced beef
1 onion, chopped
2 garlic cloves, crushed
2 large fresh tomatoes, chopped, or 200g/7oz canned chopped tomatoes
120ml/4fl oz/½ cup dry white wine
45ml/3 tbsp chopped fresh parsley
45ml/3 tbsp fresh breadcrumbs
2 egg whites
salt and ground black pepper

For the Topping
40g/1½oz/3 tbsp butter
40g/1½oz/⅓ cup plain flour
400ml/14fl oz/1⅔ cups milk
2.5ml/½ tsp freshly grated nutmeg
150g/5oz/1¼ cups grated Kefalotiri cheese
2 egg yolks, plus 1 whole egg

Serves 6

1 Layer the aubergines in a colander, sprinkling each layer with salt. Drain over a sink for 20 minutes, then rinse and pat dry with kitchen paper.

2 Preheat the oven to 190°C/375°F/Gas 5. Spread out the aubergines in a roasting tin. Brush them with olive oil, then bake for 10 minutes until just softened. Remove and cool. Leave the oven on.

3 Make the meat sauce. Heat the olive oil in a large saucepan and brown the minced beef, stirring frequently. When the meat is no longer pink and looks crumbly, add the onion and garlic and cook for 5 minutes.

4 Add the chopped fresh or canned tomatoes to the pan and stir in the wine. Season with plenty of salt and pepper to taste.

5 Bring to the boil, then lower the heat, cover and simmer for 15 minutes. Remove the pan from the heat, leave to cool for about 10 minutes, then stir in the chopped parsley, fresh bread-crumbs and egg whites.

VARIATION

Use sliced par-boiled potatoes instead of the aubergines and substitute grated mature Cheddar or Gruyère for the Kefalotiri.

6 Lightly grease a large baking dish, then spread out half the sliced aubergines in an even layer on the base. Spoon over the meat sauce, spread it evenly, then top with the remaining aubergines.

7 To make the topping, put the butter, flour and milk in a saucepan. Bring to the boil over a low heat, whisking all the time until the mixture thickens to form a smooth, creamy sauce. Lower the heat and simmer for 2 minutes. Remove the pan from the heat, season, then stir in the nutmeg and half the cheese.

8 Cool for 5 minutes, then beat in the egg yolks and the whole egg. Pour the sauce over the aubergine topping and sprinkle with the remaining cheese. Bake for 30–40 minutes or until golden brown. Allow the dish to stand for 10 minutes before serving.

Veal Scalloppine with Anchovies and Mozzarella

Scaloppine are thin escalopes of veal cut across the grain from the top rump so that they hold their shape while cooking. For this Italian dish, they are rolled around a filling of anchovies, tomatoes and mozzarella before being pan fried and served with a rich Marsala sauce.

50g/2oz/¼ cup unsalted butter
50g/2oz can anchovies
4 fresh tomatoes, peeled and chopped
30ml/2 tbsp chopped fresh flat leaf parsley
6 veal escalopes, about 100g/3¾oz each
200g/7oz mozzarella cheese, cut in thin slices
30ml/2 tbsp olive oil
175ml/6fl oz/¾ cup Marsala or medium dry sherry
30–45ml/2–3 tbsp whipping cream
salt and ground black pepper
fresh herbs, to garnish
cooked pasta, to serve

Serves 6

VARIATIONS

Try smoked mozzarella or Provolone or Bel Paese instead of regular mozzarella. If you prefer not to eat veal, substitute thinly sliced pork escalopes or turkey steaks.

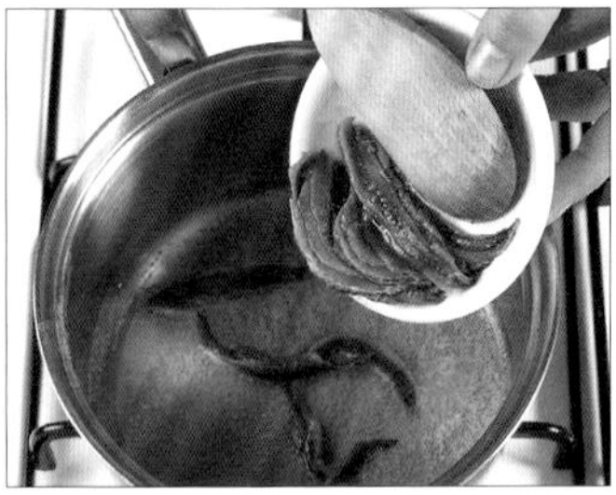

1 Melt half the butter in a small saucepan. Drain the anchovies and add them to the pan. Cook gently, stirring with a wooden spoon, until they break down to a pulp. Stir in the tomatoes and cook for about 5 minutes until they have softened and reduced. Tip into a bowl, cool, then stir in the parsley.

2 Place each veal escalope in turn between two sheets of greaseproof paper and beat with a mallet or rolling pin until thin. Spread the escalopes out on a board and sprinkle with ground black pepper. Divide the anchovy and tomato mixture among them, leaving the edges free.

3 Top with the slices of cheese. Fold the long edges of each escalope towards the centre, then bring up the sides to form a neat parcel. Secure with kitchen string or cocktail sticks.

4 Heat the remaining butter with the oil in a frying pan. Brown the rolled escalopes, in batches if necessary, then pour in the Marsala or sherry. Cook, uncovered, for 5 minutes or until the Marsala or sherry has reduced and thickened. Transfer the rolls to a serving plate, stir the pan juices to incorporate any sediment, then pour in the cream. Reheat without boiling, then strain over the rolls. Garnish with fresh herbs and serve with pasta.

Chicken Cordon Bleu

A classic that is perennially popular, this consists of breasts of chicken stuffed with smoked ham and Gruyère, then coated in egg and breadcrumbs and fried until golden.

4 skinless, boneless chicken breasts, about 130g/4½oz each
4 very thin smoked ham slices, halved and rind removed
about 90g/3½oz Gruyère cheese, thinly sliced
plain flour, for coating
2 eggs, beaten
75g/3oz/¾ cup natural-coloured dried breadcrumbs
5ml/1 tsp dried thyme
40g/1½oz/3 tbsp butter
30ml/2 tbsp olive oil
salt and ground black pepper
mixed leaf side salad, to serve

Serves 4

1 Slit the chicken breasts about three-quarters of the way through, then open them up and lay them flat. Place a slice of ham on each cut side of the chicken, trimming to fit if necessary so that the ham does not hang over the edge.

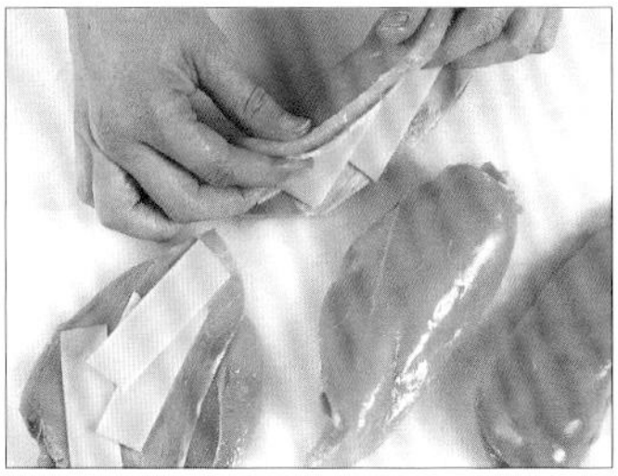

2 Top with the Gruyère slices, making sure that they are well within the ham slices. Fold over the chicken and reshape, pressing well to seal and ensuring that no cheese is visible.

3 Spoon the flour for coating into a shallow bowl. Pour the beaten eggs into another shallow bowl and mix the breadcrumbs with the thyme and seasoning in a third bowl. Toss each stuffed breast in the flour, then coat in egg and breadcrumbs, shaking off any excess. Lay the crumbed breasts flat on a plate, cover and chill for at least 1 hour in the fridge to set the coating.

4 To cook, heat the butter and oil in a frying pan. When the fat stops foaming, gently slide in the coated breasts, two at a time. Shallow fry over a medium-low heat for about 5 minutes each side, turning over carefully with a fish slice. Drain on kitchen paper and keep hot while you cook the remaining breasts. Serve with a side salad.

VARIATION
Instead of Gruyère, try one of the herb-flavoured hard cheeses, such as Double Gloucester with Chives.

French Roast Chicken with Comte Cheese

Comte is excellent for cooking as it melts easily to a creamy, glossy texture with a good flavour. To make this French dish, you will need a large flameproof casserole plus a shallow ovenproof serving dish.

75g/3oz/6 tbsp butter
30ml/2 tbsp sunflower oil
1.75kg/4–4½lb roasting chicken
3 carrots, sliced in rings
2 leeks, sliced
2 celery sticks, sliced
1 litre/1¾ pints/4 cups chicken stock or water
300ml/½ pint/1¼ cups dry white wine
4 sprigs of thyme
250g/9oz/2¼ cups button mushrooms, halved
30ml/2 tbsp plain flour
150ml/¼ pint/⅔ cup crème fraîche or double cream
1 egg yolk
30ml/2 tbsp fresh lemon juice
freshly grated nutmeg
125g/4oz/1 cup grated Comte cheese
salt and ground black pepper

Serves 6

1 Heat a third of the butter with the oil in a large flameproof casserole. Add the chicken and turn it in the fat until it is golden brown. Remove and set aside.

2 Add the vegetables to the casserole. Sauté gently for 5 minutes, then place the bird on top. Pour in the stock or water and the wine, with 1 sprig of thyme. Season well, bring to the boil, then lower the heat and cover the casserole. Simmer very gently for about 1 hour or until the chicken is cooked through.

3 Meanwhile, melt half the remaining butter in a small pan and stir-fry the mushrooms for 2–3 minutes. Do not allow them to soften or they will give up their liquid. Lift them out with a slotted spoon and set them aside. Mix the last of the butter with the flour to make a paste. Set this aside too.

4 Preheat the oven to 220°C/425°F/Gas 7. Put the cream in a jug and stir in the egg yolk and lemon juice, with nutmeg to taste.

5 Transfer the cooked chicken to a shallow heatproof dish and cover with tented foil. Remove the sprig of thyme from the casserole and discard it.

6 Return the casserole to the heat and boil rapidly until the liquid has reduced by half, then purée the stock and vegetables together in a blender or food processor. Scrape the purée back into the casserole, return to a gentle simmer and gradually whisk in knobs of the butter-and-flour paste until the sauce has thickened and is smooth. Remove from the heat again and slowly whisk in the cream mixture.

7 Surround the chicken with the mushrooms. Press half the cheese on to the chicken breast, trickle the sauce over and sprinkle over the rest of the cheese. Bake for about 15 minutes or until the cheese is golden brown. Garnish with the remaining thyme sprigs and serve.

Salmon Kedgeree, French-style

This all-in-one supper dish is ideal for informal entertaining as it can be made ahead of time and reheated for about half an hour before being served with a tossed salad.

675g/1½lb fresh salmon fillet, skinned
1 bay leaf
a few parsley stalks
1 litre/1¾ pints/4 cups water
400g/14oz/2 cups basmati rice
30–45ml/2–3 tbsp chopped fresh parsley
175g/6oz/1½ cups grated Cheddar cheese
3 hard-boiled eggs, chopped
salt and ground black pepper

For the Sauce
1 litre/1¾ pints/4 cups milk
40g/1½oz/⅓ cup plain flour
40g/1½oz/3 tbsp butter
5ml/1 tsp mild curry paste or French mustard

Serves 6

1 Put the salmon in a wide, shallow pan. Add the bay leaf and parsley stalks, with salt and pepper. Pour in the water and poach the fish for about 12 minutes until just tender. Lift out the fish, discard the herbs and pour the liquid into a saucepan. Leave the fish to cool, then remove any bones and flake the flesh.

2 Add the rice to the saucepan containing the fish poaching liquid. Bring the liquid to the boil, then lower the heat, cover and simmer for 10 minutes without lifting the lid. Remove the pan from the heat and allow the rice to stand undisturbed for 5 minutes.

3 Meanwhile, make the sauce. Mix the milk, flour and butter in a saucepan. Bring to the boil over a low heat, whisking constantly until the sauce is smooth and thick. Stir in the curry paste or mustard, with salt and pepper to taste. Simmer for 2 minutes.

4 Preheat the grill. Remove the sauce from the heat and stir in the chopped parsley and rice, with half the cheese. Using a large metal spoon, fold in the flaked fish and eggs. Spoon into a shallow gratin dish and sprinkle with the rest of the cheese. Heat under the grill until the topping is golden brown and bubbling.

VARIATIONS

Prawns could be substituted for the salmon and Lancashire or Mahon could be used instead of Cheddar. The dish also works well with pasta shapes instead of rice.

Rump Steak with Roquefort and Walnut Butter

Make up a roll of savoury blue cheese butter to keep in the fridge to top steaks. This is also good served on pork chops.

2 shallots, chopped
75g/3oz/6 tbsp butter, slightly softened
150g/5oz Roquefort cheese
30ml/2 tbsp finely chopped walnuts
15ml/1 tbsp finely snipped fresh chives
15ml/1 tbsp olive oil or sunflower oil
4 lean rump steaks, about 125g/4oz each
120ml/4fl oz/½ cup dry white wine
30ml/2 tbsp crème fraîche or double cream
salt and ground black pepper
fresh chives, to garnish
green beans, to serve

SERVES 4

1 Sauté the shallots in a third of the butter. Tip into a bowl and add half the remaining butter, the cheese, walnuts, snipped chives and pepper to taste. Chill lightly, roll in foil to a sausage shape and chill again until firm.

2 Heat the remaining butter with the oil in a heavy-based frying pan and cook the steaks for about 3 minutes each side, or until cooked to your liking. Season the steaks and remove them from the pan.

3 Pour the wine into the pan and stir to incorporate any sediment. Bubble up for a minute or two, then stir in the crème fraîche or cream. Season and pour over the steaks. Cut pats of the Roquefort butter from the roll and put one on top of each steak. Garnish with chives. Lightly cooked green beans make the ideal accompaniment.

Pan-Roasted Cod with a Vermouth and Chèvre Sauce

Team chunky white cod with a quick pan sauce of vermouth and a light, creamy chèvre sauce. Grilled tomatoes sprinkled with herbs add colour.

4 pieces of cod fillet, about 150g/5oz each, skinned
30ml/2 tbsp olive oil
4 spring onions, chopped
150ml/¼ pint/⅔ cup dry vermouth, preferably Noilly Prat
300ml/½ pint/1¼ cups fish stock
45ml/3 tbsp crème fraîche or double cream
65g/2½ oz chèvre (goat's milk cheese), rind removed, and chopped
30ml/2 tbsp chopped fresh parsley
15ml/1 tbsp chopped fresh chervil
salt and ground black pepper
grilled plum tomatoes, to serve
flat leaf parsley, to garnish

Serves 4

VARIATION
Instead of cod you could use salmon, haddock or plaice. The cooking time may change according to the thickness of the fish fillets.

1 Remove any stray bones from the cod fillets. Rinse the fish under cold running water and pat dry with kitchen paper. Place the pieces on a plate and season generously with salt and pepper.

2 Heat a non-stick frying pan, then add 15ml/1 tbsp of the oil, swirling it around to coat the bottom. Add the pieces of cod and cook, without turning or moving them, for 4 minutes or until nicely caramelized. Turn each piece over and cook the other side for a further 3 minutes or until just firm. Remove it to a serving plate and keep hot.

3 Heat the remaining oil and stir-fry the spring onions for 1 minute. Add the vermouth and cook until reduced by half. Add the stock and cook again until reduced by half. Stir in the cream and chèvre and simmer for 3 minutes. Add salt and pepper, stir in the herbs and spoon over the fish. Garnish with parsley and serve with grilled tomatoes.

VEGETARIAN DISHES

Since cheese is a fairly rich protein food, many classic cheese dishes are also vegetarian. Some of the best come from Italy: Aubergine Parmigiana, risotto flavoured with Parmesan, crisp risotto fritters with nuggets of mozzarella inside, and polenta cooked with Gorgonzola. There are also classic recipes for a cheese soufflé, an omelette and a fabulous fondue, and Twice-baked Spinach and Cheese Roulade – a superb dinner-party dish.

Aubergine Parmigiana

A classic Italian dish, in which blissfully tender sliced aubergines are layered with melting creamy mozzarella, fresh Parmesan and a good home-made tomato sauce.

3 medium aubergines, thinly sliced
olive oil, for brushing
300g/11oz mozzarella cheese, sliced
125g/4oz/1 1/3 cups freshly grated Parmesan cheese
30–45ml/2–3 tbsp natural-coloured dried breadcrumbs
basil sprigs, to garnish
salt and ground black pepper

For the Sauce
30ml/2 tbsp olive oil
1 onion, finely chopped
2 garlic cloves, crushed
400g/14oz can chopped tomatoes
5ml/1 tsp sugar
about 6 basil leaves

Serves 4–6

1 Layer the aubergine slices in a colander, sprinkling each layer with a little salt. Drain over a sink for about 20 minutes, then rinse thoroughy under cold running water and pat dry with kitchen paper.

2 Preheat the oven to 200°C/400°F/ Gas 6. Lay the aubergine slices on non-stick baking sheets, brush the tops with olive oil and bake for 10–15 minutes until softened.

3 Make the sauce. Heat the oil in a saucepan and sauté the onion and garlic for 5 minutes. Add the canned tomatoes and sugar, with salt and pepper to taste. Bring to the boil, then lower the heat and simmer for about 10 minutes until reduced and thickened. Tear the basil leaves into small pieces and add them to the sauce.

4 Layer the aubergines in a greased shallow ovenproof dish with the sliced mozzarella, the tomato sauce and the grated Parmesan, ending with a layer of Parmesan mixed with the bread-crumbs. Bake for 20–25 minutes until golden brown and bubbling. Allow to stand for 5 minutes before cutting. Serve garnished with basil.

MALFATTI WITH ROASTED PEPPER SAUCE

The Italians use their rich but light cream cheese – ricotta – in sweet and savoury dishes. This recipe has it beaten into deliciously light spinach dumplings, called malfatti, served with a smoky pepper and tomato sauce.

500g/1¼lb young leaf spinach
1 onion, finely chopped
1 garlic clove, crushed
15ml/1 tbsp extra virgin olive oil
350g/12oz/1½ cups ricotta cheese
3 eggs, beaten
50g/2oz/½ cup natural-coloured dried breadcrumbs
50g/2oz/½ cup plain flour
50g/2oz/⅔ cup freshly grated Parmesan cheese
freshly grated nutmeg
25g/1oz/2 tbsp butter, melted
salt and ground black pepper

FOR THE SAUCE

2 red peppers, quartered and cored
30ml/2 tbsp extra virgin olive oil
1 onion, chopped
400g/14oz can chopped tomatoes
150ml/¼ pint/⅔ cup water

SERVES 4

1 Make the sauce. Preheat the grill and grill the pepper quarters skin side up until they blister and blacken. Cool slightly, then peel and chop. Heat the oil in a saucepan and lightly sauté the onion and peppers for 5 minutes. Add the tomatoes and water, with salt and pepper to taste. Bring to the boil, lower the heat and simmer gently for 15 minutes. Purée in a food processor or blender, then return to the clean pan and set aside.

2 Trim any thick stalks from the spinach, wash it well if necessary, then blanch in a pan of boiling water for about 1 minute. Drain, refresh under cold water and drain again. Squeeze dry, then chop finely.

3 Put the finely chopped onion, garlic, olive oil, ricotta, eggs and breadcrumbs in a bowl. Add the spinach and mix well. Stir in the flour and 5ml/1 tsp salt with half the Parmesan, then season to taste with pepper and nutmeg.

4 Roll the mixture into 16 small logs and chill lightly.

5 Bring a large saucepan of water to the boil. Carefully drop in the malfatti in batches and cook for 5 minutes. Remove with a fish slice and toss with the melted butter. To serve, reheat the sauce and divide it among four plates. Arrange four malfatti on each and sprinkle over the remaining Parmesan. Serve at once.

Peppers with Rice, Feta and Pine Nut Stuffing

A popular family supper dish, which can be prepared ahead and reheated. Serve it with a cheese sauce for a delicious change.

4 large red, green or yellow peppers, or a mixture
475ml/16fl oz/2 cups vegetable stock
200g/7oz/1 cup long grain rice (not easy-cook/par-boiled)
30ml/2 tbsp olive oil
1 onion, chopped
2 garlic cloves, crushed
125g/4oz/1 cup button mushrooms, chopped
1 carrot, grated
4 tomatoes, chopped
15ml/1 tbsp chopped fresh dill
90g/3½oz feta cheese, crumbled
75g/3oz/1 cup pine nuts, lightly toasted
30ml/2 tbsp currants
25g/1oz/⅓ cup freshly grated Parmesan cheese
salt and ground black pepper
salad of mixed leaves, to serve

Serves 4

1 Preheat the oven to 190°C/375°F/Gas 5. Cut the peppers in half lengthways and remove the cores and seeds. Bring a large saucepan of water to the boil, add the peppers and blanch for 5 minutes. Remove from the pan using a slotted spoon. Leave to drain upside down, then place, hollow up, in a lightly greased baking dish.

Any strong-flavoured Cheddar (right) could be used in place of the feta. Or try fresh chèvre instead.

2 Put the stock in another saucepan. Tip in the rice and bring to the boil then lower the heat. Cover the pan and simmer gently for 15 minutes. Remove the pan from the heat without lifting the lid and leave to stand in a warm place for 5 minutes.

3 Meanwhile, heat the olive oil and sauté the onion and garlic for 5 minutes. Stir in the mushrooms, carrot and tomatoes with salt and pepper to taste. Cover, cook for 5 minutes until softened, then mix in the rice, dill, feta, pine nuts and currants.

4 Divide the mixture among the pepper halves, sprinkle over the Parmesan and bake for 20 minutes or until the topping has browned. Serve with a mixed salad.

Semolina and Pesto Gnocchi

These gnocchi are cooked rounds of semolina paste, which are brushed with melted butter, topped with cheese and baked. When carefully cooked, they taste wonderful with a home-made tomato sauce.

750ml/1¼ pints/3 cups milk
200g/7oz/generous 1 cup semolina
45ml/3 tbsp pesto sauce
60ml/4 tbsp finely chopped sun-dried tomatoes, patted dry if oily
50g/2oz/¼ cup butter
75g/3oz/1 cup freshly grated Pecorino cheese
2 eggs, beaten
freshly grated nutmeg
salt and ground black pepper
tomato sauce, to serve
basil, to garnish

Serves 4–6

1 Heat the milk in a large non-stick saucepan. When it is on the point of boiling, sprinkle in the semolina, stirring constantly until the mixture is smooth and very thick. Lower the heat and simmer for 2 minutes.

2 Remove from the heat and stir in the pesto and sun-dried tomatoes, with half the butter and half the Pecorino. Add the eggs, with nutmeg, salt and pepper to taste. Spoon on to a clean shallow baking dish or tin to a depth of 1cm/½ in and level the surface. Leave to cool, then chill.

3 Preheat the oven to 190°C/375°F/Gas 5. Lightly grease a shallow baking dish. Using a 4cm/1½in scone cutter, stamp out as many rounds as possible from the semolina pasta.

4 Place the leftover semolina paste on the base of the greased dish and arrange the rounds on top in overlapping circles. Melt the remaining butter and brush it over the gnocchi. Sprinkle over the remaining Pecorino. Bake for 30–40 minutes until golden. Serve with tomato sauce and garnish with basil.

VARIATIONS

Substitute any mature hard grating cheese for the Pecorino, such as the Spanish cheeses Manchego or Mahon. Instead of pesto, use a small pack of chopped frozen spinach that has been thawed and squeezed of excess water or 90ml/6 tbsp mixed chopped herbs.

Porcini and Parmesan Risotto

The success of a good risotto depends on the quality of the rice used and the technique. For this variation of the classic risotto alla milanese, saffron, porcini mushrooms and Parmesan are stirred into the creamy cooked rice.

10g/¼oz/2 tbsp dried porcini mushrooms
300ml/½ pint/1¼ cups warm water
1.2 litres/2 pints/5 cups vegetable stock
generous pinch of saffron strands
30ml/2 tbsp olive oil
1 onion, finely chopped
1 garlic clove, crushed
250g/9oz/1¼ cups arborio or carnaroli rice
150ml/¼ pint/⅔ cup dry white wine or 45ml/3 tbsp dry vermouth
25g/1oz/2 tbsp butter
50g/2oz/⅔ cup freshly grated Parmesan cheese
salt and ground black pepper

Serves 4

VARIATIONS

There are endless variations on this delectable dish. The proportion of stock to rice, onions, garlic and butter must remain constant but you can ring the changes with the flavourings and cheese. Try Pecorino with lightly blanched baby vegetables for Risotto Primavera. Chopped bacon and peas make the famous risi e bisi.

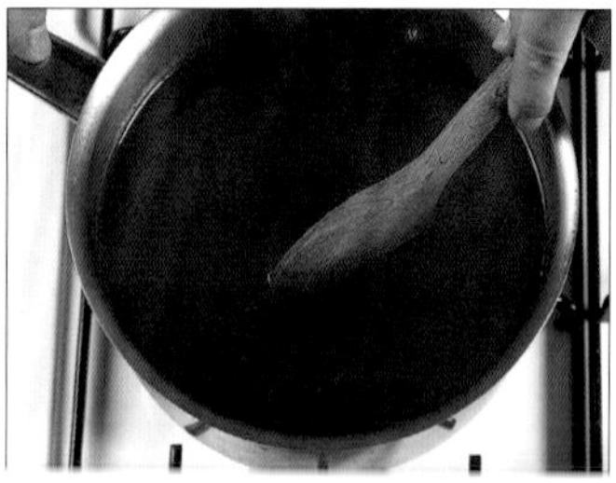

1 Soak the dried mushrooms in the warm water for 20 minutes. Lift out with a slotted spoon. Filter the soaking water through a layer of kitchen paper in a sieve, then place it in a saucepan with the stock. Bring the liquid to a gentle simmer.

2 Put about 45ml/3 tbsp of the hot stock in a cup and stir in the saffron strands. Set aside.

3 Finely chop the mushrooms. Heat the oil in a separate pan and lightly sauté the onion, garlic and mushrooms for 5 minutes. Gradually add the rice, stirring. Cook for 2 minutes, stirring. Season with salt and pepper.

4 Pour in the wine or vermouth. Cook, stirring, until it has been absorbed, then ladle in a quarter of the stock. Bring to the boil, stirring. Cook until most of the liquid has been absorbed.

5 Continue to add the stock a ladle at a time, stirring after each addition. The secret of good risotto is to add the stock gradually and to stir frequently to encourage a creamy texture from the starch grains.

6 After about 20 minutes, when all the stock has been absorbed and the rice is cooked but still has a "bite", stir in the butter, saffron water and strands and half the Parmesan. Serve, sprinkled with the remaining Parmesan.

Pecorino makes a good alternative to Parmesan in this risotto.

SUPPLI AL TELEFONO

These are risotto fritters with nuggets of mozzarella inside. When bitten into, the cheese is drawn out in thin strings, like telephone wires, hence the name.

45ml/3 tbsp finely chopped fresh parsley
1 quantity Porcini and Parmesan Risotto (see page 202), made without the saffron
200g/7oz mozzarella cheese, cut into 20 cubes
2 eggs, beaten
150g/5oz/1¼ cups natural-coloured dried breadcrumbs
corn or vegetable oil, for deep frying
fresh herbs, to garnish

MAKES 20

VARIATION
For the filling, use cubes of Emmental, Provolone or even Monterey Jack instead of mozzarella.

1 Stir the parsley into the risotto, cool, then chill until firm. Divide into 20 portions and shape each to a ball. Press a cube of cheese into each ball of rice and reshape neatly. Coat the rice balls in the beaten egg, then the breadcrumbs, and chill again for 30 minutes to set the coating.

2 Heat the oil for deep frying to 180°C/350°F. Cook about five fritters at a time for 3–5 minutes until golden brown and crisp. Drain the fritters on kitchen paper and keep warm on an uncovered plate in a warm oven so that the coating remains crisp. Serve at once, garnished with fresh herbs.

Chilli Cheese Tortilla with Fresh Tomato Salsa

Good warm or cold, this is like a quiche without the pastry base. Cheese and chillies are more than a match for each other.

45ml/3 tbsp sunflower or olive oil
1 small onion, thinly sliced
2–3 fresh green jalapeño chillies, sliced
200g/7oz cold cooked potato, thinly sliced
120g/4¼oz/generous 1 cup grated Manchego, Mexican queso blanco or Monterey Jack cheese
6 eggs, beaten
salt and ground black pepper
fresh herbs, to garnish

For the Salsa

500g/1¼lb fresh flavoursome tomatoes, peeled, seeded and finely chopped
1 fresh mild green chilli, seeded and finely chopped
2 garlic cloves, crushed
45ml/3 tbsp chopped fresh coriander
juice of 1 lime
2.5ml/½ tsp salt

Serves 4

COOK'S TIP

If you like, you can brown the top of the tortilla under a hot grill, using a frying pan with a flameproof handle.

1 Make the salsa. Put the tomatoes in a bowl and add the chopped chilli, garlic, coriander, lime juice and salt and pepper. Mix well and set aside.

2 Heat half the oil in a large omelette pan and gently fry the onion and jalapeños for 5 minutes, stirring once or twice, until softened. Add the potato and cook for a further 5 minutes until lightly browned, taking care to keep the slices whole.

3 Using a slotted spoon, transfer the vegetables to a warm plate. Wipe the pan with kitchen paper, then pour in the remaining oil. Heat well and return the vegetable mixture to the pan. Scatter the cheese over the top.

4 Pour in the beaten egg, making sure that it seeps under the vegetables. Cook the tortilla over a gentle heat until set. Serve in wedges, garnished with fresh herbs, with the salsa on the side.

Polenta with Gorgonzola and Wild Mushroom Sauce

Like semolina gnocchi, polenta is made with a ground cereal – cornmeal. After it is cooked and thickened, creamy Gorgonzola is stirred in and the mixture is left to set before being cut into wedges and grilled.

900ml/1½ pints/3¾ cups milk
900ml/1½ pints/3¾ cups water
5ml/1 tsp salt
300g/11oz/generous 2 cups polenta
50g/2oz/¼ cup butter
125g/4oz Gorgonzola cheese
sprigs of thyme, to garnish

For the Sauce

40g/1½oz dried porcini mushrooms, soaked in 150ml/¼ pint/⅔ cup hot water for 15 minutes
25g/1oz/2 tbsp butter
125g/4oz/1 cup button mushrooms, chopped
60ml/4 tbsp dry white wine
generous pinch of dried thyme
60ml/4 tbsp mascarpone cheese
salt and ground black pepper

Serves 4–6

1 Pour the milk and water into a large heavy-based saucepan. Add the salt and bring to the boil. Using a long-handled spoon, stir the liquid briskly with one hand while drizzling in the polenta with the other. When the mixture is thick and smooth, lower the heat to a gentle simmer and cook for about 20 minutes, stirring occasionally.

2 Remove from the heat and stir in the butter and Gorgonzola. Spoon the polenta into a shallow dish, level the surface and cool. Let the polenta set until solid, then cut into wedges.

3 Meanwhile, make the sauce. Drain the porcini, reserve the soaking liquid. Finely chop the porcini and strain the liquid through a sieve lined with kitchen paper.

4 Melt half the butter in a small saucepan. Sauté the chopped fresh mushrooms for about 5 minutes. Add the wine, porcini and strained soaking liquid, with the dried thyme. Season to taste. Cook for 2 minutes more. Stir in the mascarpone and simmer for a few minutes, until reduced by a third. Set the sauce aside to cool.

5 Heat a ridged grill pan or grill and grill the polenta pieces until crisp. Melt the remaining butter and brush it over the polenta. Serve hot, with the cooled sauce. Garnish with thyme.

Twice-Baked Spinach and Goat's Milk Cheese Roulade

A roulade is really a Swiss roll soufflé. Because it has air trapped inside, it magically rises again on reheating and becomes quite crisp on the outside. This is an impressive dinner-party dish.

300ml/½ pint/1¼ cups milk
50g/2oz/½ cup plain flour
150g/5oz/⅔ cup butter
100g/3¾oz chèvre (goat's milk cheese), chopped
40g/1½oz/½ cup freshly grated Parmesan cheese, plus extra for dusting
4 eggs, separated
250g/9oz/2¼ cups fresh shiitake mushrooms, sliced
275g/10oz young spinach leaves, washed
45ml/3 tbsp crème fraîche or fromage frais
salt and ground black pepper

Serves 4

1 Preheat the oven to 190°C/375°F/ Gas 5. Line a 30 × 20cm/12 × 8in Swiss roll tin with greaseproof paper, making sure that the paper rises well above the sides of the tin. Lightly grease.

2 Mix together the milk, flour and 50g/2oz/¼ cup of the butter in a large saucepan. Bring to the boil over a low heat, whisking until thick and creamy. Lower the heat and simmer for 2 minutes, then mix in the chèvre and half the Parmesan. Cool for 5 minutes, then beat in the egg yolks and plenty of salt and pepper.

3 Whisk the egg whites in a grease-free bowl until soft peaks form. Carefully fold the whites into the chèvre mixture, using a large metal spoon. Spoon the mixture into the prepared tin, spread gently to level, then bake for 15–17 minutes until the top feels just firm.

4 Let the roulade cool for a few minutes, then invert it on to a sheet of greaseproof paper dusted with Parmesan. Carefully tear off the lining paper in strips. Roll the roulade up in the greaseproof paper and leave to cool completely.

5 Make the filling. Melt the remaining butter and set aside 30ml/2 tbsp. Add the mushrooms to the pan and stir-fry for 3 minutes. Stir in the spinach and drain well, then add the crème fraîche or fromage frais. Season, then cool.

6 Preheat the oven to the original temperature. Unroll the roulade and spread over the filling. Roll it up again and place, join side down, in a baking dish. Brush with the reserved melted butter and sprinkle with the remaining Parmesan. Bake for 15 minutes or until risen and golden. Serve immediately.

Classic Cheese Soufflé

At its simplest, a soufflé is merely a thick sauce with beaten egg whites folded in – not at all difficult to achieve, especially if the base is made ahead and the whites added just before baking. Timing is the only ticklish area, as a soufflé waits for no one.

50g/2oz/¼ cup butter
30–45ml/2–3 tbsp natural-coloured dried breadcrumbs
200ml/7fl oz/scant 1 cup milk
30g/1¼oz/3 tbsp plain flour
pinch of cayenne pepper
2.5ml/½ tsp curry paste or mustard or freshly grated nutmeg
50g/2oz/½ cup grated mature Cheddar cheese
25g/1oz/⅓ cup freshly grated Parmesan cheese
4 eggs, separated, plus 1 extra egg white
salt and ground black pepper

Serves 2–3

1 Preheat the oven to 190°C/375°F/Gas 5. Melt 15ml/1 tbsp of the butter and grease a 1.2 litre/2 pint/5 cup soufflé dish.Coat the inside of the dish evenly with the breadcrumbs.

2 Put the milk in a large saucepan. Add the remaining butter, flour and cayenne, with the curry paste, mustard or nutmeg. Bring to the boil over a low heat, whisking steadily until the mixture thickens to a smooth sauce.

3 Simmer the sauce for a minute or two, then turn off the heat and whisk in all the Cheddar and half the Parmesan. Cool a little, then beat in the egg yolks and check the seasoning. The mixture should be well seasoned.

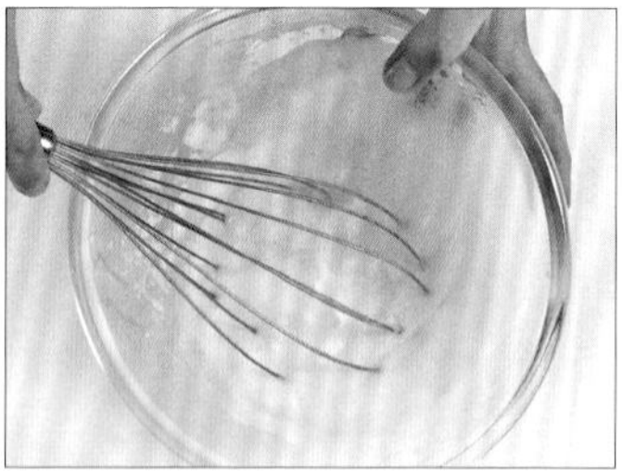

4 Whisk all the egg whites in a large grease-free bowl until they form soft, glossy peaks. Do not overbeat or the whites will become grainy and difficult to fold in.

VARIATIONS

Crumbled blue cheese, such as Stilton or Shropshire Blue or Fourme d'Ambert, make delicious flavourings. For a more substantial soufflé, put a chopped vegetable mixture, such as ratatouille or sautéed mushrooms, on the bottom of the dish before adding the cheese mixture and baking as above.

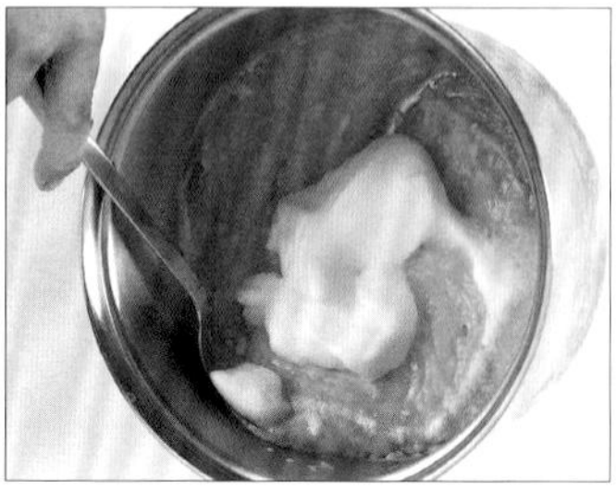

5 Spoon some of the beaten egg whites into the sauce to lighten it. Beat well, then scrape the rest of the whites into the pan and, using a figure-of-eight movement, carefully fold them into the mixture with a large metal spoon.

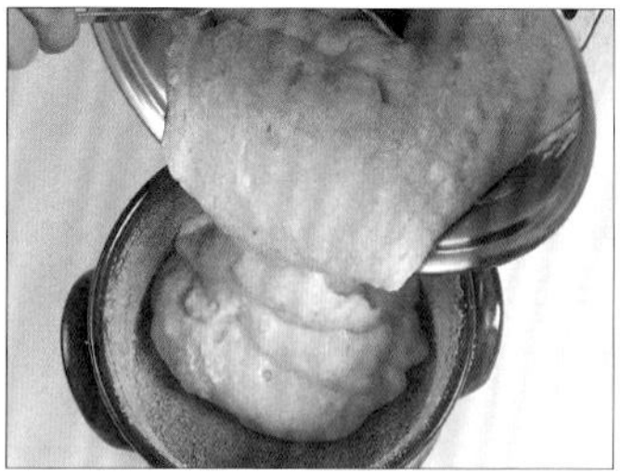

6 Pour the mixture into the prepared dish, level the top and place the dish on a baking sheet. Sprinkle on the remaining Parmesan. Bake for 20–25 minutes until risen and golden. Serve.

Stilton makes a delicious flavouring for a soufflé.

Classic Cheese Omelette

Perhaps the ultimate fast food – a couple of eggs, some nicely flavoured cheese, a knob of butter and a good pan and you have a full and satisfying meal within minutes. Technique is important with omelettes. The centre should be soft and the cheese just melted and creamy.

2 large eggs
15ml/1 tbsp chopped fresh herbs, such as chives, parsley or dill
a knob of unsalted butter
50g/2oz/1/2 cup grated full-flavoured cheese, such as Gruyère, Gouda or Cheddar
salt and ground black pepper
flat leaf parsley, to garnish
tomato wedges, to serve

Serves 1

VARIATIONS

You can add ingredients to the cheese. Crunchy garlicky croûtons are good, as are sautéed sliced mushrooms, flaked cooked smoked haddock and chopped tomatoes. As for the cheese, this is a good time to experiment.

1 Heat a 20cm/8in heavy-based omelette pan or non-stick frying pan. Break the eggs into a bowl and beat in the herbs and seasoning. It is not necessary to add water or milk, which would only dilute the egg.

2 Heat the butter in the pan. Pour in the beaten eggs, swirling the pan so that the mixture coats the base. Using a fork or spatula, pull the cooked areas of egg away from the pan sides, letting the uncooked egg run in to fill the space. When the egg at the sides is firm, but the centre still soft, scatter over the cheese.

3 Allow to cook undisturbed for about 30 seconds, then fold the edge of the omelette nearest the handle over a third. Roll the omelette over on to a warmed plate. Serve immediately, with tomato wedges and a garnish of flat leaf parsley.

Potato and Cheese Cake

This dish appears in many guises, cheese and potatoes having a natural affinity. Choose a hard, well-flavoured cheese – in France, where it is called Truffade, this cake would be made with a Tomme or Cantal. In England, Cheddar would be used, and the dish would be called Pan Haggarty.

a little sunflower oil or melted butter
675g/1 1/2lb potatoes, peeled and very thinly sliced
1 large onion, thinly sliced
150g/5oz/1 1/4 cups grated hard cheese, such as mature Cheddar, Tomme or Cantal
freshly grated nutmeg
salt and ground black pepper
mixed salad leaves, to garnish

Serves 4–6

VARIATION

In France, this is cooked with diced streaky bacon (lardons) and the cheese is chopped, not sliced or grated. The ingredients are mixed and cooked slowly in a little lard in a pan on top of the stove.

1 Preheat the oven to 190°C/375°F/Gas 5. Lightly grease the base of a shallow baking dish or roasting tin with the oil or melted butter.

2 Layer the potato, onion and cheese in the dish, brushing the potatoes with oil or butter and seasoning with nutmeg, salt and pepper. Finish with a layer of cheese. Bake for 45 minutes, or until golden brown. Leave to stand for about 5 minutes, then serve in wedges, with a salad garnish.

Sweet Pepper and Courgette Frittata

Eggs, cheese and vegetables form the basis of this excellent supper dish. Served cold, in wedges, it makes tasty picnic fare too.

45ml/3 tbsp olive oil
1 red onion, thinly sliced
1 large red pepper, cored and thinly sliced
1 large yellow pepper, cored and thinly sliced
2 garlic cloves, crushed
1 medium courgette, thinly sliced
6 eggs
150g/5oz Italian cheese, such as Fontina, Provolone or Taleggio, grated
salt and ground black pepper
dressed mixed salad leaves, to garnish

Serves 4

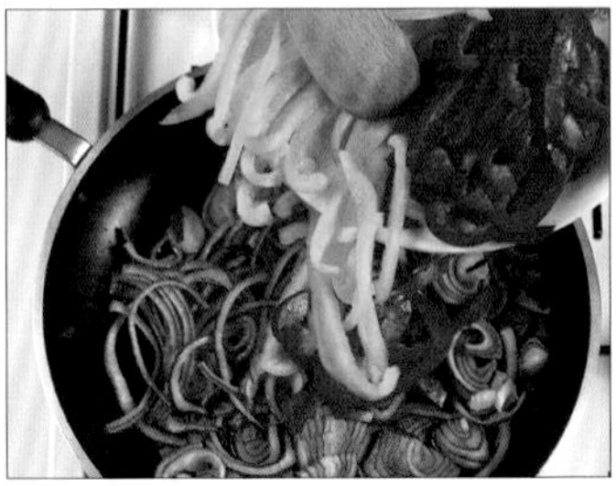

1 Heat 30ml/2 tbsp of the oil in a large heavy-based frying pan. Fry the onion and pepper slices over a low heat for about 10 minutes until softened.

2 Add the remaining oil to the pan. When it is hot, tip in the garlic and courgette slices and fry for 5 minutes, stirring constantly.

3 Beat the eggs with salt and pepper in a bowl. Mix in the cheese.

4 Pour the egg and cheese mixture over the vegetables, stirring lightly to mix. Make sure that the base of the pan is evenly covered with egg. Cook over a low heat until the mixture is just set. Traditionally, a frittata is inverted on to a plate and returned to the pan upside-down to cook the top, but it may be easier to brown the top lightly under a hot grill for a few minutes (protect the pan handle, if necessary).

5 Allow the frittata to stand in the pan for about 5 minutes before cutting. This is delicious served hot or cold, with a salad garnish.

Fondue

A fondue is simply a mixture of melted cheeses with wine to keep it liquid. Flavourless starch prevents the cheeses from separating, while garlic and Kirsch add extra flavour.

1 fat garlic clove, halved
5ml/1 tsp arrowroot or potato starch
300ml/1/2 pint/1 1/4 cups dry white wine
3 × 350g/12oz portions hard, melting cheese (see Cook's Tip), thinly sliced or coarsely grated
45–60ml/3–4 tbsp Kirsch
ground black pepper
cubes of country-style bread, for dipping

SERVES 6

1 Rub the inside of a *caquelon* (traditional fondue pan) or deep flameproof pan with the cut side of the garlic halves. If you like, you can then chop the garlic finely and place it in the pan.

2 Mix the arrowroot or potato starch with 30ml/2 tbsp of the wine in a small bowl. Set aside. Pour the rest of the wine into the pan.

3 Heat the wine very slowly. Add about a third of the sliced or grated cheese, and continue heating the mixture, stirring until the cheese starts to melt and the liquid to bubble.

4 Slowly stir in the arrowroot or potato starch mixture, then the rest of the cheese, a little at a time. Add the Kirsch and pepper. Place the fondue over a candle warmer on the table, with cubes of bread for dipping.

VARIATION

In Switzerland the cheese mixture would comprise Emmental, Gruyère and Appenzeller or raclette, while the French favour Comte or Beaufort.

Pastries, Pizzas and Pasta

Many of the world's great street foods rely on cheese. Because it melts so easily, either over direct heat or in the most rustic oven, it is ideal for slicing on to a pizza or wrapping between sheets of filo pastry. There are also dozens of cheesy pasta dishes, where the cheese is tossed into hot pasta or layered to make a mouthwatering lasagne. This sort of food is ideal for feeding crowds with speed and without fuss.

Borek

Versions of these crisp, cheese-filled pastries, are a common feature of street food throughout much of the Mediterranean. They are easy to make at home, but require a little time and patience.

250g/9oz feta cheese, crumbled
2.5ml/½ tsp freshly grated nutmeg
30ml/2 tbsp each chopped fresh parsley, dill and mint
10 filo pastry sheets, each about 30 × 18cm/12 × 7in
75g/3oz/6 tbsp melted butter or 90ml/6 tbsp olive oil
ground black pepper

Makes 10

COOK'S TIPS

When using filo pastry, it is important to keep unused sheets covered so that they don't dry out. The quantities for filo pastry in the recipe above are approximate, as the size of filo sheets varies. Any unused pastry will keep in the fridge for a week or so, if it is well wrapped.

1 Preheat the oven to 190°C/375°F/Gas 5. Mix the feta, nutmeg and herbs in a bowl. Add pepper to taste and mix to a creamy filling.

2 Brush a sheet of filo lightly with butter or oil, place another on top of it and brush that too.

3 Cut the buttered sheets in half lengthways to make 10 strips, each 30 × 9cm/12 × 3½ in. Place 5ml/1 tsp of the cheese filling at the base of a long strip, fold the corners in diagonally to enclose it, then roll the pastry up into a cigar shape.

4 Brush the end with a little butter or oil to seal, then place join side down on a non-stick baking sheet. Repeat with the remaining pastry and filling. Brush the borek with more butter or oil and bake for 20 minutes or until crisp and golden. Cool on a wire rack and serve at room temperature.

Ratatouille and Fontina Strudel

Mix a colourful jumble of ratatouille vegetables with chunks of creamy Fontina or Bel Paese, then wrap in sheets of filo and bake for a delicious, summery party pastry.

1 small aubergine, diced
45ml/3 tbsp extra virgin olive oil
1 onion, sliced
2 garlic cloves, crushed
1 red pepper, cored and sliced
1 yellow pepper, cored and sliced
2 courgettes, cut into small chunks
generous pinch of dried mixed herbs
30ml/2 tbsp pine nuts
30ml/2 tbsp raisins
8 filo pastry sheets, each about 30 × 18cm/12 × 7in
50g/2oz/¼ cup butter, melted
130g/4½oz/generous 1 cup Fontina or Bel Paese cheese, cut into small cubes
salt and ground black pepper
dressed mixed salad, to serve

Serves 6

VARIATION
Port Salut, a soft French Tomme or a Caerphilly can be used instead of Fontina or Bel Paese.

1 Layer the diced aubergine in a colander, sprinkling each layer with salt. Drain over a sink for 20 minutes, then rinse and pat dry.

2 Heat the oil in a large frying pan and gently fry the onion, garlic, peppers and aubergine for about 10 minutes.

3 Add the courgettes, herbs and salt and pepper. Cook for 5 minutes, until softened. Cool to room temperature, then stir in the pine nuts and raisins.

4 Preheat the oven to 180°C/350°F/ Gas 4. To assemble the strudel, brush two sheets of filo pastry lightly with a little of the melted butter. Lay the filo sheets side by side, overlapping them by about 5cm/2in, to make a large rectangle. Cover with the remaining filo, in the same way, brushing each layer with a little of the melted butter. Save some butter for the top. Spoon the vegetable mixture down one long side of the filo.

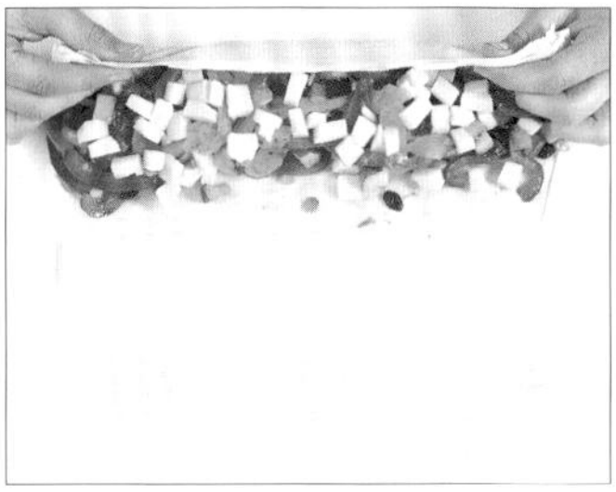

5 Scatter the cheese over, then roll up to a long sausage. Transfer the roll to a non-stick baking sheet, curling it round in a circle. Brush with the remaining melted butter and bake for 30 minutes, until golden. Cool for 10 minutes, before slicing. Serve with mixed salad.

Cheese and Onion Quiche

Perfect for picnics, parties or family suppers, this quiche celebrates a timeless combination: cheese and onion. Omit the bacon, if you prefer.

200g/7oz/1 3/4 cups plain flour
2.5ml/1/2 tsp salt
90g/3 1/2oz/scant 1/2 cup butter or sunflower margarine

For the Filling
25g/1oz/2 tbsp butter
1 large onion, thinly sliced
4 rindless streaky bacon rashers, chopped (optional)
3 eggs
300ml/1/2 pint/1 1/4 cups crème fraîche, single cream or milk
1.5ml/1/4 tsp freshly grated nutmeg
90g/3 1/2oz hard cheese, such as mature Cheddar, Gruyère or Manchego, grated
salt and ground black pepper

Serves 6–8

1 Make the pastry. Sift the flour and salt into a bowl. Rub in the fat until the mixture resembles fine crumbs. Trickle in enough water to make a firm dough, about 60ml/4 tbsp. Knead the dough lightly until smooth, wrap in clear film and chill for 20 minutes.

2 Roll out the dough on a lightly floured surface and line a 23cm/9in flan tin with a removable base. Press the pastry well into the sides and let it rise above the rim by about 1cm/1/2in to allow for shrinkage. Prick the pastry base a few times.

3 Line the flan case with foil and baking beans and chill again for about 15 minutes. Preheat the oven to 200°C/400°F/Gas 6. Place a baking sheet in the oven. Stand the flan tin on the baking sheet and bake "blind" for 15 minutes. Remove the beans and foil and return the pastry case to the oven for 5 minutes more. Reduce the oven temperature to 180°C/350°F/Gas 4.

4 Make the filling. Melt the butter in a pan and sauté the onion and bacon, if using, for 10 minutes. In a bowl, beat the eggs and crème fraîche, cream or milk. Add the nutmeg and seasoning.

5 Spoon the onion mixture into the cooked pastry case and scatter over the cheese. Pour the egg and cream liquid slowly over the filling, making sure none spills over the edge of the pastry case. Place the quiche in the oven and cook for 35–40 minutes or until the filling has just set. Remove from the oven, leave to cool, then gently ease the quiche out of the tin and place it on a plate for serving.

CALZONE

Looking like a folded pizza, a calzone consists of bread dough wrapped around a cheese and vegetable filling. The traditional tomato and garlic can be enlivened with chunks of sweet melting cheese, olives, crumbled grilled bacon, slices of pepperoni or chorizo or anchovy fillets.

30ml/2 tbsp extra virgin olive oil
1 small red onion, thinly sliced
2 garlic cloves, crushed
400g/14oz can chopped tomatoes
50g/2oz sliced chorizo sausage
50g/2oz/½ cup pitted black olives
500g/1¼lb bread dough mix
200g/7oz mozzarella or other semi-soft cheese, diced
5ml/1 tsp dried oregano
salt and ground black pepper
oregano sprigs, to garnish

MAKES 4

VARIATION

Mozzarella is the classic pizza cheese, but you may wish to experiment with other semi-soft melting cheeses, such as Fontina or Provolone.

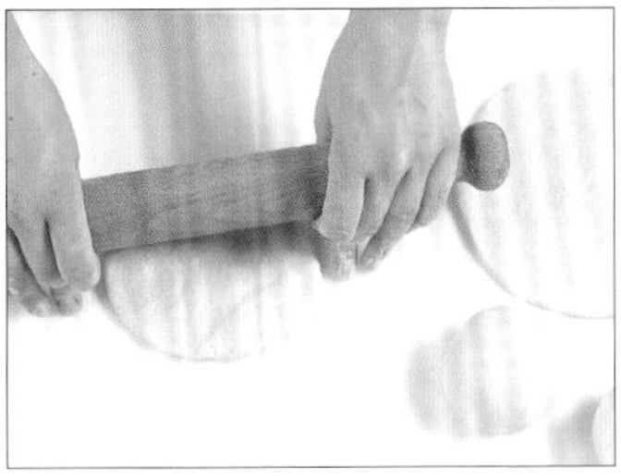

1 Heat the oil in a frying pan and sauté the onion and garlic for 5 minutes. Add the tomatoes and cook for 5 minutes more or until slightly reduced. Add the chorizo and olives. Season well.

2 Make up the dough mix according to the instructions on the packet. Cover the bowl and leave the dough to prove until it has doubled in bulk.

3 Knock back the dough and divide it into four portions. Roll out each portion of dough to a circle measuring about 20cm/8in. Preheat the oven to 200°C/400°F/Gas 6. Lightly grease two baking sheets.

4 Spread the filling on half of each dough circle, leaving a margin around the edge. Scatter over the cheese.

5 Sprinkle the filling with the dried oregano. Dampen the edges of the dough with cold water. Fold the dough in half and press well to seal.

6 Place two calzones on each baking sheet. Bake for 12–15 minutes until risen and golden. Cool for 2 minutes, then loosen with a palette knife and serve at once garnished with oregano.

CHICKEN, CHEESE AND LEEK JALOUSIE

A jalousie is a family-size lattice pastry roll with a mild, creamy filling. Ready-made puff pastry and cooked chicken make this a good choice for informal entertaining.

1.5kg/3–3½lb roasted chicken
2 large leeks, thinly sliced
2 garlic cloves, crushed
40g/1½oz/3 tbsp butter
125g/4oz/1 cup button mushrooms, sliced
200g/7oz/scant 1 cup low-fat cream cheese
grated rind of 1 small lemon
45ml/3 tbsp chopped fresh parsley
2 × 250g/9oz blocks puff pastry, thawed if frozen
1 egg, beaten
salt and ground black pepper
fresh herbs, to garnish

SERVES 6

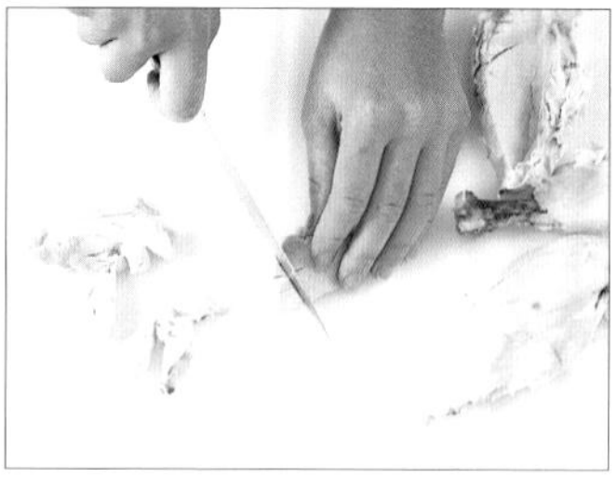

1 Strip the meat from the chicken, discarding the skin and bones. Chop or shred the meat and set it aside.

2 Sauté the leeks and garlic in the butter for 10 minutes. Stir in the mushrooms and cook for 5 minutes. Leave to cool, then add the cream cheese, lemon rind, parsley and salt and pepper. When cold, stir in the chicken.

3 Stack the blocks of pastry on top of each other and roll out on a lightly floured work surface to a large rectangle, about 35 × 25cm/14 × 10in. Lop the pastry over a rolling pin and lift it on to a non-stick baking sheet.

4 Spoon the filling on to the pastry, leaving a generous margin at top and bottom, and 10cm/4in on each side. Cut the pastry sides diagonally up to the filling at 2cm/¾in intervals.

Try a creamy blue cheese, such as Dolcellate Torta, for this jalousie.

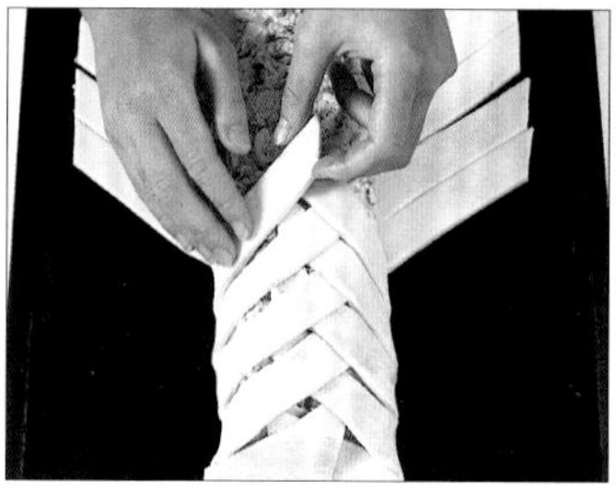

5 Brush the edges of the pastry with the beaten egg. Draw the pastry strips over each other in alternate crosses to "plait" the pastry. Seal the top and bottom edges.

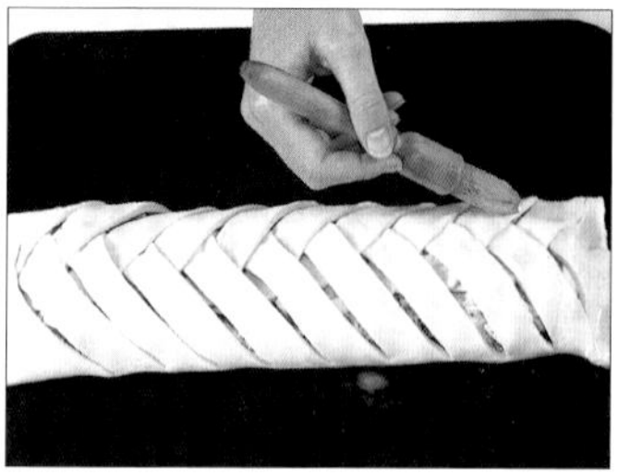

6 Glaze the jalousie with beaten egg. Allow it to rest while you preheat the oven to 200°C/400°F/Gas 6. Bake for 15 minutes, then lower the oven temperature to 190°C/375°F/Gas 5 and bake for a further 15 minutes, or until the pastry is golden brown and crisp.

7 Allow the jalousie to stand for about 10 minutes before sliding it on to a board or platter to serve. Garnish with fresh herbs.

VARIATION
Chopped cooked ham can be used instead of chicken.

Gougère

Choux pastry is very easy to make. Add cubes of hard cheese, such as Gruyère or Cheddar, and bake it in a dish with a lightly spiced haddock and mushroom filling and you have an impressive supper dish.

100g/3¾oz/scant 1 cup strong plain flour
1.5ml/¼ tsp salt
75g/3oz/6 tbsp cold butter, diced
200ml/7fl oz/scant 1 cup water
3 eggs, beaten
150g/5oz Emmental, mature Cheddar or Gruyère cheese, grated

For the Filling
250g/9oz smoked haddock fillet
1 bay leaf
250ml/8fl oz/1 cup milk
40g/1½oz/3 tbsp butter
1 small red onion, chopped
150g/5oz/1¼ cups mushrooms, sliced
5ml/1 tsp mild curry paste (optional)
25g/1oz/¼ cup plain flour
generous squeeze of fresh lemon juice
30ml/2 tbsp chopped fresh parsley
salt and ground black pepper

Serves 4

COOK'S TIP
Choose pale yellow, traditionally smoked haddock rather than vividly dyed, bright yellow fillets.

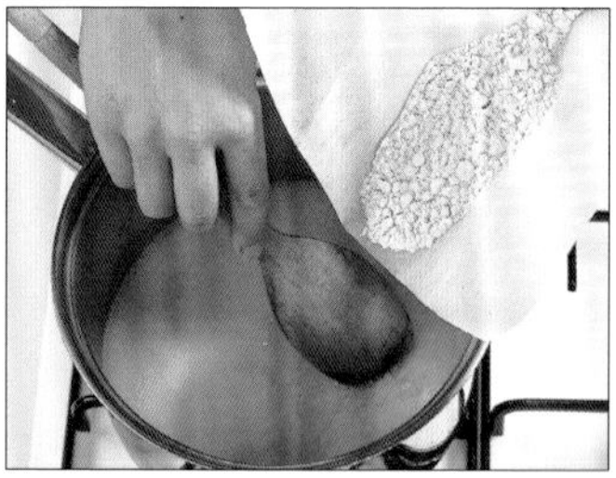

1 Lightly grease a shallow ovenproof dish. Sift the flour and salt on to a sheet of greaseproof paper. Place the butter and water in a saucepan and heat gently. As soon as the butter has melted, bring the water to the boil. Immediately tip in all the flour.

2 Beat the mixture until it comes away from the sides of the pan. (It will look alarmingly lumpy at first.) Remove the pan from the heat and cool for 5 minutes – this is important.

3 Slowly work the beaten eggs into the dough until the mixture has a good dropping consistency and holds its shape. You may not need all the egg. Stir in two-thirds of the grated cheese.

4 Spoon the choux paste around the edge of the prepared dish, making sure it comes well up the sides. Set aside. Choux paste can be made in advance and kept chilled for about 24 hours.

VARIATIONS
For an alternative filling use cooked chicken or ratatouille. Both the choux paste and the filling can be flavoured with blue cheese: use slightly less than the quantity suggested in the main recipe.

5 Preheat the oven to 180°C/350°F/Gas 4. To make the filling, put the haddock in a baking dish with the bay leaf. Pour in the milk, cover and bake for 15 minutes until just cooked. Lift out the fish. Discard the bay leaf but reserve the hot milk. Remove the skin from the haddock and flake the flesh.

6 In a saucepan, melt the butter and sauté the onion and mushrooms for 5 minutes. Mix in the curry paste, if using, then add the flour. Gradually stir in the hot milk. Heat, stirring, until the sauce is smooth. Simmer for about 2 minutes, then add the lemon juice, parsley and salt and pepper to taste.

7 Raise the oven temperature to 200°C/400°F/Gas 6. Spoon the filling into the centre of the uncooked paste. Sprinkle with the rest of the cheese. Bake for 35–40 minutes until the gougère has risen and is golden brown. Serve at once.

FOUR CHEESE CIABATTA PIZZA

Few dishes are as simple – or as satisfying – as this pizza made by topping a halved loaf of ciabatta.

1 loaf of ciabatta bread
1 garlic clove, halved
30–45ml/2–3 tbsp olive oil
about 90ml/6 tbsp tomato passata or sugocasa
1 small red onion, thinly sliced
30ml/2 tbsp chopped pitted olives
about 50g/2oz each of four cheeses, one mature (Parmesan or Cheddar), one blue-veined (Gorgonzola or Stilton), one mild (Fontina or Emmental) and a goat's cheese, sliced, grated or crumbled
pine nuts or cumin seeds, to sprinkle
salt and ground black pepper
sprigs of basil, to garnish

SERVES 2

1 Preheat the oven to 200°C/400°F/Gas 6. Split the ciabatta bread in half. Rub the cut sides with the garlic, then brush over the oil. Spread with the tomato passata or sugocasa, then add the onion slices and olives. Season.

2 Divide the cheeses between the ciabatta halves and sprinkle over the pine nuts or cumin seeds. Bake for 10–12 minutes, until bubbling and golden brown. Cut it into slices and serve immediately, garnished with basil.

CALIFORNIAN COURGETTE AND CHÈVRE PIZZA

Chefs from the West Coast of America are adventurous when it comes to making pizzas. Their wood-burning ovens give bases and cheese toppings a delicious smoky flavour. Cook this tasty pizza at a high temperature to char the vegetables lightly. Dot with goat's milk cheese for an interesting tang.

1 large ready-made, good-quality, crisp pizza base
45ml/3 tbsp drained sun-dried tomatoes in oil
45ml/3 tbsp drained roasted peppers in oil
1 courgette, thinly sliced
1 red onion, thinly sliced
250g/9oz young chèvre (goat's milk cheese), crumbled
15ml/1 tbsp chopped fresh oregano or marjoram
a little extra virgin olive oil, to drizzle
salt and ground black pepper
fresh herbs, to garnish

SERVES 2

VARIATIONS

A creamy, crumbly blue cheese such as Bleu d'Auvergne makes a good alternative to chèvre. A smoked mozzarella would also work well.

For a Greek flavour, try lightly sautéed aubergine slices in place of the courgettes and use feta rather than chèvre.

1 Preheat the oven to 220°C/425°F/ Gas 7. Place the pizza base on a baking sheet. Chop the sun-dried tomatoes and peppers and spread them over the pizza base.

2 Scatter the slices of courgette and onion on top, then dot with the crumbled chèvre. Sprinkle with oregano or marjoram, season well and drizzle a little olive oil over the top.

3 Bake the pizza for 10–12 minutes or until the cheese has melted and the vegetables have begun to char. Garnish with herbs and serve, cut into wedges.

Hard goat's milk cheese would be ideal – simply grate over the pizza.

LASAGNE AL FORNO

The classic lasagne is made with good home-made meat sauce (ragù) and a white sauce (salsa besciamella) layered with freshly grated Parmesan cheese. Keep the layers of sauces quite thin and don't make the lasagne too thick – the finished dish should hold its shape as you cut it.

about 8–10 lasagne sheets, green or white
75g/3oz/1 cup freshly grated Parmesan cheese
salt and ground black pepper
sprigs of flat leaf parsley, to garnish

For the Meat Sauce
45ml/3 tbsp olive oil
500g/1¼lb lean minced beef
75g/3oz smoked bacon or pancetta, diced
130g/4½oz chicken livers, trimmed and chopped (optional)
1 onion, finely chopped
2 garlic cloves, crushed
150ml/¼ pint/⅔ cup dry white wine (optional)
30–45ml/2–3 tbsp tomato purée
2 × 400g/14oz cans chopped tomatoes
45ml/3 tbsp single cream (optional)

For the White Sauce
600ml/1 pint/2½ cups milk
1 bay leaf
1 small onion, sliced
50g/2oz/¼ cup butter
40g/1½oz/⅓ cup plain flour
freshly grated nutmeg

Serves 6

1 Bring a large saucepan of water to the boil and blanch the pasta sheets, a few at a time, for at least 2 minutes, taking care to keep them separate. Stir the pasta during cooking to stop it sticking. Drain the blanched sheets and set them aside in a bowl of cold water.

2 Make the meat sauce. Heat the oil in a large frying pan and brown the minced beef. Add the bacon or pancetta and chicken livers, if using, and cook for 3–4 minutes. Add the onion and garlic, cook for 5 minutes more. Stir in the wine, if using. Cook until well reduced.

3 Stir in the tomato purée and tomatoes, with salt and pepper to taste. Bring to the boil, then lower the heat and simmer for 15–20 minutes until thickened. Stir in the cream, if using, and set aside.

4 While the meat sauce is simmering, make the white sauce. Pour the milk into a saucepan and add the bay leaf and sliced onion. Heat gently until the milk is just below boiling point, then remove the pan from the heat and leave to infuse for 10 minutes. Strain the milk into a jug and discard the bay leaf and onion.

5 Melt the butter in a saucepan and stir in the flour. Cook for 1 minute, stirring, then gradually whisk in the milk until the mixture boils and thickens to a smooth sauce. Season and add nutmeg to taste. Drain the pasta sheets and pat them dry with kitchen paper.

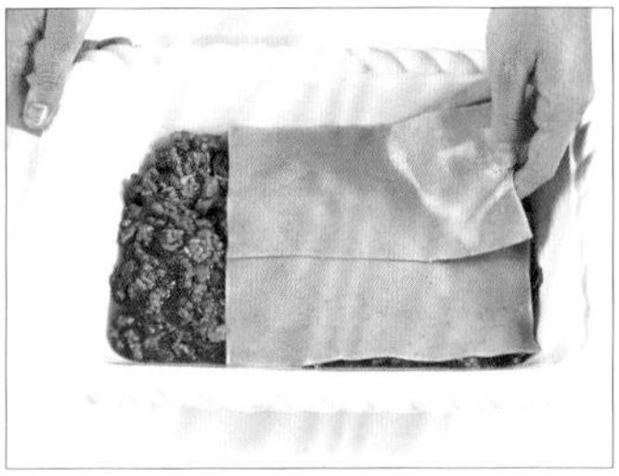

6 Spread some meat sauce on the base of a rectangular baking dish. Top with a single layer of pasta sheets. Trickle over some white sauce and sprinkle with Parmesan. Repeat the layers until all the ingredients have been used, finishing with a layer made by swirling the last of the two sauces together. Sprinkle liberally with Parmesan.

7 Preheat the oven to 190°C/375°F/Gas 5 and bake the lasagne for about 30 minutes until bubbling and golden brown. Allow to stand for 10 minutes before cutting. Serve garnished with flat leaf parsley.

New York-style Lasagne

This more sophisticated lasagne is made layering the meat sauce with ricotta cheese, spinach and sliced pepperoni or chorizo sausage. A mixture of minced beef and pork gives a good flavour.

about 8–10 lasagne sheets, green or white
400g/14oz fresh spinach
500g/1¼lb/2½ cups ricotta cheese
125g/4oz thinly sliced pepperoni or chorizo or kabanos sausage
50g/2oz/⅔ cup freshly grated Parmesan cheese
fresh herbs, to garnish

For the Meat Sauce
30ml/2 tbsp olive oil
250g/9oz lean minced beef
250g/9oz lean minced pork
1 onion, chopped
2 garlic cloves, crushed
150ml/¼ pint/⅔ cup dry white wine or 60ml/4 tbsp dry vermouth
400g/14oz can chopped tomatoes
45ml/3 tbsp tomato purée
150ml/¼ pint/⅔ cup beef stock or water
2.5ml/½ tsp dried oregano
salt and ground black pepper

Serves 6

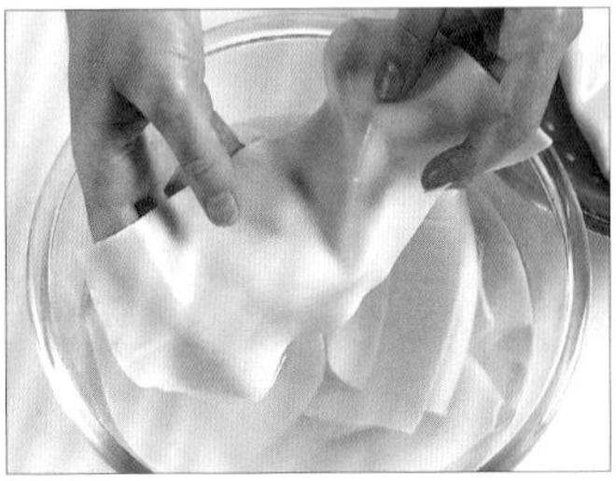

1 Bring a large saucepan of water to the boil and blanch the pasta sheets, a few at a time, for at least 2 minutes, taking care to keep them separate. Stir the pasta during cooking to stop it sticking. Drain and set aside in a bowl of cold water.

2 Snap off any thick stalks from the spinach, then blanch the leaves in a pan containing a small amount of boiling water for 2 minutes, until just wilted. Drain the spinach and refresh under cold water. Drain again, then squeeze dry and chop the leaves.

3 Put the ricotta on a plate and break it up with a fork.

4 To make the meat sauce, heat the oil in a large frying pan, then add both types of mince and cook over a high heat for about 5 minutes, until well browned, stirring to break up any lumps. Add the onion and garlic and cook for 5 minutes more.

COOK'S TIP

Ricotta can sometimes be difficult to come by, especially if you live in the country. However, it freezes well, so it is worth stocking up when you do locate a supply.

5 Pour the wine or vermouth into the frying pan and cook over a high heat until well reduced. Stir in the chopped tomatoes, tomato purée, beef stock or water and dried oregano, then season to taste with salt and pepper. Bring to the boil, then lower the heat and simmer gently without a lid for about 15 minutes until thickened.

6 Preheat the oven to 190°C/375°F/Gas 5. In a large baking dish, layer the meat sauce with the pasta sheets, chopped spinach and sliced sausage. Dot each layer of spinach and sausage with the ricotta and sprinkle with the Parmesan. Finish with a generous topping of Parmesan.

7 Bake the lasagne for 35–40 minutes until bubbling and golden brown. Allow to stand in a warm place for about 10 minutes before cutting and serving. Garnish with fresh herbs.

Spanakopitta

This popular spinach and filo pastry pie comes from Greece. There are several ways of making it, but feta or Kefalotiri is inevitably included. Go easy on the seasoning as these cheeses are salty.

1kg/2¼lb fresh spinach
4 spring onions, chopped
300g/11oz feta or Kefalotiri cheese, crumbled or coarsely grated
2 large eggs, beaten
30ml/2 tbsp chopped fresh parsley
15ml/1 tbsp chopped fresh dill
45ml/3 tbsp currants (optional)
about 8 filo pastry sheets, each about 30 × 18cm/12 × 7in
150ml/¼ pint/⅔ cup olive oil
ground black pepper

SERVES 6

VARIATION

Graviera or Kasseri can be used instead of feta or Kefalotiri. A crumbly English cheese, such as Lancashire, also works well, even though it is not strictly authentic.

1 Preheat the oven to 190°C/375°F/ Gas 5. Break off any thick stalks from the spinach, then blanch the leaves in a pan containing a very small amount of boiling water for 1–2 minutes, until just wilted. Drain and refresh under cold water. Drain again, squeeze dry and chop roughly.

2 Place the spinach in a bowl with the spring onions and cheese, then pour in the eggs. Mix in the herbs and currants (if using). Season with pepper.

3 Brush a filo sheet with oil and fit it into a 23cm/9in pie dish, allowing it to hang over the edges. Top with 3–4 more sheets; place these at different angles and brush each one with more oil, to make a roughly shaped pie case.

4 Spoon in the filling, then top with all but one of the remaining filo sheets. Brush each filo sheet with oil. Fold in the overhanging filo to seal in the filling. Brush the reserved filo with oil and scrunch it over the top of the pie.

5 Brush the pie with oil. Sprinkle with a little water to stop the filo edges from curling, then place on a baking sheet. Bake for about 40 minutes, until golden and crisp. Cool the pie for 15 minutes before serving.

PUMPKIN AND PARMESAN PASTA

The sweet flavour of pumpkins is nicely balanced by the mature flavour of Parmesan. Instead of being sprinkled on top of the pasta dish, this grated cheese is used in the sauce, and the crunch comes from garlic breadcrumbs.

800g/1¾lb fresh pumpkin flesh, cut into small cubes
65g/2½oz/5 tbsp butter
15ml/1 tbsp olive oil
2 garlic cloves, crushed
75g/3oz/1½ cups fresh white breadcrumbs
300g/11oz tagliatelle
125g/4oz rindless smoked back bacon, diced
1 onion, sliced
150ml/¼ pint/⅔ cup single cream
50g/2oz/⅔ cup freshly grated Parmesan cheese
freshly grated nutmeg
30ml/2 tbsp chopped fresh parsley
15ml/1 tbsp snipped fresh chives
salt and ground black pepper
sprigs of flat leaf parsley, to garnish

SERVES 4

1 Bring a large saucepan of water to the boil. Tip in the pumpkin cubes. Cook for about 10 minutes until just tender, then drain and set aside.

2 Melt two-thirds of the butter with the oil in a frying pan. Add the garlic and breadcrumbs. Fry gently until the crumbs are golden brown and crisp. Drain on kitchen paper and keep warm.

3 Cook the tagliatelle according to the packet instructions. Drain and set aside. Heat the remaining butter in a clean pan and fry the bacon and onion for 5 minutes. Stir in the cream and bring to just below boiling point. Add the pasta and reheat. Stir in the pumpkin, Parmesan, nutmeg, parsley, chives and seasoning. Serve sprinkled with garlic breadcrumbs and garnished with parsley.

Cheese Sauces for Pasta

Here are three quick and easy sauces – all using cheese – to toss with cooked pasta. Each is sufficient for about 250g/9oz pasta strands or shapes.

Mushroom and Gorgonzola Sauce

Gorgonzola melts easily with cream to make a delicious, quick sauce.

30ml/2 tbsp olive oil
250g/9oz/2¼ cups mushrooms, sliced
1 garlic clove, crushed
300ml/½ pint/1¼ cups single cream
175g/6oz Gorgonzola cheese, rind removed, crumbled
salt and ground black pepper
15ml/1 tbsp chopped fresh parsley and 50g/2oz/½ cup chopped walnuts, to serve

1 Heat the olive oil in a pan and sauté the mushrooms for 5 minutes. Add the garlic and cook for 1–2 minutes more.

2 Stir in the cream, bring to the boil and cook for 1 minute. Stir in the Gorgonzola. Reheat gently to melt the cheese, but do not boil. Season and toss with cooked pasta. Serve at once, sprinkled with the parsley and walnuts.

Home-made Pesto

The ideal no-cook pasta sauce, this is best made by hand with a pestle and mortar, although a food processor can be used if time is short. Use a mixture of Parmesan and Pecorino cheeses. Pine nuts are a recent addition and butter makes it enjoyably smooth.

75g/3oz/1½ cups fresh basil leaves, stalks removed
25g/1oz/2 tbsp pine nuts
2–3 garlic cloves, roughly chopped
125g/4oz/1⅓ cups mixed freshly grated Parmesan and Pecorino cheese
120ml/4fl oz/½ cup olive oil
25g/1oz/2 tbsp butter, softened
salt

1 Put the basil, pine nuts and garlic into a mortar. Add 2.5ml/½ tsp salt and grind with a pestle until the mixture forms a chunky paste.

2 Work in the cheeses until smooth. Beat the paste with a wooden spoon, gradually trickling in the olive oil as when making mayonnaise. Finally, beat in the butter.

3 Store pesto in a screw-top jar in the fridge. When you toss it into cooked pasta, thin it slightly, if you wish, by adding a little of the hot water used for cooking the pasta.

Fonduta

This Italian answer to fondue is also used as a sauce for pasta, rice and polenta. If you can't find Fontina cheese, Gruyère will do.

400g/14oz Fontina cheese, cut into small cubes
250ml/8fl oz/1 cup creamy milk
50g/2oz/¼ cup butter, cut into pieces
4 egg yolks
ground white pepper

1 Mix together the cheese and milk in a heavy-based saucepan or the top of a double boiler. Heat very gently on the hob or over simmering water, stirring frequently until the cheese has completely melted. Stir in the butter. The cheese will go into thin threads.

2 Beat the egg yolks in a large bowl with pepper. Pour the cheesy milk on to them, beating as you pour. Return the mixture to the clean pan and reheat very, very gently. Do not let the mixture boil or it will curdle. Pour over pasta, cooked rice or grilled polenta and eat quickly. The sauce is also good served cold, with chunks of bread to scoop it up.

Opposite (from left): Fonduta, Home-made Pesto and Mushroom and Gorgonzola Sauce.

DESSERTS AND BAKES

Fresh young cheeses were created to be used in cooking or mixed with other ingredients, and their mild taste and slight astringency means that they are delicious sweetened with sugar or honey to make classic desserts such as Coeur à la Crème and Tiramisù, delectable cheesecakes and a cream cheese-iced carrot cake. Full-flavoured hard cheeses make delicious, moist breads and scones.

Refrigerator Cheesecake

This dessert is so simple, anyone could make it. Serve the cheesecake with seasonal fruits. In late summer, poached plums or apricots cooked in a spiced syrup are particularly good, although soft red berry fruits are also excellent. Make sure the cheese is at room temperature when you mix it.

200g/7oz/3½ cups digestive biscuits
90g/3½oz/7 tbsp butter
15ml/1 tbsp golden syrup
seasonal fruit and raspberry coulis, to serve
strawberry leaves, to serve

For the Filling

grated rind and juice of 1 lemon or 2 limes
1 sachet powdered gelatine
200g/7oz/scant 1 cup low fat cream cheese, at room temperature
200g/7oz/scant 1 cup quark or fromage frais
150g/5oz/⅔ cup natural yogurt
50g/2oz/¼ cup caster sugar
5ml/1 tsp pure vanilla essence

Serves 4–6

COOK'S TIP
The gelatine can be dissolved in a suitable bowl in the microwave. Follow the instructions on the packet.

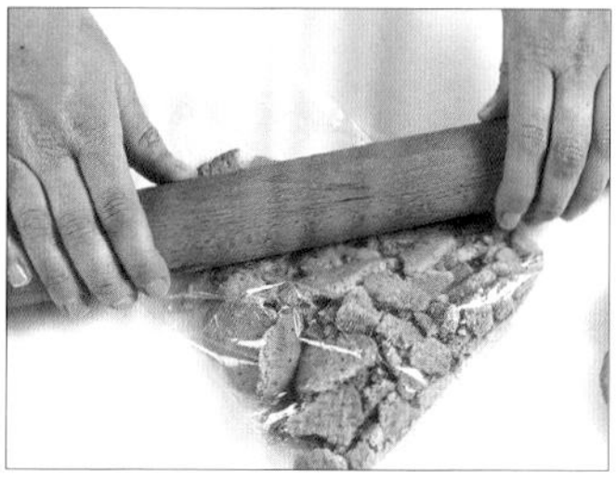

1 Crush the biscuits to fine crumbs: either place them in a polythene food bag and crush with a rolling pin or use a food processor fitted with a metal blade. Melt the butter and syrup in a saucepan, then mix with the crumbs.

2 Press the buttery crumbs into the base and up the sides of a 20cm/8in loose-based flan tin. Chill for 1 hour.

3 Make the filling. Pour the lemon or lime juice into a small heatproof dish and sprinkle over the gelatine. Leave the mixture until the gelatine absorbs the liquid and looks spongy, then place the dish in a saucepan of barely simmering water and stir occasionally until the gelatine dissolves.

4 Mix the cheese and quark or fromage frais. Add the yogurt, citrus rind, sugar and vanilla. Beat until smooth, then beat some of the mixture into the dissolved gelatine. Add this to the cheesecake filling and beat well. Pour into the crumb crust and chill for 3 hours until set. Remove the cheesecake from the tin. Serve with fruit and raspberry coulis. Garnish with strawberry leaves.

Velvety Cheesecake

The secret of a perfect baked cheesecake is to take as much care over the cooling as you do with the cooking. If you do not overbake the mixture, it will stay beautifully moist and will firm as it cools.

25cm/10in sponge cake flan base
500g/1¼lb/2 cups cream cheese, softened
600ml/1 pint/2½ cups soured cream
200g/7oz/scant 1 cup caster sugar
3 eggs, beaten
juice of 1 lemon
10ml/2 tsp pure vanilla essence
45–60ml/3–4 tbsp crushed digestive biscuit crumbs
icing sugar, for dusting
fresh fruits, to serve

Serves 6–8

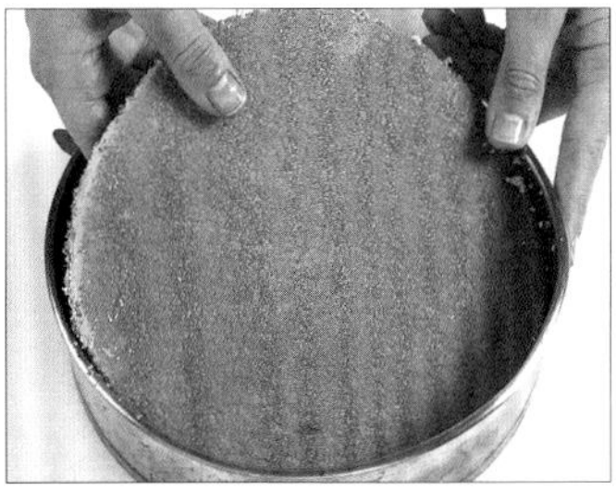

1 Preheat the oven to 160°C/325°F/ Gas 3. Lightly grease a 23cm/9in springform cake tin. Using the base of the tin as a guide, cut out a round from the flan cake base and fit this into the tin. It should fit snugly, without any gaps.

2 Mix the cream cheese, soured cream and sugar in a food processor. Process until smooth and creamy, then mix in the eggs, lemon juice and vanilla essence. Process briefly to blend.

3 Pour the filling on top of the flan base and level the surface. Bake for about 40 minutes, until the top is golden brown. Turn off the oven and leave the cake inside for another hour. Remove, allow the cake to cool to room temperature, then chill in the fridge overnight until firm. Run a table knife around the cheesecake and remove the sides of the tin. Slide a palette knife under the cake and lift it on to a serving plate.

4 Sprinkle the crushed biscuit crumbs evenly over the cheesecake and dust with a little sifted icing sugar. Serve with fresh fruits.

VARIATIONS

Make the cheesecake without a base, if you prefer. If you like sultanas in your cheesecake, add a generous handful.

Coeur à la Crème

This dessert is sheer simplicity – a curd cheese blended with crème fraîche, then sweetened and drained. Traditionally, perforated heart-shaped moulds are used (hence the name), but the mixture can be served in ramekins.

250g/9oz/generous 1 cup curd cheese
300ml/½ pint/1¼ cups crème fraîche or natural yogurt
30–45ml/2–3 tbsp vanilla-flavoured caster sugar
raspberry leaves, to decorate

For the Raspberry Coulis
250g/9oz/1½ cups fresh raspberries, hulled
icing sugar, to sweeten

Makes 8

COOK'S TIP

If using ramekins, spoon the cheese mixture into a muslin-lined sieve set over a bowl. Leave to drain in the fridge for up to 2 days, then press into eight lightly greased ramekins. Turn out the moulded cheese immediately.

1 Beat the curd cheese and crème fraîche or natural yogurt in a bowl. Add vanilla sugar to taste.

2 Set eight traditional perforated moulds on a wire rack over a roasting tin. Spoon the cheese mixture into the moulds, filling each one to the brim.

3 Transfer the roasting tin to the fridge and leave the moulds to drain for up to 2 days.

4 To make the coulis, sieve the raspberries, then sweeten with icing sugar. Turn out the moulds and serve with the coulis, decorated with raspberry leaves.

Tiramisù

The Italians consider this the ultimate "pick-me-up", which is what the name means. It makes marvellous use of silky smooth mascarpone.

2 eggs, separated, plus 2 egg yolks
90g/3½oz/7 tbsp caster sugar
5ml/1 tsp pure vanilla essence
500g/1¼lb mascarpone cheese
250ml/8fl oz/1 cup freshly brewed strong black coffee
60ml/4 tbsp rum or brandy
about 24 Italian Savoiardi or Boudoir biscuits
60ml/4 tbsp finely grated dark chocolate

Serves 6–8

VARIATION

Dispense with the biscuit base, if you prefer, and serve the Tiramisù cream over a mixture of fresh, prepared summer fruit.

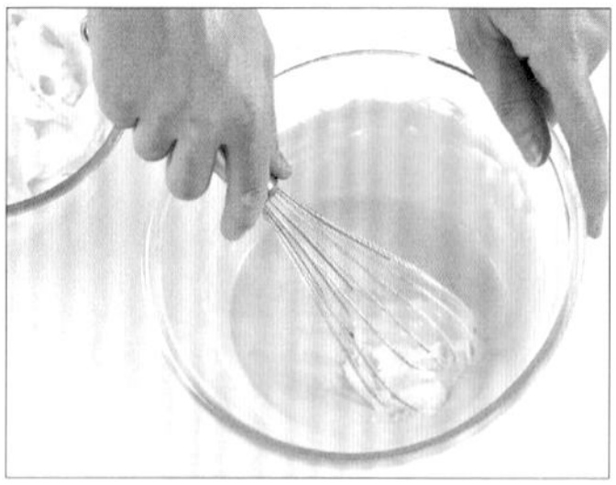

1 Whisk the egg yolks, sugar and vanilla in a heatproof bowl. Place over a pan of simmering water and whisk until the mixture is pale and thick and the whisk leaves a clear trail on the surface when lifted up. Remove the bowl from the pan and allow to cool, beating the mixture occasionally to prevent the formation of a skin.

2 When the mixture is cold, beat in the mascarpone. Whisk the egg whites in a large grease-free bowl until they form soft peaks, then carefully fold them into the mixture.

3 Mix the coffee and rum or brandy in a bowl. Dip the Savoiardi or Boudoir biscuits quickly in the liquid, then arrange them in a glass dish. Spoon the mascarpone mixture over the top, then sprinkle with the grated chocolate. Chill for at least an hour before serving.

COOK'S TIP

If you prefer to avoid using uncooked egg whites, substitute albumen powder.

Lemon Cheese Mousse with Brandy Snap Baskets

A delicious combination of a light cheesecake-style mousse with biscuit cups. Assemble the individual desserts at the last minute, so that they stay crisp.

50g/2oz/¼ cup butter
30ml/2 tbsp golden syrup
50g/2oz/¼ cup granulated sugar
grated rind and juice of 2 lemons
50g/2oz/½ cup plain flour
1 orange, for shaping the biscuits
45ml/3 tbsp water
10ml/2 tsp powdered gelatine
250g/9oz/generous 1 cup curd cheese
150ml/¼ pint/⅔ cup natural yogurt
30ml/2 tbsp clear honey, or to taste
15ml/1 tbsp grated crystallized ginger
2 egg whites
mint sprigs, to decorate
selection of soft fruit, to serve

Makes 6–8

COOK'S TIP
To save time, use bought brandy snaps to make the baskets. Simply warm them in a low oven until they uncurl, then shape them over an orange. If the brandy snaps harden before you have a chance to shape them, then simply pop them back in the oven briefly to soften.

1 Make the baskets. Preheat the oven to 190°C/375°F/Gas 5. Line a large baking sheet with non-stick baking paper. Melt the butter, syrup and sugar in a saucepan, then remove from the heat and stir in half the lemon rind and all the flour. Beat until smooth.

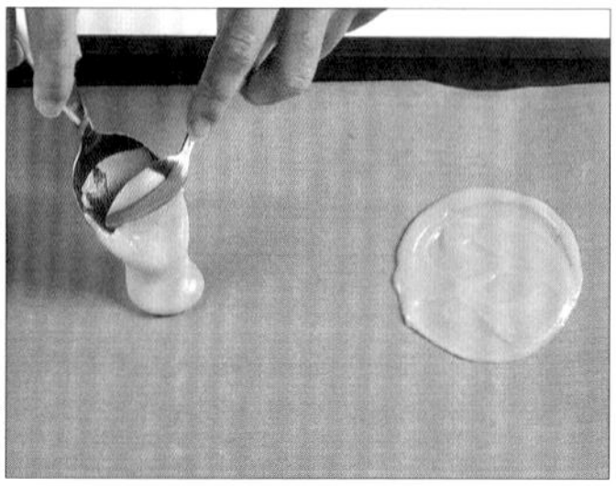

2 Put about 30ml/2 tbsp of mixture on the prepared baking sheet. Using a small palette knife, spread out the mixture to a 13cm/5in circle. Add a second circle, some distance from the first to allow room for spreading. Bake for 5–7 minutes until the biscuits have spread out and are lacy and light golden brown.

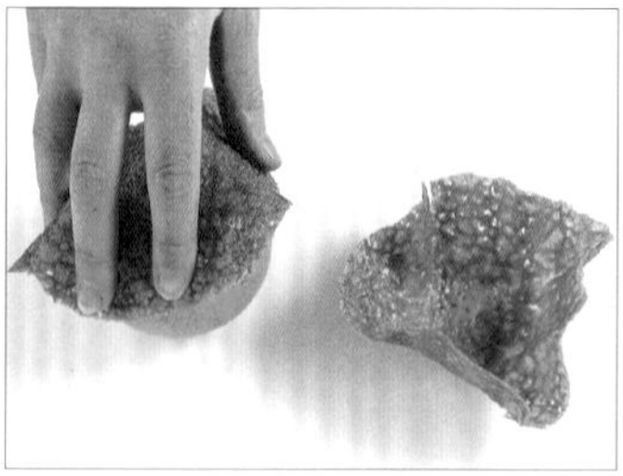

3 Allow the biscuits to cool for about 1 minute to firm slightly, but not harden, then lift each in turn off the baking sheet using a palette knife. Gently press the biscuits over the orange, carefully fluting the edges, and protecting your hands with a clean dish towel, if necessary.

4 Remove the baskets when shaped and leave them to cool on a wire rack. Repeat the entire cooking and shaping process with the remaining mixture until you have used it all.

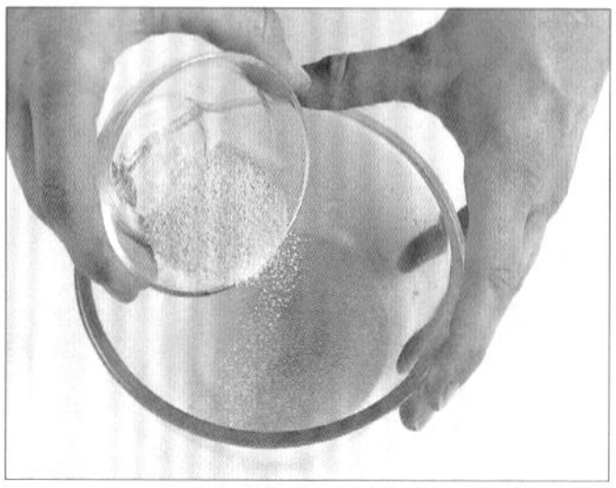

5 Make the mousse. Pour the water into a bowl and sprinkle the gelatine over the surface. Leave until spongy, then dissolve over simmering water.

6 Blend the cheese, yogurt, remaining lemon rind, lemon juice, honey and ginger in a food processor. Add the gelatine, blend briefly and pour into a bowl. Chill until just beginning to set.

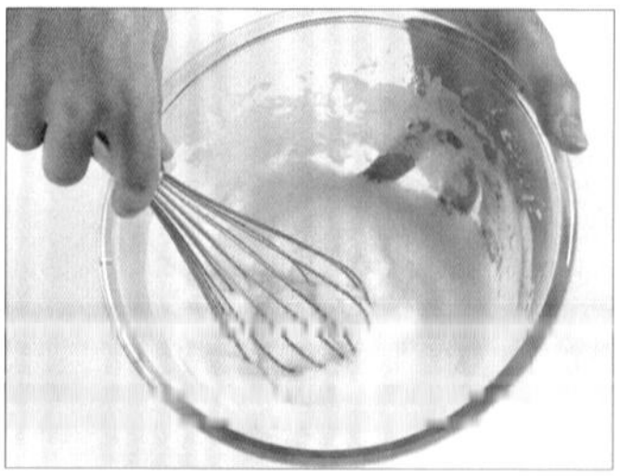

7 Whisk the egg whites to soft peaks and fold into the mousse. Spoon into the baskets and serve, decorated with mint and accompanied by fruit.

Sicilian Cassata

Is this world-famous cheese dessert a chocolate-coated ice cream or a rum syrup-soaked cake? The answer is that it can be both, and a number of other variations too. Try to track down authentic Savoiardi biscuits as they hold their shape better than Boudoir biscuits or ordinary trifle sponges.

500g/1¼lb/2½ cups ricotta cheese
75g/3oz/¾ cup icing sugar, plus extra for dusting
2.5ml/½ tsp pure vanilla essence
grated rind and juice of 1 small orange
50g/2oz dark chocolate, grated
250g/9oz/1½ cups mixed candied fruits, including orange, pineapple, citron, cherries and angelica
250ml/8fl oz/1 cup freshly brewed strong black coffee
120ml/4fl oz/½ cup rum
24 Savoiardi biscuits
geranium leaves, to decorate

Serves 8

1 Line the base and sides of a 20cm/8in round cake tin with clear film. Put the ricotta in a bowl. Sift in the icing sugar, then add the vanilla essence with the orange rind and juice. Beat until smooth, then stir in the chocolate.

2 Cut the candied fruits into small pieces and stir into the ricotta.

3 Mix the coffee and rum in a bowl. Line the base of the tin with biscuits, dipping each biscuit in turn in the coffee mixture before fitting it in place. Cut the remaining biscuits in half, dip them in the liquid and arrange around the sides of the tin.

4 Spoon the cassata mixture into the centre and level the top. Cover with more clear film, then place a plate on top that exactly fits inside the rim of the tin. Weight this with a bag of dried beans or sugar, then chill overnight until firm.

5 Turn out to serve, shaking the tin firmly if necessary and tugging the clear film gently. Dust with a little sifted icing sugar and serve in wedges, decorated with geranium leaves.

PASHKA

This traditional Russian Easter dessert is made with curd cheese and served with slices of kulich, a sweet yeast bread. The cheese mixture is pressed into a muslin-lined wooden mould so that whey drains out to leave a rich and delectably creamy mousse. In the absence of a pashka mould, use a flower pot.

500g/1 1/4lb/2 1/2 cups curd cheese, at room temperature
130g/4 1/2oz/9 tbsp butter, softened
2 large egg yolks, optional
125g/4oz/1/2 cup caster sugar
75g/3oz/1/2 cup candied fruit peel, chopped
50g/2oz/1/3 cup raisins
50g/2oz/1/2 cup chopped blanched almonds
grated rind of 1 lemon
5ml/1 tsp pure vanilla essence
pared lemon rind and geranium leaves, to decorate
sliced fresh kulich or fruited brioche, to serve

SERVES 8

VARIATION
A mixture of ricotta and mascarpone can be used instead of the curd cheese, and chopped pistachio nuts instead of the almonds.

1 Put the curd cheese, softened butter, egg yolks and caster sugar in a bowl. Whisk until smooth, then mix in the candied fruits, raisins, almonds, lemon rind and vanilla essence.

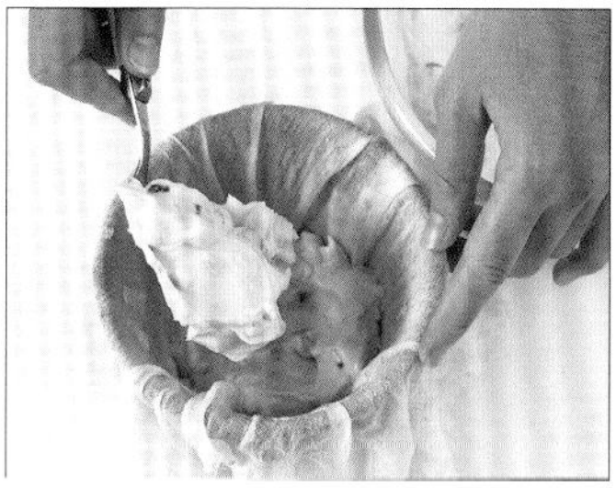

2 Line a clean, new 18cm/7in flower pot with wet muslin. Pack in the cheese mixture. Cover with a plate that exactly fits the top and weigh down with heavy cans or weights.

3 Place the flower pot on a deep plate and leave to drain overnight at cool room temperature or for a full day in the fridge.

4 Discard the whey, then uncover the flower pot and turn it out on to a pretty serving plate. Decorate with pared lemon rind and geranium leaves. To serve, slice horizontally from the top down or cut into thin wedges. Offer sliced fresh kulich or fruited brioche with the pashka.

Carrot Cake with Cream Cheese Icing

This moist cut-and-come-again cake has a delicious cream cheese icing. It makes a rather good grown-up birthday cake.

90g/3½oz/scant 1 cup wholemeal flour
150g/5oz/1¼ cups plain flour
10ml/2 tsp baking powder
5ml/1 tsp bicarbonate of soda
5ml/1 tsp ground cinnamon
2.5ml/½ tsp ground allspice
250g/9oz/1½ cups soft light brown sugar
3 carrots, coarsely grated
125g/4oz/1 cup chopped walnuts
3 large eggs
juice of 1 orange
120ml/4fl oz/½ cup sunflower oil
shreds of pared orange rind, to decorate

For the Icing
50g/2oz/¼ cup butter, softened
200g/7oz/scant 1 cup cream cheese, softened
grated rind of 1 orange
200g/7oz/1¾ cups icing sugar
5ml/1 tsp pure vanilla essence

Serves 8

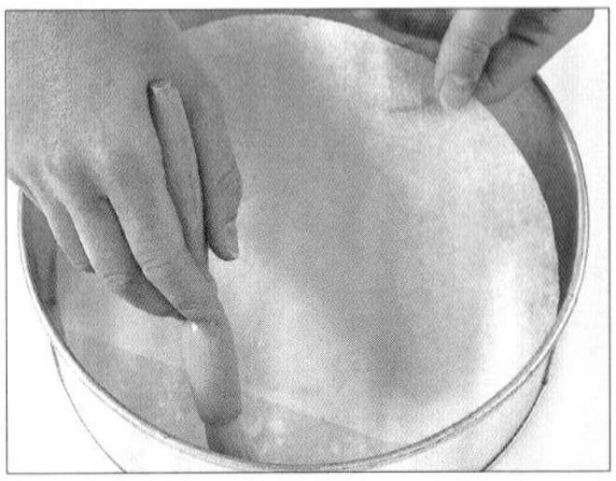

1 Preheat the oven to 180°C/350°F/Gas 4. Lightly grease a 23cm/9in round cake tin and line the base with non-stick baking paper. Grease the paper.

2 Sift all the dry ingredients except the brown sugar into a bowl, then tip in the bran from the sieve. Add the brown sugar, carrots and walnuts.

3 Beat the eggs and orange juice in a bowl. Make a well in the dry mixture and add the egg mixture and oil. Mix well. Spoon into the prepared tin and level the top. Bake for about 1 hour until risen and springy to the touch.

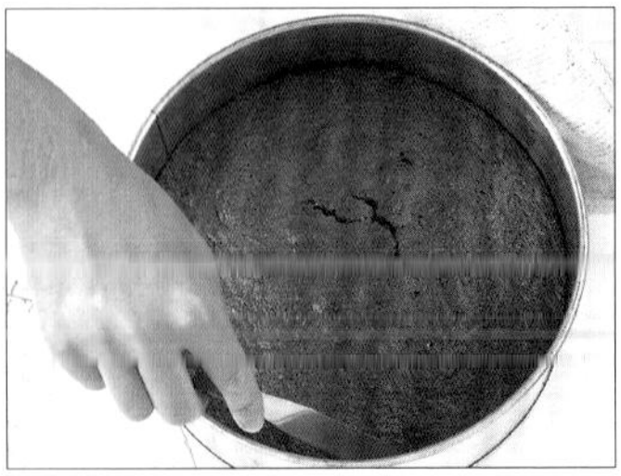

4 Slide a knife between the cake and the tin to loosen it, then turn the cake out on a rack and remove the lining paper.

5 To make the icing, beat the butter, cream cheese and grated orange rind in a large bowl. Sift the icing sugar, then gradually add to the bowl with the vanilla essence, beating well after each addition, until the mixture is creamy.

6 Split the cake in half widthways using a large serrated knife. Sandwich the cake together with about half the icing, then spread the rest of the icing on the top, swirling it attractively with a palette knife. Scatter the shreds of orange rind around the edge of the iced cake to decorate.

VARIATION

Instead of using shreds of orange rind to decorate the cake, sprinkle the iced cake with a little ground cinnamon, finely chopped walnuts or coffee sugar crystals.

CHEESE AND COURGETTE CLUSTER BREAD

Home baking is enjoying renewed popularity, thanks to the convenience of easy-blend dried yeast. This unusual bread owes its moistness to grated courgettes, and its depth of flavour to freshly grated Parmesan.

4 courgettes, coarsely grated
675g/1½lb/6 cups strong white bread flour
2 sachets easy-blend dried yeast
50g/2oz/⅔ cup freshly grated Parmesan cheese
30ml/2 tbsp olive oil
milk, to glaze
poppy seeds or sesame seeds, to sprinkle
salt and ground black pepper

SERVES 8

1 Put the grated courgettes into a colander and sprinkle with salt. Stand in a sink for about 20 minutes to drain the juices, then rinse thoroughly. Drain and pat dry with kitchen paper.

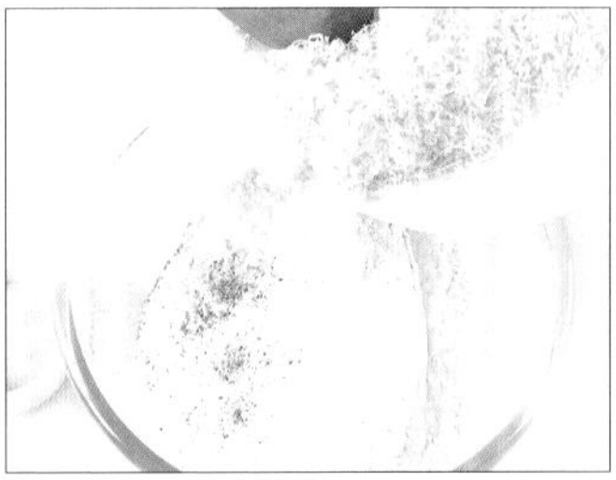

2 In a large bowl, mix the flour with the yeast, Parmesan and 2.5ml/½ tsp salt. Add pepper to taste. Stir in the oil and courgettes, then add enough hand-hot water to make a firm, but still soft dough. How much water you need depends on how wet the courgettes are, but start with about 45ml/3 tbsp.

3 Gather the dough together with your hand, then turn it out on a lightly floured surface. Knead the dough for 5–10 minutes, or until it is smooth and elastic. Return to the bowl, cover with lightly oiled clear film and leave to rise in a warm place for about until doubled in bulk.

4 Punch down the dough and knead again. Divide it into eight pieces and roll into smooth balls.

5 Lightly grease a deep 23cm/9in cake tin. Fit the balls into the tin, placing one in the centre and the remainder around the outside.

6 Glaze the loaf with a little milk and sprinkle over poppy seeds or sesame seeds. Cover the tin lightly with oiled clear film and leave to rise in a warm place until the balls of dough have doubled in size.

7 Meanwhile, preheat the oven to 200°C/400°F/Gas 6. Bake the loaf for 35–45 minutes, until it is golden brown and sounds hollow when tapped on the base. Cool on a wire rack and eat as soon as possible.

Dry Jack (left) could be used in place of Parmesan in this bread. Or try an aged Gouda or Pecorino.

Cheese and Mustard Scones

Depending on their size, these cheese scones can be served as little canapé bases, tea-time treats or even as a quick pie topping or cobbler.

250g/9oz/2 1/4 cups self-raising flour
5ml/1 tsp baking powder
2.5ml/1/2 tsp salt
40g/1 1/2oz/3 tbsp butter or sunflower margarine
175g/6oz/1 1/2 cups grated mature Cheddar cheese, plus extra for sprinkling
10ml/2 tsp wholegrain mustard
about 150ml/1/4 pint/2/3 cup milk, buttermilk or natural yogurt
1 egg yolk beaten with 5ml/1 tsp water, to glaze (optional)
ground black pepper
garlic-flavoured cream cheese, chopped fresh chives and sliced radishes, to serve (optional)

Makes 12 medium scones

1 Preheat the oven to 220°C/425°F/Gas 7. Sift the flour, baking powder and salt into a bowl, then rub in the butter or margarine until the mixture resembles fine breadcrumbs. Use a food processor if you prefer. Season with pepper and stir in the cheese.

2 Mix the mustard with the milk, buttermilk or yogurt. Add to the dry ingredients and mix quickly until the mixture just comes together. Do not over-mix or the scones will be tough.

3 Knead the dough lightly on a lightly floured surface, then pat it out with your hands to a depth of 2cm/3/4in. Cut into squares, or use a 5cm/2in cutter to stamp out rounds, re-rolling the dough as necessary.

4 Place the squares or rounds on a non-stick baking sheet. Brush with the egg glaze, if using, and sprinkle with extra grated cheese.

5 Bake for about 10 minutes until risen and golden. You can test scones by pressing the sides, which should spring back. Remove to a wire rack to cool. Serve spread with garlic-flavoured cream cheese. Top with chopped chives and sliced radish, if used.

Ricotta and Marsala Tarts

These sweet, melt-in-the mouth tarts have a crisp puff pastry base. The light cheese filling is flavoured in the Italian way with Marsala.

375g/13oz packet ready-rolled puff pastry, thawed
250g/9oz/generous 1 cup ricotta cheese
1 egg, plus 2 egg yolks
45–60ml/3–4 tbsp caster sugar
30ml/2 tbsp Marsala
grated rind of 1 lemon
50g/2oz/1/3 cup sultanas

Makes 12

VARIATIONS

Shortcrust pastry can be used instead of puff, but no other cheese will give the same texture as ricotta. Instead of Marsala you could add 5ml/1 tsp pure vanilla essence.

1 Cut out twelve 9cm/3½in rounds of pastry and line a tray of deep muffin cups. Allow to rest for 20 minutes. Preheat the oven to 190°C/375°F/Gas 5.

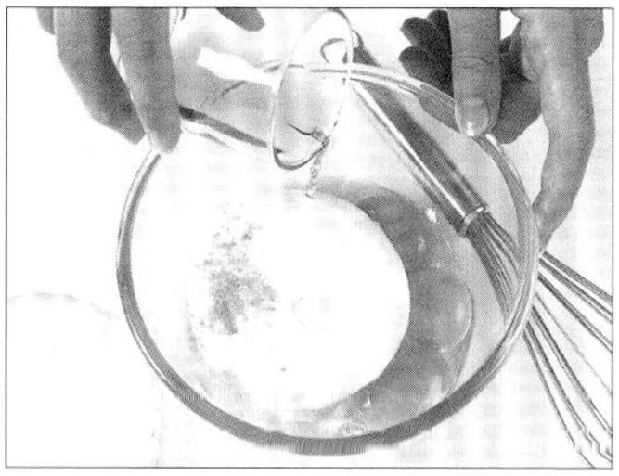

2 Put the ricotta cheese in a bowl and add the egg, extra yolks, sugar, Marsala and lemon rind. Whisk until smooth, then stir in the sultanas.

3 Spoon the mixture into the lined tins. Bake for about 20 minutes or until the filling has risen and the pastry is golden and crisp.

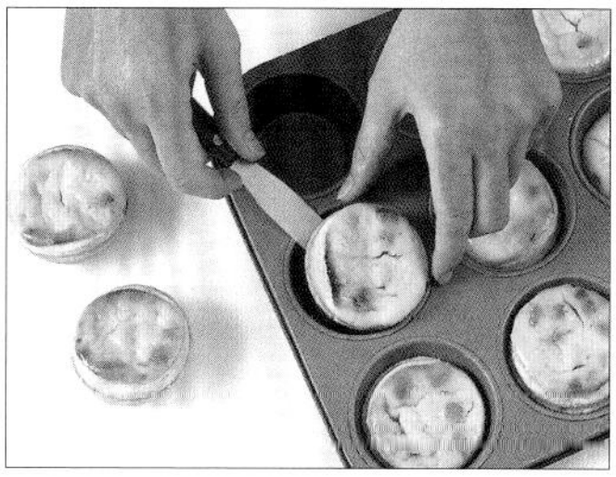

4 Cool the tarts slightly before easing each one out with a small spatula. Serve warm.

Shopping for Cheese

For most of us, finding a good cheese means first finding a good cheese shop. The best shops are those that buy in immature cheeses and nurture them until they are ready to reveal their true character and subtlties of flavour. Regrettably, most shops simply order cheese and sell them with little thought as to their ripeness.

Try to buy cheese as near to the time you want to eat it as possible. If there is a particular cheese that you want, order it well in advance to give the cheesemonger time to find it and ripen it, or ask his or her advice about what will be at its best on the day that you need it. Maturing cheese is a time-consuming labour of love, so do not expect to pay the same for a cheese from an affineur as you would from a supermarket. Shop where you are allowed to taste before you buy, and where the assistant can suggest a choice of cheeses that provides a balance of mild and strong, hard and soft, with differing flavours, types of milk, shapes and characters.

If the cheese is strangled in plastic film it will become sweaty and develop bitter flavours. A good cheese shop will use plastic film sparingly on the cut-surfaces, so that the cheese can breathe. They will know the name of the cheese, the name of the farm or creamery where it is made, and perhaps even how it was made.

In recent years, mail order has become a popular way for small producers and retailers to reach a wider audience. It is an extremely effective way of obtaining hard-to-find cheeses, and, in general, if the cheeses are well packed and sent overnight, they seem to suffer no ill-effects. Some companies will send the cheese by refrigerated transport, but this adds to the cost.

The following cheese shops are worth visiting.

Australia

Bottega Rotolo
7 Osmond Terrace
Norwood SA 5067
Tel: (08) 8362 0455
www.bottegarotolo.com.au

Simon Johnson, Purveyor of Quality Foods
181 Harris Street
Pyrmont
Sydney NSW 2009
Tel: (02) 9552 2522
and branches in NSW, VIC and WA
www.simonjohnson.com.au

David Jones Food Hall
65–77 Market Street
Sydney NSW 2000
Tel: (02) 9266 5544
www.davidjones.com.au

Myer Food Hall – Perth City
200 Murray Street
Perth WA 6000
Tel: (08) 9265 5600
www.myer.com.au

Richmond Hill Cafe and Larder
48–50 Bridge Road
Richmond
Melbourne VIC
Tel: (03) 9421 2808
www.rhcl.com.au

Canada

Denninger's
284 King Street East
Hamilton
Ontario
Tel: 905 528 8468
and branches in Oakville, Hamilton and Burlington
www.denningers.com

England

Blue Bird
350 Kings Road
Chelsea
London SW3 5UU
Tel: 020 7559 1140
www.bluebird-store.co.uk

Cambridge Cheese Company
4 All Saints Passage
Cambridge, CB2 3LS
Tel: 01223 328 672
cambridgecheese.googlepages.com

Fortnum and Mason
181 Piccadilly
London W1A 1ER
Tel: 020 7734 8040
www.fortnumandmason.com

La Fromagerie (below)
30 Highbury Park
London N5 2AA
Tel: 020 7359 7440
and 2–6 Moxon Street
London W1U 4EW
Tel: 020 7935 0341
www.lafromagerie.co.uk

Harvey Nichols
109 Knightsbridge
London SW1X 7JR
Tel: 020 7235 5000
www.harveynichols.com

Jeroboams
96 Holland Park Avenue
London W11 3RB
Tel: 020 7727 9359
and branches across London
www.jeroboams.co.uk

Neals Yard Dairy
17 Shorts Gardens
London WC2H 9AT
Tel: 020 7379 7646
www.nealsyarddairy.co.uk

Paxton and Whitfield
93 Jermyn Street
London SW1Y 6JE
Tel: 020 7930 0259
and branches in Bath and Stratford-upon-Avon
www.paxtonandwhitfield.co.uk

Ticklemore Cheese Shop
1 Ticklemore Street
Totnes, Devon
TQ9 5EJ
Tel: 01803 865 926

Vivian's
2 Worple Way
Richmond, Surrey
TW10 6DF
Tel: 020 8940 3600
www.viviansdeli.co.uk

Wensleydale Creamery
Gayles Lane
Hawes, North Yorkshire
DL8 3RN
Tel: 01969 667 664
www.wensleydale.co.uk

France

Fromagerie Barthélémy
92 rue Grande
77300 Fontainebleu
and 51 rue de Grenelle
75007 Paris

Le Bon Marché – La Grande Epicerie de Paris
38 rue Sevres
75007 Paris
www.lagrandeepicerie.fr

Fromagerie Boujon
7 rue Saint-Sebastien
74200 Thonon-les-Bains
www.fromagerie-boujon.com

Marie Cantin
12 rue du Champ de Mars
75007 Paris
www.cantin.fr

La Ferme Savoyarde
22 rue Meynadier
06400 Cannes

Fromagerie Maréchal
Halle de Lyon
112 cours Lafayette
69003 Lyon

La Fromagerie Phillippe Olivier
43 rue Thiers
62200 Boulogne-sur-Mer

Galeries Lafayette
48 boulevard Haussmann
75009 Paris
www2.galerieslafayette.com/international

Crèmerie Quatrehomme
62 rue Sèvres
75007 Paris

IRELAND

Cavistons Food Emporium
58–59 Glasthule Road
Sandycove
Co Dublin
Tel: 01 280 9120
www.cavistons.com

SCOTLAND

I.J. Mellis Cheesemonger
492 Great Western Road
Glasgow G12 8EW
Tel: 0141 339 8998
and branches in Edinburgh, Aberdeen and St Andrews
www.mellischeese.co.uk

Valvona and Crolla
19 Elm Row
Edinburgh
EH7 4AA
Tel: 0131 556 6066
and foodhalls in Jenners Loch Lomond and Edinburgh
www.valvonacrolla.co.uk

NEW ZEALAND

Canterbury Cheesemongers
44 Salisbury Street
Christchurch
Tel: 64 3 379 0075
www.cheesemongers.co.nz

Kapiti Cheeses
Lindale Centre
State Highway 1
Paraparaumu 6450
Tel: 04 298 1352
www.kff.co.nz

UNITED STATES OF AMERICA

Balducci's
81 Eighth Avenue (14th Street)
New York NY 10011
Tel: 212 741 3700
and branches in NY, CT, MD, NY and Washington DC
www.balduccis.com

Dean and Deluca
560 Broadway (Prince Street)
New York NY 10012
Tel: 212 226 6800
and branches in NY, CA, KS, NC and Washington DC
www.deandeluca.com

Grace's Marketplace
1237 3rd Avenue (71st Street)
New York NY 10021
Tel: 212 737 0600
and 81 Glen Cove Road
Greenvale, Long Island NY 11548
Tel: 516 621 5100
www.gracesmarketplace.com

Wholefoods
Branches across Canada and the USA. Some stores in London, England
www.wholefoodsmarket.com

Zabar's
2245 Broadway (80th Street)
New York NY 10024
Tel: 212 787 2000
www.zabars.com

Zingerman's
422 Detroit Street
Ann Arbor
Michigan 48104
Tel: 734 663 3354
www.zingermansdeli.com
and 3723 Plaza Drive
Ann Arbor
Michigan 48108
Tel: 734 929 0500
www.zingermanscreamery.com

WALES

Llangloffan Farm Shop
Castle Morris
Haverford West
Pembrokeshire
SA62 5ET
Tel: 01348 891 241
www.welshcheese.co.uk

BIBLIOGRAPHY

Androuet, Pierre, *Guide du Fromage* (Aidan Ellis, 1973)

Basan, Ghillie, *Classic Turkish Cookery* (Tauris Parke, 1997)

Bilson, Tony, *Cheeses – The Australian Kitchen (Buying, Preparing and Cooking)* (Barbara Beckett, 1995)

Boxer, Arabella, *Mediterranean Cookbook* (Penguin, 1983)

Burton, David, *The New Zealand Cheese Book – Cooking and Serving Dairy Produce* (Reed Methuen, 1988)

Carr, Sandy, *The Mitchell Beazley Pocket Guide to Cheese* (Mitchell Beazley, 1986)

Cheke, Val, *The Story of Cheese-Making in Britain* (Routledge & Kegan Paul, 1959)

Chenel, Laura and Siegfried, Linda, *American Country Cheese* (Aris, 1989)

Corato, Ricardo di, *Italian Cheeses – A Pocket Guide* (Idealibri, 1985)

Del Conte, Anna, *Secrets from an Italian Kitchen* (Corgi, 1993)

Halliday, James, *Australian Wine Guide* (Angus and Robertson, 1990)

Hickman, Trevor, *The History of Stilton Cheese* (Alan Sutton, 1995)

Jenkins, Steven, *Cheese Primer* (Workman, 1996)

Jones, Evans, *The Book of Cheese* (Macmillan, 1981)

Lambert, Gilles and Roche, Narcisse, *La Cuisine au Fromage* (Stock, 1971)

Montagné, Prospe, *Larousse Gastronomique* (Crown, 1965)

Nichols, Lourdes, *Mexican Cookery* (Fontana, 1986)

Rance, Patrick (foreword), *Cheeses of the World* (Little, Brown, 1993)

Rance, Patrick, *The French Cheese Book* (Macmillan, 1989)

Rance, Patrick, *The Great British Cheese Book* (Macmillan, 1982)

Rewi, Adrienne and Nicholas, Juliet, *Fine Cheese – Gourmet Cheesemaking in New Zealand* (Hazard, 1995)

Robuchon, Joel, *French Cheese* (Dorling Kindersley, 1996)

Scott, R., *Cheesemaking Practice* (2nd edn, Elsevier Applied Science, 1986)

Simon, André, *Cheeses of the World* (Faber and Faber, 1961)

Smith, John, *Cheesemaking in Scotland – A History* (Scottish Dairy Association, 1995)

Stubbs, William, *Guide to the Cheese of France* (Apple Press, 1984)

UNALAT (ed), *DOC Cheese of Italy – A Great Heritage* (Angeli, Franco, 1992)

United States Department of Agriculture, *Cheeses of the World* (Dover, 1969)

Whittle Fiona (ed), *Australian Farmhouse and Speciality Cheese Book* (Publicity, 1992)

INDEX

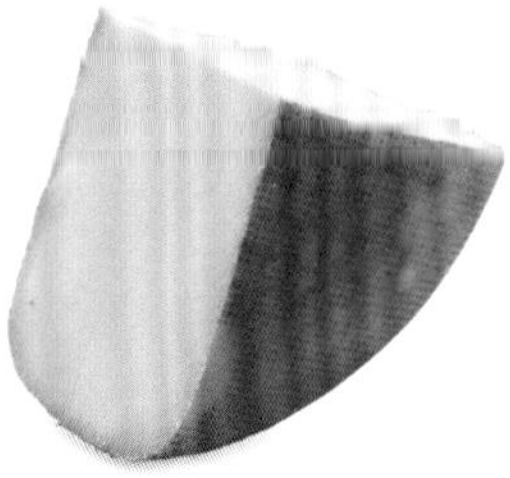

ACKNOWLEDGEMENTS

AUTHOR'S ACKNOWLEDGEMENTS

The task of creating this book almost cured me of my desire to communicate the joy of cheese to others through the written word. Had it not been for the support of cheesemakers from around the world, and their wonderful letters of encouragement, I would not have completed it. I should also like to thank all the friends who lent me books, brought back cheeses from strange places and tasted cheeses with me; Patrick Rance and Pierre Androuet, whose books first inspired in me a love of cheese; the owners and patrons of the Tite Inn in Chadington, whose *joie de vivre* and enthusiam to know more about cheese has given me much pleasure after the long nights at the word processor; the cheese team at Tesco, who helped me track down cheeses; and my staff, who put up with me and kept me on the straight and narrow.

Finally, the recipes, which include many of my favourites, have renewed my interest in cooking with cheese. Written by my friend, Roz Denny, they demonstrate her skills and her passion for cooking.

PUBLISHER'S ACKNOWLEDGEMENTS

The publisher would like to thank Jenni Fleetwood, who edited the text with such skill, Carol Tennant for tracking down the cheeses for photography; Nicki Dowey, William Lingwood and his assistant Louise Dare, who tirelessly photographed all of the cheeses; Patricia Michelson at La Fromagerie in north London for her help; and the following companies who very generously supplied many of the cheeses and props for purposes of photography:

Cambridge Cheese Company
All Saints Passage
Cambridge
Cambridgeshire CB2 3LS
Tel: 01223 328 672
cambridgecheese.google
pages.com/

La Fromagerie
30 Highbury Park
London N5 2AA
Tel: 020 7359 7440
www.lafromagerie.co.uk

Harvey Nichols
109 Knightsbridge
London SW1X 7JR
Tel: 020 7235 5000
www.harveynichols.com

I.J. Mellis
Cheesemonger
492 Great Western Road
Glasgow G12 8EW
Tel: 0141 339 8998
www.mellischeese.co.uk

Kapiti Cheeses
Lindale Centre
State Highway 1
Paraparaumu 6450
Tel: 04 298 1352
www.kii.co.nz

Jeroboams
96 Holland Park Avenue
London W11 3RB
Tel: 020 7727 9359
www.jeroboams.co.uk

Neals Yard Dairy
17 Shorts Gardens
London WC2H 9AT
Tel: 020 7379 7646
www.nealsyarddairy.co.uk

Paxton and Whitfield
93 Jermyn Street
London SW1Y 6JE
Tel: 020 7930 0259
www.paxtonandwhitfield.co.uk

Richmond Hill Cafe and Larder
48–50 Bridge Road
Richmond
Melbourne VIC
Tel: (03) 9421 2808
www.rhcl.com.au

PHOTOGRAPHY ACKNOWLEDGEMENTS

Pictures in the recipe section (except cut-outs) are by John Heseltine, and those in the reference section are by William Lingwood, except for the following:
p6 Sopexa; p7 The Italian Trade Centre; p9 Sopexa; p10 (top left) Cheeses from Switzerland, (top right) J.P. Quicke, (bottom) The Italian Trade Centre; p11 (top left) Cheeses from Switzerland, (top right and bottom) Sopexa; p12 and 13 Sopexa; pp62 (bottom left), 65 (top right), 66 (top), 67 (top) and 69 (top and bottom left) Nicki Dowey; p70 (bottom right) Juliet Harbutt; pp71 (bottom right), 72 (top left), 73 (bottom), 74 (bottom left), 75 (top left and bottom), 76 (bottom left), 77 (top right and bottom left), 79 (bottom), 80 and 81 Nicki Dowey; p83 Cooleeney Cheese; pp 85 and 90 (top) Nicki Dowey; pp128 (bottom left), 129, 130, 131 and 133 (top left)Walt Chrynwski; p134 William Milliot; p135 Walt Chrynwski; p136 (top) the Mozzarella Company; 136 (bottom) Uplands Cheese Company; 137 (top left) Cowgirl Creamery; 137 (top right and bottom) Walt Chrynwski; 138 (top) Bravo Farms; 139 (top) Walt Chrynwski; 139 (bottom) Juniper Grove; 140 (top) Artisanal Cheese; 140 (bottom right) and 141 Walt Chrynwski; p142 Gabriella Kervella; p150 Russ McCullum

Notes

Notes

Notes

Notes

Notes

Notes

Notes

Notes